Belzec:

Stepping Stone to Genocide

Aktion Reinhardt Personnel on Parade: Belzec 1942

By Robin O'Neil

Salisbury, England

Published by JewishGen, Inc.
An Affiliate of
The Museum of Jewish Heritage - A Living Memorial to the Holocaust

Belzec: Stepping Stone to Genocide

By: Robin O'Neil

Copyright © JewishGen, Inc. 2008

All rights reserved.

First Printing: July 2008

Editors: Beth Galleto and Joyce Field
Layout: Beth Galleto and Joel Alpert
Cover Design: M. Peters, Germany

JewishGen, Inc.
An Affiliate of
The Museum of Jewish Heritage - A Living Memorial to the Holocaust
36 Battery Place
New York, NY 10280

Printed in the United States of America by Lightning Source, Inc.
Library of Congress Control Number (LCCN): 2008931566
ISBN: 978-0-9764759-3-4 (hard cover: 374 pages, alk. paper)

Published by JewishGen, Inc.
An Affiliate of
The Museum of Jewish Heritage - A Living Memorial to the Holocaust

Front cover created by M. Peters, Germany
Photograph of author: John Adler, Bristol, U.K.
Back cover created by M. Peters, based on a painting from Waclaw Kolodziejczyk
Photograph of Aktion Reinhardt: United States Holocaust Memorial Museum and Tomaszow Lubelski Regional Museum

2

Contents

Dedication

This book is dedicated to the memory of Professor John D. Klier and to Martin Gilbert and my fellow students who, together, endured a journey of discovery and sadness.

Photograph Ann O'Neil

Above: the Post Graduate (MA Holocaust Studies) students of the Hebrew and Jewish Department, University College London, 1996. Left to Right: Sir Martin Gilbert, the late Professor John Klier, the author, Caroline Harris, Herute Hoskin, Jon Boyd, Paul Neville, Angela Jayson, Petra Wöstefeld, and Rosalind Morris.

In the background is a Silver Birch tree, brought back by the author from the Parczew forest in Poland, which Sir Martin had just planted in the grounds of the Imperial War Museum, London. The tree was a gift to Sir Martin by the students at the conclusion of their "Holocaust Journey." (See Martin Gilbert: *Holocaust Journey: Travelling in search of the past*, London, 1997).

4

Acknowledgments

To personally thank the many individuals who have helped and contributed to my research over many years was an impossible task. From the poor isolated residents in Poland-Ukraine, to close friends, archivists, and academia in general, I pay due acknowledgment. My sincere thanks for photographic support go to the Tomaszow Lubelski Regional Museum, the Wacław Kołodziejczyk trust, Belzec, Chris Webb and Melvyn Conroy (www.Holocaust Research Project.org), and the United States Holocaust Memorial Museum.

Special mention, however, cannot go unrecorded: To my colleague and friend for many years Michael Tregenza in Lublin, who, without his generous help, this book would not have been possible. My thanks are extended to the late John D. Klier and Michael Berkowitz (University College London): My Editors-in-Chief; Lance Ackerfeld, Joyce Field (CJ), Joel Alpert, Beth Galleto and Michael Peters (Germany).

Biography of the Author

Robin O'Neil, Investigator of Nazi War Crimes in Poland

Robin O'Neil is a former police major crimes investigator who worked at the sharp end of major criminal investigations in the United Kingdom and Central Europe. Formerly of Scotland Yard, the Metropolitan and Home Counties Police service, he then took up the challenge of Academia.

After obtaining his Masters degree at the University of London under Sir Martin Gilbert, the renowned and distinguished writer and researcher of the Holocaust, O'Neil continues his academic work with a Doctoral thesis on Belzec extermination camp, specializing in investigating Nazi war crimes. A Russian speaker, he has pursued his work to the Baltic States and former USSR. He has launched a number of major investigations into the perpetrators of the Holocaust, particularly those individuals who carried out and engineered the destruction of European Jewry in Lithuania and Poland. His past police service and rank enable him to look closely into the characters of the SS and death camp commandants of Belzec, Sobibor and Treblinka.

Robin O'Neil is universally acknowledged as the central research source for the Schindler story. A historical consultant to several TV documentaries and radio broadcasts in the UK and abroad, he is an honored guest of Schindler's home town, Svitavy in the Czech Republic, and is a regular lecturer at universities in the United Kingdom, United States, Israel and Eastern Europe.

In his spare time and to counteract the intensity of Holocaust research he diversifies his interests into the Habsburg dynasty of nineteenth century Vienna and Shakespeare's England. He is currently engaged in researching the Paston family correspondence from Norfolk 1420-1510 and associated English texts of that time.

"Yidn, shreibt un farschreibt! (Jews, write and record!)"

State of Current Research

The research that constitutes the basis of this study was undertaken on a number of different but related fronts. It includes critically important data derived from an archaeological survey of the mass graves at Belzec by forensic archaeologists from Torun University in Poland. By comparing this information with other data of the transports to Belzec from the Jewish communities of the Lublin district, Galicia, and elsewhere, we are able to envisage the scale of murder committed in the name of the "Final Solution" in a way that is independent of eyewitness testimony. Consequently, this evidence constitutes substantial proofs of Nazi war crimes against the Jewish people and an incontrovertible body of evidence to confront Holocaust denial.

In the context of a number of important and hotly debated studies of recent years, which deal with the background, indoctrination and ideological commitment of those who carried out Nazi war crimes, the evidence of this study provides an important perspective. The detailed investigation of the German and Austrian personnel who ran the camp provides a number of insights into the way in which *Aktion Reinhardt* and its precursor, the euthanasia program, were staffed.

Belzec was commissioned by the highest authority of the Nazi State and acted outside the law of both civil and military conventions of the time. Under the code Aktion Reinhardt, the death camps were organized, staffed, and administered by a leadership of middle-ranking police officers and a specially selected civilian cadre who, in the first instance, had been initiated into the euthanasia program. Their expertise was then transferred to operational duties in the death camps. The hands-on extermination of European Jewry in the death camps of Reinhardt, the author suggests, was police-led, from start to finish.

While this was a top-secret operation, many of those involved were not committed Nazis or even members of the SS, but ordinary Germans engaged not so much in gratifying congenital murderous, anti-Semitic impulses, but either under personal threat from the leadership or as opportunists hoping to avoid combat duties and amass personal wealth looted from their victims. Aktion Reinhardt staff was protected by the highest authority from military and civilian discipline or regulation. They were, in effect—for the duration of the war—a band of brothers.

The principle of police leadership in the Reinhardt camps was unprecedented and was never extended or repeated in any other penal establishment in the areas of German occupation. The combination of police and civilians appears to have been a direct policy of the Nazi State. The majority of Reinhardt personnel operating in these camps became a maverick unit and were given the spurious cover of SS insignia to facilitate their objective. These men, operating under a *Geheime Reichssache* (Secret Reich Affair) became "the untouchables." All outside influences concerning rank, status and human decency meant absolutely nothing to this group. Within the Reinhardt establishment there was a complete negation of any recognised principles of law and order, discipline or basic humanitarian considerations.

The men engaged in Reinhardt were practiced in institutional murder since 1940 and were psychologically conditioned to continue similar duties elsewhere. After all, if they could engage in the murder of their "own" through euthanasia, they could hardly be expected to have any inner moral conflict with murdering Jews. Even so, in practice, clinical institutionalized murder was a far cry from what these men were later faced with in Belzec—which called for an extra dimension of personal commitment. Among the Reinhardt personnel, the motivation for carrying out the base murder of men, women and children varied according to the individual. Fear predominated among the lower echelons of the leadership, but others were attracted by generous pay and conditions of service with extra leave, allowances and opportunities for further advancement. Others were motivated by the spoils of extermination: corruption, greed, and in some cases crude prejudices and sadistic self-gratification. Exemption from frontline duty was an added inducement. In due course all these men, even those who self-righteously proclaimed abhorrence of Belzec's purpose, became corrupted when given the power of life and death over people whom they were encouraged to treat as sub-human.

In the lower ranks, Nazi ideology and anti-Semitism were not the prime driving forces behind the majority of the mass murderers. It is in the leadership that political indoctrination and rabid anti-Semitism were to be found. One man in particular, the Stuttgart police officer Christian Wirth, exemplifies this. He will be shown to be the central cog in the destruction process, even more so than his immediate superior, the designated overlord of Reinhardt, SS-Brigadeführer Odilo Globocnik. Unlike Himmler and his immediate following, who were driven by a pseudo-religious ideology, or a "holy" mission, Wirth remained an enigma, a crude man with uncouth habits spurred on by an old-fashioned sense of "duty" and a hatred for Jews.

Recent Scholarship and Study

Books on Holocaust related subjects are not the only means by which informed scholarship is measured. Individual scholars, working quietly in the background and out of the academic and public eye, have written many of the most provoking research papers In Melbourne, Australia, independent researcher Joseph Poprzeczny is about to publish the results of 20 years' work on researching the life of Odilo Globocnik. Lukas Pribyl in the Czech Republic is nearing completion of his research project concerning the deportation transports from Bohemia and Moravia. There are many more.

The destruction of European Jewry has been treated in a number of ways by specialists who are at the cutting edge of Holocaust research: Gerald Reitlinger's The Final Solution (originally published in 1953) is thought-provoking but focused primarily on Jewish extermination and gives little indication of the inner power struggles within the General Government.[1] Reitlinger's work has been superseded by Raul Hilberg's magisterial three-volume Destruction of the European Jews (1985), which in my view remains the definitive work. It is breathtaking in scope and systematically deals with every aspect of the mechanics of destruction, including German material on this tragedy. Hilberg also includes an excellent account of the administrative conflict in the General Government. Martin Gilbert's Holocaust (1987) considers Reinhardt from a broader perspective, while Daniel Goldhagen's widely-discussed, well-documented and controversial Hitler's Willing Executioners (1997) only refers to Belzec on three occasions within its references to Reinhardt. Only Yitzhak Arad's Belzec, Sobibór, Treblinka - The Operation Reinhard Death Camps (1987), and the latest published research by Michael Tregenza in Lublin, Belzec - Das Vergessene Lager des Holocaust (2000) focuses on Belzec in some depth within the context of Reinhardt. Christopher C. Browning's prolific scholarship—Fateful Months (1985); Path to Genocide (1992); Essays on the Final Solution (1995); The Final Solution and the German Foreign Office (1978); Ordinary Men; The Reigner Telegramme Reconstructed; Nazi Policy, Jewish Questions, and Policies; Nazi Policy, Jewish Workers, German Killers—are major contributions. The SS training camp at Trawniki near Lublin was the most important element in providing manpower for Reinhardt. The interesting and most welcome research paper by David Rich et al enhances our understanding of this subject.

Among the Polish sources, of particular interest are the works of E. Szrojt, and T. Chrosciewicz. For the deportation operations from the Galician District see T. Berenstein. Other useful sources are An Outline History of the Lwów Railways 1942-3, which contains interesting facts regarding the deportation transports from Lvov to Belzec. See also Dr. Janusz Peter (Kordian), W Belzcu podczas okupacji (In Belzec during the Occupation). When discussing the Generalplan Ost see Czeslaw Madajczyk's Forschungsstelle für Ostunterkunft (Research Center for Eastern Resettlement) and the European-wide Jewish extermination program. On the fate of the Christian Poles who were left to face the German and Russian onslaughts, there are thought-provoking personal recollections of this period in Tomasz Piesakowski's The Fate of Poles in the USSR, 1939-1989 and the Zygmunt Klukowski Diary 1939-44. See also Zoë Zajderowa's The Dark Side of the Moon. For the fate of German Jews in Dresden, see the Victor Klemperer diaries.

From the German side see the diary of Alex Hohenstein, Oberbügermeister (Senior District Mayor) of Poniatowec in the Warthegau 1941/2; Das

Diensttagebuch des deutschen Generalgouverneurs in Polen (Hans Frank Diaries); Die Tagebücher von Joseph Goebbels (Goebbels Diaries); [Diensttagebuch Himmler] Der Dienstkalender Heinrich Himmler 1941/2. These are rich sources indeed.

Dr Hans Frank's Diary, Tagebuch des Herrn Generalgouverneurs für dies Besetzten Polnischen Gebiete, 25 Oktober 1939 bis 3. April 1945 is crucial for understanding the power struggle within the General Government between Himmler, Frank and Krüger. The original Frank Diaries can be found in the archives of the former Archiwum Glownej Komisji Badania Zbrodni Hitlerowskich w Polsce (Main Commission for Investigation of Nazi Crimes in Poland), today the Izba Pamiêci Narodowej (Institute of National Memory) in Warsaw, Poland. The Tagebuch is a detailed although not personal record of the civil administration divided into 38 volumes. The diary is compartmentalized according to subject matter—agriculture, labor, security, etc. There is an abridged English translation of this work (Hans Frank's Diary, Pañstwowe Wydawnictwo Naukowe, Warsaw 1961). See also International Military Tribunal, Trial of the Major German War Criminals (42 volumes). Vol. XX1X, Document Number 2233-PS, 356-725 contains material from the Tagebuch.

For the purposes of this study the author has been selective when quoting the Tagebuch, usually citing secondary sources as indicated, where appropriate. The main source of material used in this study is Larry V. Thompson, Nazi Administrative Conflict: The Struggle for Executive Power in the General Government of Poland, 1939-1945 (unpublished thesis), University of Wisconsin, USA, 1967. Importance is attributed to this work because the central theme focuses on the personal and institutional conflict, or SS & Police v Gouverneur, General Government, Poland 1941-1943. See also Robert L. Koehl, German Resettlement and Population Policy, 1939 – 1945, Cambridge (HUP) 1957.

More recent material concerning the Frank Diaries can be seen at the Deutsches Historisches Institute (German Historical Institute) in London, under references SH 5/9030 and SH 2/149. Other recent publications deal with the subject or parts thereof from different viewpoints. When placed in context, Browning's Ordinary Men (1991), together with Goldhagen's Willing Executioners, deal controversially with events outside Reinhardt that have no direct bearing on events within the death camps. Browning's thesis suggests a mundane perspective of the Nazi decimation of the Jews, explaining how ordinary men, once engaged in unbridled mass killing, went about their task with diligence and efficiency. The Reinhardt personnel were no less ordinary and they, too, took on the role of executioners in T4; and then, in a far more deadly environment, became the principals in a brutal industrialized genocide. What we have, therefore, are "ordinary men" outside Reinhardt, committing mass murders with the protection of the Reich Security Main Office Executive, with the choice of being engaged or not in mass killings. Conversely, within Reinhardt, these "ordinary men" had no protection, right of appeal, or choice of withdrawing from the slaughter. They were ruthlessly driven in their terrible mission by an untouchable, heartless police leadership, which acted on orders from the highest authority, whose purpose was the complete extermination of Jewry. One particular aspect that will be discussed is the scholarly consensus that perpetrators had the choice of refusing to obey an order to kill. This contention is largely supported and underpinned by judicial pronouncements by SS courts and in subsequent post-war criminal trials. It will be argued that these conclusions do not hold with regard to Reinhardt.

Another important contribution to be assessed here is the only published account of the Belzec death camp by a Jewish survivor, Rudolf Reder's Belzec. Reder's account, recently translated, has been liberally used by historians simply because it is the only comprehensive record by one of two sole victims who escaped and survived the camp.

Oddly, no major German scholarship, although represented elsewhere, has emerged about Belzec *per se*.

Although the euthanasia program in general has been well documented, especially from the medical aspect (Klee, Burleigh, Friedlander, Platten-Hallermund, Mitscherlich and Mielke, *et al.*), it is worth bringing into perspective its relevance to Reinhardt. The mechanics and principles of euthanasia were to emerge finally as the answer to fulfilling the Nazi genocidal policies. Mass shootings had been ruled out due to the enormous numbers of victims involved, its impracticality, and the adverse psychological effects on the executioners. There was the additional factor that secrecy could not be guaranteed. The methods and technical advances of the euthanasia program as the precursor to genocide are noted.

The central issue discussed in this reappraisal is the focus on the middle and lower echelons of recruits to the euthanasia program and their subsequent transfer to Reinhardt. Henry Friedlander in Origins of Nazi Genocide pursues a similar line of inquiry but he restricts his research to the opening phase of T4, whereas this inquiry is a more robust and comprehensive analysis. More extensive treatment of the psychiatric institutions has been explored in Michael Burleigh's Death and Deliverance: 'Euthanasia' in Germany 1900-1945, Ernst Klee's Euthanasie im NS-Staat: Die Vernichtung lebensunwerten Lebens, and more recently in Patricia Heberer's Targeting the Unfit and 'Exitus Heute' in Hadamar. See also Conference paper, Lublin, 8 November 2002: A Continuity in Killing Operations: T4 Perpetrators and Aktion Reinhard.

A new generation of German scholars has emerged and continues to emerge—Götz Aly, Peter Chroust, Christian Pross, *et al*, who are penetrating and opening up past Nazi medical crimes and forcing a certain amount of soul-searching by the present day medical establishment in Germany. For a useful background to the psychiatric institutions during the Nazi period, see

Bronwyn McFarland-Icke's <u>Nurses in Nazi Germany</u>. Gitta Sereny's <u>Into the Darkness: the Mind of a Mass Murderer</u> (personal interviews with Franz Stangl), is an extraordinary exposure of the Nazi system and genocidal policies in Reinhardt. Regarding archival material, the voluminous files relating to perpetrators prosecuted for the crimes committed during the euthanasia and Reinhardt operations are of the utmost importance.

Exploring the literature relating to events during and after the euthanasia (T4) period is vital for an understanding of Reinhardt. Attention has again focused on the new generation of German scholars—Dieter Pohl, Götz Aly, Thomas Sandküler, Peter Longerich, Karen Orth, Ulrich Herbert, Peter Witte, and Bogdan Musial, to name but a few—who have directed their research in a wide-ranging re-assessment of the circumstances surrounding the Final Solution. The Nazi crimes committed in Galicia in particular have attracted a lively and wide divergence of opinion. Contributions by Christian Gerlach were of immense value when discussing the fate of European Jews, especially those from the Greater Reich.

Other scholars, whose significant contributions in the wider context, particularly in dating the decision-making process of the Final Solution, have also been helpful. When discussing the German Security Services I have very much depended on George Browder's <u>Hitler's Enforcers.</u>

One of the difficulties encountered during the course of this research was coming to terms with the actuality of events that occurred in Belzec. It is only now, after a joint initiative by the Polish government, the United States Holocaust Memorial Museum in Washington, D.C., and the American Jewish Committee to carry out an archaeological survey at the site of the Belzec death camp, that we have the first scholarly topographical report of the camp. I was both fortunate and privileged to have been present during the course of these investigations. This work resulted in the publication of a unique archaeological document by Andrzej Kola (Professor of the University of Toruñ), <u>Belzec: the Nazi Camp for Jews in the Light of Archaeological Sources. Excavations 1997 - 1999</u> (English version), which, for the first time, exposes—without fear of contradiction—the purpose and enormity of this perhaps greatest and most brutal of crimes. In addition, a number of short histories of the Lublin ghetto and Lublin district are of interest.

In unravelling the facts and circumstances, several protagonists whose activities are of the utmost importance emerge from this period. High on the list are the subordinate leadership, the "hands-on" perpetrators of genocide: SS-Brigadeführer Odilo Globocnik and SS-Obersturmführer/ Kriminalkommissar Christian Wirth. Extensive works about the subordinate leadership are rare. A number of German language biographical outlines and studies have been devoted to Globocnik, who is also the topic of ongoing but to-date unpublished research. In the secondary literature, Globocnik is described as a "Nazi arch-bloodhound and privateer," a "professional murderer," "unbalanced," and "unscrupulous." Contemporaries observed his "strong ambition" and "organizational talent." Gerald Reitlinger asserts that, "He had a good appearance but his eyes and mouth were untruthful and brutal. During his duty in Lublin he lived in constant drunkenness and unlimited craving for pleasure. His talent for conspiracy was his only real merit."

Regarding Christian Wirth, the published literature is dismally absent. One of my objectives is to expose the importance of the character of Wirth within the framework of Reinhardt. It will be emphasized that Reinhardt was working to its own rules and regulations outside the State conventions at the time. This was due to the way in which it was set up, but particularly with respect to Wirth, who was operating without referral to his immediate superiors and with direct and unobstructed access to the Führer's Chancellery (KdF). Miscellaneous papers were presented at the conference "Aktion Reinhardt; Der Völkermord an den Juden im Generalgouvernement, Lublin, 8 November 2002." In particular, I draw attention to the article by Tomasz Kranz, "Das Konzentrationslager Majdanek und 'Aktion Reinhardt'," which produces a rich kaleidoscope of the latest research.

Note on Language

Terminology was a crucial device of the Nazis. In the words of Raul Hilberg, their policy was, "Never utter the words appropriate to the action." The euphemistic language spoken within the Nazi Police State conveyed the climate of "order" and "intention." This is the language of deception that helped shape the pattern of society, which is pertinently explored by Hans Paechter and Victor Klemperer. The Nazis thought up new terms and used old words contrary to their original meaning. By euphemistic presentation, they misled their enemies, victims, and those hovering on the periphery, to divert and obscure the most hideous of crimes.

It is very easy to be drawn into the Nazi code of euphemistic language. Indeed, it is difficult to avoid it and mean what we say. These double meanings were introduced as the system of genocide was perfected. Thus, from October 1941 onwards, we find *Judenaussiedlung* (emigration of Jews), *Judenumsiedlung* (Jewish resettlement) and *Judenevakuierung* (evacuation)—all synonyms for mass murder. When Globocnik defined his purpose we find *Aussiedling* (evacuation); *Verwertung der Arbeitscharft* (utilization of labor); *Sachverwertung* (seizure and utilization of personal belongings); and *Einbringung verborgener Werte und Immobilien* (confiscation of hidden assets and real estate). When the instruments of murder moved from T4 to the concentration camps—*Konzentrationslager* (KZs, 14f13), we find *abspritzen* (to spray—administering a lethal injection), or *Totbaden* (death baths).

The euphemistic bureaucratic terminology was perfected by the Sicherheitsdienst (SD) as the persecution progressed: *Aktionen* (operations), *Säuberung* (cleansing), *Sonderbehandlung* (special treatment), *Ausschaltung* (elimination), or *Exekutivmassnahme* (executive measure).[2] After each mass execution in Auschwitz, camp commandant Rudolf Höß submitted a report to the RSHA in a disguised formula: "... *so und so viel Personen gesondert untergebracht worden seien*" (... such and such a number of people separated, or segregated). These terms create the illusion of a bureaucratic paper chase, not genocide, where euphemistic "double-speak" was an essential ingredient in the Nazi war against the Jews. The illusion of "plain speak" contaminated, and indeed indoctrinated, the minor functionaries caught up in State racial persecution policies. Any sense of moral perspective was abandoned to conceal the true meaning of the word employed. Another aspect of this was the euphemistic jargon of the KZ guards, police, and male psychiatric nurses. They used such terms as "not worth keeping," "'treat' the child," "processed," "authorization," "put on the grill," which all simply meant "to kill." All persons at every level of the mass murder became used to communicating in this "sanitized" language. Although it might appear to be but a minor point, it had immense relevance in smoothing the day-to-day workings in both the euthanasia institutions and the death camps.

The euphemistic language was constantly being refined. When Eichmann's office was relieved of the task of compiling statistical reports pertaining to Reinhardt, these duties were passed over to Dr. Richard Korherr, the SS Chief statistician, who drafted a report for Himmler on the progress of the Final Solution. He noted that 1,449,692 Polish Jews had already received *Sonderbehandlung* (special treatment). Himmler returned the document and demanded a more appropriate phrase, *"durchgeschleust"* (passed through), thereby suggesting that the numbers of Jews referred to in the report "passed through" unnamed *"Durchgangslagers"* (transit camps). Himmler was a past master of euphemistic language and used it continually. The only time he appears to have dropped this camouflage was in his speech in Posen (Poznań) in October 1943, when he spoke directly to his SS in a protected environment.

Historians too have differed over the exact terminology appropriate to defining the Jewish catastrophe. When attempting to come to terms with the horrific events that are laid out before us, I favor a simpler and more direct approach—"destruction" or "genocide." The Holocaust should be treated in its widest context. It may be defined as the history of the criminal acts committed by the Nazis, criminals, not the destruction of the Jews *per se*. A more appropriate description of the extermination of the Jews is conveyed by the Hebrew word "Shoah," which means "destruction."

The destruction of the Jews (and Gypsies) was politically led and was a unique and special case and should be treated as such, the difference being that Jews and Gypsies were incarcerated and murdered as family groups, regardless of age. In the camps, as individuals, they did not as a group differ fundamentally from others; they differed in their fate. The Nazis killed entire families of Jews and Gypsies, including the children and the aged, purely on the basis of race. The Jews were referred to as "vermin" who, therefore, had to be exterminated. Jews were referred to by the Nazis as "Jews"— regardless of nationality, which has sometimes led to a misunderstanding in the literature, particularly when referring to Jews from Poland and Germany. Jews were a section of Polish or other nationalities that were destined for destruction. (Being a "Jew" referred to *religion*, not a particular nationality. This is the point missed by many historians, and others.) The Jews were the first victims of this nefarious and brutal policy.

Local History

If the Second World War had not occurred, Belzec village would to this day be just a name on a map like so many other obscure border locations in south-eastern Poland. Remove the notoriety of Belzec as a place of the most gruesome murders, and there is very little to report. It was not until about the 1850s that records mention a Jewish presence in Belzec, which remained static while far more vibrant Jewish communities were emerging in the neighboring towns of Tomaszów-Lubelski and Lubycza Krowleska. Belzec is situated between Tomaszow-Lubelski and Lubycza and is the main trading route between the now Polish and Ukrainian centers of commerce, Zamosc and Rawa Ruska.

There were 14,000 inhabitants living in Tomaszow, including 6,000 Jews (43 percent), 4,500 of whom managed to escape over the river Bug to the Soviet Union before the Nazis arrived on September 13, 1939, when Belzec became a border customs post separating the German-occupied area and the Soviet Union. In Claude Lanzmann's documentary film *Shoah*, he uniquely captures the social setting of communities where Jews decided to settle: very quickly indeed, Jewish entrepreneurial skills and cultural finesse subordinated the indigenous communities. Within a very short time, Jews occupied the best house and shops and rose to be the dominating influences in Polish-Ukrainian society—envied but respected by the less fortunate. Despite the social and religious difficulties, this uneasy relationship prospered. Belzec village and the adjacent town of Tomaszow-Lubelski were no exception to this social hierarchy.

In November 1939, all Jews were sent into the ghetto that had been set up in Tomaszow-Lubelski; and in July 1942, the ghetto was closed when many of the Jews were sent down the road to the extermination camp or to the Cieszanow labor camp. A number of Jews escaped to the forest, where they survived living off the land, eating turnips and fruit; their only shelter was holes they dug in the ground covered with brushwood. They remained hidden until the Russians arrived, while others joined partisan units operating in the area. From 1943 until the liberation of the area by the Red Army in July 1944, skirmishes between the "OUN," the "AK," and other militias against the German occupation forces were a regular occurrence. Relief came to the entrapped Polish communities on July 21, 1944, when Soviet and AK units seized the area from the fleeing Germans. By this time all traces of the Belzec Death Camp had been obliterated, landscaped, and planted with firs. A Ukrainian farmer was now resident in premises hastily built by the Germans before they left the area.

The eastern part of Poland was now occupied by the Russians and would remain so until 1991, when a legitimate government emerged. There are no major industries in the district, few shops, high unemployment and no sign of improvement. Belzec and the surrounding villages remain a quiet backwater content with their lot but with one important element missing: there are no Jews—and the inhabitants, Poles and Ukrainians, are all the poorer for it. The residents of Belzec are still burdened by the notoriety of the former death camp on their doorstep. Not only is it the forgotten camp, it was the deadliest and most brutal of all the Nazi killing grounds.

The construction and establishment of the Belzec death camp was the Nazis' answer to killing *en mass*. It will be shown that Belzec was the prototype camp, an experimental gassing establishment where the deceptions and procedures developed from the euthanasia experience were implemented. This expertise enabled many thousands of victims to be quietly killed without outside interference and in complete secrecy.

Belzec is the forgotten camp of the Holocaust and has not been treated extensively by historians despite being the blueprint and precursor to Sobibór and Treblinka.

This account discusses many aspects surrounding the destruction of European Jewry and clarifies several major points concerning the character and historiography of the Final Solution, which up to now may have been misinterpreted or their significance underestimated. Other conclusions contained within are based, in part, on the archaeological investigations at the site of the former Belzec camp. It provides a forensic rebuttal of Holocaust revisionist claims and shows these claims for what they are: a malicious, deliberately orchestrated and sinister distortion of the truth.

Geographical Aspects

Belzec was the receiving death camp for the Jews of the Lublin district and the entire area of east and west Galicia.

The Austrians originally referred to Galicia as "Galicia-Lodomeria" after they expropriated that territory from the Polish-Lithuanian Commonwealth during the First Partition of Poland in 1772. Over the years, the borders varied slightly, especially during the Napoleonic Wars, following which Krakow and the surrounding lands were eventually added to Galicia. Galicia became the largest province of the Austro-Hungarian Empire, and bordered Moravia in the west and the Ottoman Empire (Moldavia) to the south. For a time, Bukovina was included in Galicia. This area today forms a part of Romania. Galicia was returned to Poland when the Polish Republic was re-established after the First World War.

Today, the eastern half of Galicia is part of the Republic of the Ukraine, while the western half lies in the Polish Republic. The term Galicia therefore no longer describes an administrative or political region in either country. By far the largest proportion of the rural population in agricultural eastern pre-war Galicia was of Ukrainian nationality, followed by Poles and Jews, the latter dominating commerce and trade. This very large area contained the biggest concentration of Polish Jewry, including some devoutly religious, traditionalist sects.

It was not until the German invasion of the Soviet Union that east Galicia was integrated into the Generalgouvernement, an area where all manner of experiments directed at the Jewish population took place. It was also the area where the most affluent Jews and the poorest lived alongside the wise men and the simple, the intelligentsia, artisans, beggars, and bankers alongside the Hasidim. Regardless of their social standing and circumstances, they all found their final resting place in Belzec. The region was a center and spiritual home of the Diaspora, which was to have its heart torn out in the gas chambers of Belzec. Largely annihilated, the Jews of Galicia and their culture never recovered ... and are now the world of yesterday.

Introduction and Beginnings

On an impulse holiday in June 1974, I travelled by train to Poland and Ukraine (former Polish province of East Galicia). I was honoring a pledge I had given some years earlier to an elderly Jew I had dealt with (as a police officer) at the Central Criminal Court in London, when he was sentenced to five years' imprisonment for committing serious fraud. Despite his criminal record, he was a decent man who told me the story about his parents and relatives who had all died in the Holocaust. Then he was on his own, without family, relatives, or friends.

During the course of many interviews he pleaded with me to find the men responsible and expose the tragedy of Galician Jewry—particularly the men responsible for the demise of his own family, who had lived in the Galician town of Kolomyja. It transpired that just before the German onslaught in June 1941 into East Galicia, this elderly Jew fled east to Kiev. After the war he returned to Kolomyja where he discovered his loss: 37 near and dear relatives had perished, believed murdered in local forests, the Lvov- Janowska camp, and the extermination camp of Belzec.

At the time, I had no real interest and other priorities. Thus I had no reason to pick up the challenge. Belzec, Galicia, Kolomyja had not yet come into my vocabulary, but the more I thought about it, the more I dabbled in Holocaust literature and the more I sensed the injustice of post-war retribution for the men who had committed what appeared to me as the world's greatest crime.

Sadly, after two years of serving his sentence my friend died suddenly from natural causes. As it turned out, I took up the challenge and after 30 years of Holocaust research I have to admit defeat, as I never traced any record of his named family or any record of their final demise. But what follows is, perhaps, second best: a reappraisal of historical facts focusing on Belzec as a vehicle plotting the *modus operandi* of the total destruction of European Jewry, particularly in East Galicia, and the identification of the main perpetrators.

I have done my best: the prosecutor had become his friend and had honored his pledge—too late for the old man to know.

My search for the truth began at the gates of Belzec in November 1975. Walking out of Belzec railway station I turned left. After walking for about 400 meters, I came across the site designated as the former camp. There were iron gates and a map of the area in Polish. Local youths were playing football on the grass. People were walking and cycling on a well worn diagonal footpath to the next village. Further on, in a wooded area, a group of local youths entertained themselves with alcohol and a barbecue. Bottles, tins, and wrappings of all descriptions were strewn all over. It looked like a discarded piece of wasteland that could be found in any town.

To the left, on a sloping escarpment, my hands sifted through the sand, picking out minute pieces of what I presumed to be human bone that had been brought to the surface by the weather. Scuffing the earth with my shoe, I uncovered a kneecap, a collar bone, and pieces of skull. Under my feet, and the feet of all those socially enjoying themselves at that time, was the resting place of 500,000 Jews—men, women and small children—and this is how it remained for the next 30 years.

When the scale of catastrophe of the Holocaust was revealed and western civilization came under the magnifying glass, the symbolic icon chosen to signify this indelible stain on world history was Auschwitz. To a significant extent Auschwitz-Birkenau stamped its name on the consciousness of the world because its combined role as a labor camp and death camp enabled a significant number of people to survive and tell their story. Also, the camp itself remained largely intact to become a site of pilgrimage; whereas by the end of the war Belzec had done its murderous deeds and had been entirely obliterated. Yet in terms of historical reality, the role of symbol for The Final Solution could equally be ascribed to the largely forgotten Belzec.

This account is a reassessment of the history of the Holocaust in Galicia with particular reference to the genesis and function of the Nazi death camps.

The construction and establishment of the Belzec death camp was the Nazis' answer to killing *en mass*. It will be shown that Belzec was the prototype camp, an experimental gassing establishment where the deceptions and procedures developed from the euthanasia experience were implemented. This expertise enabled many thousands of victims to be quietly killed without outside interference and in complete secrecy.

Belzec is the forgotten camp of the Holocaust and has not been treated extensively by historians despite being the blueprint and precursor to Sobibór and Treblinka.

Chapter 1. German Security Services

The police emerge as the middle managers in euthanasia and leaders in the death camps.

Heinrich Himmler **Reinhard Heydrich**

"The task entrusted to us is to guarantee security, law and order in the territories allocated to us, especially in the rear of the German front. This task demands of us that we eliminate ruthlessly every center of resistance and impose in the most drastic way the just death penalty upon the enemies of the German people.

It is the holy duty of senior leaders and commanders to ensure personally that none of our men who have to fulfill this heavy duty should suffer emotional and personal damage thereby. This task is to be fulfilled through the strictest discipline in the execution of official duties and through comradely gatherings at the end of each day that has included such difficult task. The comradely gathering must on no account, however, end in abuse of alcohol. It should be all evening in which they sit and eat at tables, as far as possible in the best German domestic style, with music, speeches and the beauties of German intellectual and emotional life to occupy the hour.

I regard it as important and as a matter of priority to relieve our men from their heavy duties at the right moment. They are to be sent on holiday and then transferred if possible, to other areas and commissioned with new tasks which fully occupy their life.

However, I do not wish that our men mention and talk about (certain) facts and figures. This is out of the question and must be regarded as indecent. Orders and duties of vital importance for a people must be carried out. Afterwards they are not a topic for discussion and conversation." *Reichsführer SS Heinrich Himmler*

The "industrialized" mass murder integral to the Final Solution was instigated and supervised by a relatively small group of politically motivated state and security functionaries. Although it was ultimately accomplished by combined expertise, there was a clear delineation of function and its progression may be divided into two quite separate elements. The first was within the euthanasia program, in which the methodology of the extermination of groups of people was first perfected and the perpetrators retained for subsequent duty within *Reinhardt*. The second element was the delegation of authority by the KdF to the RSHA in order to implement genocidal policies outside of the death camps.

The Nazi "New Order" with its visionary concepts was generally conducted openly and was answerable to the protocols of government. However, *Aktion Reinhardt* was an exception. This distinction is important for a basic understanding of the integral parts of the Nazi genocidal machine.

The catastrophic consequences of the Final Solution are of such magnitude that it is difficult to comprehend how it was possible for such a small group of men to implement it so successfully. Of course, in the wider sense, a multitude of sympathetic or apathetic government personnel were also essential to its implementation, and indeed many were eager to rally around the Nazi flag.

Architects, Planners, Organizers and Perpetrators

The architects and planners: *Führer's* Chancellery (KdF): *Reichsführer-SS* Heinrich Himmler and *SS-Obergruppenführer* Reinhardt Heydrich and associates (HHE).

The organizers: *Sipo-und SD* (*Gestapo/Kripo* and working SD).

The perpetrators: Globocnik's *Reinhardt* Organization, police leadership, Ukrainian Guard units.

Architects and Planners: The Nazi Police State

The degree to which the activities of the Nazi State contravened all normal models of judicial and police procedure meant that a significant number of different state-sponsored organizations were involved in its various actions. With this in mind, some explanatory notes may be helpful.

There is a very apparent difference between the police service of the Weimar Republic, before the Nazis came to power in 1933, and the National Police State (NPS), which evolved under Himmler's direction during the years 1936-1939. The police state after 1933 and the uncontrolled terror which accompanied it could not have evolved the way it did from its existing form pre-1933. Therefore the HHE's reorganization of the security apparatus was an important change of direction, which guided the NPS towards carrying out one of its primary objectives—solving the "Jewish Question."

It is neither assumed nor concluded that the Nazi Police State was driven solely by the "Jewish Question." In fact, its early priorities were directed equally against other sections of society: perceived enemies of the State, sects and churches (including Jews), Party Affairs, the Occupied Territories, counter-intelligence and the frontier police—all targeted in accordance with the Nazi *Weltanschauung* (world view).[3] It would take some time for the NPS, under the cover of the Sipo-SD, to evolve as the main perpetrators of the Nazi genocidal policies. In 1936, Himmler bestowed on himself the title of *"Reichsführer-SS* (a Party function)-*und Chef der Deutschen Polizei"* (a State function).

The abbreviation for the title of Himmler's SS leaders in Nazi-occupied Europe, *SS-und Polizeiführer* - SSPF, likewise reflected the dual origin of a unified police apparatus—SS (Party) and *Polizeiführer* (State). The amalgamation was sealed when Himmler issued a decree on 27 September 1939, establishing the *Reichssicherheitshauptamt* (RSHA.), the *Reich* Main Security Office.

Security Organizations

The Reich Ministry for the Occupied Eastern Territories was organized according to a structure in which an *SS-und Polizeiführer* was directly subordinate to the relevant civil administration (i.e. Dr Hans Frank in the *Generalgouvernement*). Accordingly, there was a *Höhere SS-und Polizeiführer* (HSSPF, Higher SS and Police Leader) at *Reich Kommissariat* level (HSSPF – Friedrich Wilhelm Krüger in Kraków), an SSPF at General *Kommissariat* level (Globocnik in Lublin) and a *Kommandeur der Sipo* (KdS, Commander of the Sipo), the police commander at the local government level.

With the reconstruction of the security services in 1936, there were all kinds of difficulties to overcome. In the early days, the SD had to contend with an identity crisis involving their image and acceptance by the public; it was something of a ramshackle organization with no budget, borrowed typewriters, cardboard boxes for files and very few personnel.[4] Winds of change were sweeping across Germany and many officials of all ranks who were considered to be politically unreliable were being purged. Others, who had shown their loyalty and commitment, were accepted for inclusion in the "New Order." In general, it was predictable that the Nazi State would adopt radical measures to improve the operational efficiency of the police and security agencies which were so central to its program.[5] High on the agenda of this radical thinking was the dispersal of "old wood" —officers who did not measure up—to the outer reaches, bringing in convinced Nazis to replace them.[6]

Security Amalgamation

Himmler, as the supreme police commander, immediately divided the *Kriminalpolizei* (Kripo), the Criminal Police (equivalent to the British CID) into two departments, 1) the Kripo, and 2) the *Sicherheitspolizei* (Sipo), the Security Police. Their combined operational activities brought together the *Geheime Staatspolizei* (Gestapo), the Secret State (Political) Police—with the Kripo, thereby ensuring that the two departments worked closely together. [7] This was a situation that displeased many professional officers of the Kripo. The joint security agency was headed by *SS-Obergruppenführer* Reinhardt Heydrich and became known as *Sipo und SD*.

SD (Security Service) [8] - SIPO (Security Police)

The Security Service or *Sicherheitsdienst* was usually referred to in official German police documents under the abbreviation "SD." It originated as a profoundly conspiratorial espionage organization of German fascism within the Party and the SS, under the leadership of the HHE (Himmler, Heydrich and associates).

The SD was a secret organization within the SS system which, after the seizure of power by the Nazis, had been the first to merge with police agencies both before and after the organization of the RSHA. The SD was very close to the center of power and participated most actively in planning and leading the political functions of the HHE.

The staff of the SD consisted entirely of SS men, since the SD originated from the SS and up to the end of the war was referred to as the SD of the *Reichsführer- SS*. To most people, the SD was the guardian of Nazi policy and a despised and hated section of the security services. They were referred to as the "black power." In occupied Poland and Ukraine the SD became an unyielding octopus, with tentacles reaching to the outermost parts of the occupied territories. No one liked the SD; the *Wehrmacht* commanders cursed it and civilian government officials wrote poison-pen letters to Berlin about it. Yet the SD was all-powerful. It is not known that anyone ever prevailed against it in the *Generalgouvernment*, or elsewhere. The Jewish Question and all that surrounded it was emphatically in the hands of the SD.[9] The functions of the SD can be subdivided as follows:

> **(1)** "General Information," which literally covered everything, as shown by the SD official documents—the *"Lebensgebiete"* or spheres vital to the Nazi government, all government offices, and social circles in Germany.
>
> **(2)** "Special Functions," referring to the elaboration of special files and lists of persons (primarily in countries which were to be invaded). The filing cards and lists

contained names of people who were to be subjected to the "special regime," i.e., either to be physically destroyed or confined to concentration camps.

(3) The function of supplying personnel for the special criminal organizations directly concerned with the realization of German plans for the annihilation of the politically undesirable elements and of the intellectuals in the occupied territories, and for conducting savage executions and "actions." [10]

In addition to the above, the SD was primarily charged with the commission of solving the "Jewish Question."

The SD always retained its character as a Party organization, as distinguished from the *Gestapo*, which was a State organization. The "Jewish Question," and all that came to surround it, was unequivocally in the hands of the SD. This is powerfully illustrated by the fact that the SD was the organization that created the *Einsatzgruppen* (Operational Groups), the mobile killing squads that roamed the rear areas behind the advancing *Wehrmacht*, murdering their victims by shooting in the vicinity of the victim's homes. Later, when the policy changed, the victims were deported to the death camps, which paved the way for the near total destruction of the Jews of mainland Europe.

By 1939, with police amalgamations, the SD made great strides in establishing its credentials as the foremost security service in the *Reich*. After the outbreak of war on 1 September 1939, the SD quickly moved into Poland. To help widen security operations in the occupied areas, the HHE set up a Training Academy in Zakopane, and later at Bad Rabka,[11] with the unwieldy title of *Befehlshaber der Sicherheitspolizei und des SD im GG Schule des Sicherheitspolizei*. By the outbreak of the German-Soviet war in 1941, the Sipo-SD had become an élite and thoroughly politicized security organization.[12]

The SD always managed to keep ahead of their military partners, as the transfer and general movement of their members within the *Reich* was relatively infrequent; whereas the turn over of troops and administrative officers of the military was more rapid. This was the policy within the SD; wherever possible the SD leaders remained in the same location. As a result, the SD was significantly better organized than everyone else, with knowledge and information about local situations and particular individuals. Following Operation Barbarossa (the invasion of the Soviet Union), it was the only stable arm of the military in the *Generalgouvernment*.

The relationship between the *Gestapo* and the SD was sometimes ambiguous. Measures in the *Reich* were carried out under the direction of the *Gestapo*. The SD assisted them. Measures in the occupied regions were under the leadership of the SD, which was the most important link to the SS police machinery. It was a unique espionage and intelligence organization spread over the entire territory of the "Old Reich" as well as throughout the occupied regions and countries.

The 'SS'

Until 1940 the SS was an entirely voluntary organization. After the formation of the *Waffen* SS in 1940 there was a gradual increase in the number of conscripts. It appears that about a third of the total number of people joining the *Waffen* SS were conscripted, and that the proportion of conscripts was higher at the end of the war than at the beginning. However, there continued to be a high proportion of volunteers right up until the end of the war.

SS units were active participants in the steps leading up to aggressive war. The *Verfügungstruppe* was used in the occupation of the Sudetenland, of Bohemia and Moravia, and of Memel. The Henlein Free Corps was under the jurisdiction of the *Reichsführer SS* for operations in the Sudetenland in 1938, and the *Volksdeutschemittelstelle* financed fifth-column activities there.

The SS was particularly involved in the commission of war crimes and crimes against humanity. Through its control over the organization of the Police (HHE), particularly the Sipo und SD, the SS were effectively involved in all the crimes which are outlined within this account.

There is evidence that the shooting of unarmed prisoners of war was the general practice in some *Waffen* SS divisions. On 1 October 1944 the custody of prisoners of war and interned persons was transferred to Himmler, who in turn transferred prisoner-of-war affairs to *SS Obergruppenführer* Berger and *SS Obergruppenführer* Pohl. The Race and Settlement Office of the SS together with the *Volksdeutschemittelstelle* were active in carrying out schemes for Germanization of occupied territories according to the racial principles of the Nazi Party and were involved in the deportation of Jews and other foreign nationals. Units of the *Waffen* SS and *Einsatzgruppen* operating directly under the SS main office were used to carry out these plans. These units were also involved in the widespread murder and ill-treatment of the civilian population of occupied territories. Under the guise of combating partisan units, the SS exterminated Jews and people deemed politically undesirable; their reports record the execution of enormous numbers of people. *Waffen* SS divisions were responsible for many atrocities in occupied territories, such as the massacres at Oradour-sur-Glane and Lidice.

From 1934 onwards the SS was responsible for the guarding and administration of concentration camps. The evidence leaves no doubt that the consistently brutal treatment of the inmates of concentration camps was carried out as a result of the general policy of the SS, which was that the inmates were racial inferiors to be treated only with contempt. There is evidence that where manpower considerations permitted, Himmler wanted to rotate guard battalions so that all members of the SS would be instructed as to the proper attitude to take towards inferior races. After 1942 when the concentration camps were placed under the control of the WVHA they were used as a source of slave labor. An agreement made with the Ministry of Justice on 18 September 1942 provided that antisocial elements that had completed prison sentences were to be delivered to the SS to be worked to death. Steps were continually taken, involving the use of the Security Police and SD and even the *Waffen* SS, to insure that the SS had an adequate supply of concentration camp labor for its projects.

Along with the Sipo-SD, the SS played a particularly significant role in the persecution of the Jews. The evacuation of Jews from occupied territories was carried out under the directions of the SS with the assistance of SS Police units. The extermination of the Jews was carried out under the direction of the SS Central Organizations.

It is impossible to single out any one portion of the SS that was not involved in these criminal activities. The *Allgemeine* SS was an active participant in the persecution of the Jews and was used as a source for concentration camp guard staffing. It supplied personnel for the *Einsatzgruppen* and had command over the concentration camp guards after its absorption of the *Totenkopf* SS, which originally fed the system. Various SS Police units were also widely utilized in the commission of atrocities and the extermination of Jews in the occupied countries.

Police in German Society

It is a generally agreed maxim that a police force can only operate in a free society with the consent of the people. Prior to the ascent of the Nazis, the German police was no exception to this principle and had remained a fully professional and proud service from its inception. Throughout the Weimar Republic until the arrival of National Socialism in 1933 and the major reconstruction of all security services in 1936, the police strove to retain their independence as the guardians of civil law and public order. Yet a large majority of *Schupo* and *Kripo* officers secretly backed the Nazis long before 1933; they saw Nazism as the only authoritarian way of getting rid of the "red menace" and solving Germany's internal problems, and they welcomed the Nazi seizure of power.

To ensure that both the police and public accepted this "New Order," the State hierarchy formulated its own rules and regulations, which broke down many of the traditional boundaries of police and judicial power. To a hard-pressed police service, there were distinct advantages in these increased powers. For a start, it untied their hands from cumbersome ethics when negotiating the intricacies of criminal law and procedure. Search warrants, judges' rules for the interrogation of suspects and applications for bail were dispensed with; complaints against the police were prohibited. Instead, executive search orders, and orders for arrest and detention without any proper legal grounds were introduced and freely applied; statutory appearances before the courts were replaced by orders for committal to the newly established concentration camps for indefinite periods. Consequently, the police were now outside the very law they had previously sworn to uphold and were overtly encouraged by Heydrich to act ruthlessly.

This new turn of events may not have been completely acceptable to every police officer, but the camaraderie and the subculture of the police service held them together through these initial draconian changes. Eventually, by gradual involvement, the police found themselves so deeply involved in their work for the NPS that there was little opportunity of escape. They found themselves caught up in events which they had no power to change. We have a clear view of the difficulties facing a professional police officer from interviews conducted in 1971 by Gitta Sereny with Franz Stangl, the former commandant of Sobibór and Treblinka.[13] Stangl, a native Austrian, exemplifies the pressure brought to bear upon the waverers in the NPS.

Ideological Differences

The Sipo-SD, in its role as the main security service, was now the effective defender of the Party and State, and it was impressed upon its members that the Party was the State and the State the Party. Some disaffected career detectives did not welcome this all-embracing security system[14] and consequently suffered from a crisis of image and identity. They found themselves on the receiving end of SD penetration into their hitherto closely guarded police culture and struggled to resist Nazification and retain their professionalism and self-esteem. According to the Himmler dictum, the transfers between the SS and Sipo-SD were essential for an integrated *Reich* Security Service. To the immense annoyance of long-established career detectives, the *Gestapo*, which they considered an inferior branch of the police service, plundered the ranks of the Kripo of its finest men. Further resentment was caused by the transfer of "inadequate" officers from the *Gestapo* to normal detective duties in the Kripo; these were usually the poorly trained elements considered unfit even for *Gestapo* service. Such was the concern within the Kripo that these *Gestapo* misfits were not permitted to enter the service with the same rank. However, the Kripo were more receptive to those *Gestapo* officers who had been rejected as "politically unreliable." The overall impression formed by the majority of Kripo officers was that these rejects from the *Gestapo* were arrogant and tended to lord it over fellow officers, considering themselves untouchable. As far as the Kripo were concerned, such men were fundamentally unsuitable for normal detective work.[15] Despite the high-minded attitude of the Kripo, which implied a sense of moral standards and incorruptibility, it must be remembered that it was from Kripo ranks that the personnel were drawn for leadership in the death camps: Wirth, Hering, Stangl and Reichleitner were all serving officers of the Kripo at the time of their engagement in T4 and *Reinhardt*. The reorganization resulted in many police officers becoming disillusioned and frustrated, and consequently seeking transfer or retirement rather than serving under the HHE "umbrella." This is perhaps the reason why several of the Kripo were encouraged to transfer to other agencies, one of which was T4. These misgivings were fully understood by Heydrich, who appreciated that his ideas would only be fully accepted by future generations of security personnel. Only later, when his policies had time to become established, would his vision of a fully integrated security apparatus be accomplished.

The era of the career detective was almost over with the introduction of career civil servants and academics of the higher social order, the officer class, appointed from outside to senior command posts in the security services and police. The majority of Sipo-SD personnel who filled the lower ranks were of a lower social status and had a lower standard of education.[16] Considerable emphasis was therefore placed on education and training that would continue throughout a candidate's career. Officer training lasted many months, during which time the candidates would serve in all sections of the security offices (*Abwehr*, Sipo-SS, SD, Kripo, etc) in order to obtain the necessary experience, earn the entitlement to wear the uniform, and gain the respect of their subordinates.[17]

The HHE maintained tight control of Sipo-SD recruitment. Catholicism, adherents of which were continually being purged, was a distinct disadvantage to joining or remaining in the Sipo-SD. In the Sereny-Stangl interviews, it is interesting to note Stangl's observations on this point. Known to be a Catholic and of suspect loyalty to the Nazis, Stangl was targeted for demotion. After the police re-organization of 1939, when he moved to *Gestapo* headquarters in Linz, he was re-designated from *Kriminalbeamter* (established Detective and Civil Servant with pension rights) to *Kriminalassistent* (temporary appointment with no pension rights). Stangl successfully challenged this realignment of rank and was reinstated with the rank of *Kriminaloberassistent*.

Having tried and failed to downgrade him, the establishment then attacked his religious views. As it was known that he was a regular church-goer, Stangl was served with an official document to sign, which confirmed that he was a *Gottgläubiger* (no religious affiliation), and that he had relinquished his religion and all further contacts with the Catholic Church.[18] After some misgivings—or so he claims—Stangl signed as directed. By thus surrendering his religious principles to the Nazi creed, Stangl had compromised himself and was set on a slippery slope.[19]

With the plundering of other related agencies for recruits to the security services, it was accepted initially that some candidates would compromise the philosophy of the Sipo-SD. These elements, such as the rowdy uneducated members of the SA, as well as the "Old Guard," were therefore purged. To maintain the momentum of the recruitment drive, those who were physically sub-standard or unmilitary in demeanour were not automatically excluded from membership of the Sipo-SD. In order to emphasize the obsession with the notion of a pure German *Volk*, Himmler set genealogical requirements: Sipo-SD non-commissioned officers and their wives were required to supply certified details of family blood lines going back to 1750. Refusal to comply or unacceptable results meant dismissal.[20]

There was such a degree of overlap between the SS, SD and Sipo that it was often difficult to establish the difference; for example, although Eichmann was a *Gestapo* officer, he wore an SD uniform. *Gestapo* officers serving in Germany tended to wear civilian clothes, while those serving in the occupied territories usually wore SD uniforms. With few differences, the color of the uniforms was the regulation *Wehrmacht Feldgrau* (field grey), the same as the *Waffen*-SS. The shirt was yellowish to indicate Nazi Party affiliation. A telltale sign of a Sipo-SD officer was the high-brimmed field-grey cap with a black band bearing the silver *Totenkopf* (Death's Head) insignia. Most of the personnel serving in the *Einsatzgruppen*, regardless of whether or not they were members of the SD, wore the full service uniform of the SS. Those who were actually SD men wore a small black diamond-shaped insignia containing the letters "SD" embroidered in silver on the left sleeve. Those who had served in the *Gestapo* wore similar badges, but with a silver cord edging. The Sipo-SD held the mantle of leadership in the *Einsatzgruppen* in Poland and Russia, and in many wartime photographs of executions it is often difficult to differentiate between uniforms.[21]

At the end of the day, the Sipo-SD under the guidance of the HHE would be the main body responsible for guiding and organizing the mass extermination of the Jews—men, women, and children.

Police Leadership[22]

One of the cornerstones of this account is the role played by the police in the euthanasia program and the progression to the "Final Solution."

The leadership and management in T4, and later of all three *Reinhardt* death camps, was placed in the hands of co-opted middle-ranking Kripo officers who had all previously been engaged in T4.[23] This employment of the police in the State-sanctioned euthanasia operation and the death camp system marks the emergence of a dramatic change in police functions and structures. It perhaps emphasizes the contrast between their roles in "normal society" and in the "racial state," where their function included "purification" and "racial hygiene." This led logically to euthanasia and genocide.

The middle-ranking police officers were the business managers of euthanasia; they supervised many aspects of the killing operation as registrars, office chiefs, accountants, compilers of statistics, and managers of the victims' estates. When transferred to *Reinhardt,* they undertook similar tasks in the Lublin HQ of *Reinhardt* and the *Kommandantur* in Belzec, Sobibór and Treblinka. Of course, in the death camps their management duties assumed a much more lethal role. In Belzec a few of the lower-ranking police officers were engaged in office duties: Erwin Fichtner, Werner Borowski and Rudi Bär were all office bound.[24] Police officers Fritz Hirsch and Ernst Schemmel were permanently engaged in the administration office in Belzec and seldom if ever entered the camp. Another police officer, Arthur Dachsel, was an on-site maintenance worker in Belzec and was rarely involved in the killing process. It is interesting to note that although these men were serving police officers initially seconded to T4 and later to *Reinhardt*, they continued to wear their police uniforms well into the destruction program. It was in December 1942 that all camp commanders were issued with *Waffen*-SS uniforms. This suggests that it was only at this stage that they were finally consolidated as a collective uniformed presence n the death camps. By this time, of course, although Belzec had ceased to function as a death camp, there was plenty of "work" still to be done.

Death Camp Commandants[25]

Left to right, Christian Wirth (Belzec, Sobibor, Treblinka); Franz Stangl (Sobibor, Treblinka); Gottlieb Hering (Belzec); Franz Karl Reichleitner (Sobibor).

Throughout its short history the Belzec death camp was completely dominated by the personalities of its two commandants, SS-*Obersturm-führer/Kriminalkommissar* Christian Wirth[26] and *Kriminalobersekretar* Gottlieb Hering.[27] Both men came from Württemberg in southwest Germany and had remarkably similar backgrounds, characters and temperaments. Wirth was born on 24 November 1885 in Oberbalz-heim, a small market town in Upper Swabia, 25 km south of Ulm, and Hering on 2 June 1887 in the town of Leonberg, 15 km west of Stuttgart. After leaving school at the age of 14 they each attended vocational courses for two years, Wirth in carpentry and joinery, and Hering in agriculture. Upon conscription into the Kaiser's Imperial Army, Wirth served with Grenadier Regiment 123 ('*Konig Karl*') in the old garrison city of Ulm from 1905-1907, and Hering with Uhlan (cavalry) Regiment 20, also in Ulm, from 1907-1909. After discharge, they both reenlisted with their old regiments, Wirth for another two years of service— until 1910, and Hering for another three years—until 1912. On their final return to civilian life, both of them joined the Württemberg *Schutzpolizei* and served as constables in Heilbronn. Hering, however, first attended a police training school. Wirth transferred to the Kriminalpolizei (Kripo)—the plain clothes detective force—in Stuttgart in 1913, and in October the following year enlisted with Reserve Infantry Regiment 246 in Ulm for active service on the Western Front. He spent three years in the trenches a few km northeast of Ypres, and was invalided home twice. The last time was in December 1917, after which he remained in Stuttgart as a military policeman with Reserve Infantry Regiment 119, guarding an army supply dump. During this duty he earned the praise of his superiors for protecting the dump against "revolutionary forces."

Hering stayed in the police until his call-up in 1915, and then served on the Western Front with a machine-gun company of Grenadier Regiment 119. He did not return home until after the Armistice in November 1918. Both men were highly decorated for bravery in the field and received field promotions to NCO rank, Wirth to the rank of *Offizier Stellvertreter*.

On Armistice Day, Sunday, 11 November 1918, Wirth was so distraught with events in Germany and the final capitulation that he tried to shoot himself. His suicide was prevented by his mother.

After demobilization from the army, both Wirth and Hering rejoined the Stuttgart police force. Until this time their lives had been very similar, even to the extent that they were both obliged to marry their respective lady friends when the ladies were six months pregnant: Wirth married in 1910 and Hering in 1914. Wirth had two sons, Eugen, born in 1911, and Kurt in 1922; in the intervening years another child died in infancy. Hering had one son, Willy, born in 1914. They differed only in religion. Wirth was a Protestant and Hering a Catholic.

During the turbulent post-war years, however, the two men followed very different political paths. In 1922, Wirth illegally became a very early member of the Nazi Party (NSDAP), while Hering—also illegally—joined the Social Democrats (SPD). Their acts were illegal because in the Weimar Republic civil servants, including members of the police, were prohibited from joining political organizations. After the failure of Hitler's "Beer Hall *Putsch*" in Munich in 1923 and the banning of the Nazi Party, Wirth—and many other hard-line Nazis—joined the German National People's Party (DNVP), another extreme right wing organization. During the years of the Weimar Republic, Wirth was based at *Dienststelle* II (Precinct II) situated at Büchsenstraße 37 in Stuttgart as a detective with the theft, robbery and extortion squad. Early on, he had been made station chief and attained the rank of *Kriminalkommissar*. In 1931, Wirth again illegally rejoined the Nazi Party.

In the Weimar Republic, Hering also attained the rank of *Kriminal-kommissar*, but only after attending an officers' training course, and was posted in turn to the Kripo offices in Göppingen and Schwenningen in the Stuttgart area. During this period he earned the name of *"Nazifresser"* (Nazi Eater), because of his vigorous acts against Party members and uniformed members of the *Sturmabteilungen* (SA), the Stormtroopers. After the Nazi seizure of power in January 1933, local SS and SA leaders demanded Hering's dismissal from the police, and several court actions were brought against him. However, at the official investigation into his anti-Nazi past, Wirth spoke up for him and the charges were dropped. Overnight, Gottlieb Hering became a fervent Nazi and in Wirth's debt.

On 30 June 1933, Wirth joined the staff of SA-*Sturmbann* 119 in Stuttgart with the rank of *Sturmführer*. At this time the SA had about a half million members, and in Wurttemberg only 50 percent belonged to the Nazi Party. Wirth, then aged 48, was something of a rarity—there were very few Stormtroopers over 40. But his membership did not prevent him from arresting and charging SA and SS leaders in the Stuttgart area with criminal offences, notably for attacking members of the public, damage to private property, and the illegal imprisonment of innocent people in the so-called "wild" concentration camps set up by the SA. He even obtained the release of several people incarcerated in such camps at Heuberg, Obere Kuberg Welzheim and Hohenasperg. During the arrests of SA and SS leaders, Wirth instructed his men to use their weapons if they encountered resistance. His explanation for such actions was that he was fulfilling his duty as an impartial officer of the law.

By the mid-1930s Wirth had acquired a reputation as a good criminologist with exceptional organizational and administrative abilities, and complete dedication to duty. In consequence, he was appointed the head or deputy head of virtually every police and Party organization in Stuttgart and the State of Württemberg. However, unlike a great many police officers who wished to further their careers, he did not join the SS in 1936 when by decree Himmler became *Reichsführer-SS und Chef der Deutsche Polizei* (Reich Leader of the SS and Chief of the German Police). The decree placed all branches of the German police in SS hands while granting the SS full police powers, thus ensuring that the two organizations henceforth worked in close cooperation. The complete takeover of all the forces of law and order in the *Reich* and their incorporation into the SS had the extraordinary result of placing the police outside the law—the very law that all officers had taken an oath to uphold.

Wirth's influential functions within the Party and police, however, had attracted the attention of *SS-Obergruppenführer* Reinhard Heydrich's *Sicherheitsdienst* (SD), the Security Service of the SS, and he was recruited into their ranks, primarily to pass on information about the political attitudes and reliability of Party members and fellow police officers.

In 1938 Wirth received an important appointment, that of head of *Kommissariat* 5, the Stuttgart serious crimes squad, which included the murder squad. In October he joined the SS with the rank of *Untersturmfuhrer*.

Wirth's career with the Stuttgart Kripo was almost legendary and spanned a period of 20 years, 1919-1939; to his superiors he was "unquestionably irreproachable on duty and morally impeccable." *Kriminalkommissar* Hermann Schaaf, one of Wirth's close friends on the detective squads, described him thus:

> He was a criminologist from head to toe, energetic and methodical, unflinching in his fight against the criminal underworld and was the most hated man in criminal circles ... Ruthless to himself he sacrificed innumerable nights and Sundays to lead the fight against the criminal underworld. Through this, he had the trust of the Stuttgart Kripo, and not only in Wurttemberg but also further afield ... he was always in demand, which earned him a considerable reputation.

Wirth, according to Schaaf, was equally ruthless with his own men if they exceeded their authority or took advantage of their position as a police officer.

Wirth's impartiality as a police officer has been stressed by a secretary employed at the Stuttgart Kripo headquarters, Frau Hedwig Roller, who for a time was also Wirth's secretary: "In his official dealings he let himself be guided by his sense of duty and not by the appearance of the person."

Kriminalobersekretar Georg Ziegler, who worked with Wirth throughout his entire police career, summed him up as follows:

> He was a frank and sincere man as well as a zealous, unshakable and energetic officer. He was a soldier from top to bottom, and every wish of his superiors was his command.
>
> In the fight against the criminal underworld he had, through his untiring hard work, his fearlessness, and through his cunning and skill achieved the biggest results and so took the reputation of the Stuttgart Kripo far across the State borders. He unselfishly and energetically stood up for the welfare and grievances of his subordinates and comrades.
>
> Wirth, above all, was respected and was called in to deal with all serious cases because he was the kind of exceedingly efficient officer who is seldom found.

On 28 February, Wirth was appointed Chairman of the Police Disciplinary Court in Stuttgart, a post he was to hold until 30 June 1940.

In the spring of 1939, Wirth was sent to Vienna on a special police mission "of a political nature," and at this time his personal file was marked: "z. V. *Fuhrer*" (*zum Verfugung Fuhrer*), i.e. "at the disposal of the *Fuhrer*". SS-*Untersturmfuhrer/Kriminalinspektor* Christian Wirth had been earmarked for future important "special tasks." After Vienna he was attached to the staff of the Chief of the *Sicherheitsdienst* and SD in Prague and sent to Olmitz (Olomouc) in Czechoslovakia to set up a *Reich* Kripo office and to investigate anti-Nazi activities in the area.

On 27 September, Hitler signed a decree for the creation of the *Reichssicherheitshauptamt* (RSHA, Reich Security Main Office) which formally united the police forces of the Third Reich and the security services of the SS unto one mammoth bureaucratic organization with Reinhard Heydrich at its head. Shortly afterwards, Wirth's personal file was transferred at the request of the SD from Stuttgart to *Amt* I (Legal and Administration) at the RSHA in Berlin. From then on, his superiors at the Police Presidium and Kripo headquarters in Stuttgart had little to do with him beyond paying his monthly salary and noting his nominations for promotion and advancement through the ranks. On 1 October, Wirth was promoted to *SS-Obersturmfuhrer* and shortly thereafter left Stuttgart to begin the "special task" for which he had been selected in the spring. He never returned to normal Kripo duty in Stuttgart, and returned to the city only rarely on leave.

In the meantime Hering had also fared well under the Nazis since his radical change of political allegiance. In 1934 he was appointed head of the Kripo office in Göppingen before being attached to the Police Presidium in Stuttgart where his skills as a detective were also recognized, and in 1937 he was appointed *Kriminalbezirksekretär* (Regional Crime Officer) at the Police Presidium. He was briefly transferred back to Schwenningen in 1939 before he too was posted away on "special duty."

Leutnant der Schutzpolizei Franz Stangl

Stangl graduated from the Vienna Police Academy in 1933. By 1934, he was an ordinary uniformed constable with no particular career aspirations. His subsequent career and ultimate fate were guided by the simple premise of luck and opportunity. In 1935 he transferred to the Kripo as a Detective Constable in the Political Police dealing on a day-to-day basis with political agitators and other subversive elements.[28] Basically an intelligent man but not gifted academically, he was capable enough in his daily duties, and in normal times would have progressed through the ranks until his retirement, causing few ripples. However, these were not normal times, even in the tranquillity of Wels, where he was stationed, and to which he commuted daily from his home in Linz.

In March 1938 the "*Anschluss*" of Austria took place, with the introduction of Nazism on a scale even more fanatical than in Germany. However, although there was generally an overwhelming welcome for the "New Order," some were not so happy. The HHE had carried out their preparatory intelligence work and were in a position to stamp out any dissent by using their previously prepared lists of opponents. The Austrian Police were high on the list. In Stangl's office, three out of the five detectives on duty were arrested by the *Gestapo* and removed to a concentration camp.[29] In the Police headquarters in Linz, two senior officers were shot without arrest or trial.[30] What is interesting about Stangl's recollections of those times is the way he took precautions to head off trouble. He states that he removed all evidence from the police files that implicated him and his colleagues in any anti-Nazi activity. By calling in past favors, Stangl managed to falsify official records by adding his name and a false membership number to the list of the Nazi Party in Austria which, prior to the *"Anschluss"* had been a proscribed political Party. Stangl backdated his membership by two years. He thus would appear more committed to the Nazi party than he actually was at that time.[31]

By October 1938 Stangl was fully integrated into the Nazi system. In January 1939, with the reorganization of the German security services, he was now established in the *Gestapo* HQ in Linz, the first step on the ladder towards the "Final Solution." The police and security services had changed from being an authority administered (State-by-State) by the individual *Länder* (States) in Germany to a national security force that extended throughout the entire *Reich* to root out and eliminate all opposition to the Nazi regime. The Kripo was now the protector of "social order," backed up by the Schupo.[32]

When the Reich security services were amalgamated in September 1939, Stangl found himself entangled in the politicization of the police, and according to him, this was a most unhappy time as he was in direct conflict with his immediate superior, Georg Prohaska, the chief of the Linz *Gestapo*. Despite Stangl's emphatic assertion in the Gitta Sereny interviews that he was never a Nazi sympathiser, he certainly showed his conversion to Nazi ideology when he voluntarily transferred to the *Judenreferat* (Jewish Department), moving about the country registering Jewish communities.[33] Then, inexplicably (so he claims), a transfer order signed personally by Himmler instructed Stangl to report to *SS-Oberführer* Viktor Brack[34] at Tiergartenstrasse 4 in Berlin, where he was interviewed for duty in T4.[35]

When, in a later interview, Sereny asked Stangl if he knew at that time what Tiergartenstrasse 4 was, he replied, *"I had no idea. I had heard it vaguely referred to now and then as T4, but I didn't know what their specific function was."*[36]

Stangl's accounts of his involvement with T4 are replete with contradictions. It was perhaps the product of years of thinking through convenient answers to probing questions, which he knew would arise at some time. About the time of Stangl's appointment, other police officers were also seconded to T4, among them Franz Reichleitner, who succeeded Stangl at Sobibór, and in the lower ranks, Friedrich Tauscher, Fritz Hirsche, Franz Schemmel and Kurt Küttner, who were all prominent police appointments in T4 and *Reinhardt*.

Stangl had taken the bait of promises of promotion and other rewards, the kudos of working under the auspices of the KdF, accelerated promotion and extra pay. T4 must have considered that they had the right man (no doubt on Wirth's recommendation) for the work envisaged, as these were clear bribes to induce him to accept the appointment. It certainly worked, as Stangl was duly promoted to *Leutnant der Polizei* (Police Lieutenant)—above his then current rank—and sent back to Linz to await further orders. (All the Kripo officers assigned to T4 killing institutions had to have at least one rank above the local police chief; so that no local officer could question or argue with a higher-ranking officer). In November 1940 he was sent to the Schloss Hartheim euthanasia institute where he met *Kriminalkommissar* Wirth and later became his deputy. This was a decisive moment for Stangl. He had now crossed the line to become employed in State-sponsored mass murder.[37] A final seal of approval from the KdF came when Globocnik eventually appointed him as commandant of Sobibór (to replace *SS-Hauptsturmführer* Richard Thomalla who had built the Belzec and Sobibór camps[38]).

Stangl is an interesting example when examining the question of motivation. As the commandant of Sobibór, he proved his worth to the system and was transferred to the higher profile Treblinka camp on 2 August 1942, the day after Wirth's appointment as Inspector of the *SS-Sonderkommandos* of *Aktion Reinhardt*.[39]

Stangl's duty at Sobibór and later Treblinka was, in the first place, to obey orders and efficiently carry out his duties.[40] He intimated in conversation with Sereny that he was indifferent to the fate of the Jews and only saw them as "material objects" which had to be "dealt with." By keeping his distance from the victims he was able to recede into the background, attending the inferno only when he chose to or in the event of an emergency. He then returned to his quarters and indulged himself in self-recrimination and heavy drinking, leaving the everyday unpleasant tasks to his staff.

The few survivors from Sobibór and Treblinka—mainly long-term prisoners— refer to him as being softly-spoken, courteous and impeccably dressed. Stangl was never seen with or known to carry firearms, only a short riding crop as part of his dress. The point to enforce here is that overt actions of cruelty were neither encouraged nor discouraged, as "Jews were Jews" and not considered human within the political doctrine of Nazism.

In my view, Stangl was an ardent Nazi well before the "*Anschluss*" and remained committed throughout the entire war, although his personality was not suited to the special role for which he had been selected. He found himself in the wrong job but was too weak to rebuff the inducements offered; having accepted them, it was too late, there was no way back. In a sense, he too may be considered a victim, albeit a victim of circumstances, occasioned by his own human frailty and moral weakness. As for the thousands of Jews in whose murder he was directly implicated on a daily basis, Stangl was completely unconcerned about their fate. Whatever Stangl's attempts may have been to weasel his way out of the accusations by Gitta Sereny, there is one particular damning incident which, in my opinion, places him at the forefront of Jewish extermination: he personally designed and ordered the construction of the fake railway station at Treblinka to allay the fears of arriving victims. A mini-industry evolved in Treblinka which was to be a life-saving project for Jewish artists and sign-writers. Stangl supervised the design and painting of a sign, with black letters on a white background:

"Bahnhof Obermajdan! Umsteigen nach Bialystok und Wolkowysk!"
(Obermajdan Station! Change here for Bialystok and Volkovysk!). Other
signs announced First Class, Second Class, Third Class, Waiting Room,
Cashier, etc. The Jews arriving at "Obermajdan" saw what appeared to be
railway workers in uniform performing normal jobs. The final touch was a
large round station clock. The reception area at Treblinka had been
transformed into what appeared to be an ordinary railway station like any
other in order cruelly to deceive the victims into believing they were *en-route*
to sunnier places.[41]

Police Motivation

The police had a certain amount of choice regarding transfers to other duties.
They were not conscripted, they were recruited. No pressure was applied to
induce them to join the euthanasia program and subsequently *Reinhardt;* but
once the transfer to *Reinhardt* had been accomplished, the situation changed.
An example is the career of Jacob Wöger. In 1936, Wöger was a serving
Kriminalsekretär (Detective Sergeant) in the Stuttgart Kripo, the same force
in which Wirth and Hering had served and from which they had been
recruited to T4. In 1939, he was called-up by the KdF and offered a transfer
to T4 at Grafeneck, (one of the two euthanasia centers operating at that time).
Upon completion of his duty at Grafeneck he returned to the Stuttgart Kripo
without any complications. Hermann Holzschuh in 1937 was also a
Kriminalsekretär in the Stuttgart Kripo. In 1940, like Wöger and many
others, he was selected for T4, which he also accepted. Holzschuh also
served in Grafeneck as Wöger's deputy and succeeded him when Wöger
returned to normal duties. Holzschuh served in T4 until he was also
transferred to other duties and replaced by Franz Stangl. Neither Wöger nor
Holzschuh reappeared in the Jewish extermination operation and as far as can
be established, their transfers back to normal duties did not compromise
them.[42]

The method of recruitment does suggest some kind of complicity conducted
by the management. Wirth was probably at the center of this and was no
doubt influential in these appointments. It is also probable that the senior
police officers engaged in T4 and then *Reinhardt* were fully briefed as to the
nature of their duties. That is, they knew that T4 and *Reinhardt* were centers
for group and mass murder. Because these men had come from a disciplined
service, much reliance was placed on their ability to conduct themselves
without supervision and their capacity for improvisation in matters of great
secrecy. The police officers had proved their loyalty and abilities to the HHE
and were now trusted and given autonomy in organizing and carrying out
their duties. As shown in the early days of T4, they were prepared to forego
their professional training and join the *Führer's* clique in their quest for
personal advancement, even if it included in the process the cold-blooded
murder of men, women and children.

The importance of the German police service within the framework of both T4 and *Reinhardt* should not be underestimated. It is plausible that the police superseded the SD in the death camps because of Wirth's influence with the KdF and his contention that he required his own men to be the controlling factor. The police remained the leading group in *Reinhardt*, even above the *Allgemeine* (General) and *Waffen* (Armed) SS/SD who, although operationally involved on the outside, had no say or influence inside the camps or on how the mass murder was to be carried out.

Chapter 2. Embracing Euthanasia [43]
Euthanasia Centers

Euthanasia Centers and their intermediate Mental Homes

Bernburg ☐
Alt-Scherbitz, Görden, Jerichow, Königslutter, Neuruppin, Sachsenberg, Teubitz, Uchtspringe
Brandenburg ☐

Grafeneck ☐
Schussenried, Weinsberg, Weißenau, Winnental, Zwiefalten
Hadamar ☐
Andernach, Eichberg, Galkhausen, Herborn, Idstein, Scheuern, Weilmünster, Weinsberg, Wiesloch
Hartheim ☐

Sonnenstein ☐
Arnsdorf, Großschweidnitz, Waldheim, Zschadrass

Establishment of 'Charitable Foundation'

The ultimate authority for the euthanasia operation was *Hauptamt* II (Main Office II) of the *Führer's* Chancellery, headed by *SS-Oberführer* Viktor Brack, at Voss Strasse 4 in Berlin; and the organization set up specifically to administer the operation was given the innocuous name of the *Gemeinnützige Stiftung für Anstaltspflege* (Charitable Foundation for Institutional Care). This was simply the cover name allowing the KdF to conceal its direct involvement in the killing operation, and all personnel employed were members of the Foundation. At the beginning of December 1939 the Foundation moved into offices on the top floor of the "Columbus Haus," an eight-story office block on Potsdamer Platz, not far from Voss Strasse. It could only be contacted through a Post Office Box Number at the Post Office nearby: PO Box 261, Berlin W9. [44]

It is estimated that there were approximately 5,000 child deaths within the children's euthanasia program. In the killing centers of T4, no less than 70,273 adults and juveniles were killed. In the program 14f13 from April 1941 to 1944, it is estimated that 50,000 concentration camp prisoners were killed.[45]

Overview and Introduction

Prior to the camps of *Reinhardt* the Nazis established a policy of direct medical killing: that is, killing arranged within medical channels, by means of medical decisions, and carried out by medical professionals. The program was known as "euthanasia," a camouflage for its real meaning and purpose—mass murder. "Their aim was to induce death, and experiments on poison gas were a test bed for the Final Solution."[46]

"Life unworthy of life" *(lebenunwertes Leben)* was the concept adhered to by the Nazi mandarins when pursuing their biological, racial and "therapeutic" ideology to its maximum. The prosecution at Nuremberg saw euthanasia as the cruel culmination of racial medicine.

There appear to be four identifiable steps: coercive sterilization; killing of "impaired" children in hospitals; killing of physically "impaired" adults; the extended program to euthanase "impaired" inmates of concentration and extermination camps with a clear emphasis on the murder of Jews.

As with the Holocaust that followed, medical killing of psychiatric patients was an open secret with gradations of collective knowledge. Perpetrators were impelled by pressure from peers and superiors, unquestioning obedience, racist ideology and careerism. Perpetrators and bystanders' denial was facilitated by use of deceptive language, bureaucratic and technical proficiency, and notions such as a "greater cause" or a "sacred mission."

Dissociation and numbing were common. Psychiatrists were the main medical specialists involved because Nazi race and eugenic ideology (accepted by many psychiatrists) targeted mentally ill people for sterilization and euthanasia, and because psychiatrists were state-controlled and tended to objectify patients. Few psychiatrists resisted.

The grant of a "mercy death" is conditional upon either the consent of the individual, that of the next-of-kin, or failing the availability of either, expert medical opinion. It may sometimes consist of a combination of any two, or even all three of these parties. To an extent, it may often be described as voluntary, which indeed was the meaning originally given to the word. But Nazi "euthanasia" was quite different in conception and practice from the dictionary definition, old or new. It was derived not from humanitarian or compassionate reasoning, but from pseudo-scientific theory and ruthless economic policy.

The Nazis destroyed "life unworthy of life," as they termed it, not as an act of mercy, but as part of a strategy to murder that part of the population least able to defend itself. That policy was directed not only at German citizens, but at those of eastern European countries that fell under Nazi hegemony, particularly Poland. The "euthanasia" program formed an essential part of the evolving Nazi policy of extermination on a massive scale. That policy reached its apogee with the murder of the Jews; but had the program arrived at its intended conclusion, the eventual death toll would have been immeasurably greater.

The Nazis did not create this twisted version of euthanasia. Its roots lay in a selective reading of the evolutionary theories of Charles Darwin, and the distorted "scientific" thinking to which this gave birth. The term "eugenics," has no scientific basis. It was coined in 1881 by the British naturalist and mathematician Francis Galton, who described it as "the science of the improvement of the human race by better breeding." This took the concept of "survival of the fittest," a fundamental element of Nazi ideology, to its logical conclusion. Eugenics developed within the larger movement of Social Darwinism, which applied Darwin's "struggle for survival" to human affairs.

The fundamental tenet of the eugenics movement was that restricting the ability of "inferior" people to procreate, while maximizing that of "superior individuals," would benefit society. Attention was focused on the feebleminded (an inaccurate term covering everything from mental retardation to alcoholism), labelled as idiots, imbeciles, or morons. It was suggested that there existed a relationship between low intelligence and both immorality and crime.

Against such a background of pernicious nonsense masquerading as legitimate scholarly research, it is hardly surprising that Adolf Hitler became an early and enthusiastic supporter of this "euthanasia." In Germany the term "Race Hygiene" was in use long before the label of "eugenics" became common, and the German Society for Race Hygiene (*Deutsche Gesellschaft für Rassenhygiene*) was eventually to represent all eugenicists. It took Samuel Beckett to point out the irony in this Nazi obsession with the creation of a race of "supermen." An "Aryan," he wrote, must be blonde like Hitler, thin like Göring, handsome like Goebbels, virile like Röhm—and be named Rosenberg.[47]

After attaining power in 1933, the Nazis began an extensive propaganda campaign with the object of acquainting the German people with the benefits of "euthanasia." Via newspapers and magazines, radio and film, the suggestion was made that life could be so much better for the productive many if the non-productive few, who were such a burden to the nation, were simply eliminated.[48]

But the road to state sanctioned murder was to be a gradual one. With the early introduction of legislation ("Law for the Restoration of the Professional Civil Service" of 7 April 1933) the Nazis thoroughly purged long-established ethical and administrative public supervisory bodies. Less than six months after his election in 1933, Hitler introduced the "Law for the Prevention of Genetically Diseased Offspring." It decreed compulsory sterilization for persons characterized by a wide variety of disabilities. In the same year the Nazis enacted the "Law Against Dangerous Habitual Criminals," which further blurred the distinction between actual criminal behavior and the inappropriate social behavior that characterized many people with disabilities.

The law stipulated that these criminal asocials *(asozialen)* could be committed to state asylums, held in indeterminate protective custody, and, in the case of sex offenders, officially castrated. These and other laws prepared the ground for the Nuremberg Laws of 1935, which, while directed primarily at Jews, also regulated marriage among people with disabilities. For example, the "Marriage Health Law" prohibited marriage between two people if either party suffered from some form of mental disability, had a "hereditary disease" as previously defined by law, or suffered from a contagious disease, particularly tuberculosis or venereal disease.

By the end of 1938, the regime was receiving requests from the families of newborn or very young children with severe deformities and brain damage for the grant of a "mercy killing" *(Gnadentod)*. In particular, a petition was received with respect to an infant named Gerhard Herbert Kretschmar,[49] the so-called "Knauer"[50] child, who had been born on 20 February 1939, blind, with one leg and part of one arm missing, and who was described as an "idiot."[51] Hitler ordered Karl Brandt, his personal physician, to visit the child in a hospital at Leipzig. Brandt testified at his post-war Nürnberg trial that he had been instructed that if the facts provided by the child's father proved to be correct, he was to inform the physicians in Hitler's name that euthanasia could be carried out—which it was, on 25 July 1939. It is arguable that the Knauer case was the catalyst for all that followed, although it could equally be argued that Hitler's dedication to euthanasia was such that its introduction was inevitable at some point in the mercifully brief history of National Socialism.

On his return to Berlin, Brandt was authorized by Hitler to proceed in the same fashion with similar cases. Hitler did not wish to be publicly associated with what even he considered to be a delicate matter; and so Brandt was ordered to organize a program with the aid of Philip Bouhler, head of the Chancellery of the *Führer* (an agency created by Hitler in 1934, ostensibly to keep him in direct touch with the concerns of the population, but acting in practice as Hitler's private office). Under the direction of Bouhler, the KdF was to acquire a more sinister purpose, for it was to be the conduit through which first the euthanasia program and subsequently the planned mass extermination of Jews and others was to operate. Answerable to nobody except Hitler, in 1939 Bouhler seized the opportunity to acquire authorization to administer the euthanasia program through his deputy, Viktor Brack.

In May 1939 Hitler had instructed Brandt to pave the way for the killing of children by setting up a body entitled the "Reich Committee for the Scientific Registering of Serious Hereditary and Congenital Illnesses." By a decree dated 18 August 1939, doctors and midwives were ordered to report all cases of "deformed" newborns. Even before war came in September 1939, the Nazis had thus established a government-sanctioned process for murder. Two laymen made a preliminary selection of cases, which was then reviewed by three medical professors who determined the fate of the child. If selected for "euthanasia," the child was transferred to one of a list of special hospital wards for killing.

As early as July 1939, Werner Heyde, who was to play a prominent role in the euthanasia program, attended a meeting at which he learned of the imminent killing of the adult mentally ill. As with the "Final Solution," "euthanasia" provided a perfect confluence of the two essential elements of National Socialist ideology—the biological and the economic.

It was clear that the regime could expect no great negative reaction to the program from the general populace. A survey conducted in April 1941 revealed that 80 percent of the relatives of those murdered by the program were in agreement with the decision, 10 percent spoke out against it, and 10 percent were indifferent. It has been suggested that this policy of "official secrecy," where people knew while pretending not to know, and only a very few protested, was an invitation to denial and moral indifference on the part of both the German establishment and the German nation as a whole. It laid the foundation for a similar reaction to the "Final Solution." If people did not protest at the murder of their own relatives, they were hardly likely to do so when Jews, Gypsies, and foreigners were slaughtered.

Although Hitler had already given verbal authorization to the euthanasia enthusiasts, he wished to avoid the passing of an official law. However, he was pressed to confirm his instructions. In a dictatorship, no debate was necessary, no act of government required. It was enough for Hitler simply to issue a command (rarely explicit, and even more infrequently in writing) for his wishes to attain the force of law. And so, in October 1939, a brief decree was issued on Hitler's private stationery and signed by him.[52]

The decree was backdated to 1 September to coincide with the date of commencement of the Second World War. After operating from a number of different addresses, a permanent headquarters for the new organization was established at *Tiergartenstrasse* 4 in Berlin. The premises were rented by the KdF in early 1940 under bogus representation.

Viktor Brack's office was the decision-making agency for all aspects of the euthanasia and the subsequent *Aktion Reinhardt* policies. Although Bouhler was titular head of the whole operation, in fact he had little to do with it unless his authority was needed in dealing with other government agencies. Brandt dealt only with the medical aspect of the operation, and continued to run his medical practice. Heinrich Lammers was head of the *Reich* Chancellery and constantly carped about the lack of a legally proclaimed decree for euthanasia, something Hitler absolutely refused to do. Martin Bormann, head of the Party Chancellery, was kept well away from euthanasia matters because it was well-known at the KdF that in his hands "euthanasia would not stop at mental patients." He was displeased at being excluded because his brother Albert worked for the KdF and was also one of Hitler's adjutants. Brack's deputy was Werner Blankenburg. Hans Hefelmann and Richard von Hegener were the leading lights at the Kdf for children's euthanasia. All the KdF staff involved in euthanasia took the job on in addition to their normal functions, and all were completely immersed in the business of murder.

Individuals recruited for the project were asked if they were prepared to participate. None were coerced. All were required to confirm, by one means or another, their understanding of the necessity to maintain absolute secrecy. Some were told that a euthanasia law existed but could not be shown to them for the same reason of secrecy. Few of those approached declined an invitation to become involved. It was possible to refuse to participate in killing, or to end one's participation, as some did. So far as is known, nobody was executed or sent to a concentration camp for doing so. All the T4 personnel were initially interviewed by Brack or Blankenburg, "even down to the tea-ladies." The recruitment of Dieter Allers may be regarded as typical. In 1939 Allers, a young lawyer, was sent to Poland as an army training sergeant. In November 1940 his mother met Blankenburg in the street and when she told him that her son was in the army, Blankenburg offered to give him a job at the KdF and arranged for his discharge from the military. In January 1941 Allers was appointed managing director of T4 by Brack. "Find men with courage to implement," and "nerves to endure" was mentioned in a speech by Brack recorded by the State Court President (Alexander Bergmann) on 23 April 1941.

Mid-level bureaucrats or desk murderers (*Schreibtischtäter*) best describes the motley clique that administered T4. A surprisingly small number of individuals managed and ran not only T4, but also the *Reinhardt* killing centers. What is extraordinary is the recruiting system adopted to fill the top and middle order of high profile management posts. Very much like the recruitment of the *Reinhardt* personnel via T4, they were a mixture with no particular emphasis or required expertise.

Five of them, Brack, Blankenburg, Hefelmann, von Hegener, and Vorberg, were also working for the KdF but with additional remuneration were persuaded to split their time accordingly. The management installed in T4 resembled musical chairs rather than a well-oiled department managing the *Reich's* most closely guarded secrets.

These unexceptional men were all of similar age, born between 1900 and 1910. The majority came from middle class families. Five received post graduate education: Bohn (with a doctorate) and Allers became lawyers; Hefelmann received a doctorate in agriculture; Brack obtained a diploma in economics, and Schmiedel a diploma in engineering. Others received an average secondary school education and appeared to have had no specific aspirations. None of them showed any interest in furthering a program of state murder.

The single thread that holds these men together would appear to be their political affiliation to the Nazi party and their commitment to euthanasia. All appeared to have embraced Nazi ideology, including its racial and eugenic component.[53] These men were the innovators who operated the first technical killing centers.

Leading KdF functionaries did not sit in their offices and direct operations from their desks. They were hands-on supervisors who travelled widely to T4 institutions and the killing centers in the east to inspect the results of their deadly work.

T4 Non-medical personnel

The clear picture that emerges in respect of the lower echelon of recruits is that to a man, they presumed that they would be continuing their normal trade. It was only when they were faced with the reality of T4 that they realized it was too late. Each man received a "summons or order to report" to T4, where they were interviewed and assessed. Within days, these civilians had been selected, conscripted, sworn to secrecy and inducted into T4.[54] Among those selected were individuals possessing various skills: drivers, mechanics, male nurses, typists, cooks, carpenters, electricians, plumbers etc.

Of 37 staff who served at Bełżec, only four or five were bona-fide *Waffen*-SS and three of these were T4 practitioners. At Sobibór, out of a slightly higher number of garrison personnel, only seven were *Waffen*-SS, the rest (the majority) according to Stangl, were civilians: "There were only five SS in Sobibór, the rest were civilians."[55]

These men, in the majority, were not politically motivated Nazis, ideologues, sadists or anti-Semites. It is only among the greater part of the leadership that we find this trait. Cruelty became endemic in all of the support personnel, a characteristic they adopted either in fear of Wirth, or by being numbed into submission by repetition of their murderous duties. The fact that the majority were members of the Nazi Party should not be taken as a token of their Nazi ideological thinking.

Most considered that this was a chance to become more professional in their political engagement with the movement to which they were devoted since their youth. For the majority of the civilian staff of T4, their backgrounds suggest they were completely average (some below average), of basic educational standard and totally lacking in the attributes that would lead them to become members of the SS or the police. The overall impression obtained from their testimonies was that they were initially surprised at being selected. Most considered that the attractions of working for the government were greatly enhanced by all the trappings: extra pay, prestige, family security and duty away from the front. This was enough to tempt them. By the time they arrived at T4 and later in the *Reinhardt* camps, government employment had taken on a new meaning and was not so attractive.

For the SS-candidates, it seems to have been a lottery. Luck and the circumstances of the day would select them for this duty. There was one concern that affected them all, which was not lost on them. Their own families and relatives could, one day, come within the criteria of euthanasia. The KdF knew of this concern and quickly allayed their fears by exempting four groups from the euthanasia program: the senile; those who had served in the armed forces; those who had been decorated with the "*Mutterkreuz*" (to glorify motherhood), and relatives of euthanasia action staff.[56] It would have been inconceivable if the Nazi hierarchy were not also exempted and protected. Exemptions were extended to anyone with any possible connection to people around Hitler or the leadership in the armed services.[57]

The logic of these selections, particularly concerning the artisans, suggests a policy of need by T4. Setting aside the KZ guards and the nurses (for the moment), the backgrounds of these men appears more relevant to their selection. In fact, the whole *Reinhardt* conglomerate, in my view, was run like one large business. The Bełżec garrison were not just geared for construction and murder, there were ancillary support services that were there but took no part in direct genocidal camp activities. This cadre were the business managers, the office workers, accountants, compilers of statistics, property movers, and the clerks who occupied the Lublin HQ and the *Komandetuer* in Bełżec, Sobibór and Treblinka.

Pay and Allowances

At the euthanasia centers a "stoker" (T4 personnel who fuelled the crematoria ovens) received 170 RM per month, plus 50 RM family separation allowance, 35 RM stoker's allowance, 35 RM bonus for keeping quiet, and for stokers in particular, with their unpleasant work, a quarter liter of schnapps every day.[58] In *Reinhardt* the pay varied: non commissioned officers (the majority) earned normal army pay of 58 RM per month, but this was increased with bonuses (when in the east) of a minimum of 600 RM, with three weeks leave every three months. There were also generous holiday facilities, which could be enjoyed with their families at the T4 vacation resort in Weissenbach at the Attersee in Austria. These considerations did not take into account "Jewish gold," which was to be plentiful when the time came.[59] Generally the camp commandants turned a blind eye to their German kin, who were stealing valuables from the Jewish warehouses and sending the "goodies" home. This did not apply to the Ukrainians, who were dealing on a daily basis with the Jews and bartering with local villagers with wads of foreign currency notes, extricated from each clammy heap of corpses. They were harshly treated if caught and very often shot in front of their comrades, as happened in Sobibór.[60]

Induction and Duties - T4

As mentioned above there was an interim stage: these were all individuals; all must have been affected differently and interpreted their situation in disparate ways once confronted with the killing process. If we look closer at other T4 personnel (outside of the Bełżec nine),[61] we do find situations where certain circumstances allowed for deviation. Although as a general rule, once in the T4 system there was no way out, and the KZ (concentration camp), the Gestapo, or even worse was threatened to would-be leavers, when newly recruited Matthias Buchberger told his bosses that he was deeply opposed to these actions against defenseless victims, he was moved from "stoking" duties to cleaning the yard and stables.[62] For a woman, it was sometimes possible to get out of T4; one female nurse who became pregnant was discharged.[63] Emil Reisenberger, a mechanic, was given an emergency service assignment to Hartheim Institution. He found the work so repugnant that he spread dissent among his co-workers, with the result that he was demoted. He made further breaches of the security rules by showing a friend around the building. Realizing what was now in store for him, he shot but failed to kill himself. While waiting for the ambulance, the bosses of T4 persuaded Reisenberger to say it was an accident. On his release from the hospital he was further threatened with a KZ, but after some time he was drafted to the war zone.[64]

Efforts by the establishment to justify the euthanasia killings were part of the general training. In addition to lectures by medical experts, films taken of the seriously crippled and insane patients being gassed were shown.[65] This all enforced the notion of the state's kindness and care, by removing in perpetuity this burden in the interests of everyone: the victims, their families, and German blood and honor.

In the extended phase of euthanasia and the *Reinhardt* death camps in the east, the qualification for this duty was the individual's unquestionable loyalty and discipline and the capacity to cope unemotionally with day-to-day operations. Heading the list for automatic *Reinhardt* duty were the "cremators" and "burners," the SS and police. These were the most psychologically hardened men by the very nature of their duties, devoid of feeling and totally callous in their conduct; they behaved like all "troopers" in a closed canteen type culture. This was more to Wirth's liking, as he could identify with them. Oddly enough, the established SS were not the cruellest according to the evidence.[66] In the lower ranks, which were not established SS and Ukrainian guard units, the most undisciplined could be found—men who abused the power given to them, usually under the influence of alcohol. Wirth, despite his own personal deficiencies, hatred of Jews and contempt for most of his own men, did take action against excesses of brutality when he was confronted with them. One of the youngest guards in SS uniform was the 20-year-old Paul Groth. Because of his perpetual drunkenness and sadistic cruelty in Bełżec, Wirth disciplined him by removing him to Sobibór in the hope that he would mend his ways. This was not to be, and Groth continued to abuse his position to such an extent that the smooth workings of the gassings were being compromised.

There are similar instances of sadistic cruelty, usually alcohol-related, by other non-established SS, in which the camp administrators took action to quell this behaviour. Heinrich Barbl, 42 years of age, with a bulbous red nose and known as the "idiot," was additionally in a perpetually drunken state in Bełżec. Believed to be simple minded, Barbl was often whipped personally by Wirth for his drunken behavior.[67]

There is no doubt that SS leadership personnel did shoot Jews, but apart from a few exceptions they did not add cruelty to their crimes. On the other hand, cruelty by the Ukrainians and civilian SS was a daily occurrence: Gustav Munzberger, a Sudeten German, a carpenter at T4 (Sonnenstein), and in charge of driving the Jews into the gas chambers at Treblinka, acted with much unnecessary cruelty.[68]

Boredom?

It is not difficult to find an answer for many of these acts of cruelty in the camps by otherwise well disciplined personnel. I would suggest the main factor was boredom. There were many periods of inactivity when guards patrolled their beats. Looking to pass the time, many resorted to making fun of the inmates, ordering them to perform all kinds of unnatural acts and dangerous exercises. Paul Groth (above) ordered Jews in Bełżec to jump off barrack roofs with an open umbrella, causing much injury and distress. The files are replete with such incidents, not only in the death camps but throughout the *Reich's* KZ regime. If these same men had been let loose on the eastern front, I have no doubt that they would have fought like tigers.

For examples of such behavior we need only refer to recent happenings by our own military forces in Iraq and other centers of prisoner incarceration. Supervisors not only failed their leaders and charges but also failed to maintain their professional impartiality and thus damaged the integrity of their homeland.

It is interesting to note that throughout their duty in the death camps, and then in Italy, the camp personnel remained a distinct body of men, held together because of their knowledge of the state's most secret activities. These men, closely administered by T4 for all pay and allowances, also had all their communications—personal or otherwise—dealt with by T4. Families of these men addressed their communications, not to the institutions or death camps where they served, but to T4. Likewise, all post from the east was delivered to their homes via T4.[69]

As discussed, in the beginning these men were not fanatical anti-Semites, committed Nazis, or killers *per se*. In 1939, if we selected nine males, aged 30 years or thereabouts, at random off the street in any average-sized town in Germany or Great Britain, we would probably catch a group with a not too dissimilar profile to the "Bełżec Nine." Disregarding wartime conditions, this sample would, on average, represent the norm of male persons with diverse occupations and marital statuses. To place these nine randomly selected personnel in the service of the state, under military discipline, and then coerce them into taking human life in legally unclear situations, I suggest, would be so abhorrent that it would have been impossible to continue without serious repercussions—unless, that is, they were completely ideologically indoctrinated; or, alternatively, threatened with serious harm or imprisonment to themselves or to their families.

For our "Bełżec Nine's" activities in T4, we have corroboration from a number of other sources that the system of recruitment to T4 was haphazard and informal. Dr. Dieter Allers and his wife (a typist in T4 recruited by informal means) say just this in conversations with Gitta Sereny in the Stangl investigation. One interesting comment by the author Henry Friedlander, when probing the reasons why Stangl accepted this appointment to T4, was the conclusion that the conflict between Stangl and his boss Prohaska couldn't have been as bad as Stangl had suggested, as he must have been recommended by Prohaska for the T4 appointment. I think Friedlander has missed the point of a well-established solution to bad feelings and personality clashes between ranks. To get rid of a nuisance in the office, to promote him or to get him moved to another department (even to his advantage), is one answer and solves the personality problem. I suggest that this is what occurred.

If we accept the basic truth of these depositions in this respect (i.e. complete ignorance of their impending duty with T4), then we can be reasonably confident that what followed in the AR camps was also basically true, that it was a pre-determined policy by T4 that the men should be kept in ignorance. It is also probable that each man was acting under orders and in direct fear of serious personal harm should these orders be disobeyed. All manner of inducements and "blind-eyes" were introduced and turned to keep the killing machine going—whatever the cost.[70] This does not, of course, excuse in any way each man's complicity in mass murder, and they must be so judged.

The above examples, which have been taken from court testimonies, are so similar that suggestions of conspiracy, i.e., co-ordination of evidence by the defendants, must not be excluded. However, the statements made by these men were all taken independently by senior and experienced police investigators and under the strictest supervision. This investigation was probably the most important and serious matter to have been scrutinized in West Germany since the end of the war. In addition, the statements were taken months and even years apart in different locations, many miles apart. Nonetheless, these crimes were so horrific and committed so long ago that it could be expected of the witnesses that they would adopt a line of self preservation. In so doing, a certain amount of personal re-assessment as to their personal involvement was inevitable.

They must have been aware of the evidence piling-up against them, not from the victims, as such testimonies were negligible in respect of Bełżec, but from their friends and co- defendants. One of the traits exposed in the interrogation statements is that they all remembered a colleague doing something, which they thought might please and perhaps direct the investigator away from their own involvement, but at the same time, implicated themselves on the periphery of events. What little they did say that might implicate them in the indictments was just about adequate to satisfy the interrogator, but not enough to identify them as leading the genocide. By directing the balance of responsibility away, they saw themselves as relatively minor contributors, admitting as little as they thought they could get away with. The one exception amongst the "nine" was Dubois, who openly confessed to his full part in the overall murder policy. Oberhauser is a good example of the contrary position, ducking and diving to make himself present but only as a minor contributor to events.

I have reservations with regard to the depositions of Oberhauser, who in my opinion, because of his closeness to Wirth and Globocnik, manipulated many of the facts to diminish his personal involvement during the maximum resettlement period. (Bełżec Verdict.)[71]

If Werner Dubois, who was the only one of the "nine" to admit his complicity in mass murder at Bełżec and Sobibór (the others claimed "orders" and fear of personal bodily harm should they refuse) to the court, why should he lie about an insignificant point regarding entry into T4? Dubois was a shattered man and knew full well that before his god and his conscience there was no alternative. The premise that these men were trained by the state in the art of killing at T4, which they took with them to AR, would put them in the bracket of willing participants and thus destroy their defense. I think the truth of this lies somewhere in between, and is stated quite frankly by Franz Suchomel, who served in T4 and at Treblinka. In conversation with Sereny and in answer to the question: "Were you trained for killing at T4, which ultimately helped you in Treblinka?" Suchomel replied, "There was no need for training, but the work at the euthanasia institutes did 'inure' all of us to a feeling and thus prepare us unknowingly for the next phase." It may be argued that they too, were victims.[72]

There is no denying the fact that despite their earlier ignorance of their engagement to T4 and AR, once the initial phase was over and they had become accustomed to murder, they were as grasping as the next man, and the killing became acceptable—even enjoyed. It was only in the criss-cross of defendants in similar *Reinhardt* court proceedings (Sobibór and Treblinka trials) where other convictions were obtained, that justice was eventually regained, however minuscule in relation to the crimes. Their common duties and their readiness in carrying out the genocide composed the defining impetus that translated the genocidal policy of the National Socialist Government into practice.[73]

Chapter 3. Hitler's Man in the East: Odilo Globocnik

Odilo Globocnik

SS Stronghold

While the Final Solution of the Jewish Question was an issue of the highest priority on the Nazi agenda, the context in which the destruction of Polish and Galician Jewry took place points to a far wider and equally sinister scheme on the part of the *Reichsführer-SS*, Himmler. In the east, he endeavored to use the policy as the means to consolidate the position of the SS as the dominant and unchallenged force in the Nazi "New Order" in Europe. Furthermore, the widely-shared perception that the organization of the Nazi State was implemented with a universal sense of commitment and common purpose by the leadership is clearly not borne out by the evidence of *Reinhardt*. It was a hierarchy plagued by intrigue, counter-intrigue, jealousy and above all, the striving for power.

After the assumption of authority by Governor General Dr. Hans Frank on 26 October 1939, Frank's activities demonstrate that he chose to interpret quite literally the sweeping but ambiguous powers bestowed upon him by Hitler. He sought to establish a unified government completely subordinate to himself and autonomous from all Reich authority, with the exception of directives received from Hitler. This single-minded arrogant attitude inevitably resulted in direct conflict with the *Reichsführer SS* and his most senior SS/Police representative in the *Generalgouvernment*, Friedrich Wilhelm Krüger; and by mid 1941 cooperation between the SS/Police and the civil government in the *Generalgouvernment* was breaking down in acrimonious disarray.

The two mighty protagonists of the Third Reich, Heinrich Himmler and Dr. Hans Frank, were locked in a progressive and long-term dispute over territorial accountability. The dispute between them centered on the SS/Police responsibilities in the *Generalgouvernment* and who was to initiate policy. Standing in the middle was Friedrich Wilhelm Krüger, who was at the very heart of Frank's domain in Kraków as the highest-ranking representative of the *Reichsführer-SS* in Berlin. The result was conflict between the SS and police and the civil administration.

The year 1942 brought mixed and unpredictable blessings for the German war effort, but by the end of the year German reverses were becoming apparent. The failure to take Moscow in December 1941 and the deteriorating situation around Stalingrad had brought serious doubts about German invincibility. None of the military setbacks, however, affected the deportation of the Jews to the gas chambers at Belzec, Sobibór and Treblinka, which continued unabated.

The success of *Reinhardt* can be attributed to tightly controlled criteria set down by a close circle of people who were able to keep the "Final Solution" secret to a certain extent, and protected from any outside interference. Thus, within the overall concept of *Reinhardt* and the unfolding anti-Jewish measures, we can see that the core leadership was fighting on two fronts: implementing the destruction of European Jewry, regardless of happenings elsewhere; and combating resistance and meddling from outside the SS.

The key factor in this internal tug-of-war was the Himmler-Frank conflict for control of the police in the *Generalgouvernment*. Loyalties were divided and friendships stretched to the limit during this period when the SS (HHE) was contesting the civilian authority of Governor General Hans Frank.[74]

Conflict among the leadership of the Nazi government is well known; in the *Generalgouvernment* it was endemic, rotting and rocking the nerve center of Nazi policies in the east, including the ongoing population and extermination policies.

The background to this Himmler-Frank tug-of-war is complex and incorporates many aspects and side issues which cannot be discussed here at length. Suffice to say that there were three distinct phases:

1) Frank's initial independent mastery of the civil administration in the *Generalgouvernment*, which relied on the power invested in him by Hitler;

2) corruption scandals within the SS and the failure by Himmler/Krüger to penetrate Frank's kingdom, resulting in their attempts to engineer his downfall by blackmail or other means;

3) the deteriorating situation regarding security and population resettlement, which damaged SS prestige and was highlighted by Frank at every opportunity.

In the spring of 1943 Himmler retaliated by attempting to secure the permanent removal of the Governor General through the sinister services of the SD.

Frank's legalistic web of administration was no bar to Himmler's visionary concepts: resettlement, deportations, confiscations, concentration camp administration, and all persecution measures against the Jews were operations which Himmler considered to be outside the influence of any civil authorities.[75] There were no winners in this protracted fight for supremacy in which Frank and Himmler competed only in ruthlessness. The Jews hardly noticed the change as they were doomed anyway, whoever won. This running fight between the two powerful opponents was an additional reason why Wirth and Globocnik ignored direct accountability to their superiors and reported directly to the KdF and HHE in Berlin. In any case the extermination of the Jews was an entirely SS-controlled operation from the start as ordered by Hitler, so that Frank could therefore only do what he was told in that respect. Wirth, in possession of the *Führer's fiat*, had no reason to bother about anybody and Globocnik, as usual, went his own way. To say the least, the climate operating at the time was not conducive to co-operation, and eventually the SS managed successfully to discredit Frank.

There were accusations that Frank's sister had had illegal property transactions with Jews and the proceeds were evident in Wawel Castle, his headquarters in Krakow. Even more dangerous for Frank was his attempt to discover what was happening in Belzec and Auschwitz. His curiosity, however, was blocked by Globocnik and Höß, who jealously guarded their SS secrets from those not privy to them, no matter what their position or rank.

Frank's complaint to the *Führer*, that he was being deliberately prevented from knowing what was going on in his own territory, met with no success either. He was referred to Himmler. Hitler was not prepared to tolerate any interference in the extermination plans, not even from such a loyal supporter as Frank. Hans Frank got the message: he had lost the fight, and he abandoned any further attempts to interfere in SS matters. His influence and credibility were seriously damaged and resulted in his being stripped of his Party offices.

Although Himmler had come out on top, political repercussions followed in November, 1941, when HSSPF Krüger instigated some high profile prosecutions. Lorenz Löv, a relatively high civil servant as Chief of the Central Administration Office for the Warsaw District, was arrested on the grounds of black market activities, especially with Jews living in the Warsaw ghetto. The Governor of East Galicia, Dr. Karl Lasch, had been caught "misappropriating" Jewish property and despite the intervention of Frank on his behalf, he was arrested. Given the choice of baring his soul to Himmler and perhaps a lenient end to his "unauthorized" activities, or an SS court, Lasch chose the latter. Despite all the pleadings and maneuverings, the evidence of theft, corruption and Party disloyalty was overwhelming. Convicted on all counts, Lasch was unceremoniously place before a firing squad and shot. Further investigations and reports by the SD resulted in additional prosecutions.[76]

Meanwhile, resettlement issues continued to occupy Nazi minds; and in an effort to put an end to the rancor in the senior leadership, on 1 February 1943 Dr. Josef Goebbels suggested ending these internecine squabbles.

Dr. Hans Frank, however, was far from finished. He had ideas for making a more conciliatory approach to the Poles, especially those in the Lublin District under Globocnik, who were the most savagely suppressed in the entire Government General. Frank suggested making concessions regarding, for example, education, banned for Poles since 1939, with a view to encouraging collaboration with the occupying forces. It was to be expected that such ideas were rejected out of hand by Hitler. Frank was reprimanded but continued in his assault against Globocnik by accusing him of failure to notify Frank about the barbarous "resettlements" and punitive "operations" conducted by Globocnik's units in the Zamosc area in particular, which began in November 1942.

After several months of verbal wrangling, accusation and counter accusation, Himmler finally removed two of his most trusted officers from the Government General—HSSPF Krüger and SSPF Globocnik. Globocnik was transferred to Trieste in northern Italy in September 1943 as the HSSPF for the Adriatic Coast Region. He was replaced in Lublin by SSPF Jakob Sporrenberg. In November, Krüger was succeeded by the more compliant Wilhelm Koppe.

Now in the ascendant and in complete control of the security forces, Himmler commenced to purge his SS in the *Generalgouvernment* for corrupt practices. The first to fall were SS personnel whom he considered had been "tainted" by Frank's influence. By the end of 1943, many of the top SS leadership in the *Generalgouvernment* had been disciplined, transferred, imprisoned, or shot. Others in the lower ranks who had been employed in *Reinhardt* escaped retribution as they were on duty in northern Italy, still under Wirth's command.

It is difficult to imagine a more uncoordinated group than the one we find in the higher leadership of the Nazi Party. Besmirched by intrigues, jealousies, or tactical obstruction, the outside was working against the center, ignoring the accepted norms of communication, but surprisingly achieving their aims with comparatively few personal casualties.

Globocnik's Lublin[77]

In the drive for "*Lebensraum*" (territorial expansion to acquire living space for the German race), the Nazis decimated Poland's political and cultural élite. Poland was used as the laboratory for a great demographic experiment based on Nazi racial ideology that involved the eviction of millions of people. The Poles, as Slavs, were at the bottom end of the scale of racial purity and were turned into a nation of slaves for their German masters in preparation for the colonization of their lands. The HHE seized control of the eastern part of the Government General by placing their officers in charge before the civil authorities could establish themselves.

The first significant step was the arrival in Lublin in November 1939 of SS-*Brigadeführer* Globocnik with his own political agenda, and the full support of his sponsor in Berlin, *Reichsführer-SS* Himmler. Whereas *SS-Obersturmführer* Christian Wirth was the central protagonist in the specific operation of the *Reinhardt* death camps, Globocnik stands out as the most influential instigator of the Nazi vision of *"Lebensraum-und Rasse"* (Living Space and Race). Despite the magnitude of the indiscriminate mass murder of Poles, these liquidations were in fact of secondary consideration and simply the means by which Globocnik and the HHE's wider aspirations would be accomplished.

The expulsion of the Jews satisfied two distinct purposes: to make room for incoming *Volksdeutsche* settlers, and the Nazi policy to solve the "Jewish Question." Globocnik strived to adhere to orders for the evacuation of the indigenous populations to be carried out within the period specified by Himmler. The resettlement of *Volksdeutsche* from Volhynia, Łódź, (Litzmannstadt) and Lubartów to Lublin was coming under strain and Globocnik found he was unable to keep to the schedule. He requested more time to complete the task, but this was refused. Further negotiations—which now included the intervention of Adolf Eichmann—failed to solve the problem and Globocnik came under pressure from many directions, which is one likely reason we find Christian Wirth saddled with such power in *Reinhardt.* [78]

Globocnik was entrusted first of all with evacuations and resettlement, long before Wirth appeared or any orders were given to either of them to exterminate the Jews. These early operations involving the shuffling of populations were not at first connected with *Reinhardt*, they simply evolved in that direction; and at first Globocnik was against extermination. He had visions of employing the Jews in "his" vast labor force in his SS-enterprises in the Lublin District. Wirth came later, about five months after he and Globocnik received their orders from Himmler in July 1941.

Generalplan Ost

Historical evidence accumulated since the war supports the view that the German invasion and occupation of Poland was simply the first step in a far broader plan. The extensive research of Czesław Madajczyk [79] of the Polish Academy of Sciences has concluded that Hitler's aim was to expel virtually the entire indigenous Polish population to the forests and marshlands of western Siberia, or some other equally distant and inaccessible region, and to repopulate the area with millions of *Reichs-* and *Volksdeutsche.* The strategy underlying these draconian measures was based on a carefully structured plan.

In late 1939 and early 1940, Himmler established offices and personnel to plan in detail the eventual German resettlement. He presented his ideas to Hitler in May 1940 in a six-page memorandum for a *"Generalplan Ost."* [80] The planning agency was the *Planungs- und Zentralbodenamt des Stabshauptamtes des RKFDV* (Planning and Central Land Registry Office of the Staff Headquarters of the RKFDV). The overall plan mirrored the imperialistic dreams that Himmler harbored for Germany, and above all for his beloved SS, to be realized after the successful completion of the war.

The basic idea of the plan was to turn Lublin, as the most easterly city in Poland, into a major SS/Police center from which the tentacles of SS power could inexorably spread eastwards as far as the Ural Mountains, the geographical division between Europe and Asia.

In late 1942 the Lublin District—which included Zamojszczyzna, the area around the town of Zamosc, acquired from the Soviet Union in October 1939 in exchange for a free hand in Lithuania—became the focal point of *Generalplan Ost.* It was envisaged by Himmler's planners that over a period of some 25 years Ukrainians and a large proportion of the Baltic peoples would be resettled.

In the period following the partitioning of Poland between Germany and the Soviet Union in 1939, the Soviet NKVD—Stalin's secret police—deported 1.2-1.7 million Polish citizens from eastern Poland to the far northern and eastern parts of the Soviet Union,[81] together with Ukrainians, Jews and Lithuanians. The deportees included large numbers of the intelligentsia. They were deported mainly to remove a potential threat to Soviet rule. This huge operation, carried out from early 1940 until mid-1941, provided the Soviet Union with a vast new source of slave labor, many of whom died in the labor camps and mines due to the harsh conditions of hard physical labor, starvation, illness, and maltreatment by the guards. Ironically, Soviet deportations served Hitler's plans remarkably well. A further irony is that they saved some Jews from the "Final Solution."

Germanization Policy

Globocnik and Himmler saw the appropriation of Zamojszczyzna as the first stage of Germanizing the entire *Generalgouvernment.* *Reichs-* and *Volksdeutsche* farmers were settled there. It was through this act of "ethnic cleansing" that Globocnik set out to wrest control of the entire *Generalgouvernment* from Hans Frank. The intention was to erect a demographic block of settlements linking Transylvania with Estonia. This would have been the second such bastion. The first was in western Poland where, since October 1939, the Germanization of the lands incorporated into the *Reich* had been in progress. The deportation of the Jews and subsequent implementation of *Reinhardt* cannot be entirely divorced from this strategy.

In order to facilitate the "New Order" in Poland, Globocnik set up in Lublin the *Forschungsamt für Ostsiedlung* (Research Office for Eastern Settlement), where many young German and Austrian academics in the fields of architecture, demography, linguistics, ethnography, agriculture, forestry, and the social sciences were engaged as teachers and researchers. The head of the project was *SS-Hauptsturmführer* Gustav Hanelt, a native of Holstein and a lawyer with a keen interest in history and archaeology. A prominent role was also played by Richard Walter Darré, the Argentinean-born Nazi theorist of farming settlements in Slavic lands, and the first head of the SS *Rasse-und Siedlungsamt* (SS Race and Settlement Office) from 1931-1938.[82] Hanelt and the *Forschungsamt* were concerned with the planning and establishment of *SS-und Polizei Stützpunkte* (SS and Police Strongpoints)—partially fortified farm complexes from which it was envisaged that German peasant farmers would steadily occupy more and more adjoining land across Poland and eventually the entire western region of the Soviet Union, right up to the Urals.[83] Himmler visited the Research Center (*Forschungsmat*) in Lublin several times and, like Darré, was deeply influenced and guided by *völkisch* ideas that romanticised the vision of German farmer settlements in the East.[84]

Running parallel with *Generalplan Ost*, and a necessary ingredient in the overall plan, was the solution to the "Jewish Question." In this area Globocnik was answerable directly to Himmler as the latter's plenipotentiary for the extermination of the Jews, while Wirth acted as Globocnik's executive officer in the *Reinhardt* death camps.

The plan to eventually incorporate Poland into the Greater *Reich* had far-reaching and tragic consequences for the Poles, and in particular for the Jewish population, who before the war numbered around three million. The *Generalgouvernment* was overflowing with Jewish deportees as a consequence of the 1939-1940 purges of the western Polish lands that had been annexed to the *Reich*, when some 340,000 people had been transported into Hans Frank's domain. Notwithstanding this, a further 237,000 were earmarked by the German Armed Forces to join them from other locations that had been seized as military training grounds.[85]

The Jewish slave laborers employed on the "Otto Line" were already in the *Generalgouvernment*, not brought in from elsewhere. There is also a distinction between the "Otto Line" and the "Otto Program." The "Line" was the construction of border defenses, while the "program" consisted of river regulation and the repair and widening of an extensive network of strategic roads leading towards the German-Soviet border (a good indication that the "eastward expansion" was already well in mind at the beginning of 1940). After the invasion of the Soviet Union in 1941, the main arterial route across the Ukraine was the "DG-4" (*Durchgangsstrasse* No. 4), heading for the Crimea.

Poles, of course, did not escape this vast movement of people and they too were expelled from certain city districts to make way for German occupiers. In November 1941 Globocnik carried out his first experimental expulsions, as a feasibility study for the impending *General Plan Ost,* clearing eight villages of indigenous Poles in the Zamosc area[86] and replacing them with *Volksdeutsche*.

Zamosc

By November 1942, through deportations to the death camps and summary shootings, the Zamosc district was *Judenrein* (clean of Jews). On 28 November 1942 the inhabitants of Skierbieszów, a village 17-kilometers northeast of Zamosc, were forcibly expelled from their homes. Within a few hours their dwellings were occupied by *Volksdeutsche*. The same pattern of expulsion and repopulation was soon to be repeated throughout the region.

During the period beginning with the Skierbieszów deportations and ending late in the following summer of 1943, a total of 297 villages were "ethnically cleansed" by the expulsion from their homes of about 110,000 Poles, mainly peasant farmers and their families.[87] For political reasons, the large Ukrainian population in the area was left untouched.[88] However, Globocnik's experiment in population movements backfired. By the beginning of 1943, the brutality with which the "ethnic cleansing" was carried out resulted in increased partisan activity in the region with skirmishes and even battles with German troops. The AK was the biggest fighting unit of the several rival groups of Polish partisans and the Zamosc region was divided into several "Area Commands," with each unit having its own territory. It is most unlikely that a local commander who had seen his family, friends and neighbors suffering at the hands of Globocnik's men would take much notice of an order from Warsaw Command not to react.

Since Globocnik had initiated the expulsion operation in the Zamosc area while he was still the head of *Reinhardt*, it is probable that this was a contributory factor in his subsequent removal to Trieste in September 1943, since the all-out war resulting from his experiment drew Ukrainian nationalists and other anti-Nazi elements into direct conflict with the occupiers. This is evidenced by an entry in the diary of Zygmunt Krakowski on 10 April 1943. On a visit to see the *Kreislandwirt* in Biłgoraj in the Zamosc area, he caught sight of a confidential communiqué from Governor General Frank to the Polish Relief Committee in which it was stated that several low-ranking German officials made big mistakes over the enforced evacuations and that some would be relieved of their posts, including Lublin Police Chief Globocnik.[89]

The German authorities were desperate to supplement their auxiliary administrative forces and intimidatory tactics were used on selected Poles to induce them to register as *Volksdeutsche*. Door-to-door visits were made by uniformed German officers who attempted to persuade the occupants to sign-up as *Volksdeutsche*.[90] The questionnaire presented to the applicant was headed in German, *"Antrag auf Erleitung eines Ausweiss für Deutschstämmige"* (Application for Issuing an Identity Card for Persons of German Extraction). This was repeated below in Polish.[91] The recruiting drive was a result of the seizure of men and women for forced labor in Germany, which had decimated the local population.

East Galician Deportations

The friction between the civilian hierarchy of the *Generalgouvernment* and the SS/Police was still simmering. Meanwhile the internal conflict between the civilian administration in the Lublin District and the SS/Police was virtually duplicated in east Galicia where the SSPF for Galicia, *SS-Brigadeführer* Fritz Katzmann, and the governor, Dr Karl Lasch, were at loggerheads. The relationship between Frank and Krüger had deteriorated even further since their initial disagreements in 1940, and Katzmann was caught in between the two. His position was further complicated by his subordination to the authority of Governor Lasch in Lemberg (Lvov.) Katzmann, a confirmed Jew-hater, had witnessed what he perceived as Lasch consorting with Jews by protecting those who could afford to pay to stay out of the ghetto, or worse still, avoid deportation. There were added complications for Katzmann concerning the "Jewish Question" when an order to round up and deport several thousand Poles for forced labor in Germany was compromised. Lasch's corruption and his apparent friendly relations with the Jews had seriously undermined Katzmann's efforts to carry out the evacuation of the Jews into ghettos and satisfy the ever-increasing demands for non-Jewish labor. These tasks, undertaken by the SS, *Gestapo* and police, were made even more difficult because the Jews had not yet been completely segregated from the rest of the population.

The Polish labor force consisted of volunteers as well as those forcibly rounded up and was intended to supplement agricultural workers and as labor for the oil refining industry in Boryslau (Borysław) and Drohobycz in Galicia. The Ukrainian Nationalists were exempt for political reasons, to avoid provoking them into hostile nationalistic activity.

The scandal surrounding Lasch and his friendship with Governor General Frank was used by Himmler and Katzmann to bring matters to a head and further Katzmann's ambitions. Finally, on 5 March 1942, Himmler confronted Frank with the evidence intended to discredit and destroy him.[92]

Globocnik's Powerbase

Before and after the *"Anschluss"* Globocnik was steeped in illegal political activity, first on behalf of the Carinthians in their border dispute with Yugoslavia (Slovenia) and later on behalf of the proscribed Austrian Nazi Party and SS. A month after the *Anschluss* of March 1938, Globocnik was rewarded for his years of illegal Nazi activities by being nominated *Gauleiter* (Party District Leader) of Vienna. The nomination was confirmed by Hitler on 22 May 1938, when Globocnik was sworn-in by the *Führer* in the *Grosser Wappensaal des Klagenfurter Landhauses* (Larger Heraldic Room of the Klagenfurt Mansion).

During his early days as *Gauleiter*, Globocnik, a rabid Jew-hater, proclaimed: "I will not recoil from radical interventions for the solution of Jewish Question(s)."[93] Later that same year he opened Vienna's first anti-Semitic exhibition, which was attended by 10,000 visitors on the first day alone. Prominent at the exhibition, and received enthusiastically by the public, was the notoriously anti-Semitic film *"Der Ewige Jude."*[94]

Globocnik's personality, although pleasing to some Nazis, did not go down well with the Viennese, not least because he was an outsider from Carinthia. His arrogance, inept administration, disregard of his advisors, mishandling of relations with the Church and poor public speaking ability did him no good. He was eventually accused of misappropriating Party funds, misusing civic funds, corrupt dealings with Jewish property among his cronies, and black market speculation. Hitler saw it as politic to relieve him of his post as *Gauleiter*.

Globocnik nevertheless remained utterly devoted to Himmler who in turn knew he could make later use of a tough-minded, independent and unscrupulous individual who was so devoted to the Nazi cause. Accordingly, on 1 February 1939, the RFSS appointed Globocnik to his personal staff.

If Globocnik thought that he was now part of the inner sanctum of the Nazi party, he was soon disappointed. Himmler transferred him to the *Waffen-SS* with the lowly rank of *SS-Unterscharführer* for a period of basic military training, which he withstood with some credit. At the outbreak of war, *SS-Unterscharführer* Globocnik served in the Polish campaign.[95]

On 9 November 1939 Globocnik was elevated from *SS-Unterscharführer* to *SS-Brigadeführer* and appointed the *SS-und Polizeiführer* in Lublin, a key position in the grandiose SS plans for eastward expansion. His ruthlessness and singularity of purpose were appropriate to the task, while his acquiescence could be relied upon. A man with a criminal mentality was needed to undertake the tasks of the SS in the east, the ultimate of which was to be *Aktion Reinhardt*—the extermination of the Jews of Poland.

Reinhardt HQ Lublin

Aktion Reinhardt was administered from a former Polish school building on the corner of Distrikt Strasse and Litauer Strasse close to the city center in Lublin. The chief executive officer was *SS-Hauptsturmführer* Hermann Höfle, another pre-Anschluss Austrian Nazi, who was Globocnik's chief-of-staff. His function within *Reinhardt* was organizing the deportation of the Jews from the ghettos and transit ghettos, first to Belzec and later to Sobibór and Treblinka.

Globocnik's reign in Lublin was also not without controversy. He brazenly built his own forced labor camps for Jews and assembled quasi-military units to his own specifications for local anti-Jewish operations, which included the confiscation of Jewish property on a grand scale. Later, as he engaged in the progressive war against the Jews, he built-up a massive SS-run industrial empire financed entirely by the confiscated assets of the people he was destroying by the thousands every day in *Reinhardt*.

Although Globocnik had a lifelong propensity for murder, corruption and theft, in early 1943 he suffered a brief nervous breakdown, brought on by maudlin thoughts induced by a surfeit of alcohol. Globocnik left the office one winter night without his hat or coat and fled to the residence of his subordinate and friend, *SS-Sturmbannführer* Georg Wippern, who handed him over to Globocnik's adjutant, Max Runhof:

> Globocnik told me that everything was "frightful"; he could not tell me anything—he alone had to bear it. He asked that if anything should happen to him that I should take care of his family.[96]

Later, in 1944 in Italy, Globocnik explained to a colleague:

> I am no longer in it with all my heart. I am so deeply implicated in the matter that I have no choice—I must win, or perish with Hitler.[97]

Globocnik had considered it an honor when Himmler originally entrusted him with the implementation of the Final Solution, placing him at the forefront of the fight to make Europe free of Jews. His survival in this conspiracy was entirely due to Himmler's support, and to ensure its continuance he exerted all his loyalty and strength.[98] Globocnik had overcome all difficulties and opposition from the outside by ignoring many of the orders emanating from the Governor General Frank in Krakow, the *Reich* armament industries, and the *Wehrmacht*.

This independent action by Globocnik during *Reinhardt*, aided and abetted by Wirth, was not as extraordinary as it might appear. The whole Nazi establishment was characterized by intrigue, secrecy and information provided on a need-to-know basis. Thus, with something as laden with jeopardy as the extermination of the Jews of Europe, it was predictably rare for the protagonists to communicate in writing, unless absolutely necessary. This is reflected in the paucity of documentary evidence authorizing the Final

Solution. The fact that the overall direction and co-ordination of *Reinhardt* was undertaken from Hitler's private Chancellery certainly implicates Hitler in the genocide. There are several pieces of evidence that make it extremely difficult for anyone to defend the claim that Hitler was ignorant of Globocnik's activities or *Reinhardt.*

Firstly, Hitler and Globocnik knew each other well from the mid-1930s when the latter acted, with Friedrich Rainer, as a courier between the Nazi Party HQ in the *"Braun Haus"* in Munich and the illegal Austrian Nazis. It is also known that Globocnik made trips to wartime Berlin, and one of his adjutants, Max Runhof, has testified that Hitler and Globocnik had private meetings while *Reinhardt* was in progress. It is therefore most unlikely that a major and monumental demographic operation, carried out as government policy, was not discussed by these two ardent anti-Semites. Globocnik, of course, was close to Himmler and they consulted often on shifts in direction of policy during the two pivotal years 1941 and 1942. This included at least one well-publicized visit by Himmler to Lublin.

In addition, there is an indirect and unexpected piece of evidence that supports the view that a close liaison existed between Hitler and Globocnik regarding both the extermination of the Jews and the "ethnic cleansing" of Poles from the Zamosc area. This contention emerges by analogy from the research by Dr. Werner Warmbrunn and his analysis of the Nazi occupation of the Netherlands, where Globocnik's counterpart was Hans Albin Rauter, a fellow- Austrian.

In Rauter's case, as in occupied Poland, there existed the question of who, specifically, was in overall charge of government—the civilian administration under Seyss-Inquart, or the SS. Rauter, in much the same way as Globocnik, tended to act unilaterally, a pattern adopted by all of Himmler's SSPFs in occupied countries. According to Dr. Warmbrunn, Rauter's position was anomalous (not uncommon in the German hierarchy) since, in his capacity as SS and Police Leader, he received his orders directly from Himmler, although he was supposed to clear them with Seyss-Inquart. After the war, Rauter claimed that he was simply subordinate to Seyss-Inquart, and that Hitler and Himmler had told him so. Others, including some of Rauter's subordinates, also believed that Rauter frequently had better access to Hitler, through Himmler, than Seyss-Inquart. The latter could give orders to the police via Rauter, who would execute them if they were compatible with Himmler's directives. Actually, conflicts did occur, which were resolved only after much discussion in The Hague and at the Führer's headquarters.[99]

It is therefore probable that Globocnik's situation in Lublin was very much the same. In view of the fact that the Jewish Question was so central and pivotal to the aims of both Hitler and Himmler, and that the future of German settlement in the east was a fundamental reason for the invasion of Poland, it would thus be quite remarkable if Hitler did not take a great interest in Globocnik's activities, since they were so central to both issues.

Fate of the *Reich* Jews?

In June 1940, after the halt of the "Nisko Plan," the "Madagascar Plan" was put forward—the deportation of Europe's Jews to the island of Madagascar off the east coast of Africa. On hearing this, Governor General Hans Frank in Poland sighed with "colossal relief" *(kolossale Entlastung)*.[100] His elation was premature as deportations to the island proved impractical and by the end of the year the plan had been dropped.[101] Hitler decided to distribute several thousand *Volksdeutsche* within Greater Germany, and in order to implement this, to carry out further deportations of Poles and Jews from the annexed western territories to the *Generalgouvernment*.[102] The resettling of *Volksdeutsche* and expulsion of Poles and Jews was temporarily halted on 15 March 1941 because of the military preparations for the invasion of the Soviet Union.[103]

During a two-day conference (16-17 September 1941) Hitler and Himmler decided to deport the Jews from the Greater German *Reich* to ghettos in Eastern Europe.[104] No sooner had this decision been taken than Hitler changed his mind, citing various reasons why the expulsions should not be carried out immediately. However, by early October1941, in another moment of military euphoria at the fall of Kiev, the expulsion issue was raised again. On 10 October 1941, Heydrich drew up plans for the deportation of *Reich* Jews to Riga and Minsk, as well as to the Litzmannstadt (Łódź) ghetto in the Wartheland. The deportations began five days later, and on 18 October, Jews were forbidden to emigrate from the *Reich*.[105]

After America's entry into the war on 7 December 1941, according to Goebbels, Hitler assured him that the Berlin Jews would be deported east and that transport was available.[106] The key to the decision-making regarding the fate of the *Reich* Jews is reflected in just two measures: the halt to Jewish emigration and the establishment of the death camps at Kulmhof (Chełmno) and Belzec.[107]

The deportation of Reich *Jews* to the ghettos in the Lublin district resumed in March 1942 but their extermination was only decided in mid-April.[108] On 25 April 1942, 995 Jewish inhabitants from the German city of Würzburg were deported to Trawniki and Izbica for onward transport to Belzec.

Further deportations of *Reich* Jews from Litzmannstadt *(Łódź)* to Chełmno also commenced and between 4 and 15 May, twelve trains took over 10,000 *Reich* Jews to their death.[109]

By July 1942, the point of no return had been reached with an all-out extermination policy, which was to engulf Jews from the whole of Europe. Only one class of Jew was to be spared: fit young men between the ages of

16 and 32 who would be held in selected KZs for forced labor.[110] In September 1942, Hitler strongly intimated that the last remnants of Jewish forced laborers in the armament industry were to be replaced by foreign labor. By the beginning of 1943, in Berlin alone, 7,000 Jews had been arrested during the so-called "factory operation" and deported.[111]

Chapter 4. Sources of Manpower

Auxiliaries

In the period before and immediately following the invasion of Poland, the Nazis had taken the measure of setting up *Einsatzgruppen*, quasi-military auxiliary SS units, to secure the areas captured by the *Wehrmacht* and to undertake special duties. The *Einsatzgruppen* were quite distinct from other established security units, as their creation as a separate force added a political dimension to the agenda; a function that was only to be utilized in cases of State emergency. The control of these units was in the hands of a small élite band of high officials within the Nazi leadership. Within a very short time, a number of these armed units started to appear in the *Generalgouvernment*. They were called *Kommandostab Reichsführer - SS*:[112] the *Sonderdienst*,[113] *Schutzmannschaften* (Police Auxiliary),[114] and *Schutzpolizei*.[115]

The HHE was continually competing with the *Wehrmacht* for manpower and requested state funding in order to complement and bolster their special requirements. As the *Wehrmacht* had priority in amassing manpower through direct conscription, Himmler was well aware that this was depleting his SS of potential material. Therefore, to satisfy the demands of the *Waffen-SS*, the *Reich* Interior Ministry turned to the occupied territories to fill the gaps.[116] In this way, the problems surrounding matters of recruitment were solved, since the Army High Command was now able to maintain their first call on personnel within the borders of Germany.[117]

The best that Globocnik and the KdF could hope for by way of satisfying their own special requirements was to select men from the KZs and the police. It is more than likely that it was this policy that was the main reason we find police officers and KZ guards being incorporated into T4 and *Reinhardt*.[118] Globocnik also subsumed the nearby Trawniki training establishment into his empire and set up the Trawniki training camp in the buildings and grounds of a pre-war sugar refinery in the village of Trawniki, 25 km. SE of Lublin.

This was the central training camp for para-military auxiliaries drawn from Soviet collaborators, the majority of whom were Ukrainian, and came to be known as the *"Trawnikimänner"* (Trawnikimen). In addition, he was able to call on highly-trained personnel from the Sipo-SD Academy at Bad Rabka in southern Poland.[119] When the time came, all these support units were integrated into the organization created to expedite *Reinhardt*.

The Lublin *Selbstschutz*—Precursor to *Trawnikimänner*

Prior to the recruitment of the *Trawnikimänner*, Himmler authorized Globocnik to form *Selbstschutz* units for auxiliary security duties in order at least partially to overcome his shortage of manpower for auxiliary security duties. These units comprised *Volksdeutsche* youths rejected by the SS who, nevertheless, were entitled to many of the same privileges the SS enjoyed. Fervently aroused by political indoctrination, the recruits willingly aligned themselves with the *Führer's* vision of the "battle for the racial re-alignment of Europe." The *Selbstschutz* were placed under the supervision of the *Befehlshaber der Ordnungspolizei* (BdO), the Commander of the Order Police (Orpo) in Kraków, and used by Globocnik as his own personal police force. He molded them into a ruthless body of ghetto clearers and perpetrators of anti-Jewish atrocities in the Lublin District.[120] In this way he was able to demonstrate to Himmler how he could take 1,000 *Volksdeutsche* farmhands and convert them into brutal torturers and killers.[121] In the period of November 1939 to April 1940, the *Selbstschutz* grew to a body of over 12,000 men.[122] Governor Frank, it would seem, had recognized the warning signs and refused to take any responsibility for police units acting outside regular police channels. He referred to them contemptuously as "the murder gang of the SSPF Lublin."[123]

In mid-March 1942, when Belzec opened, Hans Frank, in a series of lectures, warned that a police state was emerging.[124] Such pronouncements were the beginning of his demise, exclusion from the inner sanctum of the Party and fall from absolute power in the *Generalgouvernment*. Frank had meddled too much in SS business. Although he was to remain official head of the *Generalgouvernment* for the rest of the war, his position was increasingly compromised and his power greatly reduced. Germany now appeared to be embarking on a system of administration that was effectively evolving into a "State-within-a-State," the consequence of which, should events have continued in its favor, would have resulted in the SS emerging as the supreme leadership in Germany and the conquered territories. With the implementation of *Reinhardt,* a third structure emerged, which also acted independently of both the civil government and the SS. *Reinhardt* would sweep aside all established conventions, rules and principles, and pursue its own unique agenda.

As the war progressed and operations against the Jews increased, greater use was made of the auxiliary units, particularly in the towns and villages of the Lublin District and the area between the Bug and the Vistula rivers in eastern Poland. During its short but distinctive existence, the members of the *Selbstschutz* distinguishing themselves by their extreme brutality, shooting, raping, and plundering when rounding up Poles and Jews for forced labor to satisfy the economic demands of the *Reich*.

The *Selbstschutz* were the main policing resource for the arrest and detention of Jews and Gypsies prior to deportation to the Lipowa transit camp in Lublin, and were additionally responsible to a large degree for deportations to the "Otto Line" fortifications at Belzec. [125]

The manner in which the *Selbstschutz* operated came under severe scrutiny by the HHE, who were concerned at the brutal way these units were carrying out their duties; and Governor General Frank, not missing a chance to snipe at the SS, demanded that his HSSPF, Krüger, justify their actions.[126] Matters came to a head when reports of atrocities committed in the town of Jozefów[127] reached the desk of Hermann Göring, Reich Minister for Defense.

By the end of June 1940, the *Selbstschutz* were so completely out of control that Ernst Zörner, the Governor of Lublin District, informed Frank of their undisciplined behavior, prompting Frank to instigate further inquiries. The result was that on 31 August 1940, the *Selbstschutz* was disbanded and the best recruits transferred to the *Waffen -SS* and the *Wehrmacht*.[128] Globocnik, however, would neither submit nor accept this as a *fait accompli*.[129] With the probable backing of Himmler, Globocnik ensured that he could retain his most trusted lieutenants for the future.

The Gloves Come Off

In October 1941 an extermination campaign was launched against the Jewish population of East Galicia and the Lublin District that was possibly only surpassed by the SS murder squads operating under the aegis of SS-*Hauptsturmführer* Hans Krüger in Nadworna and Stanisławów.

On instructions from Globocnik, *Hauptmann* (Captain) Kleinschmidt, the company leader of a transport unit, reported with 15 men to the Lublin barracks. Each one was given a truck and instructed to drive to a nearby Jewish labor camp. A total of 450 Jewish men, women and children were loaded onto trucks and driven to an abandoned airfield 25 miles outside of Lublin. The prisoners were forced to dig ditches six cubic meters in size. After finishing the ditches, the victims had to undress and were given corrugated-paper shirts to wear. In batches of 10, they then had to lie in the bottom of the ditches, which were lined with straw. Grenades were tossed into the ditches, and body parts flew everywhere. Any survivors were shot. Lime was then spread over the remains and the next 10 victims, who had been watching, were forced to submit to the same treatment. Women were kicked in the stomach and breasts, and children's heads smashed against rocks. According to witnesses, Globocnik's men subsequently killed many Jews in this manner,[130] which was about as far as one could go in streamlining the process of mass murder, in the absence of more advanced technology.[131]

Establishment of the Trawniki training camp [132]

On 21 October 1941, Globocnik received authority to set up a training establishment at Trawniki. The manpower consisted of captured Soviet troops who had until recently been held in conditions of the utmost squalor.[133] These renegade troops signed up for duty with the Germans primarily from a sense of self-preservation rather than from ideological reasons, and were to prove an invaluable asset to the Nazis. They were used to brutal effect in the KZs, ghettos and in all of the ongoing Jewish actions.[134] Their primary role, however, was as additional manpower to guard the *Reinhardt* death camps, while other units performed security duties in SS-run enterprises, guarded supply dumps and manned checkpoints on the main roads.

German-Ukrainian Partnership

The Third Reich could not have benefited from a more firmly established and historically rooted source of anti-Semitic manpower than the Ukrainians. This was partly due to their mistaken belief that the Germans would grant them an independent state once the war had been won. In the pre-war years, Ukraine had been subjected to German propaganda designed to encourage them towards self-determination and the Ukrainians had been encouraged to perceive themselves as an ally, with the tacit suggestion that Germany would reward them once the military situation had stabilised. This deception by the Germans was for purely pragmatic reasons since they had no intention of offering the Ukrainians an independent state. Once this deception became apparent, the consequence among the ex-POW collaborators was a state of mutual mistrust and suspicion. Despite their misgivings, the Ukrainians engaged in a cooperative relationship, albeit lethargically. Easily contaminated by the Nazi racial virus, the Ukrainian militias joined the Germans in their *"Drang nach Osten"* (Drive to the East) and all that it entailed. The Nazis had found a reticent but acceptable partner to pursue their aims of domination and Jewish destruction, even though their hatred and contempt for "racially inferior" beings also encompassed the Slavs.

Ukrainian collaboration in the *Generalgouvernment* can be divided into two categories: collaboration by the indigenous population of western Ukraine, and the Ukrainians who had fought under the Soviet banner and had been taken prisoner or surrendered during the Germans' eastward thrust. It is the second group that is of particular interest, since these were the men selected for service within the KZ system and the death camps.

The Ukrainians now collaborated with the Germans in a conspiracy to engage in mass murder, with each dependent on the other, although motivated by entirely different goals.[135] While the Germans were driven by their policies of rabid anti-Semitism and genocide, the Ukrainians were prepared to do their dirty work in return for immediate and future economic reward.

Trawniki: Recruitment

It is important to understand the circumstances through which the Soviet auxiliaries—the majority of whom were Ukrainians—came to be involved at the heart of the genocidal activity in *Reinhardt*.[136]

By the end of 1941, about 3,350,000 Soviet soldiers had been taken prisoner or had surrendered to the Germans. They were incarcerated in primitive enclosures known as "cages" in the towns of Zhitomir, Belaya Tserkov and Rovno in the Soviet Union, and Chełm and Zamosc in eastern Poland, where the conditions were primitive in the extreme—the prisoners were simply herded by the thousand into open fields surrounded by barbed wire and guarded by *Wehrmacht* sentries. There was no shelter of any kind and the inmates resorted to digging holes in the ground with their bare hands.[137] The selections among these prisoners to become auxiliaries took place before the onset of winter; which was a decisive factor for the "volunteers," who had no wish to starve or freeze to death. No food, water, or the most basic sanitation was provided, which reduced the starving prisoners to eating the grass in the "cages." Cannibalism was a fact.[138] The fate of many had been provisionally sealed by virtue of the "Operation Orders" issued by the Chief of the Sipo and SD, Reinhardt Heydrich, before the commencement of *Operation Barbarossa* in June 1941.[139]

However, the SS recruiting officers were very exacting in choosing suitable volunteers from the many hundreds of thousands of prisoners available. Once selected, they were removed to two "cages" in the city of Chełm in eastern Poland for further assessment. The criteria for selection were age, fitness, appearance, and a willingness to serve the *Reich*. An added advantage was knowledge of the German language.

In September 1941, many of these prisoners were scrutinized in order to assess their allegiance. When reviewing their fate, as a gesture of "friendship," the Germans showed special preference for prisoners identified as Ukrainians. German military documents seized after the war show that by the end of January 1942, of a total of 280,108 prisoners released, not a single one was Russian—but an astonishing 270,095 were Ukrainian.[140] The rest came from annexed countries. Other POWs identified as Jews were handed over to the SD for "special treatment," i.e. immediate execution.

In the early autumn of 1941, *SS-Hauptsturmführer* Karl Streibel,[141] commandant of the Trawniki camp, toured the "cages" with a team of his officers, searching for *Volksdeutsche,* who proved to be few and far between. Of the 100 prisoners selected by the end of the month, only five were *Volksdeutsche*. Groups of 50 to 300 politically suitable prisoners were eventually selected to be trained in Trawniki as auxiliary guards.[142] A final filter in the selection process was a medical team, which examined each "volunteer."

None of these Soviet prisoners knew why they had been selected or for what purpose, and those who survived the war have stated that they were prompted to "volunteer" to escape from their situation, in which many thousands were dying each day from starvation, typhus and dysentery.[143] The "volunteer" Sergei Vasilenko stated, "I did so for a crust of bread ... *I did not think the Red Army could defeat the German Army.*"[144]

Those who had passed the test as suitable for training were taken in small groups to the Trawniki camp. Only then were they told that they were being inducted as SS-*Wachmänner* (guards) for military establishments, KZs, and operational duties in the Jewish ghettos.[145] There was no mention of death camps. Objectors were threatened with "KZ Majdanek," and although they had no idea what this meant, they had no desire to return to any kind of camp.[146]

In Trawniki, each man had to fill in a *Personalbogen* (personal questionnaire), written in German and Russian, concerning his military postings, disciplinary record, transfers, promotions, and linguistic abilities, to which was added his photograph, thumb print and an *Erkennungsmarke* (identity number). After signing a *Dienstverpflichtung* (obligation to duty) each one was sworn in, welcomed as a soldier of the SS[147] and swore an oath of allegiance to Himmler.[148]

Globocnik, having retained his SS/Police officers and NCOs as instructors, opened the SS Training Camp Trawniki on 27 October 1941, and with the experience gained with his *Selbstschutz* and *Sonderdienst* units, had now created another band of murderous willing helpers. Over 5,000 auxiliary guards were trained at this camp.[149]

This special unit was extremely useful to the Germans because its members could be relied upon to carry out on-site mass murder shooting operations, and thus spare the German murder squads the ordeal of shooting men, women and children face-to-face. While German SS/Police officers undertook the initial preparations for rounding up the victims, it was usually the *Trawnikimänner* who carried out the actual shooting, and the Germans would often wait patiently while the *Trawnikimänner* first consumed quantities of vodka, usually in the presence of their victims, before commencing their murderous work.[150]

Training

The basic training at Trawniki usually lasted four to six weeks with three companies of 120 men each, divided into several *Züge* (platoons) led by a *Zugführer.* By the beginning of 1942 there were 720 recruits undergoing training at the camp with bi-lingual *Zugführers* acting as interpreters.[151]

During this period, the recruits underwent courses by German SS/Police instructors in understanding basic military commands in German, singing German songs, small arms and marching drill, guard procedures and ghetto-clearance techniques.[152] Each man was issued a captured Russian rifle;[153] only the *Zugführers* had pistols.

When a Jewish labor camp was constructed adjacent to the Trawniki training compound, the trainee guards were sent out on exercises, rounding up Jews in towns in the Lublin District and bringing them into the labor camp. Trawniki had become a central staging point for daily *"Judenaktionen"* (Jewish operations). As Wachmann Engelgard recalled, the final part of the training course consisted of each Ukrainian shooting individual Jews selected from the labor camp.

On completing their training, the bi-lingual *Trawnikimänner* were designated *Oberwachmann* and *Zugwachmann*[154] and posted to various establishments.[155] Others were simply designated as *Wachmann* and posted in groups to military establishments as armed auxiliaries to support the German security services. The majority were assigned to *Reinhardt* camps.

Once the Jewish destruction commenced, the Ukrainians were liberally used in "Jewish operations"—ghetto clearances, the preparation of killing sites, execution duties, and manning the death camps. The 20-30 strong Ukrainian guard at the Sipo/SD School in Rabka and the nearby Płaszów labor camp were all posted from Trawniki. Although their duties were assigned at the discretion of the commander on the site at which they served, they remained under Trawniki camp administration for all transfers, records, discipline, pay and uniforms. In the places where they served they were known as *Trawnikimänner*, *Askaris*, *Hiwis*, or *Czarni* ("Blacks" in Polish).[156] There was always a residue of Ukrainian tradesmen stationed at Trawniki, engaged in building and maintenance projects. However, these men were often called upon to dig mass graves in various locations and guard the killing sites until the SS delivered the victims for shooting operations.[157] Once this had been accomplished, they returned to Trawniki awaiting their next call-out.[158] Much use was made of this cadre by police regiments who were active in the Lublin area for Jewish operations, especially during mid- to late 1942.

Assignment to *Reinhardt*

At each of the three *Reinhardt* death camps 70-120 *Trawnikimänner* were selected to act as the guard unit and came under the jurisdiction of the relevant camp commandant. Although these guards remained under the auspices of Trawniki camp, in the death camps they were under the control of SS-*Obersturmführer/ Kriminalkommissat* Wirth, who also arranged their transfers between the camps.

For administrative purposes, the three Reinhardt camps at Belzec, Sobibór and Treblinka were treated as a single unit with interchangeable personnel—

both Ukrainian guards and SS/Police[159]—although the *Trawnikimänner* were also available for transfer to other establishments in the *Generalgouvernement*.[160]

During the opening phase of the Jewish deportations in March 1942, Globocnik relied on the *Trawnikimänner* to carry out these operations. The first was the clearing of the Lublin ghetto spearheaded by Worthoff, Höfle, *et al*. The Jews were driven out of their houses to the Lublin slaughter yards where they boarded the trains which took them to Belzec.

As Globocnik continued to establish new Jewish labor camps in the Lublin District, *Trawnikimänner* provided the guard units. Such camps in Lublin included the *SS-Bekleidungswerke*, located on the pre-war Lublin airfield; and the *Linden Strasse* camp, also known as the *Lipowerlager* after the Polish name for the street.[161]

By mid-1942, this team of seasoned thugs was at the forefront of all Jewish operations, including the emergency fire brigade operations during the suppression of the uprisings in the major ghettos of Warsaw, Bialystok and Częstochowa.

Duties in *Reinhardt*

A much clearer picture of the activities and lives of the Ukrainian *Trawnikimänner* has emerged in the wake of the much-publicised John Demjanjuk trial in Israel, which began on 16 February 1987 and concluded on 25 April 1988. Demjanjuk was found guilty and sentenced to death; but, remarkably, on appeal the conviction was reversed. The evidence presented by the prosecution covered the method of recruitment and activities of these guard units in the *Reinhardt* camps. This previously obscure and murky aspect of the Holocaust has had further light shed on it as the result of recently-developed co-operation between Israel, the United States and the former Soviet Union, in the course of which the post-war testimonies of several hundred Ukrainian former guards recalling their time in the *Reinhardt* death camps have been made available to the West.

The first contingent of 70 *Trawnikimänner*, mostly Ukrainians, arrived in Belzec at the beginning of 1942.[162] They were to claim subsequently that the purpose of Belzec was unknown to them. Initially brought to the camp by *SS-Oberscharführer* Josef Oberhauser, they were trained for their special duty by other nominated SS staff (i.e. *SS-Untersturmführer Schwarz*) under the express directions of Wirth.[163]

The *SS-Scharführer* at Trawniki, Reinhold Feix, was placed in charge of the Ukrainians. He had been brought in from Trawniki to maintain order and discipline. Feix set the standard for cruelty, and with the Latvian *Volksdeutsche*, Schmidt, was unsurpassed in brutality in the treatment of Jewish victims.[164] As a mark of the respect with which this brute was regarded, a road leading from the Ukrainian barracks to the high watchtower overlooking the camp in Phase Two of Belzec was named Feixstrasse.[165]

The *Volksdeutsche*NCOs were very close to the camp SS and later deputized for them in killing operations. The Ukrainian overseers and supervisors were given wide discretion by the camp leadership in their daily duties, including the carrying-out of executions, which were sometimes accompanied by brutal and intense cruelty.[166] The most favored Ukrainians—those of proven loyalty —were armed with a pistol.[167] The lower rank guards were all housed in barracks inside the camp and were delegated for duties such as patrols, manning watch-towers, guarding the rail sidings between Belzec station and the camp, and the supervision of the Jewish victims on arrival.[168]

Even though these guards had undergone extensive training in Trawniki, a different interpretation of their duties manifested itself once they had arrived in Belzec. The procedure for training them was set out in detail by Wirth. It was designed to complement the duties of his SS personnel and Jewish "work brigades." Throughout the entire period of genocide in all three *Reinhardt* camps, it was the *Volksdeutsche* NCOs and Ukrainians, assisted by the Jewish "death brigades," who—under the supervision of the camp SS— carried out the process of genocide, from start to finish. The role of the Jewish "death brigades" was vital for the extermination operation: they were the ones who had to handle the corpses daily. Wirth, in conversation with the SS investigating Judge *SS-Obersturmführer* Konrad Morgan, said, *"Give me my Jewish work brigades and I could send everyone else home and do the job myself."*[169] It is clearly evident that the auxiliary element in Belzec and elsewhere were carefully selected for this duty.

The bilingual *Volksdeutsche Zugführers* were the backbone of the camp operation. Working immediately below Wirth and his team of T4 operatives, these platoon leaders held complete power over life and death. They were the principal supervisors who handled their Trawniki guard personnel with strict discipline. Each of the three platoons in Belzec was organized on a 24-hour shift system that changed each day at noon. One platoon was designated duty at the incoming transports, another to general guard duties, while the third had rest day *("Zug bei Freiheit")*. As the slaughter progressed, the *Volksdeutsche* NCOs, who had made themselves indispensable to the death machine, were given more power and responsibility.

There are many accounts that graphically illustrate how these *Volksdeutsche Oberwachmänner* treated the Jews, who were shot, axed, and beaten to death. In front of the Treblinka gas chambers, they were beaten with clubs and iron bars by the gas chamber operators, Nikolay Shaleyev and Ivan Marchenko. Shaleyev had a cavalryman's sabre and used this weapon to cut off the breasts of Jewish women, and sever their noses and ears. He was capable of cutting a person in half with one stroke of the saber. He enjoyed setting his dog on naked people walking to the gas chamber. This creature would tear off pieces of flesh from men, women and children. Marchenko walked around the camp dispensing violence with a two-meter-long water pipe with which he was expert at killing, and with one blow could slay a physically strong man. The Ukrainian guard Pavel Vladimirovich Leleko was a witness to such atrocities.[170]

In a statement to Soviet investigators immediately after the war, Leleko described the daily gassing operations:[171]

> When the procession of the condemned approached the gas chambers, the motorists (engine operators) would shout: *"Go quickly or the water will get cold."* Each group of women and men were hurried along from the rear by some Germans and very often the Commandant himself (In Treblinka this was *SS-Untersturmführer* Kurt Franz, who was accompanied by a dog.) As they approached the gas chambers the people began to back away in terror. Often they tried to turn back. At that point whips and clubs were used. Franz immediately set his dog on the condemned which was specially trained to snap at their sex organs. At each gas chamber there were five to six Germans besides the "motorists." They drove the people into the corridor of the gas chamber with clubs and whips and then into the chambers. In this, the Germans would compete with the operators in brutality towards the people selected to die.
>
> After the chambers were filled they were slammed shut with hermetically sealed doors. The operators would turn on the motors. The exhaust gas was fed through pipes into the chambers and the process of asphyxiation began. Sometime after starting the motors, the operators would look into the chambers through special observation slits alongside each door to see how the killing process was going. When questioned what they saw there, they answered that the people were writhing and twisting among one another. I also tried to look in through the little window into the chamber, but somehow I did not succeed in seeing anything. Gradually the noise in the chambers subsided. After about 15 minutes the motors were turned off.[172]

It is interesting to note that those Ukrainian guards who were trusted by the camp leadership were issued with the black uniform of the German SS and allowed to carry arms. These favored individuals were also taken to northern Italy when *Reinhardt* was disbanded in late 1943.[173]

By mid-1942, there were very few Jews in the Lublin District who did not know what was awaiting them when they were deported. The guards were poised for action as soon as the victims stepped down from the transports in the arrival area and set upon them subduing any agitators or protestors, especially in the undressing barracks, from where the victims were driven into the gas chambers. In the course of these activities, several of the camp SS and auxiliary personnel were injured or killed: in Treblinka, *Zugwachmann* David Robertus suffered serious injury while attacking a Jew with an axe,[174] and *Wachmann* Tscherniawsky was set upon by a Jew he was beating, and had his hand shot off by another guard in the tower.[175]

Once Belzec had been organized to Wirth's satisfaction, the Ukrainians controlled most of the gassing actions under the eye of the SS. The Jewish "death brigade" experienced considerable personal stress when these actions unfolded before them. On one occasion when the Ukrainians were forcing victims into the gas chambers, the Jewish "death brigade" attacked their guards—and were immediately shot.[176]

The victims who were the subject of this revolt were probably Jews who had arrived on the first transports from Kraków. Tadeusz Miśiewicz, the Russian-speaking cashier at Belzec station, recalls many conversations he had with the "Blacks" (Ukrainians) relating to happenings in the camps:

> One boasted about how he seized a young Jewish girl by the hair and beat her against a post so that her spine was broken, killing the girl instantly. When Jews were being driven into the gas chamber, one of them hit him with a piece of wood so he shot the Jew. Another Jew was tied to a post and rubbed with goose feather spines so hard that his bare bones protruded.[177]

On another occasion, the Pole, Tadeusz Sloboda, who shared a house with a Ukrainian in Belzec village, recalled that several Ukrainian guards from the camp came to his house exhausted and told him that there had been a revolt in the camp. Two wagons (freight cars) of Polish (non-Jewish) political prisoners arrived to be gassed. The Poles had refused to undress and ran amok. They were hunted down in the camp and shot. The guards remarked that if ever a larger transport arrived at the camp they would be unable to cope.[178]

The brutal and sadistic behaviour of the Ukrainians was important in establishing their personal prestige, not only with the German SS, but also their comrades. It also sent a message to the Jewish workers that life was cheap.

Despite all this and in general, the Ukrainians' relationship with the Jewish "death brigades" in the *Reinhardt* camps was one of mutual toleration, as each benefited materially from the other. The guards had no real loyalty to the SS, and were never under any illusions as to their own ultimate fate. Despite all this, they continued with their partnership in genocide, with short-term stakes on offer for all participants.

Social Activities of the Ukrainian guards

Although each of the *Reinhardt* camps was allocated up to 120 guards, they were not all on duty in the camp at the same time but worked to a duty rota as discussed above. On rest days there was very little by way of entertainment for these men, and in Belzec they spent much of their time drinking in the local Belzec bars. The nearby town of Sobibór Lubelski offered similar fare, only more so. Even drinking in bars was not without danger. In November 1941 Anatolie Rige, an ethnic German from Siberia who had transferred to Treblinka (labor camp), died from alcoholic poisoning by drinking a locally-brewed concoction, which was substantially benzene spirit masquerading as vodka.[179]

Although it may be thought insignificant, Belzec had become an important trading center attracting many outsiders, including "loose" women. The death camp had become an integral part of the local economy.[180]

The guards, who were given 10 Reichmarks a week for tobacco, had many other sources of income, including the warehouses containing the property of the Jewish victims, which they pilfered and bartered with the local population. Even within the confines of the camp, the Ukrainian guards supplied food and vodka to "work Jews" in exchange for cash or valuables. Delivering illegal messages from one part of the camp to the other was another source of enrichment.

For example, a Polish police officer has reported that when a Ukrainian guard visited him he had a stack of money in notes, watches, gold, and all kinds of articles he had stolen from the locomotive shed where Jewish clothing was sorted.[181] They paid for vodka and women with bank notes stained with body fluids.

Although the Ukrainian guards were threatened with death by Wirth if they dared talk about their work while outside the camp, loose talk inevitably increased when the guards were drunk in the village.

Ukrainian Relationships with German Supervisors

The undisciplined behaviour of the Ukrainians caused a lot of problems for the SS/Police in the camp. Although Wirth tolerated many misdemeanors by the men under his command—including the SS-NCOs—he did not tolerate any action that placed the smooth running of the camps in jeopardy. *"We were a 'pile of conspirators' (verschworener Haufen) in a foreign land, surrounded by Ukrainian volunteers in whom we could not trust,"* according to *SS-Scharführer* Erich Bauer, the *"Gasmeister"* (gassing expert) of Sobibór.[182]

Much of the evidence concerning the activities of the Ukrainian guards originates from the Polish Commission of Enquiry at Belzec immediately after the war, when many local villagers, both Polish and Ukrainian, who had worked in the camp, relayed their accounts to the Commission. The Ukrainian guard Edward Własiuk married a 17-year-old local girl in 1942.[183] Another Ukrainian guard (name not known) told his woman friend what was going on in Belzec. She was so horrified that she gave details to the *Judenrat* in the Lvov ghetto. Consequently, when the selections for the *"Grossaktion"* (big operation) commenced there on 10 August 1942, the Jews already knew what awaited them.[184]

Security Risks

Because the Ukrainian guards were a security risk to the Germans they were treated accordingly. There appears to have been only one revolt planned by the Ukrainian guard unit in Belzec, in early 1943, when 50 guards mutinied and made an attempt to seize valuables and firearms from the garrison—an act that ended with disastrous results. One of the guards informed on his colleagues with the result that the SS were waiting and arrested them. The guards were removed under close watch to Trawniki, where it is believed they were all shot.[185]

In Auschwitz, 15 Ukrainians fled the camp, taking their weapons with them. In the following manhunt three German officers were shot. Soon after, all the Ukrainians in Auschwitz were dispersed to other KZs where it is presumed they were also shot.[186]

Because the Ukrainian guards were so mistrusted they were not issued with machine pistols. In Sobibór, the SS withdrew their ammunition on one occasion as they suspected treachery; a fact that was noticed by the Jews when planning their famous revolt.[187] German fears of betrayal proved to be well-founded: on 22 October 1943, while accompanying 30 Ukrainians from Sobibór to Trawniki by train between Chełm and the village of Zawadowska, *SS-Oberscharführer* Herbert Floss was murdered by the guard, Wasil Hetmaniec, with his own machine-pistol. The other 25 guards escaped but were hunted down by the SS, arrested in Rejowiec, disarmed, manacled, and returned to Trawniki. Their fate is not known and can only be presumed.[188]

On many occasions, Wirth, and later Hering (who replaced him as commandant from 1 August 1942) reacted to the excesses of these guards by beating, whipping and imprisoning them in a punishment bunker near the *Kommandantur,* where they remained for several days without food or water.[189] The leadership, however, were pragmatists and in return for their collaboration, turned a blind-eye on some occasions to the corruption and thefts committed by the Ukrainians. On other occasions, for serious breaches of security, the leadership did not hesitate to shoot them on the spot, or return them to Trawniki to be executed.[190] Two Ukrainians who crossed Wirth by loose talk to outsiders were reportedly arrested, dressed in clothing bearing the Jewish yellow star, and then gassed with the victims on the next transport. This incident broke many of the watching Ukrainians, who cried out in despair.[191]

Late one evening in October 1942, after two Ukrainians had been incarcerated in the punishment bunker for the theft of valuables from the *Kommandantur, SS-Scharführer* Heinrich Gley and Fritz Irrmann were intimidated by Hering into shooting them. Gley waited several meters away while Irrmann entered the bunker, where he was set upon by the prisoners; and in the darkness, Gley panicked and opened fire. He killed Irrmann, and the Ukrainian guards escaped. Irrmann was taken to the administration building where he was examined by a Jewish doctor summoned from the camp, who pronounced him dead.[192] Although the shooting of Irrmann was confirmed as accidental, Gley experienced the wrath of both Wirth and Hering, and recalled: "I could certainly have been executed without a court martial or further ado. Out of anxiety for these fearful measures, I bowed to their will."[193]

In the *Reinhardt* camps generally, a number of Ukrainian guards were summarily shot by the SS for varying reasons.[194] When Ukrainians were caught dealing with "work Jews," Wirth had three Jews shot as a warning. In Sobibór, two Ukrainian guards were shot in front of their comrades;[195] in Treblinka, Wirth dealt with the Ukrainians with extreme severity, beating and whipping them into submission in a way that even disturbed the SS.[196] Wirth's treatment of the Ukrainians was discussed by the SS who came to the conclusion that, should the guards join up with the Jews, they—the SS— would all be killed.[197] When Commandant Franz Stangl at Treblinka continued Wirth's policy of hard discipline with the guards, two attempts were made to murder him: a shot was fired at him one night, narrowly missing him as he lay in bed, and on another occasion a primed hand-grenade was found under the seat of his car.[198]

Final Stages at Trawniki

At the turn of 1942-43, serious German military setbacks resulted in a temporary halt to *Reinhardt* operations because the freight cars were needed at the front. The Ukrainian guards started to hedge their bets and several deserted, taking their weapons with them.

The worsening military situation on the eastern front resulted in such a demand for extra manpower that the standard of recruit had to be lowered. Such an additional source of manpower were the Carpathian Gorals—Poles, who with other civilian elements were utilised for auxiliary service. Until the liberation of the Lublin District by the Red Army in July 1944, the SS training camp remained the central training establishment in the *Generalgouvernment*.

The Ukrainians, in some respects, were also victims, the victims of circumstance; nevertheless, they paid a high price for their collaboration. It could be argued that they were more psychologically conditioned for their operations against the Jews by their long-standing background of anti-Semitism. If we accept that Ukrainian anti-Semitism was far more ingrained in the national psyche than among the Germans, then why did the Germans perpetrate this relentless genocidal policy with far more fervor than their

Ukrainian counterparts? It is apparent that the protagonists viewed the "Jewish Question" from different standpoints. The Germans, with their ideological perceptions of race *per se*, placed the Jews, Gypsies and Negroes at the bottom of the list of those who were "racially 'unclean'," with the Slavic nations, Russians, Poles and Ukrainians, only slightly less "tainted." The Jews, having been economically dispensable from the beginning, were the first destined for total destruction. The Ukrainians and Poles were regarded as beasts of burden and, in the short term, were to be exploited accordingly as slave nations.

In the *Reinhardt* camps, the attitudes of Germans and Ukrainians towards the Jews differed fundamentally, even if they vied with one another in the depths of their depravity. With their age-old tradition of pogroms, the Ukrainian *Trawnikimänner* took the path of collaboration with the Germans, and in so doing became subservient tools in a policy of coercion, cruelty, deprivation and mass murder. The whole process was initiated and supervised by the Germans, with Ukrainian collaboration. More to the point, easy access to untold valuables stolen from their victims gave the Ukrainians an unprecedented chance of gaining wealth, however risky. The systematic wholesale murder of a people, however, was another matter. It is most unlikely that they would ever have entertained such a course on their own initiative. That was something peculiar to the Germans.

There is some evidence to suggest that due to the situation in which the Ukrainian guards found themselves in Belzec, they were lethargic and greedy, and generally indifferent to Jewish persecution. Although they were willing to go along with the program of murder, they were not committed to the fanatical, ultimate aims of the Germans. Many Ukrainians who had loyally served the Germans attempted to escape when they sensed a reversal of German fortunes and the possibility of being accused as collaborators. At the conclusion of *Reinhardt,* the majority of Ukrainians were transferred to the SS *Galizien* Division in whose ranks they fought until defeated and destroyed by the Soviets at Brody in 1944.

Jewish Enforced Collaboration

Fig 1: Jewish workers in Belzec 1942.

During the second extermination phase in Belzec, a group of five persons (three male and two female) were photographed in front of three large sheds identified as part of the camp. I take the view that this was a contrived but factual photograph. The men are well-clothed, wearing collar, tie and caps. One man displays an armband on his left sleeve. All the men are wearing highly polished boots and flat caps. Two (center and right) appear to be exhibiting the Jewish star on their left breast. The male figure on the right is holding a whip in his right hand. The male figure (left) is also probably holding a whip clasped behind his back. The woman on the left appears to be wearing an armband on her right arm. There are indications that the woman on the right may also be wearing an armband. All five appear well nourished and well dressed. These people are Jews working in Belzec.[199]

Fig 2: SS- Scharführer Rudi Kamm in Belzec 1942.

The photograph above was almost certainly taken on the same day as Figure 1 and by the same photographer. (The SS officer is Rudi Kamm, first supervisor of the sorting/storage depot in the old locomotive shed). He is wearing the standard uniform of the *Waffen-SS* issued to members of the SS-garrison. The woman in the background appears to be the same one as in Figure 1 (second from the right). To the right of her, and standing by a barrack door, could be one of the men also shown in Figure 1. The buildings shown in Figures 1 and 2 are of special interest. The survivor Reder referred to the southern part of the camp, where a series of five detached wooden buildings stood facing the square, closed by a camouflaged fence of firs and mixed chicken and barbed wire. The wooden buildings are identical to those wooden barracks shown in Figure 2. It is the opinion of the investigation team (1997-9) that the buildings shown in the photographs (Figures 1 and 2) were the reception buildings where the women's hair was cut, and the undressing barrack.[200]

A key element in Christian Wirth's organization of the extermination program that was to prevail at Belzec, Sobibór and Treblinka, was his appointment and training of Jewish prisoners as an integral part of the extermination process. They were called "work brigades." Wirth selected two senior *Oberzugführer* who selected 15 *Zugführer*, who in turn selected the members of their individual work brigades. Under the supervision of the SS/Police leadership they had definite power. Apart from the Jewish *Zugführers* and members of the work brigades there were no "prisoners" in Belzec—only victims to be gassed or shot.

They were given adequate rations, allowed to select decent clothing taken from the victims, and were well-treated as long as the killing operation ran smoothly. The surviving photographs show them in riding breeches, black knee-length boots, and wearing cloth caps, which were a sign of authority.

They enforced their authority with whips, which they used freely, especially when the Germans were in sight.[201] The team of *Zugführers* supervised the Jewish work brigades in the death camps and assisted the SS.[202]

To place Jewish cooperation in the *Reinhardt* camps in perspective, it will be appreciated that the Jewish population in the ghettos and camps were under immense pressure to carry out the orders of the SS.[203] In Belzec, during the second phase, the Jewish work brigades were divided into two distinct and segregated groups of 500 Jews each. The "work Jews" in Camp I, the arrival and reception area, attended to the unloading of the wagons at the ramps, the undressing of the victims, and finally the collection and sorting/storage of the victims' clothing and belongings.

In Camp II, the extermination area, the "work Jews" unloaded the bodies from the gas chambers and buried them in the mass graves; later, they also cremated the exhumed bodies. Because of their gruesome work handling the bodies they were known as the "death brigade." A small team of Jewish mechanics also helped operate the gassing engines. A Jewish taxi driver from Kraków, remembered only as "Moniek" is said to have assisted.[204] Rudolf Reder, the roaming engineer and fixer of most things in Belzec, was often called upon to tinker with the gassing engine when there were "technical difficulties."[205] He also delivered the fuel. Jews certainly attended to the gassing engines in Treblinka, which they also refuelled.[206]

There were also Jewish specialists in each *Reinhardt* camp, such as gold- and silversmiths, jewellers, bankers, tailors, cobblers and doctors.[207] Other workers sorted the cash, valuables, clothing and footwear left by the victims. A separate work brigade attached to Camp I maintained the camouflage on the camp fences, supervised by an SS-NCO and Ukrainian guards. A smaller group, the "*Putzer*," (lit. 'cleaner' or in military terms a 'batman') materialised later in Treblinka and Sobibór; their duty was to clean the uniforms and boots of the SS and act as waiters in the canteen. The duties were governed by the schedules of incoming transports, at the arrival of which the prisoners reported to their assigned and permanent posts within the work brigades: haircutters, ramp duties, the luggage and clothing commando and fire specialists, who destroyed all personal possessions and spoilt items by burning them.[208]

Among the SS/Police garrisons in the *Reinhardt* camps there was a general mood of pessimism and apprehension, especially in Belzec under Wirth's command, a mood that was occasionally lightened by football matches between the SS and "work Jews" on days when no transports arrived. According to post-war German and Polish testimonies, there was no rancor should the Jews win the match.[209] In the bigger game they had lost anyway. For them, it was only a matter of time.

"Collaboration" is an emotive word and should be dealt with within the context of the circumstances at the time. Were the Jews who carried out the orders of the Germans in the death camps "collaborators"? There is a difference between the work Jews in the death camps and the rest of the Jewish population outside. In the death camps, according to the SS, the *Zugführers* "were particularly cruel to their own people," and the Jewish *Ordnungsdienst* in the ghettos were not exactly gentle.

In an overview of the war, there were, of course, individuals from nation states who willingly collaborated with the German occupiers. This is evident and generally not in dispute. No nation can claim "exceptional status" by stating that there was no willing co-operation by their nationals.

In the ghettos and camps of the *Generalgouvernment*, the focus for collaboration fell mainly on the *Judenrat* (Jewish Council) and the *Ordnungsdienst* (OD), the ghetto Jewish "police." From the position of friendly and helpful protectors of their kin, the members of each *Judenrat*, in a progressively deteriorating situation, were finally forced to act as mere puppets of their German masters. This change from altruistic benefactors to sometimes brutal and uncaring tools of destruction was brought about by threats to their own lives and those of their families. Should they not fulfill the wishes of their German oppressors to the letter, they too faced resettlement or immediate summary execution. In the end, they met the same fate as every other Jew in the ghettos.

The whole question of Jewish collaboration in the *Reinhardt* death camps must be viewed objectively in the light of the situation confronting them at that time. It is now generally accepted that far from being willing collaborators, they were very much the victims of circumstances, living in daily fear for their lives and clinging desperately to a slim hope of survival.

As an indication of the appalling reality that the Jewish "death brigades" endured as the forlorn price for temporary survival, one need only consider the case of Heinz "Heini" Schmidt, the Latvian *Volksdeutsche Zugwachmann*, who was in charge daily of the "death brigade" in Camp II in Belzec. He meted out regular vicious beatings to the "work Jews" who very often did not survive such treatment. It was common for Schmidt to kill 30-40 Jews a day, who were immediately replaced from the next transport. A daily register was kept by the *Oberzugführer* to ensure that the complement of 500 "death brigade" workers was always maintained.[210]

On another occasion, in the freezing cold, when the "death brigade" could not cope with the burial of the corpses, Schmidt selected 100 (naked) Jews who had arrived from the Janowska camp in Lemberg (Lvov) and forced them to work naked all day at the mass graves. In the evening, Schmidt took them to a grave and shot them one by one. When he ran out of ammunition, he took a pick-axe handle and beat the rest to death.[211] There are on record the arrival in Belzec of two small transports which contained only young children and babies. As it would have been difficult, if not impossible, to arrange the gassing of such small children, Schmidt ordered the Ukrainian guards to throw them into the pit and bury them alive.[212]

Once the gassing had been completed the "death brigade" dragged the bodies out of the chambers onto the unloading ramps. [213] Leather straps were wrapped around the wrists of each corpse and they were then dragged to a mass grave; *en route*, a brief halt was made for a "dentist" to remove any gold dental work from the mouths of the victims. The gold was melted down, fashioned into small ingots, and collected at regular intervals by a courier from T4 in Berlin.[214] Children who had been gassed together with their mothers were carried out two at a time,[215] slung over the shoulders of the "work Jews."

At the graves, a standard procedure for the disposal of the bodies was followed, as described by Rudolf Reder, one of the very few survivors of the death brigade:

> We were made to pile the corpses one meter above the rim of the already full grave, and then cover them with sand. Thick, black blood seeped from the graves and poured over the surface like a sea. We had to move from one side of the grave to the other in order to reach another grave. Our legs were immersed in the blood of our brothers. We stepped on mounds of corpses. That was the worst, the most dreadful thing of all... [216]

The story of the Jewish elements in the *Reinhardt* camps—the teams of *Zugführers*, "work Jews" and members of the "death brigades" —who found themselves involved in the genocide of their fellow Jews, is perhaps unsurpassed in its potency as an illustration of the power of the will to live. The desire to survive was what drove them to perform their dreadful tasks and endure the unimaginable horrors which they witnessed day after day.

Chapter 5. Suspension of T4; Crossover to *Reinhardt*

T4 personnel at Hartheim (Kurt Franz far left).

On 17 July 1941 Globocnik was appointed *Der Beauftragte des Reichsführers-SS für die Errichtung der SS- und Polizeistützpunkte im neuen Ostraum* (Plenipotentiary for the Construction of SS and Police Strongpoints in the new Eastern Area).[217] Between July 1941 and April 1942, there was a plethora of coded radio transmissions between Globocnik and commanders of the *SS- und Polizeistützpunkte* in Riga (*SS-Obersturmführer* Georg Michalsen), Bialystok/Minsk (*SS-Untersturmführer* Kurt Classen), and Mogilev (*SS-Hauptsturmführer* Hermann Höfle). Also in the Soviet Union at this time and closely involved with Globocnik were *SS-Obersturmführer* Richard Thomalla (later to be overall supervisor of the construction of Belzec, Sobibór and Treblinka) and *SS-Sturmbannführer* Hermann Dolp (in 1940, in general command of the labor camp complex centered on Belzec). When Globocnik was relieved of this construction task on 27 March 1942, all of these officers (with the exception of Dolp) played important roles in *Reinhardt*.[218]

In my view there were three steps to total genocide: *in-situ* mass killing operations post-Barbarossa (June-December 1941); first phase at Belzec (March-June 1942); second phase at Belzec, Sobibór, and Treblinka (July 1942-October 1943). This was a progressive war of annihilation against the Jews, brought to fruition gradually by a crazed anti-Semitic, all-powerful bully.[219]

Orders for Destruction

The escalation of decision-making in the "Final Solution of the Jewish Question" took place in October 1941. At a "Final Solution" conference at the RSHA on 10 October, the decision was made to deport *Reich* Jews eastwards where they would be held in camps. On 19 October, the Jews of Frankfurt were targeted for deportation by the *Gestapo*, and three months later, after the Wannsee Conference on 20 January 1942, German and Austrian Jews were dispatched in a wave of deportations to killing centers in the occupied areas of the Soviet Union (Minsk, Riga, Kovno) and Poland (Łódź, Chełmno, Sobibór, Treblinka, Majdanek, Belzec, Auschwitz.) sometimes via the *"Durchgangsghetto"* in Theresienstadt (Terežin) in Czechoslovakia.[220]

The decision makers in the Nazi hierarchy who argued for total Jewish extermination by gassing were now coming to the fore. Among the leading advocates in the *Generalgouvernment* who were in favor of this were Dr. Wilhelm Dolpheid, *SS-Obersturmbannführer* Dr. Ludwig Losacker, *SS-Obersturmbannführer* Helmut Tanzmann, and *SS-Gruppenführer* and Governor, Otto Wächter.

It is intriguing to note that in November 1941, Dr. Dolpheide negotiated with *SS-Oberführer* Viktor Brack at the *Führer's* Chancellery in Berlin to use the expertise of T4 personnel to solve the "Jewish Question" in his area. This being the case, Dolpheid apparently did not know the purpose of Belzec, which was already being constructed.[221]

The years-long debate by scholars about the decision-making process for the Final Solution has produced a wide spectrum of interpretations and overviews. No direct evidence of the "order," written or unwritten, has surfaced, or is likely to do so. The debate continues, because it is crucial for understanding the historiography of the Nazi State. One could even say it will remain the "holy grail" of Holocaust studies. New research shows that it was a gradual and complex process and that the crucial decisions were taken in the summer and autumn of 1941.[222]

Opinions vary about the most probable time that the decision was taken, but the consensus of opinion is that the likeliest period was in the latter half of 1941. Christopher Browning, who for some years has been a leading researcher on this point, argues that it was a two-stage decision, one for Soviet and another for European Jewry—based on the euphoria of victory in mid-July and early October 1941, respectively.[223] If this is so, I would add that those decisions were also implemented in two main stages: predominantly in late 1941, to rid the *Reich* of unproductive Jews (subsequently confirmed by the Wannsee conference); and in July 1942, to accelerate deportations of all Jews under German occupation, with the exception of Jews selected for labor.[224] Bogdan Musial, in his case study of Jewish persecution in the *Generalgouvernment* 1939-1944, concludes that the order was given in the first half of October 1941, based on the initiative of Globocnik and connected with his orders to Germanize first the Lublin District, and then the entire *Generalgouvernment*.[225]

Dieter Pohl,[226] Peter Witte[227] and Götz Aly, among others,[228] nominate late August and early September for the initial decision date. Certainly, there were a number of high-level communications as recorded in Himmler's diary for October: Globocnik appears in the diary on five occasions between 9 and 25 October.[229]

When Philipp Bouhler and Viktor Brack from the *Führer's* Chancellery visited Lublin at the beginning of September 1941, within two weeks of the "stop" to the T4 gassings in the *Reich*, Globocnik spoke to them about his "special task" and referred to the Jews who were to be deported from the *Reich*.[230]

Viktor Brack

The realization of the enormous task entrusted to Globocnik (and Wirth), is brought into focus by Brack, who had directed the euthanasia program. During his meeting with Globocnik, Brack decided that additional personnel from T4 would be placed at Globocnik's disposal:[231]

> In 1941, I received an oral order to discontinue the euthanasia program. I received this order either from Bouhler or from Dr. (Karl) Brandt. In order to reserve the personnel relieved of these duties and to have the opportunity of starting a new euthanasia program after the war, Bouhler requested, I think after a conference with Himmler, that I send these personnel to Lublin and put them at the disposal of SS *Brigadeführer* Globocnik. I then had the impression that these people were to be used in the extensive Jewish labor camps run by Globocnik. Later, however, at the end of 1942 or the beginning of 1943, I found out that they were used to assist in the mass extermination of the Jews, which was as then already common knowledge in the higher Party circles.[232]

In mid-1942, Brack wrote to Himmler where he again referred to Globocnik's role in this genocide. At about this time the pace of *Reinhardt* was already being markedly accelerated: Eichmann's trains were generally running to schedule and Globocnik's and Wirth's killing teams were in full swing. Brack continues:

> On the recommendation of *Reichsleiter* (Philip) Bouhler, I put my men at *Brigadeführer* Globocnik's disposal for the execution of his special tasks. Having received a further request from him I sent him more people. *Brigadeführer* Globocnik has stated that the campaign against the Jews should be carried out as quickly as possibie; as unforeseen difficulties might stop the campaign altogether and then we should be stuck in the middle of the road. You yourself, *Reichsführer*, some time ago drew my attention to the necessity of finishing this work quickly, if for no other reason than the necessity to mask it. In view of my own experience I now regard both attitudes, which after all have one and the same end in view, as all the more justified.

The very first sentence of this letter confirms that the SS-garrison (T4) was in the pay of the KdF and in no way connected to the service of the RSHA.[233]

After Wirth's experimental period at Belzec, it was apparent that the capacity of the *Reinhardt* camps was insufficient to cope with the planned increase in the volume of deportations.

Brack's use of the words, "my men" confirms the status of T4 personnel. What we are seeing here are the establishing principles and protocols as to how *Reinhardt* would operate independently and completely outside of all normal state functions. Brack was not simply an extermination planner sitting behind a desk, for he is known to have visited Lublin at least once. According to Josef Oberhauser, Brack's visit came as a surprise.[234]

I find no support for the contention of the scholars who maintain that the initial decision was made outside this period, i.e. December 1941, or even later. My own conclusions as to the decision date are in agreement with Aly, Pohl, Musial and Witte. Although concurring with many of their conclusions, one of the objectives of my own research is to pinpoint the activities of Wirth in the late summer of 1941, and to investigate the reasons for the discharge of many members of T4 on 24 August 1941, and their emergency recall two weeks later [235] when Phillip Bouhler was requested to transfer them to Globocnik in Lublin.[236] Clearly, whatever the decision and whenever it was made, once it had been taken there was no let-up, regardless of whether the killings were to take place in the execution pits in the Galician forests, or in the gas chambers at Belzec.

Much has been made of a visit to Lublin and Belzec by Adolf Eichmann— but when he made this visit is difficult to determine. According to the evidence he gave at his trial, his visit was in the late summer or early autumn (two to three months after the invasion of Russia). This is unlikely, as the construction of Belzec only commenced on 1 November 1941 (although the survey inspections must have been carried out before then, in late September or early to mid-October 1941 at the latest, as it is not usual to decide one day to build a death camp and immediately commence laying the foundations the following day). The site had to be cleared first by cutting down the trees and clearing the undergrowth. After that, concrete foundations had to be laid only for the first gas chambers—the rest of the barracks, probably no more than half-a-dozen, were assembled from prefabricated parts. The fact that it took almost two months to build such a primitive camp was due to the appalling weather conditions—blizzards, fog and temperatures as low as minus 25 °F— which halted work for days on end. The fences and watchtowers were not erected until after New Year 1942.

Whatever the date of Eichmann's visit the "decision" must have been made well before construction commenced at Belzec on 1 November, and in my view, any autumnal visits by Eichmann can be disregarded for these reasons: Eichmann clearly states that he met Wirth (a police captain) at Belzec and was taken into the camp where the final touches to the construction and sealing of the gas chambers were being made.[237] The evidence shows that Globocnik had handed Eichmann over to his deputy Höfle for a tour of inspection of the experimental camp. This entourage descended on the camp where they found Wirth, with sleeves rolled up, in the process of sealing the gassing barrack doors. After showing Eichmann the zinc-lined rooms (to facilitate cleaning) Wirth explained how the system was operated:

> When he had made everything airtight then he would hook-up a Russian U-boat engine, and the exhaust gas from this engine would be let in and the Jews would be poisoned. *(Wenn er dies alles schön dicht gemacht hätte, denn hier würde ein Motor eines russischen U-Bootes (arbeiten?) und die Gase dieses Motors würden hier hineingeführt und dann würden die Juden vergiftet werden.*[238]

After taking note of the operation, Eichmann returned to Berlin, where he submitted his report to his immediate superior, Heinrich Müller, head of the *Gestapo*, and to Heydrich.[239] Wirth did not take charge of the camp from the SS Construction team until 22 December 1941, and then he went away, returning after Christmas 1941 to convert one of the barracks into a gas chamber. Any suggestion that Eichmann was there in the autumn is without foundation. A December visit by Eichmann, as first suggested by Christian Gerlach, is most unlikely;[240] as is Philippe Burrin's conclusion that at this time he also visited Chełmno. Since the latter was functioning at the time of his visit, it must have been after December.[241] Gerlach later amends his views to a date after Wannsee.[242]

The exact date on which Eichmann visited Lublin is immaterial, apart from indicating the connection between Belzec and the decision-makers in Berlin. Any suggestion that Belzec was one of Globocnik's localized cavalier solutions to the Jewish Question can be dismissed as fanciful. It is clear that Eichmann's visit could only have been at the final phase of the construction, therefore dating it probably after the Wannsee Conference on 20 January 1942.[243]

The "order," therefore, must be calculated from circumstantial evidence. This suggests that in mid-summer 1941, the orders had been issued on a "need to know" basis. More substantial evidence appears in late 1941 and early 1942. A corroborative factor and a signpost may be gleaned from the time when Globocnik received orders from Himmler to implement *Reinhardt*. Eichmann, in his evidence at his trial in Jerusalem, stated that Heydrich informed him two or three months before the invasion of Russia that the *Führer* had ordered the physical annihilation of the Jews.[244] Later, on a date not determined, Heydrich ordered Eichmann "to drive to Globocnik. The Reichsführer has already given him corresponding orders. Look, see how far he has gone with this project."[245]

We have the autobiographical notes of Rudolf Höß, commandant of Auschwitz, who states that in the summer of 1941 he received "the order from Himmler personally," to "prepare a site for mass extermination:[246] The existing extermination camps in the East are not in a position to carry out the large 'Aktionen' which are anticipated. I have therefore earmarked Auschwitz for this purpose."[247] If Höß had been instructed during the summer of 1941, why not Globocnik, who had to perform the same tasks? It is inconceivable that Globocnik was not aware of this.[248]

One point that emerges is that the HHE/KdF had made "the decision" but were uncertain as to how it was to be carried out. T4 technology and experience was useful, but the scale of destruction now proposed required much greater technical support. This accounts for Belzec's importance as the experimental, prototype death camp.[249]

Once this problem of the mechanism for mass destruction had been solved, there was only the organization and implementation of resettlement that remained outstanding. For this, the Wannsee conference was convened as the final piece of the jigsaw. *Reinhardt,* according to Globocnik's own statements, was to be divided into separate sections dealing with deportations, exploitation of the work force, and utilization of property and the securing of the valuables.[250]

Wannsee (20 January 1942)

The SS-officers present at Wannsee included Dr. Eberhard Schöngarth, security chief in the *Generalgouvernment* (BdS). Members of other government departments concerned with the Jewish Question in their districts also attended. When Heydrich outlined his thoughts on possible solutions he could not be sure that the *Reich* departmental representatives would back him. Lurking in the background to his preamble to the conference was Heydrich's real intent: to deport the Jews to the East to the newly constructed death camp at Belzec (to which detail only the SS were privy). Coming to Heydrich's aid and helping to carry the day for the SS was *Staatsekretär* Dr Joseph Bühler, (Hans Frank's representative for the *Generalgouvernment*) and *Gauleiter* Dr. Meyer (Eastern Territories). They drew attention to the 2.5 million Jews within the *Generalgouvernment* who, they claimed, were a major health hazard and unemployable, and should thus be removed as fast as possible. Dr. Bühler emphasised to the waverers that transport and other technical difficulties were not a problem. Wannsee had the desired result, with the unanimous agreement of all those present that deportation to the East should go ahead with all that it implied.[251]

The only matter outstanding, which was to prove a major sticking point, was the definition of "Jew." To the Nazis, defining who was and who was not a Jew was important when their deportation policies were discussed. This issue was never completely resolved. It is interesting to note that in October 1941, three months before the Wansee Conference, preparations had begun to convert the old mansion at Chełmno into a killing center, and the mass gassings (in gas vans) commenced on 8 December 1941.[252]

The construction of these first death camps, in relation to the date of the Wannsee Conference, is revealing—as it shows that at Chełmno the mechanics of destruction were already in place and in operation, and Belzec was almost completed, before the conference was convened. The physical extermination of unproductive Jews was already being carried out at Chełmno.[253] As early as 1939, a few weeks into the war, Chaim Kaplan, in his diary of the Warsaw Ghetto, had foreseen and predicted exactly this tragedy with extraordinary perception—the annihilation of the Jewish people.[254]

Euthanasia and the 'Final Solution'[255]

The connection between the T4 euthanasia operation and the ultimate decision to implement the "Final Solution to the Jewish Question" are inextricably linked, as we have discussed. It cannot simply be coincidence that the technology for the destruction of those in the gas chambers of the T4 killing centers was functioning at its optimum at the moment of the decision making process for the "Final Solution" in mid to late 1941, thereby sealing the fate of the Jews of Europe. [256]

After the "suspension" and within the period I have suggested above, the "recall" of T4 personnel is very significant. This sudden reversal was unquestionably the product of policy-making within the HHE and was probably the result of several high-level meetings: Viktor Brack at the KdF; Heinrich Lohse, *Reichskommissar* of the *Ostland*; Dr. Erhard Wetzel, from 1941 Adviser on Jewish Affairs at the *Reich* Ministry for the Occupied Eastern Territories; and Adolf Eichmann, all of whom were very influential individuals advising the main planners of the "Final Solution."[257] Simultaneously, Himmler and Höß were discussing the enlargement of Auschwitz, specifically with Jewish extermination in mind.[258]

In November 1941 a high-level conference of euthanasia personnel was convened at Sonnenstein where, according to the Hadamar "gassing physician," Hans- Bodo Gorgass, "the action was not to be ended as had occurred in August 1941, but it will continue…in some other form."[259] It is clear therefore that something was being considered for the T4 operatives. While many of the T4 personnel were in limbo, decisions were being taken elsewhere. Exactly what was discussed at these meetings is not clear, but shortly afterwards, Brack committed T4 personnel to undisclosed duties in the East.[260] By January 1942, when construction of the Belzec camp was nearing completion, the T4 leadership were on the Eastern Front under the camouflage of *Organisation Todt*.[261]

The HHE/KdF were now engaged in compiling lists of other T4 personnel for "special duty."[262] One such list, entitled "*Sonderführer*," was sent to HSSPF Krüger in Kraków. It consisted of an unknown number of men probably to serve alongside the *Ordnungspolizei* who were becoming increasingly active. Although it is not known where these men were eventually sent, it is possible they went to Chełmno to assist the police units gathering there.[263] Another list of 92 T4 staff (compiled by Wirth, Brack, Blankenburg and Prof. Heyde) were designated for special duty in Lublin.[264] These men were not executives but the T4 artisans: drivers, builders, guardsmen, clerks and the SS-NCOs and policemen employed in the *Sonderstandesämter* of the killing centers. Even Wirth, and later Stangl, were at this point only intermediary cogs in this machine that was gathering momentum.

We can ascertain on the basis of post-war interrogations that the KdF for the Final Solution program, under Globocnik's direction, gathered these men to form the nucleus of gassing specialists to staff the first prototype death camp at Bełzec. To bide their time and keep this specialist unit together, many were sent to the Russian front to aid wounded German soldiers (*Aktion Brandt*).

Central to this group of medical experts was Dr. Irmfried Eberl (later commandant at Treblinka) who set up a medical unit near Minsk. Absent was Christian Wirth, the inspector and trouble-shooter of T4. Anecdotal evidence suggests that some T4 medical orderlies gave deadly injections to brain-damaged soldiers.[265] As evidence there is the statement by the nurse Pauline Kneissler, who started her career in murder at Grafeneck, that she and her unit administered lethal injections to brain-damaged, blinded, mutilated troops and amputees.[266]

Before the T4 men could finally be put to work, they had to have a killing center. Bouhler and Brack met Globocnik in Lublin in September 1941 and probably discussed *Reinhardt* and the transfer of personnel before going on to inspect the Old Lublin Airfield camp.[267]

As Brack testified at the Nuremberg Medical Trial in 1946:

> In 1941, I received an order to discontinue the euthanasia program. In order to retain the personnel that had been relieved of these duties and in order to be able to start a new euthanasia program after the war, Bouhler asked me—I think after a conference with Himmler—to send these personnel to Lublin and place them at the disposal of *Brigadeführer* Globocnik.[268]

On 25 October 1941, *Amtsgerichtstrat* Dr. Alfred Wetzel, responsible for Jewish affairs at the Ministry for the Occupied Eastern Territories, wrote to Heinrich Lohse, (the *Reichskommissar Ostland*,) with a proposal advanced by Brack.[269]) In his so-called "*Gaskammerbrief*" (Gas Chamber Letter), Wetzel suggest the "Brack remedy" for Jews no longer able to work, while Jews fit for labor might be transported east for further use.[270] Brack's suggestions were never implemented in Riga as originally planned, but

Reinhardt strategists now called in his offer to loan T4 personnel for the gassing of Jews in the *Generalgouvernement*. On 14 December 1941 Brack kept a noon-time appointment with Himmler, ostensibly to discuss his recent proposal and perhaps also to secure or arrange the delegation of T4 personnel to Lublin. The meeting was followed by a luncheon attended by Hitler, Himmler, Bouhler, and Rosenberg.[271]

The construction of Belzec did not commence until early November and the camp was not operational until December 1941 when the first trickle of T4 personnel began to appear for duty.[272] Schwarz and Oberhauser were the first SS-men to arrive in Belzec at the end of October. The rest, 10 men, arrived from Bernburg at the very beginning of January 1942. For the initial postings to *Reinhardt*, only a small group were sent. Other T4 personnel returned to their euthanasia institutions on a temporary basis.[273] In each man's pay book the red page endorsement read, "not to be employed at the front line." This was meant to protect against the possibility of their capture by the Soviets and to thereby help in preserving the secrecy of the program. Alternatively, it may have been in the nature of a reward for the service they were providing.[274]

Civilian to SS unit

The second transfer of T4 men to Reinhardt took place in July 1942 in time for the second, main gassing phase, from 1 August. As this group were civilians, of whom few had had any military experience, they were sent first to Trawniki for a two-week basic military training course before joining the SS-garrisons in the death camps.[275] In fact, during the early days at Belzec everyone wore civilian clothes. Their assimilation was further enhanced when SSPF Globocnik ordered *SS-Sturmbannführer* George Wippern, the *SS-Standortverwaltung*, to issue the men with *Waffen-SS* uniforms.[276]

The *SS-Standortverwaltung* was simply the Lublin Garrison Administration HQ that looked after accommodation, pay, leave and transfers. Wippern took on the extra duty of keeping the *Reinhardt* account books in the summer of 1942. At first he did not want to issue the uniforms as these men were not under his SS-administration. He checked with Krakow and Berlin and was told to proceed with whatever Wirth wanted without discussion or argument.

These uniforms were without SS runes on the collars. Josef Oberhauser referred to these men as "civilians in uniform."[277] The issuing of the grey *Waffen -SS* uniforms and the designation of *Scharführer* (Sergeant) rank to the Belzec garrison was to give some semblance of order and, perhaps, to set an example to the Ukrainian guard unit there who were set apart and dressed in their own distinct military uniform, one that was similar to the SS-uniform. It may also have been a direct message to the local Polish and Ukrainian inhabitants to indicate an armed presence in the district.[278] Wirth, dressed in the uniform of a Stuttgart police superintendent, enforced this message to the residents of Belzec by leading his men on frequent marches through the streets.[279] Conferring these men with the rank of *Scharführer* confirms the view that this was a special arrangement. To promote a civilian with no military background directly to rank of Scharführer was both odd and unprecedented, even in Nazi organizations. It had long been appreciated by the KdF that the T4 men assigned to *Reinhardt* would no longer be fit for euthanasia duties inside the borders of the *Reich* and were now expendable.[280]

The T4 personnel had to wear the uniform because the extermination of the Jews was an SS operation; hence only the nominal ranks of *Unterscharführer*, *Scharführer* and *Oberscharführer* were granted. Oberhauser reported the presence of "an SS-unit" in Belzec to the local commander in Sobibór as a matter of normal military courtesy. The marches in formation through and around Belzec village took place on days when there was nothing to do in the camp, simply to keep the men occupied, as well as to show themselves to the locals.

Disregard for Authority

The Berlin leadership had let the "genie out of the bottle," so to speak. *Reinhardt* was so secret in formation and extreme in its purpose, that extraordinary measures were adopted. One of the side effects was an arrogant disregard for outside authority by *Reinhardt* personnel. They had no reason to pay any attention to any authority other than the KdF, via T4, and SSPF Globocnik. They were "untouchable" and everyone knew it. This was condoned by Berlin in that no outside interference was tolerated from any quarter. This being so, any measure could be either adopted or circumvented in the interests of State secrecy

The distinction between hybrid KZ/death camps (Auschwitz and Majdanek), their subsidiary camps, and the *Reinhardt* death camps, was also apparent by virtue of the leadership personnel. In *Reinhardt*, the SSPF in Lublin, Odilo Globocnik, had specific qualifications for this task as decided by Himmler, who had clearly indicated that Auschwitz was to be used as an overflow killing facility for *Reinhardt.*

KZ Majdanek

Built under the direction of SS-*Untersturmführers* Hautz and Neumann from the SS-*Zentralbauleitung*, Lublin, Majdanek grew to be a major extermination site for Jews only in late (September) 1942. Subsequently, a third of the Jews from the Warsaw and Bialystok ghettos were gassed in Majdanek.

Himmler directed the building of Majdanek on 20 July 1941, for the purpose of holding 25-50,000 to be used for labor. Majdanek had two masters: the SS-WVHA and SSPF Globocnik. Majdanek was probably one of the most versatile penal establishments in the *Reich*. Commanded by *SS-*

Standartenführer Karl Otto Koch, who had been transferred from KZ Buchenwald, the camp was a central melting pot as a workforce reservoir for multi-national prisoners, including Jews.[281] It also acted as a clearing and economic counting house for *Reinhardt.*

Gas chambers, which were "dual-purpose" (killing and disinfection), were built in October 1942. Two chambers were converted for *Zyklon B* use and one for carbon monoxide.[282] These facilities were used sporadically for gassings until September 1943, when for some unknown reason the mass killings ceased.

Although approximately 70,000 Jews died at Majdanek, it was not, strictly speaking, a Jewish death camp. The meeting of minds there between the WVHA and *Reinhardt* was never fully realised as the WVHA was primarily concerned with labor pools, while *Reinhardt* carried out gassings of Jewish prisoners once they had proved ineffectual as labor in Globocnik's enterprises.[283]

In July 1942, Himmler ordered that all camps and ghettos in the *Generalgouvernment* must be cleared of Jews by the end of the year. As the ghettos and transit camps were emptied, many thousands arrived in Majdanek to work in SS enterprises. By the beginning of 1943, thousands of Jews deported from Greece, Holland and France arrived at the camp. Although Majdanek was outside the *Reinhardt* loop and administered by the WVHA, Globocnik utilised the camp for *Reinhardt* purposes in that the loot taken from murdered Jewish prisoners was added to the *Reinhardt* account. It is interesting to note that Majdanek is included alongside Belzec, Sobibór and Treblinka in the secret telegram SS-*Sturmbannführer* Höfle sent from Lublin to Krakow giving the numbers of victims for 1942.

Majdanek continued to operate until 1944, receiving political prisoners from other KZs in Germany and Austria. The camp functioned until early July 1944, when the Russians had crossed the Bug River. Orders to abandon the camp resulted in over 1,000 prisoners being marched towards Auschwitz and Gross-Rosen. Very few survived.

KZ-Auschwitz

Commandant Rudolf Höß, although deeply implicated in the destruction of European Jewry, was an outsider to Globocnik's camps in the East.

What the HHE/KdF were about to embark on was both unorthodox and of such magnitude that serious implications were emerging as to the integrity of the much-cherished Prussian military ethos and command structure. The German tradition of exemplary discipline and order in the military rank structure was being undermined and was disintegrating. When Rudolf Höß was summoned to see Himmler in the summer of 1941 and told of his duties in the genocidal policy, he was instructed to keep his orders absolutely secret, even from his immediate superiors.[284] When SS-*Obergruppenführer* Jakob

Sporrenberg replaced Globocnik in September 1943, he was expressly warned by Himmler to keep away from "Jewish matters." Sporrenberg, ignoring this advice, was curious to know exactly what was going on and went to Sobibór with the intention of inspecting the camp.[285] The commandant at Sobibór at that time was *SS-Hauptsturmführer Reichleitner* (a police captain and T4 graduate), who refused to open the gates and advised the *Obergruppenführer* to return to Lublin.

This action by Reichleitner in refusing to obey an officer—who was by any normal criteria his most senior local officer—emphasizes these men's complete disregard for rank and their belief that they were untouchable, above the law and only answerable to the very highest authority.[286]

The duties of T4 specialists were initially to supervise mass gassings, and they expected a certain amount of protest by the victims, even violence, for which they were well prepared. The first line of defense, instigated by Wirth, consisted of deception techniques designed to lure the victims to their fate with false promises. By this time the majority of Polish Jews knew what Belzec meant; "false promises" could only have been used with the foreign transports. If that failed, overwhelming deadly force of arms was used with brutality, cruelty and disregard for life by the Ukrainian guards who supervised the continuous flow of victims. The SS, however, rapidly became indifferent or immune to the pleadings of the victims. They had eradicated any personal feelings or moral responsibility for what they were doing to innocent people. As Franz Stangl aptly put it:

> They were cargo. It had nothing to do with humanity—it could not have, it was a mass—a mass of rotting flesh. Wirth had said, *"What shall we do with this garbage?"* I think unconsciously that started me thinking of them as cargo.[287]

The men now engaged in *Reinhardt* were not the same men who had sought career advancement and family security when they initially joined T4. They had become the butchers of men.

Shooting Operations within and outside *Reinhardt*

In contrast to *Reinhardt*, *Einsatzgruppen SS*/Police units engaged in Jewish murder operations had the personal protection of Himmler when refusing to obey execution orders. This protection was without recourse to punishment or courts martial. No such luxury of courts martial was ever entertained in Belzec, as refusal to bow to Wirth's orders was not negotiable. The system of mass murder relied on the absolute fear of retribution by the camp commandants, particularly by Wirth, should they refuse. Josef Oberhauser recalls:

> Regarding Schluch (*SS-Scharführer* in Belzec), who Wirth had assigned to the shooting of unfit Jews (in the *Lazarett*), he said to me, face to face, *"I would have dearly liked to have shot him down in the grave!"* Wirth made this remark, not for the reason that

> Schluch had not carried out an order or had completely refused (to obey it), but only that he had not shown sufficient vigor. This was Wirth. If anyone argued with him, he immediately went for his weapon. None of us were safe, not even me, a close colleague.[288]

Wirth was the kind of man who exterminated thousands of Jews *every day,* and for whom the life of one SS man who refused to obey an order meant not the slightest thing. On many occasions Wirth simply drew his pistol. He had an iron hard discipline, unconditional obedience, belief in the *Führer*, and an absolute heartlessness and ruthlessness.[289]

As the Prosecuting Counsel in the Belzec Trial later remarked, "without bothering with an SS Court, the refusal to obey orders led to certain death."[290]

The usual punishment for the SS, according to *SS-Scharführer* Heinrich Gley, was "hard probation" in Camp II, especially during the exhumation and burning of the bodies—a punishment that both Wirth and Hering liberally exercised. Gley continued, "Refusal to do this duty would mean immediate execution without courts martial. Out of anxiety for these fearful measures, I bowed to his will."[291]

If the leadership was able to shoot or gas properly inducted Ukrainian security personnel for minor infringements (as they did), threaten to whip an SS officer who was personal assistant and deputy to the commandant (Oberhauser), to pull a pistol on an *SS-Scharführer* and make moves to shoot him down where he was (Fuchs), then anything was possible.[292]

However, even Wirth had to act within certain SS regulations, especially with the pre-war professional SS-NCOs. Fuchs was a "civilian in uniform"; he could only have had Fuchs brought before a special court for "obstructing important SS business," i.e. sabotage, which carried the death sentence. There are many other incidents of this nature in the Belzec, Sobibór and Treblinka files, all of this contrary to what was happening outside of *Reinhardt,* where a much more liberal view of dissent was taken.

The circumstances outlined above may appear contradictory; but this was *Reinhardt*, in full flow in uncharted waters.

Refusal to Shoot Jews

The Nazi approach to murdering Jews was paradoxical. There were fundamental differences between what prevailed in *Reinhardt* and the general protocols practiced elsewhere. It was generally accepted within the prosecution of the war and its political objectives, that killing Jews was a lawful "duty" for the personnel given this task. However, to kill Jews with sadistic brutality, even with authority, was not lawful and could not be justified. Killing Jews without an order was unlawful and could be excused only if the circumstances warranted it. It was contended that such savage behavior brought the German people down to the level of the "savage Bolshevik hordes" with their un-German methods.[293] To murder persons who had put themselves on the side of the Germans, i.e. the Ukrainian cadres, was not acceptable without conclusive evidence against them produced in judicial proceedings. SS-Judge Konrad Morgan, a criminal investigator with a roving brief from Himmler, stipulated three kinds of acceptable murder: officially decreed murder of Jews, euthanasia killings at T4, and lawful executions in the KZ.[294] Morgan's assessment, of course, dealt with everything outside *Reinhardt*. Morgan knew well enough about *Reinhardt*; he met Wirth and spent over a year trying to prove a case of corruption against him. He also knew Wirth's orders came from the *Führer* and therefore could not do anything about the Jewish exterminations, which were not only outside his brief but authorised "from on high."

Some historians conclude that there was no real overt threat by the leadership to shoot or incarcerate those members of the security personnel who showed dissent when enmeshed in killing operations.[295] This may well have been the case for police squads engaged in mass shootings, but in *Reinhardt*, a contrary picture emerges. [296] The accepted thinking on this issue is based on judicial pronouncements made in subsequent SS prosecutions during the war, particularly in relation to the *Einsatzgruppen*, (the mobile killing squads). The consensus of the courts at the time, and in post-war years, was that the SS personnel had a choice of refusal to shoot Jews, rejecting claims that they had no choice but to kill in fear of retribution. The SS judiciary concurred that refusal was not a threat to their personal safety as they had an appeal route to their superiors. It is the general view that on this point, there is no proof that any German officer or NCO was ever punished for refusing to obey orders to kill Jews.

In this study, we are not dealing with general killing actions by the SS, *Schutzpolizei* or the *Einsatzgruppen*. The death camps were operating according to quite different rules and criteria from those prevailing for police operations in the ghettos and killing sites in the occupied areas. I draw attention to the numerous testaments made under oath by former members of the SS-garrisons of Belzec, Sobibór and Treblinka. These men were in the utmost fear of their lives should they not carry out their duties as ordered in killing operations. Of this there is no doubt as the evidence is overwhelming, as will be discussed elsewhere.

To rely on SS court pronouncements and the numerous individual statements obtained from perpetrators outside *Reinhardt* is both misleading and spurious. When *SS-Obersturmführer* Albert Hartl, a member of a mobile killing squad in Russia, was asked at the Nuremberg trials, "Was it possible to refuse to take part in a shooting?" He replied, "In my experience it depended on the mentality of the individual commander."[297] This view by Hartl is corroborated by events happening outside *Reinhardt*. After *SS-Brigaderefführer* Dr. Schöngarth had entered Lvov with his *zbV unit* (a special *Einsatzgruppen* unit which followed the *Wehrmacht* into Russia to deal with enemies of the *Reich*), he immediately commenced the mass killing of all perceived political opponents, including Jews. Schöngarth ordered his commanders personally to shoot Jews during these operations and demonstrated how this was to be done. After shooting his selected Jew into a pit, he said:

> You saw how it was done. Every man should join in the shooting. I will shoot anyone who does not agree. I will back up every SS *Führer* who shoots a man for not obeying my order.[298]

The SS officer who recalled Schöngarth's "shooting seminar" *was SS-Hauptsturmführer* Hans Krüger, who became the leader of the largest mass shootings in East Galicia.

SS Shooting Practices

As has been indicated elsewhere,[299] the men holding the power in the *Einsatzgruppen*, the KZs and *Reinhardt* camps were mostly hardened, ideologically committed Nazis who were authorized to act on their own responsibility. Although given wide discretion as to how they were to be effective in an unclear and fluctuating situation, they were not officially authorized to shoot Jews from the area of the German *Reich*.[300] However, the open-ended mass murders in the Soviet Union soon spilled over into other regions where the security services responded in kind. These regional annihilation programs were all part of a much wider scenario of deportation and decimation of the Jewish populations.[301] Some regional commanders responded by developing their own methods through experimentation during the day-to-day killings. This does not necessarily mark them all down as wanton killers, as many of them firmly believed they were acting under orders. Certainly, many of the *Einsatzgruppen* commanders carried out executions but adhered to well laid-down, recognized principles of properly convened and regulated firing squads. This principle of military honor was the well-established code of shooting at "twelve paces" with the *coup de grace* given by the squad leader. These recognized practices soon deteriorated once mass murder of the Jews began to accelerate, and when the killers became overwhelmed, exhausted and psychologically impaired by the sheer weight of numbers. This was evident in the killings on Soviet territory and in East Galicia, where the SD independently organized mass shooting operations at Nadworna and Stanisławow.[302] The interesting point here is that extermination policies at this time (autumn 1941) were very much organized at a local level, based primarily on economic conditions and not on direct orders from Berlin.

There is no doubt that the shooting operations in the East were causing serious psychological problems for the killers. Participants of firing squads/execution squads carried out their orders despite personal repugnance, many breaking down in tears when faced with killing women and children. Many had nervous breakdowns and some resorted to suicide. Himmler had taken steps to alleviate such heavy psychological pressure by offering a blanket protection for any refusals or requests not to take part in these actions. He also made available a convalescent home for those seriously affected.[303] Was this an understanding by the RFSS for the morale of his men, or was it a clever maneuver? There were certainly mixed messages coming from Berlin to the leadership in the field. Those SS personnel of the lower ranks who refused outright to obey orders and genuinely could not reconcile the action with their consciences stood their ground and put up with ridicule from their comrades.[304] They were labeled "cowards" and "un-soldierly" by their compatriots, and not worthy of the SS. Higher ranks of leadership who refused on principal to become involved in "un-German" actions avoided serious consequences, but had to forego any further advancement.[305]

Occurrences of unlawful killing of their own men by the SS leadership are illustrated by the following incident. Again, Dr. Schöngarth is involved. On 21 November 1944, the crew of an Allied bomber bailed out near Enschede in Holland. One of the crew had the misfortune to drop into the SD headquarters where Dr. Schöngarth was attending a conference. On Schöngarth's orders, the airman was taken outside and shot. He was buried in the grounds of the SD/HQ and the grave carefully camouflaged.[306]

Shortly after the war, the grave was opened. In addition to the airman's remains, three other corpses were found—with ropes around their necks, as opposed to the airman who had a bullet wound in the head. The three corpses, in SS uniform, were identified as SS/SD officers, one of them named as *SS Hauptscharführer* Peter Bell. We may assume with some certainty that these corpses had been the subject of an unofficial SS hanging party, but for what offenses it has not been ascertained. It was this one incident of shooting the British airman that resulted in Schöngarth being sentenced to death by a British military court and hanged.[307] Dr. Schöngarth's personal contribution to violent excesses in east Galicia and elsewhere are immeasurable and probably unsurpassed.

Throughout the war, the more maverick commanders of the SD, like Schöngarth, Otto Ohlendorf and Hans Krüger made up their own minds and devised their own methods of summary justice according to their idiosyncratic personalities. It would be naïve to think otherwise. In *Reinhardt*, the question of choice or uncertainty never arose—summary justice ensued for all those engaged under *Reinhardt* command.

Suicide: Reasons and Alternatives

The attitude of the majority engaged in *Reinhardt* towards the victims was contemptuous indifference. In Belzec, when two Jews, after seeing their families go to the gas chamber, pleaded to be shot, Josef Oberhauser pulled his pistol and shot them as a "mercy death."[308] Although acts of murder, whether by shooting or by gas, were carried out quickly and efficiently, there was a sadistic quirk in the system. The timing and place of death was dictated and controlled by the SS killers, and although the principle of a painless death had been practiced in T4, in *Reinhardt* there was no conscious consideration of this. The psychological circumstances surrounding the victims once in the death camps was in many cases more terrifying than the act of murder itself. The main affront to the perpetrators in the camps was the victim committing suicide at a time of his or her own choosing. Nothing was guaranteed to enrage the killers more than suicides among their prisoners, which, as a result, would set off a train of events that brought about more brutality and death for the helpless and innocent victims.[309] When a Jew attempted suicide at Sobibór in the spring of 1943, *SS- Scharführer* Karl Frenzel whipped the dying man and then shot him: "Jews have no right to kill themselves. Only Germans have the right to kill."[310] The files are replete with descriptions of occasions such as this.

Attempted suicides occurred not only among those arriving for immediate execution at the death camps, but also among those selected for temporary survival. For these crimes, execution was not enough to satisfy the persecutors who demanded torture first in the most demeaning manner. In Belzec a Jewish woman who had concealed a razor on her person assisted several Jews of the work detail to end their lives by cutting their throats. She was immediately shot by the guards. Wirth deeply regretted that the woman was already dead as in his view she should have suffered some exemplary punishment. As for the Jews the woman had aided, now wounded, they were given medical attention in the camp and this fact of concern for their welfare deceived them into thinking that they would survive. Wirth found an inexhaustible source of astonishment and amusement in the fact they (the Jews) believed in their survival: "and the fools believed it."[311]

Suicide enabled the victims to choose the time and place to beat the hangman rather than face what lay before them. Suicides were prevalent in all three *Reinhardt* camps, both among the victims and the perpetrators. This was particularly apparent in the extermination areas, where the SS leadership assigned guards to "suicide prevention duty," in the course of which they observed Jews likely to put a rope around their own necks. Failure to stem Jewish suicides merited a brutal beating or even hanging for the guards.[312] At Sobibór in the winter of 1942-3, 10 Jews chose this course rather than submit to further mental torture.[313]

In Belzec, Sobibór and Treblinka, everyone killed Jews. The question of a choice was never a possibility, unless, that is, the perpetrator committed suicide or rashly showed open dissent that could amount to the same end. Suicide was obviously a way out—but even here, it was a matter either freely entered into or it was carried out by coercion. Suicides among the SS perpetrators during actual duty were of three kinds: those who just could not stand the sight of mass murder and were in absolute fear of Wirth; those who relished the murders, but were troubled by them; and those who were persuaded by outside influences.

In the first category, at Treblinka, *SS-Scharführer* Erwin Kainer was ordered by Wirth to supervise the clearing away of a mound of decomposing corpses outside the gas chambers. Kainer was so distressed at the sight in front of him and so in fear of Wirth should he refuse, that he shot himself in desperation.[314] Erwin Kainer was looking at decomposed corpses 5 meters high beneath a 75 cm-deep cesspool, full of blood, maggots and excrement.[315]

In December that same year, *SS-Scharführer* Bauch at Sobibór shot himself in what was referred to by Franz Suchomel as a "neurosis fear" of Wirth.[316] In the second category, we have the *Volksdeutsche* Heinz Schmidt, who was the most brutal killer in Belzec and, because of it, was ostracised by the camp SS. Later in Italy Schmidt shot himself. The third category is more difficult to establish in the death camps, but we do have examples of this occurring in the HHE cadre of zbV, the pre-*Reinhardt* spearhead unit. In this case, induced suicide was the preferred method whereby the SS would shoot themselves out of fear of the consequences should they feel unable to obey orders. This category also challenges the Goldhagen theory, as discussed above. In addition it supports the concept of the third category of suicides, which were absent in the death camps but materialized later.[317] Depression in individual members of the SS was only too apparent in the death camps. In the *Deutsches Haus* (German House), the German recreation center at Rawa Ruska, an SS man from Belzec was seen "bawling like a child." The SS man said that he was on duty in Belzec and if it was going to go on for another 14 days he would kill himself because he could not stand it anymore.[318]

This was not the only occasion where we see the authority of rank determining suicide as the outcome of events. Two SS men who refused to kill Jews were driven to commit suicide by Dr. Schöngarth: "Some SS men went into the woods near Lvov in search of partisans and an SS *Führer* shot himself there. The other SS men reported that partisans had shot him." In fact, this man had shot himself on orders from Schöngarth because he did not want to kill Jews. Dr. Schöngarth gave him the choice of facing an SS court and being shot, or to kill himself so that his wife would receive a pension (which would not have been the case if the officer had appeared before an SS Court).[319] In Warsaw, an SS *Führer* refused to kill Jews and was imprisoned. Dr. Schöngarth arranged for a pistol to be placed in his cell; the man shot himself.[320] *SS-Brigadeführer* Eberhard Schöngarth was not a man to be trifled with; he was a key architect in the destruction of European Jewry who sat on Heydrich's right at the Wannsee Conference table.

SS-Discipline and 'Hard Probation'

One of the central themes of this account has been to highlight how, from its inception, the T4/*Reinhardt* personnel were held together *incommunicado* from all other wartime activities; and to examine the means the Nazis devised to protect their most secret operation. Those privy to *Reinhardt* were kept outside the norms of military discipline, regulation and punishment, and although they were financially rewarded by the KdF with extra bonuses, there would eventually be a price to pay.

At Belzec, once Wirth had thoroughly worked out the extermination procedure, the SS had little actual participation in the gassings apart from supervisory duties. Once the victims had left the undressing/haircutting barracks and entered the "Tube," the Ukrainian auxiliaries supported by the Jewish "death brigade" took over and were able to complete the whole murder process with very little SS assistance. Backed up by thoroughly camouflaged perimeters and buildings, and overseen by heavily armed guards in watchtowers, they had little need for SS interference. It was on the periphery of events—maintaining a continuous flow of transports and fulfilling the aftermath of their deadly work—that the leadership focused. Within this cauldron of mass killing, every conceivable manifestation of cruelty and murder was carried out daily.

With so many Jews rolling off the transports, the men soon became blasé, and to relieve their boredom commenced to turn the victims' plight into periods of amusement to break up the monotony of daily gassings. The SS guards were an idle lot; and providing there were no problems, wandered from post to post within the camp looking for entertainment until their shift finished. "We didn't have to do anything. There wasn't really anything for us to do. Yes, we just had to be there," said former *Scharführer* Gustav Münzberger.[321] Jews were picked on to entertain and satisfy this need, and it is within this atmosphere of idleness that many of the "work-Jews" suffered from such excesses. Many guards resorted to sadistic acts of cruelty by making the victims perform all kinds of unnatural acts. The SS repeatedly spoke about their individual actions against Jews in the mess rooms and during off-duty hours.

The punishment most favored by the SS leadership to curtail indiscipline or other misdemeanors by their own men was a period of hands-on duty at the reception ramp, where at times, several thousand Jews were found dead on arrival, their bodies bloated and infested with flies. On the Kołomyja transport of 14 September 1942 (discussed later), over 2,000 out of 8,250 Jews (25 percent) were found dead in the freight wagons after a journey that had lasted several days in unusually hot weather.[322] Another designated punishment duty ordered by Hering was assignment to execution duties, assisting the specialist *SS-Scharführer* Heinrich Gley (an original T4 member from Grafeneck). It was here that the SS shot the sick, elderly and infirm victims in the back of the neck with a small caliber pistol or machine pistol. "They didn't suffer," Gley claimed.[323] Only one SS-NCO in Belzec was excused this duty: *SS-Rottenführer Heinrich Barbl* (the metal worker at Hartheim) who was considered the "fool" of the SS-garrison (which may explain his low rank). Barbl was a 42-year-old man of low intelligence who was permanently drunk on duty. He was the subject of many jibes by his SS colleagues and was a source of constant amusement. None of them could decide whether he really was "stupid," or was just "playing the fool" in order to avoid the more onerous duties in the camp. Commandant Hering refused to allow him to participate in such executions because, "he is so daft that he would shoot us, not the Jews."[324] However, Barbl was not to escape severe punishment by Hering. For some unknown reason in the winter of 1942-43 Hering had Barbl imprisoned in a concrete bunker for several days, without food or water.[325]

For commandants Hering, Stangl and Reichleitner, their loyalty and allegiances (reluctantly) were strictly to Wirth with no possibility of compromise. They dared not oppose his authority, as the consequences would be too catastrophic to contemplate.

Attempts to Leave *Reinhardt*

None of the SS, including the police leadership, could get out of *Reinhardt*. An order from the KdF forbad any transfer even to front line duties.[326]

On a number of occasions a few men from the Belzec garrison attempted to seek release by pleading directly to Berlin; others showed reluctance when carrying out their murder duties, exhibiting a distinct lack of enthusiasm. These cases failed and only brought more trouble and grief for those concerned. Wirth knew full well that no one under his command would ever be released simply through a request to Berlin, and he reacted swiftly and harshly to any such attempts—especially with those who went behind his back. Wirth, by the very nature of Belzec's untouchability and secrecy, was free to avenge any perceived disloyalty in his own way and to resolve matters accordingly.

In October 1942, Heinrich Unverhau (another original T4 member from Grafeneck) contracted typhus in Belzec was hospitalized in Lublin and allowed to return home to Berlin to convalesce. Unverhau was already blind in one eye due to a pre-war industrial accident incurred while he was employed as a plumber. This eye was removed as a result of the typhus. On advice from a colleague, Erwin Fichtner, Unverhau applied to T4 for discharge from further duty in the camp. T4 informed him that the best they could do was offer a transfer to a euthanasia institution in the *Reich*. Declining the offer, Unverhau returned to Belzec. Immediately on reporting to the camp, he was paraded before the SS-garrison and vilified by Wirth in the crudest language. When Unverhau attempted to justify his actions, Wirth shouted, "*Halt die Goschen!*" (Shut your trap). Wirth was in such a rage that he drew his pistol and threatened to shoot Unverhau there and then.[327] Needless to say, Unverhau was given "hard probation" and was destined for permanent duty in camp 2.[328] Because both Wirth and Hering detested Unverhau from the very start for his "weakness," he was banished to supervise the locomotive shed—the farthest they could send him from the camp and out of their sight. He occasionally performed duty in the camp when particularly large transports arrived and all hands were needed.

When *SS-Scharführer* Erich Fuchs was ordered by Wirth to fix shower heads in the newly erected gassing barrack in the first phase, he questioned Wirth as to the logic of this, as there were no water pipes to which they could be fixed. Wirth exploded in a rage, beat Fuchs with a whip, and ordered two *SS-Scharführers* who were standing nearby to take him away and shoot him. Fortunately for Fuchs, the Scharführers talked Wirth out of it.[329] Wirth was certainly capable of carrying out his threats and everyone else was aware of this.[330] Erich Fuchs submitted a report of the incident, complaining about his treatment to T4, but received no reply—which is not surprising, as Wirth confiscated it. From then on Fuchs never again dared question an order from Wirth.[331] Even the loyal Oberhauser attempted to be transferred out of *Reinhardt*. While driving Wirth from Belzec to Lublin he took the opportunity to mention his request for a transfer. Wirth was so overcome with rage at hearing this that he took hold of his whip and threatened Oberhauser.[332]

During the visit to Belzec by Wilhelm Pfannenstiel, Professor of Hygiene at the University of Magdeburg/Lahn, in August 1942, several of the SS-NCOs begged him to use his influence in Berlin to get them out.

The overriding question that concentrated the minds of the SS was, "Would Wirth carry out his threats?" They just did not know! This was the fear; they dared not put it to the test. It was the view of the more experienced SS personnel that it was no longer possible to converse with Wirth, as he had ceased to be normal.[333] Even *SS-Scharführer* Bauer, the Sobibór "*Gasmeister*," a committed Nazi, anti-Semite, and a Wirth "reliable," has commented, "Wirth was a man mad with rage; he was the worst beast, a sadistic pig."[334]

Several SS-NCOs in Treblinka, affected by their duties and the way they were being treated, applied to T4 for transfer—anywhere, as long as it was away from Wirth and his work. On hearing about these requests, Wirth went to Treblinka and berated each man in turn.[335] When Werner Blankenburg, Brack's deputy at *Hauptamt II* of the KdF, visited Treblinka, Stangl also requested a transfer to normal police duties. His request, too, was denied.[336]

Outside the *Reinhardt* camps, however, Wirth adhered to normal SS disciplinary measures and procedures. Hering and Gley, who had been transferred to the Poniatowa labor camp after Belzec closed, were instrumental in prosecuting their SS medical officer, *Waffen-SS*

Sanitätsoffizier Bachaus. Bachaus had committed a grave offense— *"Rassenschande"* (lit. race shame)—by associating with a Jewish woman in the camp hospital. The inseparable duo, Wirth and Oberhauser, came to the camp and arrested Bachaus. After interrogating him for some hours, Wirth placed Bachaus before the SS/Police Court in Lublin, where he was tried, found guilty and executed.[337] If this offense had occurred in one of the *Reinhardt* camps, I doubt whether the SS court would have been considered. To shoot, torture and abuse Jews was acceptable practice. To associate with a Jewess was an anathema to the leadership and the basic principles of Nazi ideology.

In attempting to maintain intact the secrecy surrounding *Reinhardt*, the KdF leadership were confronted with a new problem. When *SS-Scharführer* Heinrich Matthes from Treblinka fell ill with typhus and was removed to a hospital, in his delirium he rambled about his work in the camp. To overcome any further incidents like this, guards were placed by the bedside of all hospitalized Reinhardt staff.[338] The *Reinhardt* staff were also entered in the Patients' Admission Book under false names.

Chapter 6. The Camp System [339]

Introduction and Overview[340]

The construction, function and operation of the Belzec death camp, the ultimate answer to Nazi genocidal plans, will now be examined. It will be shown how Belzec was inextricably entwined with the destruction of the Jewish communities in Galicia and elsewhere; and how a mainly civilian cadre of ordinary men, led by senior police officers, received their orders directly from the HHE, policy makers in Berlin.

Before reviewing the role of the perpetrators in Belzec, I propose to explore the background of the camp system and show how the death and labor camps came into being. *Reinhardt,* under Globocnik, was the central organizing vehicle by which every material aspect of Jewish destruction was performed, monitored and carried out before being finally disbanded in the latter part of 1943.

Camps within the political system of the *Reich* were both for the incarceration of political prisoners and for the exploitation of forced labor, and included a women's camp at Ravensbrück in Mecklenburg. Even the concentration camps like Mauthausen were intended as labor camps, but with an emphasis on death through labor.[341] As has been shown under the 14f13 protocols, there were many prisoner-group killings, which took place outside these camps' jurisdiction, i.e. in the T4 killing centers.

By the late summer of 1940, Belzec had become the center of a network of 35 forced labor camps in which over 10,000 predominantly Jewish prisoners were confined. Aged 14-60, they came from the SS-Districts of Lublin, Warsaw and Radom, and were kept in appalling conditions in primitive wooden barracks surrounded by barbed-wire. The prisoners from 15 of the camps were employed as slave labor by the *SS-Grenzsicherungskommando* (SS-Border Defense *Kommando*) for the "Otto Program," the construction of frontier defenses, which consisted of a 10 m wide and 6 m deep anti-tank ditch, backed on the German side by a massive earth rampart camouflaged with bushes and shrubbery. The border defense system stretched for 140 km around Belzec, and construction of the section in the immediate vicinity of the village was supervised by two SS-officers from the staff of *SS-Brigadeführer* Gobocnik in Lublin, *SS-Hauptsturmführer* Richard Thomalla and *SS-Hauptsturmführer* Georg Michalsen. Both of these SS-officers were later to play leading roles in the extermination of the Jews of the *Generalgourvernement.* The rest of the slave laborers were employed by the civil water authority on the regulation of the numerous tributaries between the rivers Vistula, San and Bug.

The entire network of camps—the main ones of which were located in Cieszanow, Dzikow Stary, Dzikow Nowy, Lipsko, Narol and Plazów—came within the jurisdiction of *SS-Brigadefuhrer* Globocnik in Lublin, and under the overall command in Belzec of *SS-Sturmbannführer* Hermann Dolp, a career SS-officer from the concentration camp service, described thus by one Belzec labor camp survivor. As the work brigades marched from the camps to the work sites each morning his favorite "sport" was shooting at Poles in the villages they passed through as well as at the columns of Jews. In Belzec, Dolp's favorite "sport" was forcing Jews into a deep pond where on his signal they had to completely submerge themselves. The guards fired their weapons above the water to make sure the Jews remained totally immersed; anyone who surfaced was immediately shot.

The first Jewish slave laborers from the Lublin District destined for Belzec were rounded up on the orders of *SS-Brigadeführer* Globocnik by Police Battalion 104, based in Lublin. The operation, in which units of the *Wehrmacht* and *Gendarmerie* also took part, was carried out in five areas: Zamosc, Chełm, Bilgoraj, Hrubieszow and Krasnystaw. At the end of July, Governor General Hans Frank inspected the "Otto Line" defenses in the vicinity of Belzec. He also visited Bilgoraj, Chełm and Hrubieszow.

A German medical commission that visited the Belzec labor camps reported further on the appalling conditions they witnessed in the grossly overcrowded barracks:

> They are dark and dirty. The infestation with lice is very high. About 30 percent of the laborers have no shoes, trousers or shirts. They all sleep on the floor, without straw. The roofs are completely dilapidated, the windows without panes; the barracks are frightfully overcrowded. For example, in one room of 5 m x 6 m, 75 people sleep on the floor, lying on top of one another ... There is a lack of soap, and water is difficult to obtain. The sick lie together with the healthy. They are not allowed to leave the barracks at night and have to perform their natural functions on the spot. It is therefore no wonder that under these circumstances there are many cases of illness.

Inevitably, a typhus epidemic further decimated their numbers. Corpses covered in maggots lay strewn around the camps and special brigades of elderly Jews were assigned to collect and hurriedly bury the dead in mass graves. Any Jew who attempted to flee to the Soviet side of the border was handed back by the Russians and immediately shot by the SS.

The vile conditions in the Belzec labor camps finally led to protests to the SS by the German military authorities in the area. Nevertheless, *SS-Brigadeführer* Globocnik officially praised commandant Dolp's efforts in completing the border defenses "under primitive conditions, without an adequate number of guards, and with an inferior labor force consisting of Jews and Gypsies."

By the end of September 1940, about 4,500 members of the labor force had either been released or ransomed; but when on 21 October the German civil administration inquired about the rest, they were unable to discover their fate because of the "lack of cooperation by Globocnik and the SS." Secrecy surrounded the whole matter. The fate of several thousand slave laborers in the Belzec area remains unknown to this day. Almost exactly a year later, the SS were to return to Belzec to begin the construction of yet another camp for Jews: the Belzec death camp.

The SS: Government in Waiting

In addition to *Reinhardt,* an intensive but politically necessary expedient of short duration, a more urgent program emerged, as referred to in remarks by *SS-Obersturmbannführer* Fähnrich. "The military victory in Poland was the foundation of a New Order. The fight really starts when the guns fall silent."[342] A number of interpretations may be drawn from these remarks, but it is certain that in addition to a massive reorganization of society there was the intended ascendance of the SS as a political elite.

The picture developing from activities at this time appears to confirm that moves were afoot in the establishment of a *"Schutzstaffel"* administration, or SS-government, centered in the city of Lublin. To feed their economic plans and reorganization of society, the SS intended to Germanize this region by experimental social engineering. They planned to build a vast network of factories and work-camps specifically geared to SS requirements. The Frank-Himmler squabbles enacted daily were at the cutting edge of SS frustration in their attempts to pursue their philosophy.

Governor Hans Frank, still smarting over the "Jewish reservation policy" and the hope that he would at last get rid of his Jews in the *Generalgouvernment,* was obviously being sidelined with the SS taking over "reservation" policy decisions. What annoyed him was the fact that the deportation of the Jews from his domain had been agreed, and he was just passing the message on.[343]

It would appear from Frank's conversations with Hitler, that the Poles were now considered a priority for deportation so as to avoid international protest after the war. Finally, in a conversation on 19 June 1941, Goebbels, Frank and Hitler appeared to be euphoric at the prospect of the Jews being expelled. [344] Despite all the set-backs and disappointments Frank had endured regarding his Jewish problem, on 16 December 1941 he informed his associates of the decision to kill the Jews: "If the Jews survive the war while Germans sacrifice their 'best blood,' then the war would only be a partial success."[345] A year later, in December 1942, he tells a different story, regretting the loss of Jewish labor: "In our time-tested Jews we have had a not insignificant source of labor manpower taken from us."[346]

There is no doubt that the SS had laid claim to the "East" and were prepared to go to any lengths to hold it, much to Frank's chagrin. The "Jewish Question" was an impediment to the greater war plan, but "solving it" was totally necessary from the ideological point of view; it would remain high on the agenda, even to the perceived detriment of economic and war considerations. As it turned out, contrary to its original purpose, *Reinhardt* was to evolve into an extensive industrial enterprise, where vast profits were made on the backs of slave labor in order to feed the ultimate aim of SS dominance.

The SS were in a great hurry to establish and protect their prominence over the civilian government, and what ultimately emerged was a two-pronged assault—one directed toward SS superiority and dominance based on economic reconstruction; and the second, to deal with the Jewish problem as quickly as possible. It was only the method of implementation that had to be resolved. Perhaps this is why we see Christian Wirth emerging as the main protagonist of Jewish destruction, while his immediate superior, Globocnik, although the nominated leader of *Reinhardt,* was largely occupied elsewhere—building up the SS Empire through a string of Jewish camps, factories and workshops in the Lublin District.

Camp Inspectorate

The father of the German concentration camp system after Dachau, the original KZ, was *SS-Obergruppenführer* Theodor Eicke.[347] Commissioned by *Reichsführer-SS* Himmler in 1933 to build up a concentration camp system within the *Reich*, Eicke, a confirmed Nazi, set about his task with vigor and single-mindeness. Initially, the local SA and local police were used to man these camps; but after a short period, because his Nazi ideas clashed with those of the German police, they were replaced by his own SS-men. A new politically hardnosed group of devoted Nazis was formed, known as the *"Totenkopf Verbände"* (Death's Head) formations. This policy of Eicke, together with his new camp SS-staff, confirm two points: the SS and the police were incompatible; and the SS camp personnel, who with their politically indoctrinated Nazi ideals would shrink at nothing when ordered, were ideal fodder for T4 and later in the death camps. *SS-Oberscharführer* Joseph Oberhauser, Christian Wirth's right-hand man and constant companion in the *Reinhardt* death camps, is an example of this new breed of tough murderous jailers.

Camp Economics

The camp system in the occupied territories was multi-faceted and complex. Oswald Pohl's *SS-Wirtschafts-und Verwaltungshauptamt* (SS Main Office for Economy and Administration), which in March 1942 absorbed the Inspectorate of Concentration Camps, was more focused on the economic requirements of the war, and because of the need for a work force developed a strategy of extermination through labor.[348]

We are left in no doubt as to the *Reinhardt* camps' purpose as self-financing human abattoirs run on the industrial principal of mass production, with the sole aim of killing Jews. No unauthorized person who entered these camps was permitted to leave, unless they escaped. As we know, of the 600,000 Jews who perished in Belzec, only five or six succeeded in escaping and surviving the war: Reder, Hirszman, Birder, Bracht, Velser and Honig.

Even though Auschwitz, Majdanek, Janowska and Plaszów were multipurpose camps, incorporating prisoners of different races, they were also to some extent committed either to Jewish exploitation through labor, or annihilation through shooting or gas chambers.

Initially, the Camp Inspectorate supervised Jewish labor and subcontracted the labor force to outside agencies, but in 1943 the SS superseded the Inspectorate in controlling and exploiting Jewish labor. The Schindler factory in Lipowa Street, Kraków, is a good example of this, where Jews from KZ Plaszów were hired-out at so many zloty per prisoner to the factory owners, who paid the SS directly. The profit was made by the differential between the costs of maintaining the prisoners in the camps and the costs charged by the SS to the industries that employed them.[349]

The camps designated as labor camps changed emphasis when the SS took over and they became *Konzentrationslager* (KZs), concentration camps. Even though mass gassings took place in Auschwitz and Majdanek, and mass shooting was the killing method in Janowska and Plaszow, these killings were completely separate from the *Reinhardt* camps, where labor was not a consideration.

The nearest Globocnik came to setting up his own profit-making hybrid camps was when he went into partnership with the German industrialists Toebbens and Schwarz, based in Warsaw, to exploit Jewish slave labor in the subsidiary camps of Dorohucza, Poniatowa and Trawniki. These centers of SS industry were connected with 14 other similar camps in the Lublin district. They were very profitable for the SS and remained so until the camps and all the workers were liquidated in November 1943 during the *"Erntefest"* (Harvest Festival) massacres at the termination of *Reinhardt*.

Globocnik's Camps

In 1940 Globocnik opened a group of labor camps specifically for supplying labor for the construction of the fortification sites that were being built in readiness for a possible drive east. The idea of erecting a defense line on the border with the Soviet Union, which came from Himmler in the autumn of 1939, received strong support from the *Wehrmacht*. Himmler realized that such a construction project would allow the concentration of several thousand Jews in the East to be placed in large labor camps for an indefinite period.[350]

Known as the "Otto Line," this fortification extended 140 kilometers in length between the Bug and San Rivers, with a 50-kilometer section from the Upper San to the Sokołija River on the border of the *Generalgouvernment* and the Soviet Union.[351] There were three main centers of rampart fortifications: at Miedzyrzec (east of Warsaw), Belzec and Cieszanow.[352] They consisted of a large anti-tank ditch on the Soviet side (before Barbarossa), backed by a solid earth rampart on the German side, which was camouflaged with bushes and trees. After the invasion of the Soviet Union in June 1941, the "Otto" program was extended to east Galicia, where it was intended to construct or repair a further 6,000 kilometers of strategic highways and other constructions. It also included the regulation of the numerous rivers and streams in the south-east part of the Lublin District and employed forced labor from 15 camps of the Belzec complex.

All these projects came under the auspices of SSPF Globocnik in Lublin, who set up a Jewish labor administration to control the movement of Jewish labor throughout eastern Poland. To oversee these major changes, *SS-Obersturmführer* Karl Hofbauer[353] was placed in command to administer the hundreds of thousands of Jews who were forcibly rounded up for the scheme. Globocnik's *Volksdeutsche* auxiliaries and the *Selbstschutz*, under the command of the *Befehlshaber der Ordnungsplizei* (BdO), Commander of the Order Police, were the tools used for the security and control of this huge labor force. On 22 April 1940 Globocnik announced that over 5,000 Jews were to be sent to the border at Belzec. A few weeks later, the first detachment of the *SS-Grenzsicherungsbaukommando* (SS Border Security Construction Detachment) arrived in the Belzec area to set up the camps. The Belzec labor camps became models for the accomplishment of "destruction through labor," and would remain so until the death camps became fully established.[354] They were closed down at least a year before the construction of the death camp began.

First Labor Camps

The first labor camps in Belzec were built in early 1940 for several thousand Jews and Sinti and Roma (Gypsies).[355] The main camps were situated on a farm in on the Narol road in Belzec and held over 2,000 people.[356]

There were three labor camps in Belzec: the farm, the mill, and the abandoned locomotive shed near the station. Already living in appalling conditions— which were the subject of much concern to the civil authorities as there were reports of typhus outbreaks—Jews and Sinti and Roma were rounded up and imprisoned in temporary camps and buildings surrounded by barbed-wire fences. [357]

There were 20 camps along the Otto line fortifications. A labor camp was constructed near the Belzec railway station in the mill and locomotive shed, 400 meters from the death campsite. Over 2,500 people, mainly Jews, were used to build this rampart and were kept imprisoned in the work camp. Jews were seized from Lublin and other towns and transported direct to the Belzec labor camps. Zygmunt Klukowski, a Polish doctor living in Zamosc, noted in his diary on 1 October 1940:

> Today was a good day for the Jews because almost all of the men
> taken a few weeks ago to the Belzec camp have returned. For this
> the Jewish community paid 20,000 zloty. [358]

In Warsaw, the Chairman of the Judenrat, Adam Czerniakow, and the diarist Chaim Kaplan, recorded in their diaries these deportations of Jews sent to supply labor for the "Otto Line" in the Belzec area. [359]

Within a few months, the whole area had become one string of labor camps serving these massive fortifications. The resident SS commander of the entire Belzec complex, *SS-Sturmbannführer* Hermann Dolp, was a cruel, sadistic and uncompromising overseer who had previously supervised the Jewish labor camp on Lipowa Street, Lublin. [360]

During the period October 1941 to February 1942, productive Jews were still being sent east to supply these massive building projects. The Jewish labor camps defense and road construction projects at that time were the predominant Nazi policy for the decimation of unskilled Jewish labor. [361] The human cost was staggering, and once the Jewish workers had been forced to work on the anti-tank ditches under the most dreadful conditions they were useless for any other kind of work. [362] Even when the death camp at Belzec opened in March 1942, the DV 1V road and several of the labor camps supporting it were still functioning, but with reduced importance.

Belzec death camp had priority as the central establishment for Jewish destruction. One of the earliest escapees from the death camp in April 1942 found sanctuary in the nearby Gypsy camp and informed the internees of the murders taking place nearby. [363] Contrary to views held by some historians that the death camp was converted from a labor camp, the death camp was purposely built. [364] Stanislaw Kozak, who was among the first Belzec construction workers employed by the Germans to build the death camp, supports this view. [365] The "Jewish labor camps" in the *Generalgouvernment* continued to function until 22-23 July 1943, when the labor camps for road construction were systematically liquidated. [366]

Himmler and Globocnik met in both Lublin and Berlin[367] on no less than six occasions in October1941 (five meetings in Lublin, one in Berlin).[368] Following these conferences gassing experts from T4 started to arrive at Belzec to assess the site.[369] It is interesting to note that on Monday 13 October 1941, Himmler conferred for two hours with Krüger, the HSSPF for the Government General, and Globocnik, SSPF for the Lublin District where Belzec was located. It is probable that the order to build Belzec was given at this conference.[370]

In a real sense the *Reinhardt* death camps were the final stage in a direct line of development from the first concentration camps founded in 1933. By 1939, a set pattern of political and labor camps was well established. In December 1941, with the expertise gained from the euthanasia program and experiments by the RSHA chemists, new mobile and static killing facilities emerged. As discussed earlier, leading these prototype-killing facilities were, in the first instance, the gas vans used in Chełmno, which were to give way to the system employed at Belzec, Sobibór and Treblinka.

Ghetto Clearing

Some thought and planning by the SS had gone into the procedures for clearing ghettos and other resettlement actions. The architect of these procedures, which were adopted in the *Generalgouvernment*, was *SS-Hauptsturmführer* Amon Leopold Goeth, who was attached to the *Reinhardt* office in Lublin. Goeth, known as "the Mad Dog of Lublin,"[371] was a great believer in getting the Jews to do the "dirty work" in the selections and loading of resettlement transports, and at the same time making them pay for the privilege of deportation. Many of Goeth's theories were so successful that they were adopted in nearly every Jewish resettlement operation in the *Generalgouvernment*, which depended on "order," "deceptions" and brutal force. Goeth was well known for his brutality and favored the "*Blitzkrieg*" method of surprise and fear, accompanied by immediate executions. It was Goeth's belief that all operational Jewish actions should be paid for by the Jews themselves—including even payment for the bullets used in mass shootings.[372] Goeth had only one equal in this regard: *SS-Hauptsturmführer* Hans Krüger, who operated in East Galicia.

From the autumn and winter of 1941, non-productive Jews, *("Arbeitsunfähige")* were massacred on a daily basis.[373] With the commissioning of Belzec in mid-March, a new system of mass murder came into operation. Even the opening of the death camps was not enough to quench the Nazi appetite for indiscriminate round-ups and shootings, which affected both Jew and Pole alike. By using the "Goeth principle" of making the Jews pay for the "privilege" of being killed, on 11 May 1942 in the small town of Szczebrzeszyn in Lublin District, the *Gestapo* ordered the *Judenrat* to pay 2,000 zloty and 3 kilos of coffee for the ammunition used to kill Jews.[374]

Chapter 7. First Phase at Belzec

Construction

The construction of the Belzec death camp was a major step towards realizing the entire *Reinhardt* extermination operation.

Belzec, although the first static death camp to be built within the *Reinhardt* complex, was not alone. In October 1941, plans were apparently made to build gas chambers in Riga, Chełmno and Sobibór. A huge cremation facility, bigger than Birkenau, was planned for Mogilev, paid for by the SS, and then abandoned. At least one of the cremation furnaces ended up in Auschwitz. With the exception of Auschwitz (where gassing experiments were already taking place) and Sobibór, gas vans were preferred as the main tool of destruction,[375] while at Fort IX in Kovno, shooting was employed. Without question, a concerted policy of multiple killing experiments by gassing and shooting had been authorized at the highest level.[376] With all this going on, it is unlikely, as has been suggested, that Belzec was one of Globocnik's innovations to solve a localized problem. As Browning has said, "Most importantly, the construction of Belzec at this time ought not be viewed in isolation but rather in conjuncture with the evidence of other Nazi plans for gassing facilities in the fall of 1941."[377] The fact that Sobibór was also being surveyed in December 1941 confirms this.[378]

In late October 1941, *SS-Hauptsturmführer* Richard Thomalla,[379] a construction engineer and building contractor at the *Zentralbauleitung der Waffen-SS und Polizei* (Central Construction Office of the Waffen-SS and Police) in Lublin, and head of the *SS-Bauleitung* (SS Construction Office) in Zamosc, arrived in Belzec. Thomalla, a career SS officer, was accompanied by *SS- Hauptscharführer* Gottfried Schwarz[380] and *SS-Oberscharführer* Josef Oberhauser, acting as liaison officers for Globocnik's office in Lublin.

Artisans and laborers were recruited from the local villages to do the work and to construct the camp buildings.[381] The locomotive shed was amalgamated into the death camp complex and used as a warehouse for sorting and storing the belongings of the murdered Jews.[382]

Construction of the Belzec camp commenced on 1 November 1941, before the arrival of the police leadership and euthanasia specialists. Under the supervision of the SS planners, locally employed tradesmen were used for skilled manual tasks and the erection of buildings. The Mayor of Belzec, Ludwig Obalek, who was responsible for supplying local labor to the SS, confirms in detail the identification and names of the Polish workers engaged in this work.[383]

The first buildings to be erected were three barracks that were linked by a walkway to the third barrack (the gas chamber). This barrack had a corridor with three compartments, each of which had an exit door. All six doors (entry and exit) were sealed. The camp itself was surrounded by a double fence of barbed wire.

A railway engine driver, Michael Kuśmierczak, had limited access to the camp; but more importantly, he became friendly with the Ukrainian guards. When Kuśmierczak asked what was going on, he was informed that the Jews were being killed with exhaust fumes produced by a 250hp engine, located a short distance from the gassing barrack.[384]

A Pole, Stanisław Kozak, the local locksmith, was employed in the early construction, including the installation of a narrow-gauge track for the removal of bodies from the gassing barracks to the mass graves.[385]

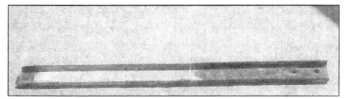

Summer 2003 at Belzec: Finding of Narrow Gauge Rail?

Kozak, who gave evidence to the Polish Commission of Enquiry after the war, has also given a detailed account of the construction of Belzec:[386]

> In October 1941, three SS men came to Belzec and requested from the municipality 20 men for work. The municipality allotted 20 workers, residents of Belzec, and I was among them. We began work on 1 November 1941. We built barracks close to the sidetrack of the railway. One barrack, which was close to the railway siding, was 50 meters long and 12.5 meters wide. The second barrack, 25 meters long and 12.5 meters wide, was for the Jews destined for the "baths."

> We built a third hut, 12 m long, 8 m wide. Inside, it was divided into three parts by wooden walls, so each part was 4 m wide and 6 m long. The height inside was 2 m. The double walls of the hut were made of boards and the space between them was filled with sand. The walls inside were covered with tarpaper and the floors and walls were covered with sheets of zinc. There was a corridor with three doors opening into the windowless rooms. Each part of the construction had another door in the north wall, about 1.8 m high. That door as well as the one inside was tightly sealed with rubber. All doors of the building opened outwards.

> The unloading doors were fastened shut from the outside by heavy wooden locking bars that fitted into big hooks on either side. The doors were sealed with rubber gaskets around the edges.

> In each of those three parts were water pipes placed at a height of 10 cm, hidden under benches. In the eastern wall of each room,

there were also water pipes with an elbow joint at a height of 1 m above the floor. There was a wooden platform at the height of 1 m along the northern part of the hut, along which ran the rails of a narrow-gauge railway. It led to the pit dug by the Ukrainians, which was situated in the very corner of north and east border of the camp.

During the time that we Poles built the barracks, the "Blacks" (Ukrainians) erected the fences of the extermination camp, which were made of dense barbed wire. After we Poles had completed building the three above-mentioned barracks, the Germans dismissed us, on 22 December 1941.

The author offers possible layouts to phases 1 and 2 gas chambers

Below: gas chambers of the first phase drawn from the testimonies of witnesses.

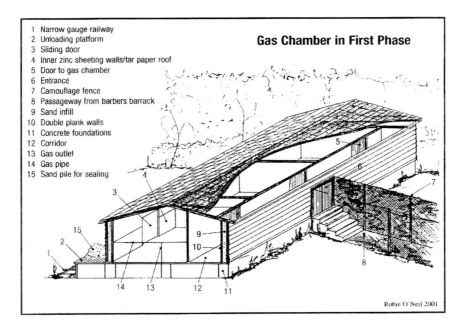

1	Narrow gauge railway
2	Unloading platform
3	Sliding door
4	Inner zinc sheeting walls/tar paper roof
5	Door to gas chamber
6	Entrance
7	Camouflage fence
8	Passageway from barbers barrack
9	Sand infill
10	Double plank walls
11	Concrete foundations
12	Corridor
13	Gas outlet
14	Gas pipe
15	Sand pile for sealing

Gas Chamber in First Phase

Robin O'Neil 2001

The Treblinka gas chambers were based on the already constructed "*Stiftung Hackenholt*" in Belzec, which served as a blueprint for the new Sobibór and Treblinka death rooms. Although the building constructed at Treblinka had a larger chamber capacity, the principle was the same in all three *Reinhardt* camps. In Sobibór, Wirth flew into a rage and ordered the gas chamber "exit" doors to be immediately changed, as they had not followed the method achieved at Belzec. The doors of these rooms were small and opened upward, much like garage doors of today. These heavy wooden doors were then supported on iron poles until the corpses had been removed.

For the first phase the gas chambers had strong wooden beams to hold the doors securely against the outer walls. The said "beams" were slotted into iron hooks set in between the bricks in these structures during construction, sealing the gas chambers, which were then faced with concrete. A sliding door method was introduced for the second phase in Sobibór and Treblinka. It has been suggested in the past that an outward single door movement took place. This is very unlikely due to the weight of these double wooden doors. Yet another suggestion is of folding doors in two sections, upward and downward. Again this is extremely unlikely as the bottom section would have been very difficult to clean after the rooms were emptied, the lower section being covered in human waste, etc.

Penultimate Operations

On 22 December 1941, Christian Wirth arrived in Belzec to finalise his staff-accommodation by requisitioning properties along the main village street close to the camp. A final inspection of the camp was carried out by *SS-Hauptsturmführer* Neumann from the Central Construction Office of the *Waffen-SS* in Lublin. After signing over the camp structures to Wirth, Neumann and Thomalla left for Sobibór to repeat the Belzec operation in the newly-surveyed site adjacent to the Sobibór railway station.[387]

There was a break-in activity at Belzec over the Christmas period when Wirth left the area and returned to Germany. At the beginning of January 1942, he returned, having selected his initial camp staff. The first T4 conscripts arrived at Belzec in three trucks, the convoy led by Wirth in his car. *SS-Hauptscharführer* Gottfried Schwarz was designated deputy commandant and held full powers of command after Wirth. *SS-Oberscharführer Josef Oberhauser* supervised the Ukrainian guards and acted as personal assistant to Wirth.[388] Among this first group of T4 specialists were Erich Fuchs, Werner Borowski, Johann Niemann, Siegfried Graetschus and later, Kurt Franz, Heinrich Barbl and Erwin Fichtner.

In late December 1941, about 70 Ukrainians arrived from Trawniki to complete other structures, erect the watchtowers and security fences and to manually dig what is believed to be the first mass grave (grave 14/aerial photo 1944), which took the Ukrainians six weeks to excavate with spades and measured approximately 75 m 35 m x 5 m deep.[389] It is probable that the earth dug from this grave (1,850 cu. m) was used to landscape and level the ground on which the Ukrainian barracks were built.

The exact location of the earliest mass graves (following grave 14) is difficult to determine. According to the witness Kozak and his description of the narrow gauge rail link on the north side, the initial batch were located to the northeast corner (see mass graves on map No.s 8, 9, 32, or 33). However, the lime content found in grave pit 14 that confronted Stangl on his visit to Belzec in early spring 1942 suggests otherwise.[390]

Another observer and witness to the building of the gassing barracks during the experimental period was the Polish mechanic Kazimierz Czerniak, who had his workshop in the nearby town of Tomaszòw-Lubelski. Czerniak, in his evidence to the Polish War Crimes Investigating Commission, recalled the Germans calling at his workshop to have pipe-work welded.[391] When he asked a Ukrainian the purpose of the building, he was told it was a storeroom (the Ukrainian smirked), but Czerniak guessed it was a gassing barrack by the way it was constructed, and had noticed that there were no windows, as well as the wooden doors that opened outward onto a ramp.[392]

On a number of occasions, the Germans took Czerniak into the camp to carry out maintenance work and to install the narrow gauge rails that linked the gas barracks to the field of mass graves.[393] Shortly after, on another occasion when he visited the camp, he saw piles of discarded clothes being sorted by Ukrainians and Jews.[394]

Although the camp was in effect one large area, there was a camouflaged division between the main reception area and grave field. Later, when the camp was reconstructed (July) in the second phase, it became two defined established areas with the grave area having moved around to fresh ground.[395] In the main reception area, there was space for 2,000 Jews to assemble before being segregated. Initially, there were no barracks for hair cutting or property storage facilities and this was done on the spot. Men, women, and children were not segregated for the first few transports. The hair was shaved from the bodies of the women, piled up alongside the gas chamber unloading ramp after gassing. The locomotive shed was used for storage from the first days. It was only after the reconstruction of the camp that separate and more permanent barracks were built for this purpose. A camouflaged corridor (the tube/walkway) joined the structures that led directly into the gassing barrack.

Early Transports

On 14 March 1942, a meeting took place in Krakow between Himmler and the two security chiefs of the *Generalgouvernment*, HSSPF Krüger and Dr. Schöngarth (BdS). As Dieter Pohl has suggested, it is probable that the discussion was centered on the early deportations to Belzec from Lublin and Lvov that were in progress.[396] Between mid-March and mid-April 1942, approximately 74,000 Jews from Lublin and Galicia were murdered in Belzec.[397]

It is known that the first mass deportations to Belzec came from two directions: Lublin and Lvov (Galicia).[398] In order to prepare the transports for deportation, Höfle and the SS in Lublin had carried out careful research. In Lvov similar arrangements were also in hand. We are able to overview the

Lvov deportations from a captured SS document. The document refers to a Jewish report concerning the first mass deportations from Lvov to Belzec, which commenced on 13-14 March 1942.[399]

The pogroms, officially called "Expulsion operations" or simply "operations," took place partly unofficially, partly officially, i.e. after informing the *Judenrat* and with the participation of the Jewish Militia subordinated to it. Herewith, in chronological order, the official "operations" in Lhg (Lemberg/Lvov).

The first official "operation" began on 13 March 1942 (before the establishment of the ghetto) and lasted nearly three weeks, with the participation of the Jewish and Ukrainian Militia but under direction of the *Gestapo* and the *Sonderdienst* of the SS. The *Judenrat* was ordered to make available 33 percent of the Jewish population, supposedly for shipment to labor camps.

A German recruiting board had its seat in the Sobieski School and Dr. Jaffe, Hader and Seidenfrau were the representatives of the *Judenrat*. Many Jews who had labor permits were exempted from expulsion. The total number of Jews was 18,000. To make it more credible that they were intended for labor camps, the people were committed to take with them the barest necessities. These people had hardly arrived at the station when they were attacked in groups by the SS and robbed. Rumors were circulating that these transports would not go to labor camps, but to execution places at Belzec, and many Jews committed suicide right there at the station.

The fact should be noted, that the bodies of the suicides and those killed in attempting to escape were transported in the same cars with the living. It has been confirmed by railway personnel, accompanying the party, that apart from the few Jews who saved themselves by jumping from the train, the party was destined for Belzec to be executed.

In the early morning of 15 March 1942, just before the commissioning date of Belzec, a small transport of 15 freight cars was brought into the camp. It is not known if the gassing system was working or not, but the Jews from this transport were all allegedly shot. Whether the SS would shoot so many people (when the gas chambers were operational) is open to question.[400] On 17 March 1942, Belzec was set to receive its first large transports.[401] In the second week of March 1942, preparations for deportations had already started, with 1,001 Jews from the Theresienstadt ghetto being sent East on "Transport Aa," which left the ghetto on 11 March and reached the Izbica-Lubelska transit ghetto two days later. Only six Jews from this transport survived the war; the remainder perished in Belzec. On 13 March, 8,000 Jews from the southern Polish town of Mielec arrived at the same transit ghetto and then went on to Belzec. There were no survivors. It is reasonably safe to assume that all resettlement transports at that time were probably destined for Belzec. The problem of identifying the end phase of these actions arises later after Sobibór opened in early May 1942, as it not possible to determine to which camp the victims from Izbica were sent—Belzec or Sobibór.

Reception of Transports

The procedure for dealing with the transports was carried out according to the detailed plan laid down by Wirth, and rarely varied. Each transport was communicated in advance to the *Kommandantur*, usually by telephone, and the information was then telephoned in turn to the camp gate-house, manned by a duty SS-NCO and several Ukrainian guards.

At the arrival of the transport at the camp, the duty SS-NCO signalled to the locomotive driver where to stop just outside the gate, which remained open during the unloading of the wagons. As soon as the line of wagons came to a halt inside a cordon of Ukrainian guards on the siding, at a given signal the Jewish work brigade pulled back the wagon doors and ordered everyone to get out and bring their luggage with them. The unloading was accompanied by much pushing, shoving and shouting by the "work Jews" and guards, who also fired their rifles in the air and used their rifle-butts to hurry the new arrivals along. The victims were given no time to look around or think about what was happening to them; their normal reactions were paralyzed by the speed of events and the sheer pandemonium around them.

At this time, the meaning of the Belzec camp was unknown outside the immediate area and the pretence that the Jews were being resettled had to be maintained for as long as possible. Of necessity, therefore, only the few agitators and voluble protesters were beaten or shot in front of the others as an example, to encourage them to hurry without protest. In Wirth's scheme of things, the speed with which the entire process was carried out served a dual purpose: not only to minimize opportunities for resistance, but also to maximize the daily killing capacity of the camp.

The Jews who were unable to climb out of the train cars unaided were carried out by "work Jews" and laid in the snow and mud beside the railway track. The dead were taken away immediately and dumped into a mass grave; those lying by the track who wailed too loudly and were likely to upset the others were also carried to a grave, where they were shot by a Ukrainian guard. The remainder—the old, the frail, the sick and infirm Jews, had to wait their turn to die, until the rest of the transport had been dealt with. This could sometimes mean a wait of two hours or more while lying on the ground in the cold open air.

At this point, one of the duty SS-NCOs accompanied by a Ukrainian guard checked each wagon to make sure that no one had remained behind. Any Jews found hiding were handed over to the Ukrainian guards, who either beat them to death or shot them. The doors of the wagons were shut and the first batch shunted out of the camp and back to the station. The camp gate was then closed until the arrival of the next batch of wagons.

The first group of 700-750 Jews in the yard were next directed into the largest of the three barracks, which until now had not been used. Inside, Wirth personally delivered a speech to reassure the bewildered new arrivals, his words translated by a *Zugsführer* and relayed to the Jews outside through a loudspeaker:

> Jews, you have been brought here to be resettled, but before we organize this future Jewish State you must, of course, learn how to work. You will learn a new trade; you will be taught that here. Our routine here is, first, everyone has to get undressed so that your clothing can be disinfected and you can have a bath to ensure that no epidemics are brought into the camp.

According to T4/SS-NCOs who supervised the undressing barrack, none of the Jews listening to the speech had any idea of the real fate that awaited them. The majority, both inside and outside the barrack, actually cheered Wirth's words and protests were rare; there were a few sceptics among them, but there was nothing they could do.

The Jews in the barrack undressed with little hesitation and were directed again in groups of 80 people, men, women and children, into the middle barrack where the adults deposited personal papers, cash and valuables into the waiting suitcases. From there, the victims ran along the enclosed passageway ("tube") to the "bathhouse," spurred on by the whips of Wirth and Schwarz, and into the three chambers. The doors were closed and the Russian tank engine started.

At first, the engine was operated by Wirth personally, assisted by *SS-Scharführer* Hackenholt; later, Wirth placed Hackenholt in charge, assisted initially by the young Ukrainian mechanic, Edward Wlasiuk, who had previously driven the gassing van. The exhaust fumes were pumped into the chambers for 20 minutes, after which time the engine was switched off and Jews from the "death brigade" opened the exit doors.

Inside the dark chambers the bodies were soiled with excrement, vomit, saliva and urine, and menstrual blood soiled the legs of some of the women and girls. At times, the workers who entered the gas chambers immediately after the doors were opened were themselves affected by the residual gas. The tangled mass of bodies was prised apart and stacked below the unloading platform in two long heaps: the women and girls with long hair in one pile and the rest in another. It took the "death brigade" about 15 minutes to empty the chambers of their load of over 1,000 bodies, urged on by blows from the Ukrainian guards.

Now the "specialists" selected on arrival at the siding began their grisly tasks: a team of barbers cut the long hair from the heads of the females that had been stacked separately and piled it into big sacks; and a team of dentists searched the lifeless mouth of each adult body for dental gold—gold to the left, without gold to the right. Gold teeth, fillings and bridges were crudely torn out with pliers and thrown into cartons. Gold and diamond rings were also removed from the fingers of the dead; if a ring could not be removed easily, the entire finger was cut off and thrown into a separate carton.

Finally, the plundered bodies were stacked in the tip-up trucks on the narrow gauge railway and pushed up the slope by "work Jews" who tipped them into the mass grave dug alongside the northern fence.

Property Disposal

The mounds of clothing, footwear and luggage left behind by the victims were collected together by a brigade of "work Jews" and piled onto the three trucks from the camp garage. From the camp everything was taken to the disused Austrian-built locomotive shed near Belzec station where T4/SS-NCO Rudi Kamm had been placed in charge by Wirth. Kamm had at his disposal a Jewish work brigade consisting mainly of German Jews who had been deported from the *Reich* and who were guarded by a squad of Ukrainian sentries. It was the task of the "work Jews" in the locomotive shed to make a start on the sorting and baling of all salvageable items for further utilization.

Already during the first two weeks of the mass killing, a major problem was experienced in Belzec. On several occasions when the exit doors of the gas chambers were opened some of the victims were still alive, and children were found crouching or lying on the floor. Air was seeping in through chinks in the plank unloading doors. Other victims, particularly pregnant women, sometimes revived in the cold, fresh air after being taken out of the fume-filled chambers. The survivors—children and adults alike—were killed by the Ukrainian guards. Wirth had issued strict orders at the very beginning that no Jew who entered the Belzec camp was to be allowed to live—especially not Jewish children. From that time onwards, the Jews of the "death brigade" had to pile sand against the outer doors to make them airtight before each gassing operation; the sand then had to be dug away again before the doors could be opened to empty the chambers, a laborious and time-consuming job—made even more difficult because the sand clogged the greased runners of the sliding doors—that often had to be repeated several times a day. And to make doubly sure that there would be no future survivors, Wirth ordered the death brigade to wait another 20-30 minutes after the engine had been switched off before opening the exit doors. New doors were not made and fitted as two or three transports were arriving every day, bringing 3-5,000 Jews to the camp for extermination; besides, the gassing barrack was only a temporary structure, to be replaced within a few weeks. In spite of this technical hitch, during the first two weeks it was in operation this primitive wooden shed with its three zinc-lined chambers claimed over 60,000 victims.

Typhus

An additional serious problem in the early days was an outbreak of typhus in the camp, brought in by the Jews who had been living in grossly overcrowded and unhygienic conditions in ghettos where malnutrition and lice were commonplace. One of the first victims among the staff was Edward Własiuk, the "death mechanic," who was taken to a German Military Reserve Hospital in Lublin. For the Jews of the work brigades who caught the disease, however, it meant an immediate death sentence. Obtaining any kind of medical treatment, or even lying down, was out of the question, and any "work Jews" found to have a high temperature or who even looked weak and unwell were shot on the spot. They were easily replaced from the next transport. While the epidemic lasted Wirth amended his speech to the newly-arrived Jews; he informed them that they had to be disinfected "because of the prevailing typhus." As we shall see later, expert advice was sought by Globocnik to counter this outbreak.

Belzec Survivors

There are only two eyewitness account of the processing of an early and late transport, that of Chaim Hirszman, a 30-year-old metal worker from Janow Lubelski, who had worked there for the German construction office; and Rudolf Reder from Lvov.

These two Jews who survived the Belzec death camp have confirmed the layout of the camp in some detail; Rudolf Reder (second phase) and Chaim Hirszman (first and second phases). When Hirszman and his wife arrived at Belzec from Janow-Lubelski, his wife went to the gas chambers but he was selected for work: *"Du bist ein Militärmensch, dich können wir brauchen"* (you are a military man, we could need you.) Hirszman's physique had impressed the SS and had saved him. Hirszman's evidence after the war is the only record by a victim of these early transport procedures.[402] Both Reder and Hirszmann were to escape: one by stealth and the other, by more desperate measures. Their recollections remain the most enlightening testaments to emerge relating to the death camp:

> At the entrance to the gas chambers stood Schmidt, a Latvian *Volksdeutsche*, who beat each woman with a club as she entered. Before the door was closed, he fired a few shots from his revolver, after which the doors closed automatically, and 40 minutes later we went in and took out the bodies and shaved off their hair which was packed into bags and taken away by the Germans … the bodies were not buried immediately; they waited until more had been collected. [403]

As it was located on the edge of the village, the local population was aware of the happenings in the camp, as many testified to the commission of inquiry after the war. Stanislaw Kozak, who helped build the camp, went to the hill above it to observe activities. Kozak, using a telescope, watched as the Ukrainians beat the Jews with whips, driving them towards the gas chamber. He could hear shouting, screaming and wailing as the Jews were driven into the gassing barrack.[404] Further descriptions of the layout of the camp in the first and second phases were provided by the perpetrators in the Belzec investigations and interrogations after the war.[405]

In the euthanasia phase and subsequent crossover to *Reinhardt*, an essential qualification of the men chosen for this duty was their capacity to cope unemotionally with day-to-day operations. Some failed this test but many adapted and some were enthusiastic. Heading the list for automatic *Reinhardt* duty were the "cremators," "burners" and the KZ guards, who were the most psychologically-hardened men due to the nature of their duties in T4. Devoid of feeling, they behaved like "troopers" in a closed canteen type culture or, as Karin Orth puts it, "*SS-Sippengemeinschaft*" (SS Clan Community):[406] obedient, efficient and single-minded. This was more to Wirth's liking, as he could identify with them. Wirth was pragmatic when allocating duties to his staff in Belzec. Regardless of rank or personality, he selected the man with the right attitude and expertise to be placed where he was most effective to get the job done: smoothly, efficiently and without problems.

Cruelty

That the SS leadership did indiscriminately shoot Jews is generally unchallenged; but apart from a few exceptions, they rarely added sadism to their functional duties. However, cruelty was a daily occurrence among the Ukrainians and some maverick *SS-Scharführers: SS-Scharführer* Gustav Münzberger, a Sudeten German and carpenter from T4 (Sonnenstein), was in charge of driving the Jews into the gas chambers at Treblinka, where he acted with much unnecessary cruelty.[407] On the other hand, the previously mentioned "idiot," *SS-Scharführer* Heinrich Barbl, was not renowned for any acts of cruelty but was often whipped by Wirth for his drunken behavior.[408] However, Barbl had his uses; in civilian life he had been a plumber, and he was later sent to Sobibór by Wirth to fit the pipe system in the gas chambers.[409] Despite all their perceived difficulties and personal worries, the SS-garrison held together, supported by over-eager auxiliary cadres and the entrapped Jewish *Sonderkommandos*, plundering and processing each transport as it entered the camp.

126

SS in Belzec

Summer 1942, outside the *Kommandantur* on the main Village road 400 meters from the camp. L - R: SS-*Oberscharführers* Oberhauser, Irrmann, and Franz (in summer dress). Note Ukrainian sentry in background.

At Belzec, the SS-garrison was all accommodated together, sharing on a communal basis the village houses along the main Belzec-Lvov road.

Perhaps the combination of male communal living and common activity was a crucial factor in welding these men together as one unit. In Sobibór, so strong was the bond between the SS, they had rings featuring SS runes made from five mark pieces for every member of the permanent staff.[410] To emphasize and endorse the fact that the men now engaged at Belzec, despite wearing the uniforms of the *Waffen-SS*, were a civilian group, we have an interesting observation of an occurrence at the railway station. When the attention of a German railway inspector from Lublin was drawn to a group of SS men behaving strangely, he questioned them. They stated that they were not SS men, but had been issued with SS uniforms for their work at the camp. They told the inspector that they were from lunatic asylums and nursing homes where they had killed the mentally ill.[411] This is corroboration from the men themselves that they were civilians and outsiders, in the military sense.

Any personal relationships between SS personnel and Jewish women, or personal friendship with Ukrainians, even for chess games, was enough for Wirth to take action. These reprisals usually occurred when the officer was either on leave or temporarily away from the camp. On return, all relationships had been "dealt with"—the targeted companion had been shot or gassed on direct orders of the camp commandant, much to the distress of the officer concerned. Very often, this completely changed the behavior of the individual involved. Some changed from a cruel and sadistic murderer to an introverted character and saw no reason to carry on, as happened to *SS-Scharführer* Paul Groth in Sobibór.[412]

Paul Groth, aged 20, was one of the youngest guards in SS-uniform. Because of his perpetual drunkenness and sadistic cruelty in Belzec, which concerned his SS colleagues and threatened to disrupt the smooth running of the camp, Wirth disciplined him by transferring him to Sobibór in the hope he would mend his ways. However, this was not to be. In Sobibór, Groth ordered Jews to carry him around the camp in an armchair.[413] On other occasions when he was supervising young boys and one became tired, he would send him to the "hospital" for a bullet.[414] Groth continued to abuse his position to such an extent that the efficiency of the camp was being compromised. Wirth recognised this and immediately curbed this talent by removing Groth's most prized possession, a Jewish girl from the kitchens. Wirth had her shot.[415] It was acceptable to kill and torture the "*Untermenschen*," but to associate with them was not permissible.

Groth's catalogue of cruelty is unending. He tormented the Jews with his dog "Barry" who was the size of a small pony. He had trained the animal to attack on the command, "Jew," whereupon the animal leapt at the victim, biting him in the groin. Now disabled, the victim was invited by Groth to go with him to the "hospital" (*Lazarett*—the grave), where he was shot. Groth ordered prisoners to eat their own excrement, even though they pleaded to be shot instead. In another instance, he ordered Jews to climb to the top of buildings and then jump holding an open umbrella. All these Jews were shot, as broken bones were a ticket to the open pit. Because of his actions, from which he took great pleasure, Groth was soon ostracized by his SS colleagues.

When Groth struck up a relationship with a Jewish cleaning girl named Ruth, he became more reasonable. A relationship with a Jewess, it appears, was a more serious affront to camp discipline than neglecting orders—and the association between Groth and Ruth was quickly dealt with, probably on Wirth's direct orders. On Groth's return from leave, he found that Ruth had been shot. Shortly after, he was transferred back to Belzec.[416] An identical situation arose in Sobibór with *SS-Scharführer* Hans-Heinz Schütt, who was associating with an Austrian Jewish woman named Gisela and her 22-year-old niece. When Schütt returned from leave, his SS colleague, *SS-Scharführer* Erich Bauer, called him to the pits in Camp III. Bauer remarked, "Enjoy the Jewess's beautiful ass." Both the women were dead, having been shot, it is alleged, by Bauer on orders from the commandant.[417]

To pass the time between gassing operations all manner of cruelties were indulged in and condoned by the leadership. Each SS man had his preference for entertainment and torture. *SS-Scharführer* Paul Bredow, in charge at the "*Lazarett*" in Sobibór, gave free rein to his hobby of target shooting. (SS or Ukrainians on duty at the "hospital" amused themselves by placing a bucket on the victims' heads, sending them into the grave for shooting practice).[418]

He boasted of shooting 50 Jews a day with his automatic pistol. He also selected young girls from the transports and whipped them. *Scharführer* Hubert Gomerski used a truncheon packed with nails to assault the victims.[419] The auxiliary ranks (*Volksdeutsche*) that were not established SS were the most undisciplined elements who abused the power given to them, usually under the influence of alcohol. Wirth, despite his hatred for Jews and contempt for his own men who showed dissent, did take action against excesses of drunkenness and brutality when it threatened the orderly killing system.

Management Lines

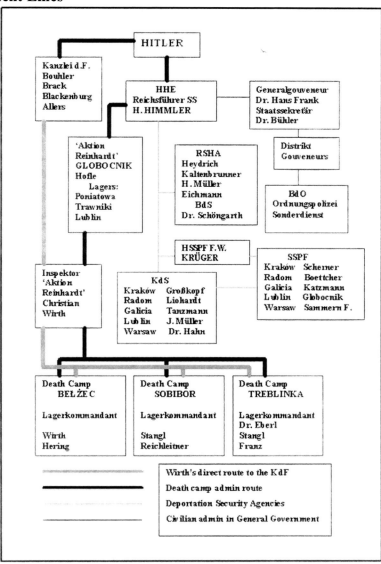

The above chart shows the lines of communication in respect of *Aktion Reinhardt*. Hitler is clearly shown as the pinnacle of power. There are two main information centers from which the Final Solution was organized and carried to fruition: *Reichsführer-SS* Himmler and the *Führer's* Chancellery. Notably, *Kriminalkommissar* Christian Wirth is shown as the major lynchpin, bypassing his superior Globocnik to gain direct access to Hitler's Chancellery.

Wirth By-passes Globocnik

One of the curious aspects to emerge within *Reinhardt* was the two-way flow of communication between the KdF, HHE and the death camps. Globocnik, as *SS-Polizeiführer*, held the overall authority for administration and control of *Reinhardt*, but when the focus centered on anything to do with the death camps, Wirth was in control and by all accounts was working to his own agenda. Both Globocnik and Wirth had different power bases, and although on good personal terms, appear to have been commissioned separately to work towards the Final Solution. This fact may explain the idiosyncratic chain of command that existed, particularly at the time of Wirth's hurried exit from Belzec after the experimental phase.

In early 1942, the experimental gassings in Belzec had come to an abrupt halt and all the Jewish workers were shot. Wirth and the rest of the German personnel left Belzec for Berlin without informing Globocnik. It was clear, even then, that Wirth was working under independent authority in respect to all operational issues concerning Belzec. Josef Oberhauser, who had arrived back from Lublin, found the camp deserted apart from a nominal security guard of Ukrainians. Within a few weeks, Wirth was back in Belzec, and with new vigor, commenced immediately to re-organize the camp. It also transpired that he had orders from the KdF to prepare for and receive Jews from the districts of Lublin and Galicia.[420] Wirth continued to bypass normal channels and go directly to the KdF for all policy decisions. The KdF, endorsing this, now sent special couriers carrying sealed instructions (bypassing Globocnik) to Wirth via T4 in Belzec.[421] Globocnik, although at times frustrated by Wirth's independent activities, was doing exactly the same in going directly to the HHE, ignoring and bypassing his superior, the HSSPF in Kraków.[422]

Chapter 8. Modus Operandi, Transports

Central Control of Deportation Trains

The administrative center of the transports to the death camps was the RSHA in Berlin. From the offices of 1V B4, the Jewish Affairs department of the *Gestapo*, Adolf Eichmann supervised a web of deportation transports. In a coordinated exercise, the offices of the Ministry of Transport and the senior police chiefs in the *Generalgouvernement* were brought together and between them planned and organized a systematic program of destruction. The Ministry, via the three regional *Reichsbahn* operational centers, administered the timetables, fare rates, concessions and arrangements for the escorting security personnel.

A commercial deal was concluded between Eichmann's 1V B 4 office and the Ministry of Transport. Exact times of departure were specified with details of the locomotives and number of cars/wagons. "*Sonderzug*" (Jewish transports) took priority over military transports. The minimum charge per transport was 200 Reichsmarks, with no charge for the return of trains after they had been emptied of their human cargo. A cargo of 1,000 persons per train was the norm, but for the *Sonderzug* the norm was 2-5,000 for short hauls (within Poland), allowing 2 sq. ft. per person, adjusted accordingly for transports elsewhere in Europe. That is one of the reasons why there was no shortage of resettlement transports—it was good business. In the final hours of the war, the Slovak Ministry was billed by the *Reichsbahn* for costs of the 1944 deportations (within the *Reich*). The trains departed as German Military Transports. The explanation was that they carried Jews who were considered essential transport of the *Reich*, and that the costs should be taken from the sale of Jewish property. The Slovak resettlement transports contained 70,000 Jews, 65,000 of whom did not return.

We have first-hand details of the resettlement transports to Belzec, of men, women and children. We also know that the organizers of these deportations were *Ordnungspolizei* (Order Police), *Schutzpolizei* (City Police), Ukrainian guards, Polish collaborators (public officials), rail personnel, Sipo – SD and the SS. The Jewish *Ordnungsdienst* (OD) Order Police on orders from the *Judenrat* were also involved.[423]

All resettlement rail transports to Belzec from the east and west Galicia districts were controlled from the Head Office of all eastbound traffic in Kraków.[424] The coordinating center for *Reinhardt* death camps was the *Aktion Reinhardt* HQ at the "Julius Schreck" barracks in Lublin.[425] The organization of a death transport of Jews from Kołomyja to Belzec received exactly the same attention as 50 wagons of freight, military personnel or armaments to any other designated location. Providing the bill was paid, it was only another entry in the ledger; and surprisingly, the movements were not marked "secret."[426]

In present day travel offices, leaflets point out the benefits of group travel. This is exactly how it was in the occupied territories in 1942: The *Reichsbahn* offered the SS "special rates" for Jewish transports. For the "resettlement" policies of *Reinhardt*, Jews were transported at discount rates from these areas. There were special rates for large parties of more than 400 people, half fare for adults and all children aged 4-10 years. Those under four years travelled free! The agency responsible for payment to *Gedob* (*Generaldirektion der Ostbahn*, Director of Eastern Rail) was of course the SD, via Eichmann's Department 1V B 4 at the RSHA in Berlin,[427] who then in turn reimbursed themselves from Jewish assets. That is why there was never any shortage of trains for Jewish transports.[428]

The RSHA was invoiced per transport at the single fare rate (return was of course not necessary), with appropriate discount adjustments for the children, plus return fares for the guard detachment accompanying the transports. There may have been other adjustments resulting from damage to rail property, including the damage caused by Jews breaking and jumping (the "jumpers" or "parachutists" as they were known) from trains *en-route* to Belzec. Another considerable cost was the labor involved in removing the dead and in cleaning transports before the return journey. All these tasks were billed and invoiced to Eichmann's department in Berlin—which made payments to the rail authorities from a special *Reinhardt* bank account, which was continually swallowing up Jewish assets.[429] The principle was very simple—Jews paid for their own demise.[430]

Transit Ghettos

Emerging as an integral part of deportation were the transit ghettos: Izbica, Piaski, Rejowiec and Trawniki. Subsequently, further ghettos in the districts of Opole Lubelski, Zamosc, Chełm, Włodawa and Miedrzyrzec Podlaski were opened to cope with the ever-increasing numbers. These establishments became the hub for the management of the onward deportations to the death camps.

Jews from the occupied territories were collected at these locations for disbursement to the killing stations of *Reinhardt*. The largest, Izbica, became the central holding ghetto for Jews in the early stages (March to June 1942), handling over 17,000 Jews. Piaski (5,000) and Rejowiec (5,000) acted as overflow centers. For the purposes of *Reinhardt*, these ghettos were strategically placed for rail transportation and significantly, places of supposed "new settlements" to fob off the sceptical Jews deported from Germany, Austria and Slovakia. Once ensconced on arrival, the fit and healthy were forwarded to Majdanek for labor and the remainder, the children, women and elderly, joined the queue for the death camps. During the period before final deportation particular care (not always successful) was taken that no postal communication was to penetrate beyond the Lublin district. Communications that did get back to their home-towns were the only indication of the subsequent fate of these people. Cultural problems added to the misery as the vastly different backgrounds of Jews from east and west, who were now in the same melting pot, were not always conducive to mutual understanding. When these ghettos were finally closed (November 1942), several thousand Jews were removed and shot in local cemeteries. [431]

Modus Operandi of Deportation to the Lublin District [432]

The Lublin District was one of the key centers in the strategy to destroy the Jewish presence in Europe. This was the area in the *Generalgouvernment* where the victims, brought from far and wide, were concentrated prior to further treatment. The deportation of Jews to the Lublin District was carried out in two phases: 1939 to 1941 and 1942 to 1943. The first period was a result of the population politics when western Jews were deported from Polish territory annexed to the *Reich* to the Lublin District.

In 1942, 14,000 Czech and Moravian Jews, 39,890 Jews from Slovakia, 19,050 Jews from the *Reich*, and 6,000 Jews from Vienna were deported to the Lublin District. In 1943, 4,000 Jews from France, 34,310 Jews from Holland, and 12,700 from the eastern *Kommissariat* of the *Reich* were deported to the Lublin District. Many went to the transit ghettos and labor camps. The majority, however, went direct to the extermination camps and Majdanek KZ.

In the Galician District, most deportations of Jews went direct to Belzec, as well as 134,700 Jews from the Kraków District and 8,330 from the Radom District. In addition, between 1942 and 1943, 45,000 Jews from Warsaw and 11,190 Jews from Bialystok were sent to the labor camps at Poniatowa, Trawniki and Lublin. A total of approximately 575,450 Jews were deported to the area around Lublin within those years. In the period of 1939 to 1943, a total of 640,000 Jews (518,430 from Polish territories and 121,450 from elsewhere) were deported to the Lublin District. The optimum period was 1942 when 473,240 Jews were deported there, the majority of whom entered the death camps and Majdanek. [433]

Deportations from the Lublin District

Himmler's visit to Lublin marked the onset of a clear and unambiguous policy of annihilation. Its purpose was to make room for the influx of Jews arriving from the outside (Germany and Slovakia), and at the same time to murder or deport the Lublin Jews to Belzec. Similar actions were being carried out simultaneously in east Galicia. [434]

At the *Reinhardt* headquarters in Lublin, Globocnik had installed a special staff under the command of his deputies, Hermann Höfle and Amon Goeth. Höfle outlined to his staff how the deportations were to commence. At terminal stations (transit camps) the Jews were to be divided into productive and non-productive workers. Non-productive and sick Jews would all go to

Belzec via transit ghettos at Izbica, Krasnik and Piaski where many thousands could be processed. Belzec was capable of receiving four to five transports per day, each containing one thousand Jews. Officially, these Jews would be "brought over the border and never again return to the *Generalgouvernement*."[435] On the evening of 16 March 1942, mass roundups of Jews in the Lublin ghetto commenced. The commanding officer for the first resettlement transport to Belzec was *SS-Obersturmführer/ Kriminalkommissar* Hermann Worthoff,[436] who, with the help of the formations of "Trawniki Men," seized 1,500 Jews from the ghetto and marched them under guard to the slaughter yards, where they were loaded, in groups of a 100, into 15 sealed freight wagons. On the morning of 17 March, the transport left for Belzec. There were no survivors.

In Lublin, the SS directed the *Judenrat* to the effect that for the next 14 days, 1,500 Jews per day, men, women and children, were to be sent to a transit camp for resettlement in the East. By the end of March 1942, over 20,000 Jews from the Lublin ghetto were already in the pits at Belzec (graves 14 and 20). A further 10,000 followed in early April. Each day, transports arrived at Belzec from two directions: the Lublin district and East Galicia.[437] In just under four weeks, from 17 March to 14 April 1942, 43,500 Jews were transported from the Lublin ghetto and the surrounding district to Belzec.[438] These transports did not go unnoticed by the observant local inhabitant Dr. Zygmunt Klukowski in Szczebrzeszyn, who made the following entry in his diary on 6 April 1942: "We know for sure that every day two trains, consisting of 20 cars each, come to Belzec, one from Lublin, the other from Lvov."[439]

From the direction of Lvov, the SS ordered the *Judenrat* to make available 18,000 Jews, who were to be immediately deported.[440] The only exemptions were those families with labor permits. This suggests a weeding out of the non-productive Jews, with the remainder held back for the war economy, which was a definite Nazi policy. On arrival at the Klaparow railway station, the Jews were immediately robbed of their possessions and herded into boxcars destined for Belzec.[441]

Further deportation "operations" were carried out in Lvov in May and August 1942. The early deportations from Lublin to Belzec were noted by Josef Goebbels in his diary:

> From the *Generalgouvernement* now, beginning in Lublin, the Jews are being deported to the East.[442] The former *Gauleiter* of Vienna, who carries out this action, is doing it with great circumspection and also with a method which does not appear too conspicuous.[443]

But it was conspicuous; in Warsaw, the Chairman of the *Judenrat*, Adam Czerniakow, and the diarist Chaim Kaplan, reported in their diaries the fate of the Jews from Lublin and Lvov.[444]

Arrival Procedures and Deceptions

Although there were many deportations to the death camps, evidence of these transports is hard to come by. In the absence of German documentation (which was the exception in the case of the Kołomyja transport of 7-10 September), we have to rely on depositions made by survivors, bystanders, or the Polish railway staff who carried the victims or deposited them. What may be considered as the best evidence (the victims) is very often unreliable for a number of reasons. These include the trauma of the initial round-ups in the ghettos and incarceration in holding pens awaiting transport, which in some cases went on for several days; and the unspeakably inhuman conditions in the overcrowded wagons without food, water, or sanitary facilities, naked, among their kin and paralyzed by fear.[445] The "jumpers" from the trains who survived the fall but were later caught very often turned on their people as informants, in order to survive. After all of this, it is very unlikely that recollections of survivors would be clear, unless that is, the occurrence happened to be on a specific holy day: first or second day of Yom Kippur, Rosh Hashanah, or Passover, which the Nazis, with their obscene sense of occasion, often chose for the beginning of an "operation."[446]

'Resettlement' Operations

All "resettlement" transports within *Reinhardt* were carefully logged: date, place, date of embarkation, numbers, destination, escorting personnel, intelligence, etc, as we shall see when the Kołomyja transport is discussed. The only absent feature, which was applicable to all transports entering Belzec, was that no names or other personal identification was ever made. The procedure for mass "resettlement" to Belzec may be divided into two separate phases: March to June 1942 and July to December 1942.[447]

In the earlier period of "resettlement" transports, thousands of bewildered Jews from the districts of Lublin and Lvov started to arrive at Belzec railway station marshalling yard. When a number of transports arrived over a short period, causing build-ups and delays in entering the camp, the wagons (freight cars) were stacked in strict order of entry on spur-lines. In rotation, the wagons were unhitched in blocks of up to 20 and shunted into the camp. If we take one average transport of 40 wagons (some were 50-60, or even 80 wagons), containing approximately 4-5,000 (some held over 8,000), the trauma and chaos can be well imagined. Transports arriving late were held over until the following day. The one small window at the top of the wagon was heavily boarded and covered with barbed wire. Even so, hands were pushed through any opening offering takers valuables in exchange for water. In order to prevent breakouts and disorder each transport was guarded by German security units until entry to the camp had been completed. It is of note that no Polish train drivers went as far as the reception ramp of any of the three death camps. It was a standard German practice that a deportation train stopped at the nearest station to the designated camp (Belzec town, Małkinia in the case of Treblinka) where a Polish crew was replaced by a German crew, which took the train inside the camp.

The scene within the camp was of devastation and utter inhumanity. Any Jews who had managed to break out from the wagons were immediately shot and left on the track until after the last wagon had been processed. The driver who shunted the train into the Belzec camp was always the same person, the *Reichsbahnsekretär* Rudolf Göckel.[448] One local observer to these early transports, Mieczysław Kudyba, probed the camouflaged fencing surrounding the camp and witnessed naked men, women and children carrying their clothing, and standing in the snow screaming.[449]

In his attempt to hide the real purpose of Belzec, Wirth went to great lengths to represent it as a transit camp.[450] This policy of verbal camouflage and deception was not only to deceive the arriving victims, but also to disguise the camp's purpose if official communications should fall into unauthorized hands. The misrepresentation and deception was achieved in two ways:

1) The camp was constructed in such a way that to outside observers and the arriving Jews nothing remotely suspicious could be seen. This was important for the several thousands of Jews waiting expectantly in the reception area.

2) Both the speech and the actions of the welcoming SS-NCOs duped the anxious, frightened, trembling mass of humanity and allayed any suspicion of their intended fate. By these methods, the Jews saw a glimmer of hope and believed for that moment, that they *were* in transit to a work camp and not to certain death as the rumors had speculated.

The euthanasia establishments, and later the death camps, were each designed as a "Potemkin Village" —a screen to hide its true purpose. As in the euthanasia establishments where Wirth had deceived the victims by false representation, he continued with and enhanced these deception techniques. In preparation for receiving the incoming transport, the camp command held a briefing session with the stand-by squad either on the previous evening or in the early morning on the day of reception. Although the SS-garrison was small in number, Wirth selected each man for the position for which he was best suited, regardless of rank.

The system that Wirth implemented at Belzec was improved upon as the killing operations progressed. By the time Sobibór and Treblinka were operating, the bogus rail platforms, false clocks and other deceiving devices had been introduced and perfected. The difficulties for the SS arose when Jews from the towns close to Belzec remained convinced of their demise. Even so, when their time came, they too, for a brief moment, succumbed to false promises until reality prevailed. Only the gas chambers awaited them.

First Large Transports

The first big transports of Jews came from the Lublin District, and from the Lublin ghetto alone, 30,000 were deported to Belzec in 16 transports between 17 March and 14 April, with a further 15,000 from Zamosc, Krasnik, and the transit ghettos in Piaski and Izbica. There were also several transports from the Lvov District, notably from Kołomyja, Stanisławow and Drohobycz—30,000 people from these Galician towns whom the Nazis termed as "non-working" Jews were gassed in three weeks. Several of these deportations were organized on a Saturday, the Jewish Sabbath, as on that day the SS were sure of finding the maximum number of Jews at home; other transports were deliberately arranged on Fridays, to ensure that the Jews would spend the following holy day locked inside the freight wagons, *en route* to Belzec. They would therefore arrive in time to be gassed on the Sabbath. Notable among such transports were the two organized on 11-12 April, the eve of Pesach (Passover), and the first day of Passover respectively. On Passover Eve, 3,000 Jews were rounded up in Zamosc, and on the first day of Passover, 2,000 in Krasnik.

The net of human destruction began to spread. In addition to Polish and Galician Jews, German Jews also began to arrive in Belzec. The first of these had been rounded up during the last week of March and in early April from the rural communities around Bad Kissingen, north of Würzburg: from Bad Kissingen itself, Pfaffenhausen, Poppenlauer, Steinach, Volkersleier, and a dozen smaller places. Towards the end of April, German Jews were also rounded up from the rural communities around the city of Würzburg: Gaukonigshaufen, Gerolzhofen, Kitzingen, Laudebach, Marktbreit, Theilheim, and a score of smaller villages. In some cases, only a single family per village was "deported to the east."

In April too, German Jews were deported from the cities of Augsburg, Bamberg, Coburg, Fürth, Landshut, Nuremberg, Schweinfurt, and Killisberg in Württemberg. Austrian Jews from Vienna, Bohemian Jews from Ceske Budejovica, and Jews from Slovakia and the Theresienstadt (Terezin) ghetto also joined those deported to the east for "resettlement." All of them were sent first to the transit ghettos in Piaski and Izbica from where they were sent in batches to Belzec. There were no survivors from any of these transports, and by the end of April over 90,000 Jews had been gassed in the Belzec camp.

Reception in the Camp (Interim Phase)

Much had been learned from the earlier transports. The appearance of Belzec to the Jews disembarking from the *Sonderzug* (special trains) was an elaborate fiction. Christian Wirth and his team had gone to great lengths to structure the reception area as a worker friendly environment, at least until the purpose of the camps became clear. Their first direct confrontation with the camp SS was when the Jews climbed down from the wagons and stood in the reception yard, bemused and frightened.

As we have observed when discussing the duties of the Ukrainians at the reception area, this was the most unpredictable time. The separation of families, men and boys from the women and children, caused much agitation and heartache and spread anxiety throughout the whole transport. Confusion, fright and realization (by some) created mass hysteria, which sometimes got out of control. In a last desperate plea, the names and addresses of Jews still in hiding in the towns they had come from were spilled out by the deportees, but fell on deaf ears. Rudolf Höß, commandant of Auschwitz recalled. "Often the confusion was so great that the selections had to begin all over again. It was often necessary to use force to restore order."[451]

The SS reception troops and dogs were ready and waiting; and as soon as there was a murmur of dissent, they assaulted the dissenters with brutal efficiency. Armed Ukrainian and SS guards watched carefully and removed persons showing anguish or defiance to a nearby building where they were shot in the back of the neck with a small calibre pistol. This was the most crucial time for the SS as it was the most likely time for revolt. Wirth had carefully weighed all this up and had personally worked out the calming speeches to be given to the masses.

The most effective form of deception was the words spoken to the victims by the Jewish *Sonderkommandos* on reception and during the haircutting and undressing stages that followed. In a whisper, "Where are you from?" In a whisper, the answer, "From Lvov," "From Kraków," "From Zamosc," "Wielicka," "Jaslo,"[452] "Tarnow," and so on. Rudolf Reder witnessed this two or three times a day, every day.[453] Speaking through a microphone and with a Yiddish interpreter, Wirth (or his deputy) welcomed them, now reassured to suit the new conditions:

> This is Belzec where your stay is temporary. You will move on to work camps where your skills are needed. There is work for everyone, even you housewives are needed to cook and keep the houses clean. First, I must have your cooperation so that we can get you on your way quickly.

There was a ripple of applause and shouts of "Thank you Mr. Commander!" Jew turned to Jew with delight and clear expressions of relief. Then, Wirth raised the essential part of the deception:

> We must have order and cleanliness. Before we feed you, you must all bathe and have your clothes disinfected and the women will have to have their hair shaved. We cannot have disease breaking out here in Belzec. Please comply with my staff's orders. The sooner we can deal with these essential requirements, the sooner you can eat and have hot coffee.

Wirth then passed on the process of gassing to the duty NCO: *"Scharführer!* Commence immediately."

While all this was going on, the "work-Jews," who were standing among the masses, were expressionless. The final gift of life was announced from the loudspeaker, directed towards the men and young boys who had now been formed into a work detail in order to collect the clothing from the assembly square and remove it to the warehouse. "Whoever does the most can stay in the work detail!" barked the loudspeaker. Then began a race to the death between these naked people under the sarcastic laughter of the camp guards.[454]

Men were requested to remove their shoes and tie them together with pieces of string being handed out by a reprieved Jewish child from a previous transport.[455] The men, now separated, were marched off in blocks of 750, five abreast, towards the "tube." At various points attended by the SS, they handed over clothing, personal property, money, etc., until they were completely naked, standing at the entrance to the "tube." With armed Ukrainian guards to the rear led by the duty *Scharführer*, the men, with arms raised, not in an act of surrender but to facilitate and maximize easy access in greater numbers, entered the gas chambers. By this time the men sensed betrayal, but by then it was too late. Paralysed with fear, and in their nakedness, they were unable to respond effectively with their full potential for resistance.

Wirth had selected the soft-spoken *SS-Scharführer*, Karl Schluch, to pacify the victims at the "tube" by answering their searching questions about was happening to them. Schluch did this very well, making the transition from the reception and undressing areas to the gas chambers orderly and mainly without incident. Should all this fail, which it did on occasion, the victims were overpowered by force of arms and forced along the tube at the point of a bayonet to the gas chambers. The "nice guy/bad guy" syndrome prevailed; if the reassurances and promises failed, the bayonet and the whip came into play. Despite all the deceptions, once the victims had arrived at the gassing barrack, their impending doom was clear to all.

In a well-rehearsed operation, the Trawniki men, armed with whips and bayonets, prodded and forced the men into the three chambers and closed the doors. At a signal from the escorting *Scharführer*, the gassing engine was started. After about 20 minutes, inspection through the peephole in the chamber door confirmed that the engine could be turned off. The SS had completed their part of the operation. Now the Jewish *Sonderkommandos* took over and removed the bodies. From the rear of the gassing barracks, the doors were opened outwards and the corpses removed. Each corpse was searched for valuables and any gold teeth extracted before the bodies were placed in the pits. Another commando entered the gas chambers to clean up, while still others raked the sandy pathways to the gassing barrack.

Immediately, the women and children who had by now been processed and were waiting their turn, suspected what was before them; but again, once in the "tube" it was too late.[456]

In Belzec, evidence is scant regarding resistance, but in Treblinka and Sobibór—and there is no reason to believe that the same did not occur in Belzec—attacks on the SS were made with grenades, pistols and razors during disembarkation from the death transports.[457]

Once the Jews had been unloaded from the wagons and were on their way, those found dead from the incoming transport were piled to one side. Jews who were sick or elderly were taken to the pit and shot.[458] Again, to promote a calming influence, these ghastly scenes were played out to the accompaniment of the camp musicians, sometimes two or three times a day, sometimes every day, from March to December 1942.

From among the thousands of Jews arriving in the camp, Wirth selected physically strong individuals (150 in the first phase; 500 in the second phase) to carry out tasks in the murder process. During the first few weeks, those "work-Jews" selected were retained for a very short period before being disposed of and replaced by others from the next transport. Under a new system, which Wirth devised, he engaged a more permanent work force—*Sonderkommandos*. Ironically, after a time, the *Sonderkommandos* knew that they too would meet exactly the same fate as that suffered by the thousands of their own race, to whose destruction they had contributed so greatly, "Yet the eagerness with which they carried out their duties never ceased to amaze me," said Rudolf Höß.[459]

Overflow of Mass Graves

In April 1942 the weather became unexpectedly warm, which speeded up the decomposition of corpses in graves that were still open. In mid-April, SS-*Obersturmführer* Franz Stangl had been sent to Belzec by Globocnik to be briefed by Wirth before taking up his (Stangl's) command at Sobibór. A horrifying sight met him:

> Wirth was standing on a hill; next to the pits...the pits.... they were full. I cannot tell you, not hundreds, thousands, thousands of corpses. Oh, God, that is where Wirth told me; he said that was what Sobibór was all about.[460]

Due to the stench of bodies, the local authorities complained to the camp SS. Truckloads of lime were brought in to cover the open graves and suppress the stench of decaying corpses. In 1998, during the course of the second stage of the Belzec survey, soil samples taken at varying depths in this area not only confirmed earlier reported sizes of the graves, but also showed a large mix of concentrated lime, soil, ashes and bones in graves numbered 14 and 20.[461]

End of First Phase - Wirth Leaves Belzec

SS-*Oberscharführer* Werner Dubois arrived at Belzec from T4 in early April 1942. From his interrogation notes we have corroboration as to the working of the gassing barrack and the difficulties experienced. Having only the three gas chambers and the general working conditions in the camp, taken together with the inadequacy of the pits to swallow up the vast numbers of Jews murdered, was hampering the facility to gas and bury the victims efficiently. Wirth concluded that nothing short of a complete overhaul of the camp would meet the requirements necessary.

About mid-April 1942, Wirth temporarily closed the camp and left for Berlin, taking with him his deputy (Schwarz) and his gassing expert (Hackenholt).[462] The reasons for this sudden departure have never been clearly explained, but no doubt it was to confer with his KdF masters regarding the gassing difficulties and to request authority to reorganize and rebuild Belzec. In view of the Nazis' projected Jewish policies, they probably agreed. We know that Globocnik, his superior, had no knowledge of Wirth's departure.[463] When Wirth returned to Belzec the re-planning and reconstruction of Belzec took another six weeks to complete.[464] Belzec did not resume full-time gassing operations until mid-summer.[465] In the meantime, the construction of Sobibór was completed and the camp commissioned on 8 May 1942. Sobibór immediately engulfed the overflow from Belzec and the residue of the Lublin Jews.

Suspension of Gassing Operations

The entire Belzec chronology, especially dates of the construction of the second set of gas chambers, is a matter of some confusion. The consensus from a variety of sources suggests that between mid-May and July,[466] the camp was reorganized and new, much larger, gas chambers were built. In my view, during the rebuilding, the old gas chambers were still in service. Although the transports during this period were much diminished, gassings were still being carried out at the same time as the new series of gas chambers were being built.

Both Arad and Rückerl follow the conclusion of the Munich court judgement, explaining the temporary cessation of operations at Belzec in mid-April by the sudden departure for Berlin of the camp commandant, Christian Wirth, and dating the construction of new gas chambers to late June or early July. In doing so, they follow Oberhauser's 1962 testimony before the Munich court. In my view, his earlier testimony is more reliable because he chose to focus on the period in which he was less involved. According to the earlier testimony, Wirth carried out experimental gassings in February, then left suddenly for Berlin and returned mid-March to begin the Lublin and Lvov "operations."

Josef Oberhauser probably manipulated times, dates and figures to misrepresent himself as only a minor cog in the wheel of mass murder. He craftily limits his activities to the periphery of events up until 1 August 1942, when he leaves Belzec with Wirth (now *Inspektor* of *Reinhardt* camps), and when the Treblinka-Sobibór-Belzec complex in the *Generalgouvernment* was coordinated at the commencement of the maximum resettlement period. In his post-war statements to the criminal investigation department inquiring into the Belzec crimes, he repeatedly refers to experimental periods when two or three small transports were processed.[467]

The only period thereafter during which new construction could have taken place at Belzec is the five-week interruption in deportations between mid-April and late May. The late-June, early-July interruption was due to transportation problems. In my view, in his 1962 testimony, Oberhauser was trying to give the false impression that until August 1942 (the period for which he was on trial) Belzec only had the capacity to carry out small experimental gassings in a single gas chamber holding up to 100 people.

There were three gas chambers in the first phase, but only one was used in conjunction with the gassing van in February and the subsequent gassing experiments with *Zyklon B* and CO gas. In reality, between mid-March and August, despite the five-week interruption for the construction of new gas chambers, many thousands of Jews had been gassed at Belzec. When one sees both statements placed together for examination, and takes into consideration all the surrounding facts, this is the picture that emerges.[468]

Franz Stangl in Sobibór

Soon after Stangl's disagreeable visit to Belzec where he had seen what was to be expected of him at Sobibór, he sought a way to get himself relieved from this duty. After some attempts to seek a transfer to other duties, he realized that once brought into this secret murder program, the only way out "was under the earth."[469] What distressed him more, and kept him at his post, was that his family would be held accountable should he be uncooperative. Therefore, with this in mind—or so he says—he continued his duties in Sobibór.[470]

It was at Sobibór that we have further evidence of Wirth's impromptu actions and complete disregard for human life. It occurred when Stangl was working on the construction of the camp and Oberhauser (Wirth's confidant) called with instructions for Stangl to go immediately to the gassing barrack. Stangl found Wirth sweating and cursing (just as in Belzec) over the seals to the doors of the gas chamber. Suddenly, Wirth pronounced, "Right, we will try it out now with those 25; get them up here." Jews who were working nearby were marched to the gassing barrack and forcibly beaten by Wirth into the gas chamber. Once satisfied that things at Sobibór were working correctly, Wirth returned to Belzec for Phase Two.

At the end of April, the Armia Krajowa (AK, Home Army), the Polish underground resistance organization, produced an intelligence report on the Belzec death camp based on eyewitness reports, mainly from Polish railway workers at Belzec station. The report stated that during the first month of its existence, the camp had received 52 transports, each containing on average of 1,500 Jews, i.e. a total of around 78,000 Jews, and that after each transport two wagonloads of clothing were removed from the camp to the locomotive shed near the station. As well as mentioning the deliveries of lime and cement, the report also named Wirth as the camp commandant and gave his correct rank.

Chapter 9. Interim Phase

June-July 1942

The reception of the next few transports in the camp was supervised by SS-*Oberscharführer* Oberhauser personally, on Wirth's orders, and from these transports fit and strong young Jewish males were selected to lead the new work brigades. Wirth selected his own *Oberzugsführers*. These Jewish supervisors in turn selected 15 *Zugsführers*, among them several women, to supervise various tasks in the camp. The Jewish work brigades in Belzec would soon number 1,000 people.

These *Zugsführers*, like their predecessors, were considered by Wirth and the T4/SS-NCOs to be completely degenerate since they too had agreed to perform their bloody work, with whips and rubber truncheons in hand, in return for the rewards offered by Wirth. They too deceived themselves with Wirth's promises that as killers of their fellow-Jews they would one day be given their freedom and resettled on their own land. Belief in this deception was encouraged, as before, by the SS, who occasionally allowed the *Zugsführers* to leave the camp under armed escort, and even to visit the nearby town of Tomaszow. Also selected at this time were the specialists needed in the camp: gold and silversmiths, dentists, barbers, tailors, cobblers, and a doctor to attend to the immediate needs of the camp staff.

The processing of the transports was now greatly speeded-up by the erection of two large barracks at the eastern end of the reception yard; these empty, hall-like buildings were the undressing barracks for the segregated males on the left, and for the females and children on the right. Attached at right-angles to the left of the far end of the females' undressing barrack there was a second barrack which contained two long rows of stools. Here, after they had undressed, the women would have their hair cut off by a team of Jewish barbers. The women selected from the transports to act as *Zugsführers* were to be employed mainly in supervising the women and children at the undressing stage and during the hair cutting. The exit doors from the males' undressing barrack and the barbers' barrack opened into a small yard surrounded by a high plank fence, which in turn led to a 2 m wide open-air corridor, hemmed-in on both sides by tall camouflaged barbed-wire fences. The 150 m long corridor led up a steep, sandy slope, through a copse of silver birch trees, to the steps of the "Hackenholt Foundation," and within a short time had acquired a similar name among the SS-garrison and "work Jews" alike: "*die Schleuse* - the sluice," or "the tube."

Up until this time the T4/SS had attempted to keep the purpose of the deportations and fate of the Jews a secret from the German civil authorities—a difficult task as the Jews of the *Generalgouvernement* were under civil jurisdiction and since mid-March the deportations had been coordinated between them and the SS. Finally, on 3 June, Governor General Dr. Hans Frank issued a directive transferring all Jewish affairs to the SS and *Sicherheitspolizei*, thereby simplifying the whole deportation procedure. From that date onwards, the fate of the the Jews of Poland was entirely in SS hands.

At this time, a total of 7,000 Jews from the Kraców ghetto were delivered to Belzec in three transports; then, during an intensive 11-day operation carried out between 9 and 19 June, 11,500 Jews from the Tarnow ghetto were brought to the camp. On 17 June, just before the end of the Tarnow operation, *SS-Hauptscharführer* "Friedl" Schwarz and SS-NCOs Werner Dubois and Rudi Kamm were attacked and injured by Jews at the railway siding while they were supervising the unloading of transports. From that day when Jews had dared attack and injure SS-men in Belzec, Wirth ordered that all SS-NCOs had to carry whips "for their own protection." The Jewish *Oberzugsführers* and *Zugsführers* were also issued with special horse whips consisting of a thick wooden handle 30 cm long, to which were attached leather thongs several meters in length.

In addition to the transports from Kraców and Tarnów, several smaller trainloads from Dabrowa Tarnowska, Kolomyja, Olkusz and Pilica, other transports of Czech, Moravian and Slovakian Jews, as well as Jews from the *Reich*, together brought the total number of victims of the new gas chambers to about 30,000 in 19 days. During the first three months of its existence, i.e. between mid-March and mid-June, over 185,000 Jews were killed in Belzec.

With the arrival of the last transport from Tarnów on 19 June the gassing operation at Belzec came to a halt for almost three weeks. An acute shortage of freight rolling stock in the *Generalgouvernment* rendered the *Gedob* offices in Lublin and Kraców powerless to provide transport for the deportation of Jews.

Consolidation and Preparations

By early June 1942 experimental and regionally based mass killings had been overtaken by the general annihilation policy of the "Final Solution." The mass killings now went into "free fall" and encompassed all districts of the *Generalgouvernment*. From mid-July the deportations from Western Europe to the death camps commenced with transports sent directly to Auschwitz.

In July 1942, groups of T4 personnel started to arrive at *Reinhardt* headquarters in Lublin, where each man was sworn to secrecy and warned to keep silent about their duties. Photography was strictly forbidden. When the police searched the home of Kurt Franz after the war, they found a photograph album containing numerous photographs taken in Treblinka. The album, *Schöne Zeiten (Beautiful Times)*, sealed his conviction.[471]

It is apparent that by May 1942 a decision had been taken for the destruction of *all* Jews.[472] After the reorganization of Belzec, and in preparation for even more transports, the camp was divided into two parts, separated by a camouflaged high fence interwoven with firs. The only entrance into Camp II was by a heavily guarded security gate and, of course, via the connecting camouflaged "tube," which ran from the undressing barracks directly to the gas chambers. Work Jews could be transferred from Camp I to Camp II but not vice versa.[473] The lower part (Camp I) was the reception area for arrivals. In Camp II there were barracks for the 500 "death brigade" Jews. This regiment of lost souls was made-up of gravediggers, body removers and specialist artisans, including dentists and technical workers.

By the time Treblinka opened on 22 July 1942, Belzec camp had been completely reorganized and restructured. The old wooden barracks containing three gas chambers had been demolished and were replaced by a solid building of brick and concrete, double the size. It is interesting to note that the new gas chambers were the only solidly constructed building in the camp.

Although Rudolf Reder did not arrive at the camp until August 1942, he had a good idea of how the camp had been originally constructed and of the reconstructed gas chambers:

> The chamber building was made of concrete and covered with a flat roof of tarpaper. It stood on a raised surface with steps leading into it from a reception yard. Along both sides of the building was an unloading platform. The small stairs ended with a door, over which was a notice: bath and inhalation room (*Bade und Inhalationsträume*), and a big vase with flowers stood there by the entrance.

> From the entrance door, a passage ran along the length of the building with three one-wing doors on each side. The doors led to rooms with no windows. Behind the building was a small room, which housed a petrol engine. The gas chambers were camouflaged with a net interwoven with leaves and branches that stretched over the roof on high poles. A one-inch diameter pipe led from the engine room directly into the windowless rooms.[474]

Probable Reconstruction of the Second Phase Gas Chambers
as Sketched by the Author

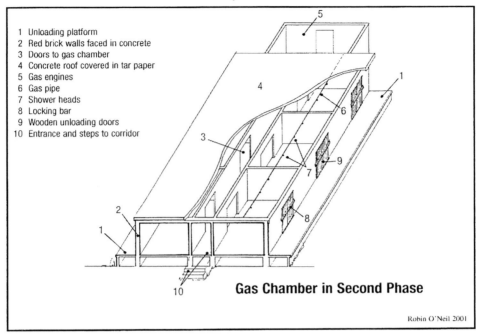

1 Unloading platform
2 Red brick walls faced in concrete
3 Doors to gas chamber
4 Concrete roof covered in tar paper
5 Gas engines
6 Gas pipe
7 Shower heads
8 Locking bar
9 Wooden unloading doors
10 Entrance and steps to corridor

Gas Chamber in Second Phase

Robin O'Neil 2001

The newly built gas chambers, measuring 24m x 10m wide, contained six gassing rooms of approximately 4 m x 8 m capable of holding 750 people simultaneously in each chamber. [475] Similar modifications were also made at Sobibór where Stangl was also experiencing problems. [476] To keep the transports moving, Stangl's new gassing barrack was also increased in size to six chambers and built next to the original gas chambers, which were kept commissioned during the rebuilding operation. [477] These improvements in capacity now opened the way to the maximum "resettlement" period in all three death camps.

Reder states that on both sides of the building, grave pits had been dug, and that the dead bodies were manhandled to the pits. There is no reference to a narrow gauge railway for the second phase gas chambers.

A description (edited by the author) of the gas chambers that corroborates Reder's account was given by T4/SS Karl Schluch when describing his duties in Belzec to his interrogators well after the war.

> They sent me to camp Belzec, June 1942. The situation there was worse than I thought. Most of us hated this job but the fear of Wirth was bigger. He ordered me for duty at the ramp and in the "tube." My job was to lead the victims through the tube to the gas

chamber building. I had to carry a whip but I never used it. I had to calm down the victims and then tell them to take a bath.

About the gc (gas chamber) building: a low house with a flat roof. There was a center corridor and three gassing rooms to the left and to the right, each for about 200 people. At the outside there were big gates and concrete ramps along the building; 80cm high and 2m wide. Over the entrance door was a big yellow Star of David. Left and right of the door were signs with the inscription: *"Stiftung Hackenholt"* and *"Bade-und Inhalationsräume."*

The doors to remove the corpses were of wood and could be lifted up. Initially they used iron sliding doors but these did not close hermetically and were replaced by these lift-up doors. At the rear gable side was the engine house. Inside were two big engines and the exhaust was piped into the chambers. The corpses were brought into the pits. The pits were dug around the gas chamber building all of different dimensions: about 50 meters long, 25 meters wide and 10 meters deep.

This job I had to do until December 1942. In this month the gassing was finished. Then I supervised the digging out and burning of about 520,000 corpses.

Hans Girtzig, the male nurse from Grafeneck, was among the first support group of 50 T4 personnel transferred to *Reinhardt* for an unknown duty. Girtzig is a good example of how T4 personnel were lured into *Reinhardt,* not knowing the purpose for which they were being engaged.[478] After induction they were handed over to Wirth and given a choice as to who they would prefer to serve under: Reichleitner (Sobibór), Stangl (Treblinka) or Wirth (Belzec). Girtzig elected to go with Stangl, as he knew him; others elected for Reichleitner, but very few elected to go with Wirth. Wirth ordered all those who had opted for Stangl or Reichleitner to be switched to his *Kommando* in Belzec. Those who had opted for Wirth were sent to Sobibór or Treblinka.[479] The reason for this is unknown, but I suspect it was just one of the ways in which Wirth stamped his authority on subordinates.[480]

SS-Scharführer Hans Girtzig was appointed Quartermaster (procuring provisions). It was only after his posting that he became fully aware of Belzec's purpose.[481] When Wirth ordered him to the Ramp to unload Jewish "resettlement transports," he refused. Wirth detained him, locked him under guard in his quarters and threatened to send him to a KZ. Girtzig maintained his position and invited the KZ option. What Wirth would have eventually decided to do with Girtzig is not known, but the situation was saved for both men with the arrival at the camp of the T4 managing director, Dieter Allers. Allers calmed the situation by advising Girtzig to hold on, as Wirth would be leaving the camp very shortly. Wirth did in fact leave two days later, on 19 August, when he was appointed Inspector of *Reinhardt* camps.[482] The interesting point here is that Girtzig, having won the moral argument with Wirth, was very soon afterwards integrated into the full extermination process by Hering, Wirth's successor.[483] Therefore, despite efforts to maintain the so-called moral high ground, the individual soon succumbed to involvement in daily mass murder.

Even Wirth's protégé, the guard/cook, *SS-Scharführer* Kurt Franz (later deputy commandant at Treblinka) could not escape vindictive attention. During the early spring gassings (1942) the pits had been filled beyond their capacity and Wirth ordered his favored NCOs, Franz and Hackenholt, to clear the overflowing corpses. When they refused, Wirth attacked them with his whip and beat them into submission.[484] For some months, Franz had been very friendly with his batman (personal butler, assistant, dresser), the Ukrainian guard, Piotr Alexejew. According to Franz, they thought alike and had the same views; much of their off-duty time was spent playing chess together.[485]

When Franz returned from home leave in late July 1942, he learned that Hering had executed Alexejew, allegedly for involvement in partisan activities. Franz had strong words with Wirth and Hering and suggested that if Alexejew was a partisan, so was he. When Wirth decided to remove Franz from kitchen duties to take command of Camp II, the gassing area, Franz refused. Wirth immediately sent him to Treblinka as deputy commandant and replaced him with *SS-Scharführer* Reinhold Feix from the Trawniki training camp.[486] The true reason for Alexejew's death was probably that the leadership had viewed the friendship as a security risk. Similar incidents occurred at Sobibór and Treblinka when SS men were entangled with Jews or Ukrainians.

Accelerated Resettlement

Having overcome the initial difficulties at Belzec, there were still concerns within the HHE as to the slow progress of the deportations. *Staatssekretär* Dr. Josef Bühler (KdF) made inquiries of the HSSPF (F.W. Krüger) in Kraków, questioning the lack of urgency of the deportations. Krüger stalled and informed Bühler that after having assessed the situation, he would reply by August.[487] The deportation transports had stalled mainly due to the *Wehrmacht* claiming priority of all trains for the war front. The situation was further complicated when the Chełm-Sobibór rail-link completely broke down, temporarily taking Sobibór out of commission. All this notwithstanding, HSSPF Krüger in Kraków made his own local arrangements and somehow kept the transports to the death camps moving. Even at the height of "Stalingrad" (December 1942 to January 1943), when the *Wehrmacht* stopped all civilian transports, Himmler managed to continue to supply victims to the death camps.

A high-level conference, convened between *SS-Obergruppenführer* Wolff (Himmler's chief-of-staff) and Dr. Ganzenmüller (Transport Minister), had the required result. Beginning on 22 July 1942, 5,000 Jews would be leaving

Warsaw twice weekly for Treblinka and another transport of 5,000 Jews would be deported on a similar schedule from Przemsyl to Belzec.[488]

The euphoria of the SS was short-lived as other delays clogged up the works, threatening to throw Himmler's calculations off course, particularly in December 1942. But by this time, Belzec had ceased resettlement operations; the bulk of East Galician Jews were no more.

On 19 July 1942 an order issued by the HHE, personally signed by Himmler, ordered the resettlement of all Jews in the *Generalgouvernment* and further commanded that the expulsions should be completed by 31 December 1942.[489] The only dissenting voices to be heard came from the military who argued successfully that losing all Jews would compromise urgent war production and present critical labor problems.[490] Himmler's answer came in a memorandum to General von Gienanth on 9 October 1942, amending his previous order but stipulating adherence to certain conditions, without exception.[491] As the result of this turn-about, there was a flurry of communications between the military and the SS, each trying to substantiate its claims for Jewish labor. For the Galician Jews, this was a respite; but it was only of a temporary nature.

A communiqué from the Military Commander in the *Generalgouvernment*, dated 17 August 1942, reported the mood of the Jews in Lvov to be exceptionally depressed, yet astonishingly composed. The report concluded: "Lvov must contain 100,000 Jews (based on food rations) but since 10 August, some 25,000 Jews were re-settled out to Belzec and another 15,000 will have to follow them before this operation is closed."[492] In the same report: "Our Jewish labor has enabled the military to continue their enterprises unaffected."[493] The Military Governor claimed success due to an understanding between Chief Field HQ 365 and HSSPF Krüger in Kraków that their Jewish workers and families would be exempted from resettlement.[494] It was added, however, that they expected further selections to take place and that those Jews retained for specialist labor would soon lose their families to "resettlement" operations in the coming weeks.[495]

The whole question of labor versus destruction was manifesting itself in different guises. Intercepted radio decodes for October 1942 indicate that Höß in Auschwitz was so concerned that his source of suitable labor was being hijacked from deportation trains (*en route* for extermination) from "*Polo-Czech-Neiderländischen,*" that he complained to Eichmann. Höß requested that the deportation trains not stop at Kosel (Kozle) but should proceed directly to Auschwitz.[496] The struggle for supremacy over "labor" was a constant source of infighting and was commonplace during this period. Apparently, *SS- Brigadeführer* Albrecht Schmelt (Kattowitz), encouraged by Albert Speer, Minister of Armaments and Munitions, was intercepting deportation transports and removing fit Jews to work in the steel and coal industries.[497]

Romanian Jews Escape Deportation

On 22 August 1942, British Intelligence intercepted German radio transmissions regarding invitations sent from the WVHA to selected officers to attend a conference on 28 August at the RSHA Berlin (Kurfürstenstrasse 116). This was Eichmann's address: IV B4, the Jewish Affairs Department of the RSHA. Those who attended included Eichmann, Höß (KZ Auschwitz), and Pister (KZ Buchenwald), among others. On 24 August, radio decodes show Globocnik contacting *SS-Sturmbannführer* Rolf Günther (Eichmann's deputy in IV B4) about the evacuation of Romanian Jews, and that all deportation trains should be directed to Trawniki from where further distribution would take place (to Belzec).[498] A further conference on the deportation logistics did not take place until 26-28 September 1942, a month later. So, even here, plans for resettlements were being sealed in advance. However, on this occasion, unfortunately for Eichmann, at the last minute the Romanian rail representatives failed to attend the conference and the deportations never took place. [499]

Deportations from Kołomyja to Belzec (1)[500]

During the period 1939-1941, thousands of Jews fled from surrounding towns to what they thought was the safety of Kołomyja and its neighboring towns and villages. The area was already heavily populated with Jews, and the Jewish population of Kołomyja swelled to over 60,000. Tragically, it was to become the central transit and extermination center for the Jewish population of that district. Mass killings had been occurring there since October 1941, the majority by shooting operations in local forests. Nevertheless, 16,000 Jews still remaining in the ghetto and surrounding districts were sent to Belzec in four large transports: two in April, and two in September 1942.

As the ghettos in Galicia were self-governing, a most essential requisite was the maintenance of law and order and the keeping up-to-date of population records, as required by the SD. This brought about the establishment of the Jewish *Ordnungsdienst* (Order Service), a paramilitary ghetto police armed with rubber truncheons and wearing a distinguishable uniform. Initially, the Jewish auxiliaries did their best to be fair and considerate when maintaining law and order, but when used by the SD for "resettlement" operations, their own people accused them of collaboration[501] and brutality. In Stanisławow, the Jewish Order Police were told that if they failed to bring the allotted quota of Jews for transports, then they and their families would make up the shortfall. In the eyes of their communities, the Jewish Order Police became corrupt tools of the murder machinery and an extension of the *Gestapo*.[502]

At the end of the war, only 200 Jews had survived from the Kołomyja deportations, and it is from a small number of these survivors that we are able to piece together the calendar of events during this period of Nazi occupation.

Deportations from Kołomyja and Zamosc - April to August 1942

Following the first transports from Lvov and Lublin to Belzec in March 1942, simultaneous mass deportations commenced from East Galicia and the regions south of Lublin.

In April 1942 deportations to Belzec began in Tarnopol and Zloczów and then moved on to other areas: Sambor, Drohobycz, Czortków, Stanisławów, Stryj and Kołomyja.[503] On 2 April 1942 the head of the Sipo-SD office in Kołomyja, *SS-Hauptsturmführer* Peter Leideritz (zbV),[504] organized the first deportation and resettlement transports for Jews in the southern part of east Galicia. Jewish workers on the way to their place of work in the German armament factories were suddenly arrested and assembled in Kasarnik Street to await an SS selection commission. The old and frail were selected for transport and separated, the others were sent back to work.

At 05:00 on 3 April, ghetto "A" was surrounded by detachments of Schupo, Jewish Police, SD and Ukrainian Auxiliary Police. Other members of the Sipo-SD, commanded by Peter Leideritz, augmented by additional forces of the Schupo from Tarnopol, entered the ghetto. All Jews were removed forcibly from their dwellings, and the sick, the old and those considered unfit for transport, were shot on the spot.[505] The remaining Jews were concentrated in the synagogue, where they underwent further selection. Those deemed fit for labor were released and sent home. Those remaining were taken to the railway station and loaded into boxcars for transportation to Belzec.[506]

On 4 April, the same procedure was repeated in ghetto "B." Elderly Jews and those classified as unfit for work were taken to boxcars where they were kept without food or water. On 6 April, ghetto "C" was targeted. As many Jews now knew the likely course of events, they went into hiding. Those found were killed on the spot without regard to age, fitness, or sex. Parts of the ghetto were set on fire to prevent any escape of those concealed in their prepared hiding places, while SS and auxiliaries stood guard near the burning houses to shoot anyone attempting to break out. During these proceedings, several hundred Jews were killed inside the ghettos; 5,000 were taken to the waiting transport where they joined the other deportees, including a small shipment of Jews brought in from the surrounding towns and villages.[507]

On 7 April 1942 all the Jews held over the past few days were loaded, 140 to a wagon, and the train departed on schedule for Belzec via Janowska (which had become the main transit point for all transports to Belzec),[508] where 100 fit Jews were off-loaded and replaced by 100 naked, unemployable Jews.[509]

Some 18 hours later, the Kołomyja transport arrived at Belzec where the deportees were destined for "special treatment." There were no survivors.

Between the 22 and 26 April 1942, a further 4,000 Jews were brought to Kołomyja from smaller towns to replenish the ghetto.[510] Approximately 1,000 were immediately sent to the local prison prior to "special treatment" in local forests. This cycle of selection and destruction then recommenced.

Zamosc Region

Jews who managed to avoid deportation fell prey to executions. They were not only hunted down like animals and shot in the streets, the Nazi-appointed Jewish Councils were also ordered to pay for the ammunition expended.[511]

On 11 April 1942 the deportation of Jews from Chełm to Belzec took place, and it was noticed by the "transport watchers" that when the empty train returned to Zamosc, it waited there. The following day, 2,500 were evacuated from Zamosc to Belzec. In the neighboring towns of Szczebrzeszyn, Biłgoraj, Frampol and Zwierzyniec there was panic.[512] Jewish women fled to the sanctuary of the cemetery, some to the forests, and others even as far as Warsaw, preferring to die there than be killed in the concentration camps or shot down in the street like dogs. There was now a lull in the evacuations for the rest of April, which was probably due to Belzec's limited reception abilities during the reconstruction of the second phase gas chambers.

Further Deportations

August 1942 saw further evacuations to Belzec from the regions of Zamosc and East Galicia. Between 10 and 23 August, 40,000 Jews from Lvov were deported to the death camp. In the Zamosc region on 9 August, 1,000 Jews were "evacuated" from Biłgoraj to Belzec.[513] The deportations and mass shootings continued until October 1942, when the Zamosc district was officially declared "*Judenrein*" (clean of Jews).[514]

In September 1942 further deportations from areas previously targeted—Tarnopol, Złoczów, Sambor, Drohobycz, Czortków, Stanisławów, Stryj and Kołomyja—rolled on continuously until the end of the year.[515] The train timetable for the Kołomyja transport on 10 September 1942 shows a number of intermediary stations between Kołomyja and Belzec. Each station *en route* was notified of all Jewish transports: "PKR" (death train), showing the number of *pieces* (passengers). A further indication of the size of the transport was also shown by the entry: "*50G - fünfzig Güterwagen*" (50 goods wagons). After reaching Belzec, where the train was unloaded and readied for return, it was annotated on the railway documents as a "*Leerzug*" (empty train). All scheduled times of arrival and departure for the incoming and return journey were shown. All "special trains" were costed on the basis of so many *pfennings* per track-kilometer. On present day rail-line maps, the distance in kilometers is shown between stopping points (Lvov to Rawa Ruska 137 km, Rawa Ruska to Belzec 36 km, etc.). By the very nature of these special transports there were, of course, exceptional problems and costs.

The policy of spreading lime in wagons before departure was a contributory factor to the number of deaths *en route.* As previously noted 25 percent (2,000) of the Kołomyja transport of 10 September was dead on arrival at Belzec. Many Jews broke out of the wagons, causing serious damage to railway property. The cost of cleaning and repairing these wagons before the return journey was taken into account in the final reckoning, as invoiced to the RSHA. Despite all of this, when Claude Lanzmann interviewed Walter Stier, head of *Abteilung* 33 of the Reichsbahn (Dept. 33 of the *Reichsbahn*) and the organizer of these transports, for his documentary film "*Shoah,*" Stier stated that he had no idea of the purpose of these transports.[516]

Modus Operandi of Deportations[517]

How did the deportations work in practice? If we take the Kołomyja resettlements of 7-10 September 1942, we find that the handling agent was the SD of the Kołomyja district. Orders received from the coordinating central command post (ARHQ)[518] to the HSSPF Galicia District in Lvov set in motion the orders for destruction.[519] Orders were then issued to the commanders of the Orpo and SD in the Kołomyja district (Hans Krüger/Stanisławow and Peter Leideritz/Kołomyja). Depending on circumstances and ongoing operations at the time, the security leaders were given a certain amount of flexibility. In the Kołomyja resettlement, orders were issued on 31 August 1942 to the Orpo command center where at this time the Orpo were engaged in "resettlement" activities in the Stryj, Skole, Tarnopol, and Chodorów districts (3-5 September). It is probable that Krüger juggled the transport dates in order for Orpo to complete their current assignment and then go directly to Kołomyja to reinforce the local SD during the impending action. Meanwhile, the SD in Kołomyja was already planning the resettlement operation to commence at 06:00 on 7 September 1942.[520]

The SD, under the direct command of *SS- Obersturmbannführer-Kriminalkommissar* Peter Leideritz, received orders (probably by phone or personal contact with Krüger) and immediately instructed the district *Arbeitsamt*, the labor office in Kołomyja, to draw up lists of the numbers to be "resettled."[521] A large group of Jews, numbers to be confirmed, were booked for "resettlement," leaving Kołomyja at 20:50 on 10 September 1942. Leideritz also contacted his Sipo-SD counterparts in the adjoining districts of Kosów,[522] Horodenka,[523] Kuty,[524] Obertyn, and Sniatyn,[525] where the sweep would extend, and placed them on stand-by.

From experience gained in other "resettled" localities, [526] and precise knowledge of the number of Jews involved, Hans Krüger in Stanisławow ordered reinforcements of the Orpo (*Ordnungspolizei)* into the Kołomyja ghetto to assist his SD and resident Schupo in this particularly large resettlement operation. Thirty-five men of the Vienna Orpo arrived in Kołomyja on 6 September to augment the local security forces. [527] Additional forces, including Reserve Police Regiment 7/24, arrived in Kołomyja on the 6 September with orders to sweep the district. The operation commenced on the morning of 7 September and lasted until the time of departure at 20:50 three days later. [528]

Security Duties

Several groups of the security forces were involved in the big operation in Kołomyja, including two police detachments brought in from outside as back-up; and on 31 August, Police Regiment 24 received orders from the Commander of the *Orpo,* to assist with the Kołomyja transport. [529] The local Schupo—operating in Kołomyja since about October 1941—whose duties until now had been mundane policing tasks in the town, were also suitably placed to assist with the "resettlement" operation. With the onset of the mass murder policies in the *Generalgouvernment,* police duties widened to include ghetto operations, escorting victims to killing sites, and eventually personal involvement in the shooting of victims in other localities. [530]

The majority of Jews marked down for this transport were already in the Kołomyja ghetto, where comprehensive lists of residents were kept. The officials of the labor office, who had a copy of the resident list, issued instructions to all Jews in the ghetto to report to the assembly area in the town square at 05:30 hours on 7 September for registration. At the designated time, 5,300 Jews reported as ordered; a further 600 were added, however, after an additional search of the ghetto, bringing the total to 5,900. The old and the sick were shot immediately after a brief selection, which reduced the total to 4,769. [531] They were then marched to the station, guarded by detachments of Jewish police and auxiliary personnel. [532] These auxiliaries, brandishing horsewhips, and with shouts of *"Jüdische Schweine!"* (Jewish Pigs!), loaded the Jews onto the transport waiting on a branch line away from the main traffic area. The number of Jews in each car was then chalked on the outside and the train finally sealed prior to departure. [533]

In Germany and Czechoslovakia in particular, many "resettlement" transports left from regular *Reichsbahn* mainline railway stations; isolation of the transports was not unusual, however, as there are many reports of transports parked in out of the way locations, especially in the larger cities. In Kraków, for example, transports left from the suburban station at Plaszòw on a specially designated platform, well out of the way of the prying eyes of the local population. In east and west Galicia, the SD was not so sensitive and made whatever arrangements were available to them. During sweeps in the outer districts of Kołomyja, all manner of transport was used: third class railway carriages, motor and horse drawn transport, and even by foot, as we shall see.[534]

At the same time as the Kołomyja round-ups, other selections were carried out in the towns of Horodenka and Sniatyn; thus, on 10 September, a further 20 wagons loaded with several thousand Jews[535] arrived in Kołomyja from these districts and were coupled to the transport already loaded and waiting in the siding. In addition, 1,500 Jews were force-marched through the streets of Kosów, 35 km away, and from Kuty, 50 km distant, in full view of the local population, to be added to the main transport. Several hundred others who were considered unfit to travel on the transport, or who had faltered on the marches, were taken out of the line and shot.

The final loading and sealing of the transport was now complete and the average designated 100 Jews per wagon well exceeded.[536] According to the official report of the supervising officer, 180-200 were crammed into each wagon. In his report of 14 September, the officer commanding the escort guard unit refers to his lack of understanding of how so many Jews could have been crammed into the 20 wagons from Horodenka and Sniatyn. He also refers to the *great heat* on that final day, the suffering the Jews must have experienced, the lack of provisions, the days of waiting in the airless wagons: "It was a catastrophe."[537] Everything considered, it was indeed a catastrophe.

Kołomyja deportation to Belzec 10 September 1942[538]

'Resettlement' Trains to Belzec

The same procedure was used for all subsequent transports from Kołomyja to Belzec. In East Galicia it was certainly the practice for detachments of Schupo personnel to guard the trains until the time of departure to prevent escapes. Extra vigilance was afforded to this particular transport because of the horrendous conditions of overloading, the heat, the lack of water and the general distress of the imprisoned Jews, many of whom had been stripped naked. As darkness fell, there were repeated attempts by the Jews to break out of the wagons. At 19:50 hours, 15 members of the Schupo, led by a Sergeant, arrived to take up positions along the track, prepared to shoot on sight any Jew who attempted to escape.

At 20:50, a second special unit of the Schupo led by *Leutnant der Reserve* Westermann arrived and joined the Jewish resettlement transport for its journey to Belzec.[539] Five men were accommodated in a single passenger carriage at the front of the train and a further five in a carriage at the rear. The supervising officer, anticipating a potential security problem, ordered the guards to deploy along the whole length of the train and to take up positions on the roof and in the brake car. This procedure was adopted for the entire journey to deal with breakouts and, as it turned out, this was well advised:

> On 9 September 1942 I received orders to take over command of the Jewish resettlement train, which was leaving Kolomyja for Belzec on 10 September 1942. On 10 September 1942 at 1930 hours in accordance with my orders, I took over command of the train together with an escort unit consisting of one officer and nine men at the railway yard in Kolomyja. The resettlement train was handed over to me by Hptw.d Schp (*Schutzpolizei Hauptwachtmeister*) Zitzmann. When it was handed over to me the train was already in a highly unsatisfactory state. Zitzmann had informed me of this fact when he handed it over to me. As the train had to depart on schedule and there was no other person who could take responsibility for loading on the Jews, there was nothing left for me to do but to take charge of the transport train in its unsatisfactory state.
>
> The condition of the train notwithstanding, the insufficient number of guards—i.e. one officer and nine men in the escort unit—would have been reason enough for me to refuse to take over command of the train. However, in accordance with my orders, I had to take over the train with the escort manpower I had. Hptw. Zitzmann stayed at the station with his guard unit until the train departed. Both units had their hands full preventing Jews escaping from the cars, since it had meanwhile become so dark that it was not possible to see the next car properly. It was not possible to establish how many Jews escaped from the train before its departure alone; however it is probable that almost all were eliminated during their escape attempts.

At 20.50 the train departed from Kolomyja on schedule. Shortly before its departure I divided up my escort squad, as had been planned beforehand, putting five men at the front and five men at the rear of the train. As the train was, however, very long—fifty-one cars with a total load of 8,200 Jews—this distribution of manpower turned out to be wrong and the next time we stopped I ordered the guards to post themselves right along the length of the train. The guards had to stay on the brake housing for the entire journey. We had only been travelling a short time when the Jews attempted to break out of the wagons on both sides and even through the roof. Some of them succeeded in doing so, with the result that five stations before Stanisławow I phoned the stationmaster in Stanisławow and asked him to have nails and boards ready so that we could board up the damaged cars temporarily and to put some of his *Bahnschutz* (track guards) at my disposal to guard the train. When the train reached Stanisławow the workers from Stanisławow station as well as the *Bahnschutz* were at the station waiting for our train. As soon as the train stopped work began. An hour and a half later I considered it adequately repaired and ordered departure.

However, all of this was of very little help, for only a few stations later when the train was stationary I established that a number of very large holes had been made and all the (barbed) wire on the ventilation windows had been ripped out. As the train was departing I even established that in one of the cars someone was using a hammer and pliers.

At 11:15 hours the train arrived in Lemberg (Lvov). As there was no replacement escort squad, my squad had to continue guarding the train to Belzec. After a short stop at Lemberg station the train went to the suburban station at Klaparow where I handed over nine wagons which had been marked with an "L" and had been designated for Lemberg compulsory labor camp to SS-Obersturmführer Schulz. He then loaded on about 1,000 more Jews and at about 13:30 hours the transport departed again. At Lemberg the engine was replaced and an old engine was attached which was not powerful enough for the weight of the train. The train driver never managed to reach top speed with his engine so that the train, particularly when travelling uphill, moved so slowly that the Jews could jump off without any risk of injury. I ordered the train driver on numerous occasions to drive faster but this was impossible. It was particularly unfortunate that the train frequently stopped in open country.

The escort squad had meanwhile used up all the ammunition that had been brought with us as well as an extra 200 bullets that I had obtained from some soldiers, with the result that we had to rely on stones when the train was moving and fixed bayonets when the train was stationary.

The ever increasing panic among the Jews caused by the intense heat, the overcrowding in the wagons... the stink of the dead bodies—when the wagons were unloaded there were about 2,000 dead in the train— made the transport impossible.

At 18:45 the transport arrived in Belzec and I handed it over to the *SS-Obersturmführer* and head of the camp at 19:30 hours.

Towards 22:00 hours the transport was unloaded. I had to be present during unloading.

I was not able to establish the number of Jews that had escaped.

(Signed) Jäcklein *Zugwachtm. D. Schutzpol.*

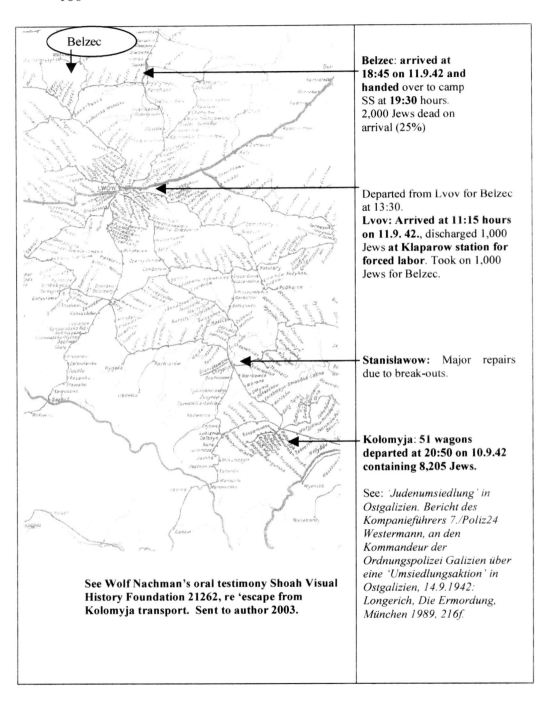

Belzec

Belzec: arrived at
**18:45 on 11.9.42 and
handed** over to camp
SS at **19:30** hours.
2,000 Jews dead on
arrival (25%)

Departed from Lvov for Belzec
at 13:30.
**Lvov: Arrived at 11:15 hours
on 11.9. 42.**, discharged 1,000
Jews **at Klaparow station for
forced labor.** Took on 1,000
Jews for Belzec.

Stanisławow: Major repairs
due to break-outs.

Kołomyja: 51 wagons
departed at 20:50 on 10.9.42
containing 8,205 Jews.

See: *'Judenumsiedlung' in
Ostgalizien. Bericht des
Kompanieführers 7./Poliz24
Westermann, an den
Kommandeur der
Ordnungspolizei Galizien über
eine 'Umsiedlungsaktion' in
Ostgalizien, 14.9.1942:
Longerich, Die Ermordung,
München 1989, 216f.*

**See Wolf Nachman's oral testimony Shoah Visual
History Foundation 21262, re 'escape from
Kolomyja transport. Sent to author 2003.**

Inside the wagons of the Kołomyja transport, which had been standing idle
now for three days, a layer of quicklime had been spread on the floor.[540]

There were no sanitary facilities whatsoever, therefore urination on the lime spread on the floor produced acidic steam, which would burn and peel away skin on contact. There was also the psychological shame of being stripped naked and performing bodily functions in the presence of others, including family, and among mixed sexes; this was more than many could endure.[541] The longer the journey, and in many cases they lasted for several days, the more perilous it became and the impetus to escape was unavoidable, whatever the risk. As a last resort, messages scribbled in haste to family and friends (or to anyone), were thrown from the small ventilating window in the very distant hope that someone might find and read them. Jewelry, shredded zloty banknotes, *Reichsmarks* and dollars were strewn along the tracks. This can be judged an attempt at defiance and resistance.

Once the train was on the move, the first shunting failed to dislodge the people in tightly-packed wagons and almost immediately work began to start on a breakout. Artisans used their tools to tear up the floorboards and remove the window bars, mesh and barbed wire that sealed them in.[542] Women removed hairpins, fasteners, and used their nails to bore and scratch between the boards to allow the smallest amount of air to enter the wagons. As the train gathered speed, decisions were made as to the best time to escape. The hours of darkness were the preferred time, especially when the train was laboring up-hill, or rounding a curve.

The occupants of the wagons were aware that they could expect no mercy from sharpshooting armed guards. The most desperate concern was whether to leave and be separated from one's family; everyone realised that the consequences of escape were unpredictable. Very often, mothers urged their children to jump; fathers would not give advice one way or the other for fear of making the wrong decision; the elderly suffered most because they considered themselves a burden to everyone else. Their will to survive had diminished and they largely accepted the fate that awaited them. We can be sure that most of the Jews from the Kołomyja district were under no illusion that they were not on a death transport. Some, however, refused to accept this and deluded themselves that not all was lost. Others had gone mad in their despair.

No sooner had the train left Kołomyja on its journey to Belzec than mayhem began: Jews broke out at every conceivable point along the train, some through the small windows and others through the roof. Five stations before Stanisławow, (probably Hotoszków), the guard radioed ahead for help, reporting considerable damage to the wagons.[543] When the transport arrived at Stanisławow, the railway guards were ready to re-seal the train for its onward journey towards Lvov, Rawa Ruska and Belzec. Just how many "jumpers" on this "resettlement" train managed to escape between Kołomyja and Stanisławow is not known, but there were several.[544] We know the names of three Jewish survivors who were to bear witness: Feder, Zenner, and Mrs. Weinheber.[545]

After a two-hour delay in Stanisławow for repairs, the transport departed for the suburban station of Klaparow-Janowska in Lvov. Several stations along the line, another mass breakout was attempted; several holes appeared in the sides of the wagons and the barbed wire securing the small ventilation windows was torn away again. *En route* to Lvov, the train was forced to stop at each station for emergency repairs until it eventually arrived at Klaparow station at 11:15 on 11 September. A total of 1,000 Jews in nine of the freight wagons, each marked with an "L," were designated forced labor for KZ Janowska[546] and were taken off the transport, to be immediately replaced by another 1,000 naked Jews brought from Janowska who had been tagged for "special treatment" at Belzec.

At 13:30 on 11 September, the "resettlement" train eventually left Klaparow for Belzec. The Jews, now in complete panic, knew that time was running out. Consequently, even more desperate and repeated attempts to break out occurred between Lvov-Rawa Ruska and Belzec.

As already noted, September 1942 was an exceptionally hot month and the majority of Jews had been imprisoned in the wagons since the early morning of 7 September. Only one station—Rawa Ruska—now separated the 8,250 Jews, men, women and children, packed into 51 wagons, from their destination. From there it was only a 30-minute journey along a single track to the death camp. Which begs the question: if the Jews *knew* the purpose of their deportation, how were they so deceived on arrival in Belzec?

On 9 September, SD officers entered the Jewish Orphans' Home in the Kołomyja ghetto, which housed approximately 400 children whose parents had either already been murdered or were waiting at that very moment in the wagons destined for Belzec. The orphanage was located in ghetto "B" and was spared when the ghetto was liquidated. It was planned to remove the children into ghetto "A," but this never materialized. The night before the transfer was to take place *Leutnant der Schupo* Hertl arrived at the orphanage with several Schupo men and shot all the children. The wife of SS-Peter Leideritz was present and assisted in this massacre.[547]

The Kołomyja transport was typical of many hundreds of resettlement transports carried out in the *Generalgouvernment*. It is known that between March and December 1942, over 400 Jewish communities were subjected to "resettlement" operations in the Galician District and transported to Belzec.[548] There are first-hand accounts of the agonies endured by the Jews during the course of these death transports to Belzec.

Deportations on Holy Days

The list of ghettos and communities in the Lvov District cleared of Jews throughout September was longer than ever before, about 70 altogether. On 3-4 September, the first Sabbath eve of the month, 8,000 Jews were deported to Belzec—4,000 from the Lvov ghetto, and 22,000 from Bolechow,

Brzozdowce, Chodorow, Dzialdoszyce, Miechow, Mikolajow, Proszowice, Rozdol, Sambor, Skalbmierz, Skale, Slomniki, Zurawno and Zydaczow. On 9 September, another 3,000 were deported from Bilgoraj in the Lublin District. Following the Nazi penchant for organizing "resettlements" on Jewish holidays, on 12 September—the first day of Rosh Hashanah, the Jewish New Year—about 5,000 Galician Jews were rounded up in the Stanisławow ghetto; and the second day of New Year, a further 8,000 in Brzesko, Tuchow, Zabno and Zakliczyn in the Kracόw District were loaded into a transport train of 45 wagons, each wagon containing around 120 people. Yom Kippur—the Day of Atonement in the Jewish calender—fell on 21 September and on that day 5,500 Jews were deported from the Rohatyn ghetto and a dozen other communities in the area, together with another 1,500 Jews from Biłgoraj in the Lublin District. During the first three weeks of the month, i.e. up until the time of the Jewish New Year, over 100,000 Jews were deported to Belzec for extermination; a further 16,000 were deported from the Lvov District during the last five days of the month. An operation that began on 26 September, a Sabbath day, brought the final total of victims for September to 116,000.

Chapter 10. Final Stage of the Journey to Belzec

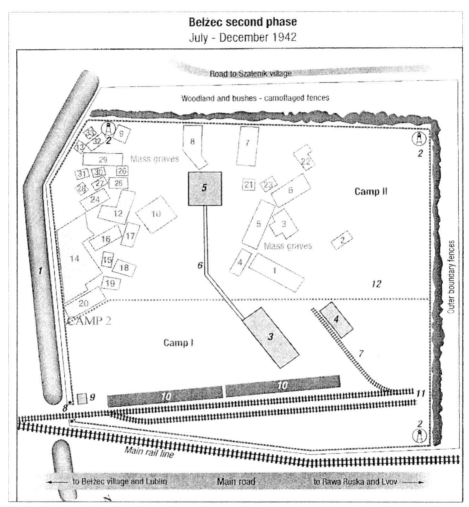

Author's reconstruction from the evidence. Key: Numbered irregular shapes 1-33 are mass graves as located. 1. Anti-tank ditch fortification 1940. 2. Watchtowers. 3. Undressing and haircutting barracks. 4. Warehouse.5. Gas Chamber. 6. The Tube. 7. Rail link. 8 Main gate. 9. Gate house. 10. Ramp. 11. Rail siding.

The Belzec Paintings

The author visited the priest's house in Belzec in 1987 and later in 1998 when engaged with the archaeological investigation. The paintings were hanging on the wall for all to see. The author photographed the paintings *in situ*. Unfortunately, the original photographs were lost in transit via the

Polish postal services and duplicates taken at a later date, with permission, are now shown.

In the 1960s, Waclaw Kolodziejczyk, a former worker at the Belzec railway station, created six paintings showing Belzec during the German occupation. In the years 1939-1944 Kolodziejczyk supervised repairs to the rail tracks, and lived with his family in buildings close by Belzec station. Because he spoke and understood German well, the Germans used him as an interpreter for the purpose of contact with the Polish railway staff. According to some testimonies by local inhabitants from Belzec, he was even temporarily employed in the Commandant's house as the person responsible for the SS store. There he had contact with the Jewish prisoners from the death camp who worked in the SS houses, and he probably learned some details about the camp from them. He never personally entered the death camp.

He and his family were witnesses to the manner in which Jews were deported to the Belzec death camp. They saw the transports at the railway station. As his son testified: "When I was a child, together with my parents I lived close to the railway and the territory of the camp. I remember transports arrived with Jews. Guarded by Ukrainians, other Jews were employed in the transport from the camp of the clothes of Jews who had been killed. The clothes were transported on small railway trolleys and the clothing was sorted. Then the clothes were loaded onto wagons and were sent by rail in the direction of Lublin. I remember transports arrived and the Jews who were sitting in the wagons begged for water."

Waclaw Kolodziejczyk retained his memories of the camp until the 1960s. After he had retired, he decided to produce the paintings in order to present both his knowledge and his visualization of the camp. Because he had never been inside the camp, many details are the product of his imagination.

Painting 1

In the first painting (above), where the arrival of a transport and the moment of unloading are visible, we can see a depiction of the speech given to the deportees by the "Jew Irrmann." This is the first incorrect piece of information. Irrmann was an SS-man who usually gave a speech to the arriving deportees, but sometimes this speech was given by the functionary prisoner from the camp, Sylko Herz, probably in Yiddish.

Painting 2

In the second painting (on the previous page), showing the moment of the burning of the deported Jews, there is no information about the gas chambers. It is probable that Waclaw Kolodziejczyk did not know about the gas chambers and since he had never seen them and did not know how they operated, he did not show them. On the painting there is a depiction of the victims being burned alive.

Painting 3

The third painting (above) is about the punishment of Bartlomiej Panasowiec, an inhabitant of Belzec who was caught by the Germans in the act of spying on the camp. SS-men on horseback from the camp chased him, setting a dog on him and beating him. Panasowiec had to run through the whole village. This was intended to be an example to all the inhabitants of what people who wanted to know too much could expect. Bartlomiej Panasowiec was seriously wounded but survived. Because he was Ukrainian, he and some of his family were resettled to Ukraine after 1944. Even today Panasowiec's story is very well known in Belzec.

Painting 4

The fourth painting (above), presents the old railway station in Belzec. All transports with Jews deported to the death camp arrived at this station. Documentation about the transports, notably the transfer telegrams, was also kept in this building. In July 1944, two weeks before the Soviet army entered Belzec, the railway station was bombed by a single Soviet airplane. A German transport loaded with ammunition was standing in the station and was destroyed. Because of the exploding ammunition, all structures within a radius of about 250 m., including the railway station, were completely demolished. It was at this time that the original documentation about the transports was lost.

Shortly before his death Waclaw Kolodziejczyk donated his paintings to the parish church in Belzec. These paintings remain in the old house of the priests today. The Catholic priests in Belzec make no problems for visitors to Belzec who wish to see the paintings. The paintings are presented as a "good original source" and good primary evidence.

Final Approach

The height of the "resettlement" traffic was during September 1942 when several trains daily were scheduled for Belzec via Lvov and Rawa Ruska. On one transport waiting in Rawa Ruska, an 11-year-old boy was thrown out of a wagon window in a futile bid to save his life. The boy was immediately shot by waiting guards.[549] Many young children were found dead or injured on the railway track between Rawa Ruska and Belzec, not after any determined escape, but simply thrown out of the wagons by their parents in a desperate bid to save them from the alternative. From all over Poland people witnessed children being thrown out of trains. Efraim Franciszek, a railway worker at Rawa Ruska station, speaks of naked Jews escaping uninjured from the transports but being offered little help by the local population:

I know of no single case in which local Poles had rescued such an escaper. At the most, they helped by giving a piece of bread. The Germans had issued special orders to the population to report if any naked Jews were found.[550]

Approaching Belzec from the direction of Lublin, the "resettlement" trains stopped at Zwierzyniec, 28 km from Belzec, where similar regulations applied. In addition, the same frantic quest for escape occupied the Jews on these transports. On a transport from the direction of Lvov several Jews jumped from a speeding train and escaped. One boy who survived the jump, Yacov Gurfein, fell to the ground and waited. When the train finally moved off after a search, Yacov walked to Jaroslaw and took a train to Przemyśl. He survived the war.[551]

One evening in late 1942, a transport arrived in Belzec railway station from Tarnòw. It had to wait all night on a siding, guarded by Ukrainians from the camp guard unit. From the inside the wagons came terrible wailing and cries for water. In some of the wagons, Jews had broken through the barred windows and jumped to the ground, where they were shot by the Ukrainian guards. In the morning, 34 bodies were counted on one side of the track. Helen Goldman, a young girl in her teens, was being transported with her family from Jawarów via Lvov to Belzec in August 1942. She, with others, broke out of the train *en route*, escaped and survived the war.[552] From the same town in September, Jadzia Beer got her skirt caught in the car window in her attempt to jump the train. She was shot. In each deportation to the death camps, Jews tried to jump from the trains. The above stories and accounts are just examples of what occurred.

Camp Entry

Once a "resettlement" train had received clearance from Belzec station, the train, on a single track, took approximately 30 minutes to reach Belzec camp. On arrival, the Kołomyja transport of 51 wagons (to which reference was previously made) was shunted onto a station siding. There commenced the ritual of entry into the camp proper—up to 20 wagons at a time, personally driven by the German station master at Belzec, Rudolf Göckel, who was the only *Reichsbahn* official permitted to enter the camp. All other personnel, including the escorting guards and Schupo, were prohibited from entering Belzec camp and were required to patrol the area between the station and the camp gates. After the unloading in the camp, Göckel, accompanied by one of the camp SS-NCOs, personally checked each wagon; and when all was clear, he waved his flag and returned to bring in the next load.[553]

Göckel was the railway intermediary with the camp administration. In 1946, he was arrested in Eisenach, E. Germany, and in May 1947 deported to Poland and sentenced as a war criminal by a court in Zamosc. He was released in 1950 due to an amnesty.

To the accompaniment of the camp musicians,[554] 20 wagons were shunted through the main gates, closely guarded by the SS and Ukrainian guards. Once inside the camp proper, the camouflaged main gates were closed until the first intake had been dealt with. Overlooking the whole process was a centrally sited watchtower manned by armed Ukrainians. Everything was now automated to deal with the transport as quickly and efficiently as possible.

Dead on Arrival[555]

As already noted, when the Kołomyja transport arrived at Belzec and was unloaded inside the camp, 2,000 Jews, men, women and children (25 percent) were found dead in the wagons.[556]

According to Rudolf Reder, who had arrived with his wife on 17 August,[557] the Jews were driven out of the wagons by the Ukrainians and had to jump one meter to the ground, where they were ordered to strip naked. The duty officer supervising this particular transport, *SS-Scharführer* Fritz Irrmann, gave the usual speech to the Jews that they had come here to work, but first they must bathe: *"Ihr geht jetzt baden, nachher werdet ihr zur Arbeit geschickt!"* (You are now going to have a bath. Afterwards you will be sent to work).[558] One of the few artifacts that survived the Nazi demolition of the camp is one of the original information boards directing the Jews to the gas chambers:

Attention!
Complete removal of clothing!
All personal belongings, except money, jewelry, documents and certificates must be left on the ground. Money, jewelry and documents must be kept until being deposited at the window. Shoes must be collected and tied in pairs and put in the place indicated.[559]

A short time later, the men marched naked towards the "tube." The women, after undressing, were driven to the haircutting barrack where a hundred "barber" chairs beckoned them to have their hair shaved. After the haircutting had been completed,[560] the women were also driven along the "tube" to the gas chambers. By this time, the men were already lying dead in the pits. To enter the chambers, the Jews had to climb up several steps to the entrance; but they could see nothing of what was going on around them as the graves and the density of trees hid all other activities including the pits. Even in winter, as the trees were firs, they maintained this camouflage.

During this period—August to September—which was the peak of the "resettlement" operations, three transports per day were arriving in Belzec.[561] The conditions at the ramp even shocked the supervising SS: piles of fly-ridden putrid-smelling bodies were just dumped on the ramp awaiting removal by the Jewish-work brigade. Those too ill or too weak to proceed through the extermination process unaided were left lying on the ramp until the rest of the transport had been dealt with. Then they were taken to the execution pit and shot.[562] Shooting of the elderly and the sick was normally carried out by a designated SS-NCO at the unloading ramp. *SS-Scharführer* Robert Jührs was posted to this area about the time the Kołomyja transports were arriving:

> On this transport, the wagons were grossly overfilled and there were very many Jews who were not able to move. It could be that … Jews had been pushed to the floor and trampled. In any case, there were Jews who in no way were able to go to the undressing barracks. As usual, Hering appeared and gave the order to shoot the Jews. "Jührs, take these people to Camp II and shoot them."[563]

Camp Reception

Once the chambers were full and the doors were sealed tight, a Jewish *Zugführer*[564] named Moniek, a cab driver from Kraków[565] signalled to the gas-engine mechanics to start the engine. During gassing operations, the camp orchestra played continuously to drown out the screams and shouts. After the engine had been running for about 20 minutes, Moniek again signalled to the mechanics to switch the engine off.[566] While this was going on, Rudolf Reder was fully engaged at working the excavator, digging graves and observing the gassing of his fellow man.[567] Reder's assessment that 33 mass graves were located within the designated area of Camp II was, incidentally, corroborated by the subsequent investigations in 1997-99. Some of these graves were enormous and it is difficult to imagine how they may have looked. On average, according to Reder, it took gravediggers a week to dig one grave and that was with the assistance of a mechanical earth removing machine and conveyor belt, which took the sandy earth from the bottom of the grave and deposited it at the rim. The investigating team in 1998 examined these graves to a depth of six meters. In grave No. 14, which was undoubtedly the biggest and dated from the first phase, it would have been possible to drop two houses into the cavity with room to spare. Others were much smaller but still large enough to contain several thousand corpses.[568]

The gassing operation in Belzec was strictly off-limits to outsiders; even to some of the SS garrison. Throughout the first and second phases of Belzec, the gassing installations and operation were in the hands of just one man, *SS-Scharführer* Lorenz Hackenholt, who worked continuously with the assistance of selected Ukrainians and Jewish Kapos.[569]

When the German visitor Professor Pfannenstiel wanted to know what was going on inside, he was invited to put his ear to a door and listen. Pfannenstiel did just this and remarked, "just like in a synagogue."[570] Glass peepholes had been inserted into the doors; but on this occasion, Pfannenstiel stated, when he attempted to look inside he could not see anything as the glass was steamed over. After the signal had been given that the gassing was over, the "death brigade," led by the *Zugführer*, immediately went to work, pulling out the corpses with leather straps. The victims lay inside the gas chambers, criss-crossed and intertwined with one another. One by one, the Jewish "death brigade" dragged the corpses to the open graves.[571] The next task was to clean the gas chambers and prepare them for the women and children who would soon arrive to be dealt with in the same way.

The property from each transport was collected and sent to the old locomotive shed near Belzec station for sorting and initial cleaning, then on to Lublin by rail. Cash and valuables were dealt with separately and collected by a special courier from T4 in Berlin.

Temporary Reprieve

In the Lvov region, plans were being made for more transports to Belzec; but the wrangle over Jewish labor between the SS, the *Wehrmacht* and the WVHA continued. On 17 September 1942 the operations officer, Chief Field HQ 365 (Beuttel), made a further report to the Military Commander of the *Generalgouvernment* concerning the continuing Jewish "resettlement," which was having a detrimental effect on the armaments industry. Once again, a compromise was reached between the wartime manufacturers and the SS;[572] although these actions relieved the situation for both the armament contractors and the Jews, neither was under any illusion about the eventual outcome. With further "resettlement" operations planned for the Jews of Lvov, the SS knew full well that political priorities would take precedence and that their Jewish workers would eventually be "resettled." The death sentence had long since been given—it was the timing that remained to be decided. The skilled Jewish workers and their families, already on borrowed time, were again reprieved from immediate "resettlement" but were in no doubt that this was only a temporary respite as they had heard rumors of the likely outcome. These circumstances induced considerable depression and even suicides among the Lvov Jews during the course of this waiting game.

'Lazarett': Execution Pit

In the death camps and the majority of KZs where instant killings were carried out, there was always a special place set aside for additional executions known as the "Lazarett," a reception area camouflaged to look like a field hospital and intended to deceive the victims that medical assistance was at hand. In Belzec during the first phase these executions may have taken place at the several small graves in the northeast corner. In the second phase, it was Grave No. 2—which fits Gley's description accurately. According to the evidence given by Reder after the war, SS-Scharführer Fritz Irrmann was a specialist at this deadly work:

> At the edge of the grave, the elderly, the children and the sick were waiting with insane expressions in their eyes, staring dully into the grave. They were waiting for death and were allowed to see their fill of the corpses, the blood, and the stench of putrefaction before SS-Scharführer Irrmann swept them into the grave with gunshots and the butt of his gun.[573]

In Sobibór and Treblinka, Wirth introduced somewhat more "sophisticated" arrangements. Rather like Dr. Schöngarth in Lvov and Hans Krüger in Stanisławow, Wirth demonstrated to his men how these executions were to be carried out.[574] Many children were liquidated in the pits rather than in the gas chambers. These victims were the toddlers, children who had no mothers to undress them and lead them to the gas chambers, and the small children of large families whose mothers had their hands full. These children were separated and taken to the graveside to be shot or bludgeoned to death. According to the Belzec survivor Chaim Hirszman, he witnessed on one occasion how many babies and very young children were just thrown alive into a pit and then covered with sand.[575] He was horrified to see the earth moving until they had all suffocated to death. In Treblinka, the duty executioner smashed children's heads against a wall and then threw the bodies into the burning ditch of the Lazarett.[576] The most important considerations were the conservation of bullets or gas. *SS-Scharführer* August Miete (who was not SS) worked in the reception camp at Treblinka selecting Jews for the *Lazarett*:

> I fired at the nape of the neck with a 9 mm. pistol. Those shot would fall ... into the pit. The number of people shot in this way from each transport varied. Sometimes two or three and sometimes 20, or even more. They included men and women, young and old, and also children.[577]

As the killing progressed in the *Lazarett*, these procedures became more sophisticated. Lessons learned in Belzec were implemented in Sobibór and Treblinka. For example, the sick and disabled Jews were now guided by a selected group of Jewish camp personnel to the *Lazarett*. In a small hut in Treblinka, manned by two members of the Jewish "work brigade," a white-coated bogus Red Cross official (an SS-NCO dressed in white doctor's coat) invited the victims into the hut.[578] Once taken behind a screen all became clear to them. Before them was a pit, several meters deep and surrounded by an earth bank. In the pit was a burning mass of decomposed bodies infested with flies. Led or stretchered by the "work brigade," and now resigned to their fate, the victims quietly walked or were carried to the edge of the pit and shot in the back of the neck by a pre-positioned executioner, usually the duty *SS-Scharführer* or Ukrainian auxiliary.[579] This was also the fate of Jewish workers in the camp who had contravened the rules, became ill, or had fallen victim to an assault by a guard and sustained serious injuries. Any injury inflicted by a cruel beating, thus making that person unable to work, was an invitation to attend the *Lazarett,* and qualified the victim for immediate attention by the duty SS-NCO. At the order, "*Komm*," the victim was then led for disposal in the pit.

We have the eye-witness accounts of these procedures in Belzec by Rudolf Reder, the Ukrainian guard Nikolai Malagon, and members of the SS-garrison who carried out these summary murders.[580] When their work had been completed the SS garrison relaxed and waited for the next transport, expected to arrive within a few hours. Commandant Franz Stangl at Treblinka would have us believe that these disgusting brutal murders were carried out with consideration, especially if one happened to meet an old acquaintance from times gone by in the *Lazarett*.

German-speaking Jews were often selected in the death camps for special tasks, and chances of survival were also greatly increased if a new arrival knew a camp official personally. It was a well-known fact that the camp SS had their favorites and afforded them special considerations. Stangl was no exception, especially with Jews who arrived in Treblinka from his native Austria. Such was the case of the Jews Blau and Singer, who both received personal attention from Stangl: Singer was appointed chief of the "*Totenjuden*" (Death Jews) and Blau and his wife were given the most sought-after work of cooks in Camp I, the lower camp. According to former

SS-Scharführer Franz Suchomel, Blau had known Stangl in Austria before the war and when he stepped off the transport in Treblinka was greeted as an old friend and immediately appointed *Oberkapo* in the kitchens... and informer.[581]

Old friends can expect favors, regardless of position, and when Blau's 80-year-old father arrived in the camp some time later, Blau sought Stangl's help to ease the inevitable by requesting that he take his father to the *Lazerett* instead of the gas chambers, whereupon Blau senior was taken by his son to the execution pit, given a meal and then shot. Blau said to Stangl: "Herr *Hauptsturmführer*, I want to thank you; I gave him a meal before taking him and now it's all over. Thank you very much."[582]

Final Deportations

November 1942 saw the final round-up of Jews in the Zamosc region for deportation to the death camps. The towns of Zwierzyniec, Szczebrzeszyn, Tarnogrod, Biłgoraj, Krasnobród and Jozefów had all been officially cleared of Jews. Only a few were still holding out in the forests but many of them were forced by hunger and the cold to give themselves up. It was a recurring fact that men, women and children came out of the forests half-dead from starvation and reported to the police posts with a request to be shot. The Germans duly obliged without recourse to higher authority.[583]

On 15 November 1942, 4,000 naked Jews arrived at Belzec from Zamosc. The entire *Judenrat* was on this transport. The men were immediately driven to the gas chambers and the women to the barracks to have their hair shaved. One male Jew, the deputy president of the Judenrat, was selected to remain behind.[584] The Latvian Schmidt ordered the Jewish band to assemble in the yard.[585] To the accompaniment of *"Es geht alles vorüber, es geht alles vorbei"* (Everything passes, everything goes by) and *"Drei Lilien, Drei Lilien, kommt ein Reiter gefahren, bringt die Lilien"* (Three lilies, comes a rider bringing lilies), the *Judenrat* representative was cruelly beaten about the head with whips and ordered to dance and jump in the process. The torture of this man who had done nothing to provoke his attackers went on for several hours, watched by the SS-garrison who stood about laughing: *"Das ist eine höhere Person, Präsident des Judenrates!"* (That is a high-ranking person, president of the *Judenrat*!). In the evening, Schmidt took him to a grave, shot him in the head, and kicked him onto a pile of gassed corpses.[586]

Field of Mass Graves

During the second phase in Belzec, at the highest point of the "resettlement" transports, three transports arrived daily and several thousand victims were "processed" in a matter of hours. A Jew who arrived in the camp at 10:00 would be dead by midday with his body lying in a grave. Simultaneously, personal property, including dental gold, was being processed in an adjoining building. Grave digging was the main task of the "death brigade," working in shifts to open the ground. So organized was the brigade that they always worked with one grave in hand, just for emergencies.[587] The death brigade of 500 Jews worked flat out to clear the corpses. (The numbers of 500 was kept constant by a head count every morning before the arrival of the first transport). When an exceptionally large transport arrived, such as the 51 wagons from Kołomyja in September 1942, when 2,000 Jews were found dead on arrival, extra help was needed. For this purpose, a further 100 naked Jews were taken off the next incoming transport to assist.[588] Once the work had been completed and the emergency was over, the *Volksdeutsche*, Schmidt, marched the 100 Jews to the open grave and shot them. When Schmidt ran out of ammunition he killed the rest with a pickaxe handle.[589] It was not economical to use the gassing facilities for only 100 victims.

A grave was not considered full until the layer of corpses exceeded one meter above ground level. The "body placers" worked to a strict routine, which necessitated their walking over the buried corpses to reach all sides of the grave, even though body fluids engulfed their feet and ankles. According to Reder, this was the worst practice they had to endure. This procedure was tolerated with only their faith to comfort them:[590] Reder stated that most had long since lost all religious belief and merely existed from one day to the next, "like robots"; only a few still prayed quietly at night:

> The brigade consisted mostly of men whose wives, children and parents had been gassed. Many of us managed to get *tallesim* and *tefillin* from the storerooms, and when the door was locked we heard the murmur of the *Kaddish* prayer.[591] We prayed for the dead. Afterwards there was silence. We did not complain as we had resigned ourselves to our fate. Maybe those 15 *Zugführers* were still under some sort of illusion, but not us.
>
> ...We all moved like people who had lost their will. We became one mass of people. I knew their names, but not many. I know that the doctor was a young general practitioner from Przemyśl; his name was Jakubowicz. I also knew a businessman from Kraków called Schlussel, and his son; also a Czech Jew whose name was Ellbogen, he apparently owned a bicycle shop; I knew a man called Goldschmidt who was a well-known chef at the famous "Bruder Hanicka" restaurant in Karlovy Vary. We went through this terrible life like robots.
>
> ...We had to sing songs before lunch and sing before evening coffee. At the same time one could hear the howling of the people being gassed—and the band playing; and opposite the kitchen stood the gallows. The final act of these macabre burials was the closure of the graves. On instructions from the *Zugführer*, the grave top was sprinkled with lime and covered with sand. It looked like a large mound but after a few days the mound had sunk to ground level.

Working conditions for these numbed souls had no let-up. Forced to work at a hard pace while continually being beaten, carrying or pulling corpses, many found life impossible to endure and collapsed, knowing full well what their own fate would be. Any infraction was met by an immediate 25 lashings with a riding whip. To receive this punishment the victim had to count off the lashes, 1 to 25, in German. Failure to keep count resulted in the whole procedure being repeated, but this time it was 50 lashes. Very few Jews were able to withstand such savage treatment and crawled back to the barrack badly injured. There they waited for the inspection and the almost inevitable bullet in the head. According to Reder, the majority died soon after such a beating. Each day after roll call the supervising SS guard recorded a list of the injured, the ill, or those considered "finished." These men were quietly taken to the grave edge and shot into the pit.[592] The scene was macabre as described by Berl Freiberg, a body remover in Sobibór: "When pulling a dead man by the foot to the pit I sat down for a rest; all of a sudden I saw the 'dead' man sit up and ask, 'is it still a long way?'" Any attempt by Freiberg to save the man would have been futile.[593]

Destruction of Evidence

When the Germans realized that their war was not quite going according to plan they began to contemplate the possible aftermath of their genocidal policies. On 30 April 1942 District Commissars throughout the occupied territories received instructions requesting them immediately to submit details of all mass graves in their district to the RSHA in Berlin.[594] The reasons were not long in becoming clear.

Because of a number of setbacks in the military sphere and the possible consequences, Himmler directed that all traces of mass killings must be obliterated throughout the occupied areas. The task of coordinating and carrying out these measures was assigned to *SS-Standartenführer* Paul Blobel.[595] Due to his reputation for drunkenness and belligerency, Blobel was regarded by the HHE as a disgraced officer who had attracted the wrath of his superiors. As a punishment he was transferred to Amt 1VB4, under the supervision of *SS-Gruppenführer* Heinrich Müller, Eichmann's immediate superior. Blobel had been a successful *Einsatzgruppen* commander in Kiev, where he had butchered 35,000 Jews during a three day period—men, women and children who had fallen victim to his command at Babi Yar.[596]

Paul Blobel was entering new and untried territory when given the task of pinpointing all the mass graves throughout the eastern territories. With a small team of operators, known as "*Sonderkommando 1005*," Blobel went to Chełmno (Kulmhof) where they investigated the mass burial sites of the many thousands of victims who had been murdered in gas vans. Blobel began his experimental burning of corpses by adopting various concoctions of fuel and pyres; even explosives were used in these experiments.[597]

On 15 September 1942, secret German radio messages decoded by British Intelligence referred for the first time to the code designation *"Aktion Reinhardt"*: "WVHA gives KZ Auschwitz authority for a vehicle to travel to Łódź and inspect *'Aktion Reinhardt'* research station for field furnaces."

At this time, Blobel was in Chełmno experimenting with the burning of corpses.[598] Depending on the magnitude of the exhumation and cremation tasks, the groups of Jews assigned for this work consisted on average of 40-80 workers. Among the group employed in Fort IX at Kovno, there were four doctors, a pharmacist, an engineer, a mechanic, an artist, a lawyer, and various other professional and working men.[599] In the camps, ghettos, the death camps and any other place of confinement, the composition of personnel was the same. The only thing they had in common was that they were all Jews.

Throughout this grisly process of exhuming and burning the bodies, *Sonderkommando 1005* were chained when carrying out their task. On completion, they were all shot and a new *Kommando* formed to take their place and move on to other designated sites.[600] A special school was set up in the Janowska camp where German camp personnel underwent instruction on how to eradicate mass graves: burn the corpses, grind the bones and plant trees on the sites of the former grave areas. Twelve officers from each area of occupation where mass graves were located attended the course and 10 groups went through the course at Janowska in five months.[601]

The task was so vast and deemed to be so urgent that camp commanders at other locations where mass killings had taken place organized their own "1005" *Kommandos*. In Plaszów KZ, *SS-Hauptsturmführer* Amon Goeth chained his Jews together, even when sleeping. When the work had been completed they too were all shot and a new team selected. In Fort IX at Kovno, Stutthof KZ, and in Vilna, the members of *"Sonderkommando 1005"* were held incommunicado and shackled each day. The chains, weighing two kilos apiece and fastened around both ankles and the waist, were worn permanently for approximately six months. Heavily guarded, the *Kommandos* were marched to the pits daily, where they worked in the most gruesome conditions, including the common occurrence of exhuming their close relatives who had been shot or gassed several months before.[602] These men became immune to all sensitivity. Caked in mud and body fluids, poisoned, depraved and lost, only their spirit drove them on in the hope that some day, vengeance would be possible.

Due to the large number of killing sites, many were overlooked. For example, at the Sipo-SD Academy at Bad Rabka, which had been used as an execution site for that area of southwest Galicia, the mass graves containing over 2,000 corpses were not considered important enough to warrant special attention.[603]

Another secret radio message sent from Lublin on the night of 24 February 1944, intercepted and decoded by British Intelligence, refers to the escape that night of 20 or so *"Geheimnisträger"* (bearers of secrets) from an unspecified camp in the Lublin District. The prisoners had removed their shackles and broken out of a tunnel beyond the camp perimeter.[604] These prisoners were most probably Jews from a *"Sonderkommando 1005"* team engaged in removing and cremating corpses.

Exhumation and Cremation

The "resettlement" transports to the Belzec death camp ceased on 11 December 1942, but preparations were already in place to trigger the corpse burnings. No outsiders entered Belzec for this task: it was carried out by members of the Jewish "death brigade" supervised by SS-NCOs. Although Paul Blobel and his *"Sonderkommando 1005"* had access to camps throughout the occupied area, he had no access to the *Reinhardt* camps.

At Belzec, commandant Hering delegated the *SS-Scharführers* Fritz Tauscher and Heinrich Gley to commence this work with the help of *SS-Scharführer* Lorenz Hackenholt, who had at his disposal the mechanical excavator to dig up the corpses.[605] The exhumation and cremation operations began during the first week of November 1942, and at the beginning of December, according to Gley, who was in charge of their construction, a second cremation pyre was assembled.

The Jewish workers of the "death brigade" labored to build the pyres and to systematically burn and then re-bury the residue of the corpses back into the emptied pits.[606] A "barbecue grill" type system had been devised, and it is noted that other cremation sites, thousands of miles apart, used the same system. Evidence was given by former *Oberscharführer* Gley, who supervised the construction of the pyres in Belzec: "The grates were made by arranging standard gauge railway line sections on top of large stones. Narrow gauge line sections were then placed crossways on top to form a close meshed solid grate."[607] Whether Belzec personnel attended the "cremation classes" in Janowska is not known, but in all probability some expert advice was given.[608]

The preparation and building of the pyres before ignition was most important. Great care was taken to ensure that the right materials were available. A narrow ditch was dug around the fire, into which the fat and fuel from the bodies together with unused fuel would drip, according to testimonies and the evidence of the archaeological dig. The pyres, now intermingled with wood and fuel, gradually rose to a height of several meters, and each contained 2,000 bodies. [609]

The number of pyres used in Belzec is not clear, as witnesses refer to two to five of them. These had been constructed in mid-November 1942 and were in continuous use until March 1943.[610] Although there appears to have been no effort to count and register victims arriving at the camp, great care was taken to note the number of corpses retrieved from the graves.[611] As the bodies were brought to the pyre, a nominated person registered the number of bodies before they were laid out in specified positions.

The Belzec trial testimonies refer to at least 300,000 bodies being cremated on the first pyre and a further 240,000 on the second pyre; therefore, at least 540,000 corpses were cremated on pyres in Belzec.[612] In Treblinka, where the burnings did not commence until February 1943 and were completed in July, at least 700,000 corpses were destroyed.

At the "school for clearing of extermination sites" in Janowska, a clear euphemistic procedure emerged where each task was given a specific name. The excavator would remove the upper layer of the light sandy soil. The "gravediggers" would then commence to uncover the "dolls" (corpses). The "drawers" who, with the help of long poles with hooks, lifted the bodies from the pits to the surface, followed the "gravediggers." "Checkers" extracted gold teeth and dentures from the mouths. After the "checkers" came the "porters" carrying makeshift stretchers, or the "draggers," who with leather belts, dragged or conveyed two "dolls" at a time to the pyres where a group of "fire-fighters" supervised the burning.[613]

According to SS-Oberscharführer Gley, who arrived at Belzec from T4 towards the end of July 1942: [614]

> When all the bodies had been removed from the graves, a special search commando sifted through the earth and extracted all the leftovers: bone, clumps of hair, etc., and threw these remains on the fire. An additional mechanical excavator was brought to accelerate the work. One excavator came from Sobibór and the other from the Warsaw district, which were operated by Hackenholt.[615]

It is interesting to note that during the excavations and burnings by Belzec's "burners," it was found that some bodies burned better than others: the recently gassed burned better than those from the first transports, fat women burned better than thin women, men did not burn well without women, as their fat is better developed than in men. For this reason, the bodies of women were used to build the base of the pyres intermixed with other bodies and combustible material. Blood, too, was found to be a very good combustible material and the young burned even better because of their softer flesh.[616]

Flames leapt into the sky and the stinking smell permeated the area. Smoke from the pyres was seen for miles around and on damp wet days would seldom rise above 10 meters, clinging to the river as it drifted on the wind. Witnesses were affected by the smell and darkened sky as far away as Susiec (15km). Belzec was engulfed in acrid smoke, so it was not difficult to trace the happenings and relate them to the Polish War Crimes Investigation Commission after the war.[617]

In conclusion, if we examine the findings of the Archaeological Investigation at Belzec 1997-99, we can corroborate that there were indeed mass excavations and cremations. The Belzec "burners" however, were not as diligent as they could have been, as a number of graves proved. During the archaeological excavations of 1998, it was proven beyond doubt that certain graves contained unburnt entire corpses, where the sandy soil had compressed corpses into slabs only a few centimeters thick. Even after all these years, when the drills penetrated the Belzec soil, gasses were released, giving the first indication that a mass grave containing corpses was below.[618]

During the course of the cremations, many thousands of Jews on incoming transports must have been met by the sight of the pyres when entering the camp, and could have been under no illusion that they would soon join this scene.[619]

Was the order to dig up and burn all the corpses in the many hundreds of execution sites in the occupied areas issued in order to destroy the evidence? Digging up corpses, burning, and grinding the bones to dust, and then re-burying the residue, would not remove the evidence. Perhaps they wanted to disguise the true numbers of victims who perished in Belzec; not to obliterate the evidence *per se*, but to hide the enormity of the crime.[620]

The Bone Mill

Another innovation that emerged to assist in the obliteration of evidence was a specially constructed machine to destroy the burnt human bones. Initially, the SS looked to the Jews in the Łódż ghetto to supply such a machine and it is not surprising that they failed.[621] Blobel eventually found a machine from the Schriever Company in Hamburg and after much use elsewhere, recommended it to Höß at Auschwitz. The Auschwitz commandant declined the offer as he found his Jewish workers were doing an adequate job with hammers and special mortars.[622]

In their efforts to destroy the evidence, in particular any large bone material, the camp command at Belzec sought outside help from the Janowska KZ by borrowing their bone crushing machine and an operator, a Hungarian Jew named Szpilke. The machine resembled a cement mixer with heavy iron balls inside the revolving drum; as the drum revolved at high speed, the metal balls crushed the bone material into small fragments.[623] At the base of the bone mill there was a sieve, which acted as a filter for the bone material—the fine dust was expelled while larger pieces of still uncrushed bone were retained inside the drum.

The Jews who operated the bone mill were known as the *"Aschkolonne"* (ash brigade). Covered completely in thick white dust, they must have looked a horrific sight.

Belzec's efforts to complete the exhumations and destruction were not devoid of problems, and it was some time before they fell in line with other murder sites in the system of digging up corpses, crushing their bones to powder and burning the corpses to ashes.[624] The destruction of the corpses was of the highest priority. The Jews engaged in this work were subjected to continual bullying and harassment by the guards in order to force them to work faster. Their only consolation was that the SS realised that to work in these conditions and to complete the task, the Jews had to be cared for and fed adequately. In the unhygienic conditions, unusual consideration was given by the SS supervisors to the supply of clothing and footwear for those engaged in this work. After each day's work, personal clothing was disinfected in Lysol, rinsed and dried before further use. Their diet was also improved. For breakfast, each prisoner received a quarter of a loaf of bread, black coffee, honey substitute and cheese spread. After work, they received two liters of thick soup with noodles and meat. The better quality food and personal care of the commando 1005 was one of Blobel's tactics to spur on the workers to finish the work as quickly as possible. Meals were eaten on-site. In the Stutthof Camp the "burners" became callous and hardened, cooking their allocation of potatoes on the burning coals of the pyre.

In Belzec between December 1942 and January 1943, the "death brigade" Jews tending the cremation pyres endured a typhus epidemic and starvation—their numbers decimated by a combination of the sick being shot with no further transports to replace those killed. It should also be noted that there was a clear difference between *Reinhardt* operations and those of Blobel's *Sonderkommando 1005* elsewhere.

Closure of Belzec

The last transports to arrive at Belzec contained the survivors from the liquidated ghettos. On 4 December 1942 a small transport of 600 Jews from Krosno was gassed in Belzec; a few days later, 1,250 Jews from the Rohatyn ghetto were killed; on 7 and 11 December, several thousand Jews from Rawa Ruska were killed. Finally, three transports of survivors from the towns of Bursztyn, Bolszewce and Bukaczowce were brought to the camp and gassed. On 12 December 1942, Belzec ceased to function as a death camp.[625]

The complete absence of transports also meant that no extra food was brought into the camp by the victims, and the heavy work of digging up the corpses, the unhygienic environment of handling the decomposing bodies in addition to the burning, took its toll. The Jews were near starvation and sick with disease but reluctant to show their condition as they knew the consequences. Typhus does not discriminate between Jew, Ukrainian, or German, and when this disease was diagnosed in the camp, there was panic. Several of the SS and Ukrainians succumbed and were hospitalised until the danger had passed. Jews who could hold off no longer and collapsed were shot and cremated on the pyres. According to the survivor Chaim Hirszman: "There were cases when the 'death brigade' were so starved that they ate pieces of flesh from the legs of corpses."[626]

Belzec had now lost its importance as a death camp as the bulk of Galician Jewry had been dealt with. With the enlargement of Auschwitz, and the efficiency of Treblinka and Sobibór, Belzec, geographically, had lost its importance and had become redundant.

With the near completion of exhumations and cremations, commandant Hering placed Fritz Tauscher in charge of the final disbandment of the camp, and left Belzec. According to Tauscher, several SS remained behind in the camp to assist him.[627] Before Hering left the camp, he had assured the "work Jews" that they were safe and would be sent to other camps of their choosing.[628]

The decommissioning of Belzec commenced with landscaping parts of the former camp area with firs and wild lupines.[629] The remaining 300 or so Jews of the last "death brigade" now awaited their fate in the hope of their survival. Among this group were Chaim Hirszman and Sylko Herc.[630] We are able to piece together the last moments of the 306 "death brigade" Jews transported from Belzec to Sobibór from the testimonies of former *SS-Scharführers* Fritz Tauscher and Heinrich Gley. According *to* Gley:

> The disbandment of the camp presented the leadership with a problem: what was to happen to the work-Jews? Their gassing at Belzec was unthinkable because it would have to be carried out by the camp personnel. There was also the question of the burning of their bodies. The camp leadership decided to transport them in railway wagons to another camp. I heard later that this camp was Sobibór. To avoid panic, Hering spoke to the Jewish kapos and told them that they were being taken to Lublin. The transport was suitably strongly guarded. I heard later that there were mass breakouts.[631]

According to Fritz Tauscher, suddenly, about 14 days before the end, in the grey light of dawn, Wirth turned up without previous warning. At the same time, a train of eight or nine wagons rolled into the camp. Wirth told them that they were now going to their chosen camp, induced all the Jews to board the train and organized their loading and departure.[632]

Leon Feldhendler, a survivor of Sobibór, was in that death camp on the day the Belzec transport arrived. He has testified:[633]

> On 30 June 1943, a transport of the last Jews from Belzec arrived at Sobibór, under the supervision of *SS Unterscharführer* Paul Groth, to be liquidated. Sobibór prisoners were suddenly locked in the barracks with strict orders not to look out.[634]

On arrival at the ramp in Sobibór, the Jews were removed selectively in small groups from the wagons and immediately shot. After the murder of the last Jewish workers from Belzec, a number of final messages written on various scraps of paper were found by a survivor, 14-year-old Tomasz (Tovi) Blatt from Izbica, who was in charge of the camp rubbish incinerator. While sorting their clothing and burning the documents, he found a diary written up to the last minute, which revealed that the transport had been made up of workers from the Belzec death camp.

I quote from the diary of an unnamed victim: "We have worked one year in Belzec. We do not know where they are transporting us. They say to Germany. There are dining tables in the wagons. We have received bread for three days, canned food, and vodka."[635]

A note on a scrap of paper read:

> We know they are killing our comrades. The third wagon has already been opened and we can hear the sound of gunfire. Whoever finds this letter is requested to warn his comrades. Place no trust in the Germans' smooth tongues and lies. They will trick you just as they tricked us. Rise up and avenge our blood! Do to the Germans what we meant to do but did not succeed in doing. From a Jew who has spent more than a year in the death camp at Belzec. These are the last moments of our lives. Avenge us![636]

In addition to Gley's statement quoted above, the decision to deal with the last remaining Jews somewhere other than in Belzec may have been in order to hide their fate from the Ukrainians, who were already edgy and suspicious of what the Germans had in mind for them.

Immediately after the SS left Belzec, the local population descended on the site of the death camp, rummaging in the earth for gold and other valuables, and in doing so unearthed parts of decomposed bodies.[637] Werner Dubois returned alone, saw the situation and reported to Lublin. Then two labor groups, one from Treblinka and the other from Sobibór, were sent to Belzec to clear up the mess and build a farm. Accommodation was created for a caretaker to live on site and prevent further incursions.

After the war, a Polish investigator visited the former camp, where he found the ground dug-up, property strewn about and body parts exposed, no doubt in the search for valuables.[638]

Escapes from Belzec

The very few Jews who escaped from Belzec managed to do so only during the first phase. No Jews escaped from the camp in the second phase. Both Hirszman and Reder made their escapes from outside the camp. Those who did manage to get out were often caught shortly afterwards and immediately shot, returned on subsequent transports to Belzec, or fell victim to some other action. The first recorded escape from inside the camp was by a 17-year-old youth who arrived in Belzec on a road transport from Lubycza Krolewska in February 1942. He was one of a group of Jews rounded up to work on the final construction of the camp and witnessed the first gassing experiment by Wirth. These Jews were suddenly pushed into one of the newly erected gas chambers and killed with *Zyklon B*. At that moment the youth had been hiding in bushes nearby, and after witnessing this gassing, he escaped. The youth later met the village blacksmith and related his story.[639] He was subsequently caught and shot.

The second escape was from one of the first transports that arrived from the town of Żółkiew in March 1942. Two women, Mina Astman and Malka Talenfeld, had taken advantage of the inexperience and confusion of the guards in the early transports. Already naked, the women jumped into a ditch where they remained until dark when they escaped back to Żółkiew.[640]

Another escape, which did not quite succeed, was by a Jew from Piaski who had arrived in March 1942, and was part of the team in the area of the gas chamber. This Jew, no doubt horrified at the scene around him, suddenly broke away, forced himself through the surrounding barbed-wire fencing, and ran off. Quickly hunted down, he was brought back to the camp and shot.

During the round-up of Jews in Zamosc on 11 April, the Welsztein family, including their 18-year-old daughter and 13-year-old son, were transported to Belzec. When the welcoming speech had been made, the SS-guard instructed them to undress, whereupon the Zamosc Jews spat and cursed the camp SS. Fearing a riot, the SS fired into the crowd. Taking advantage of the commotion, the boy fled to the latrine where he hid until darkness and then escaped. Two days later, on 13 April 1942, the boy returned to Zamosc, where he told the *Judenrat* what he had witnessed: during the few hours he was hiding in the camp, he had seen how the gassings were carried out.[641]

Another escape from the latrine in Belzec was by a dentist from Kraków named Bachner. In June 1942 Bachner was part of a large transport of several thousand Jews from Kraków. In the reception yard, Bachner also hid in the latrine cess pit. Immersed up to his neck in human waste swarming with flies, he remained there for two days before escaping from the camp. After two weeks, he returned to the Kraków ghetto where he told the *Judenrat* of what he had seen.[642] There is no record of what happened to Bachner after his return, but one of the indictments against Amon Goeth, the commandant of Plaszów camp, was the shooting of the Bachner family in Plaszòw in 1943.[643]

In October 1942 the rabbi of Blazowa, Israel Spira, was transported from Janowska to Belzec and was fortunate enough to be selected for the clothing work brigade at the old locomotive shed. After a few days, he attached himself to the escort taking a trainload of clothing back to the Janowska camp. In Janowska, Rabbi Spira (much like Reder) detached himself from the escort and mingled with the other Jews. When he loitered near a coffee stall, he was recognised by other Jews who protected him. Rabbi Spira survived Janowska and subsequent deportations to Belzec. His wife Pearl was murdered in Belzec on 18 October 1942.[644]

There were three other escapes. They included that by Rudolf Reder, who had escaped by stealth while in Lvov under guard collecting building materials; and Chaim Hirszman and Sylko Herc, two members of the last "death brigade," who escaped from the transport taking them to Sobibór for execution. Hirszman returned to Lublin, where he joined a Communist partisan unit. He was subsequently recruited by the Soviet NKVD, and reappeared in Lublin after the liberation working for the Russians.

On 19 March 1946 in Lublin, Hirszman testified before a War Crimes Investigation Commission in the District Court.[645] That same day, he was murdered in his home by members of a Polish right-wing anti-Semitic organization. It is not known what happened to Herc.[646]

Two other known escapes, again by stealth, included the five-year-old child of Sara Ritterbrand (nee Beer). Sara had arrived in Belzec on an early transport from Lvov. Her brother was a baker living in Belzec under a false Aryan identity and part of his work was delivering bread to the camp. On a date unknown, he removed his niece from the camp in his breadbasket and gave her into the care of a local Ukrainian family, who protected her throughout the war period. He was arrested by the SS and shot in the presence of his sister Sara in the camp. Sara was one of the 30 Jewish women working in the camp laundry and the last to be removed from Belzec. When the war finished, she returned to Belzec village and was reunited with her daughter.[647] Sara and her daughter Bracha came to Belzec from Lvov in about 1941: the girl was later hidden in various places in the village throughout the war by Julia Pepiak, who is now counted among the "Righteous Among the Nations" at Yad Vashem.[648]

The only other record, which has not been verified, comes from a Jew named Sanio Ferber, who was employed in one of the SS workshops in Lvov. He testified after the war:

> Towards the end of December 1942, there came to our workshop a young dentist (not Bachner, above) whose name I do not recall ... He told us that he had escaped from Belzec. This dentist was in Belzec for three months as part of the work brigade who removed the gold teeth from the victims.[649]

By the end of 1946, only six Jews from the Belzec camp were still alive. They include four who subsequently emigrated to Israel; Rudolf Reder, who changed his name to Roman Robak, went to Canada, via Israel, and was the only witness at the Belzec pre-trial hearings in Munich 1963-64; and Chaim Hirszman, who was murdered in Lublin.

VIP visitors to Belzec[650]

The *Reichsführer-SS*, Heinrich Himmler—according to his diary entry for 7 January 1942—went on a two-day tour of inspection of the Lvov and Lublin construction projects. There seems little doubt that Himmler was adopting a hands-on inspection tour ready for the impending clearing of the Lublin and

Lvov Jewish populations.[651] It is reported that Himmler visited Belzec twice. On 16 August 1942 (the day before Rudolf Reder and his wife entered the camp),[652] he arrived by car under a heavy escort.[653] In October 1942 he arrived by air, landing on an improvised strip close to the rail station. On this occasion, *SS-Gruppenführer* SSPF Katzmann accompanied Himmler from Lvov. According to Reder, the visit lasted half an hour, during which time they inspected the gas chambers in operation.[654] Himmler was obviously pleased, as he handed out commendations to the SS-garrison.[655] Himmler never returned to Belzec; but he visited Treblinka in 1943 and Sobibór both in July 1942, and in February 1943, when 300 Jewish women were gassed in his presence.[656] There is no indication in Himmler's diary that he visited Belzec on the dates intimated; but this does not negate the possibility of his visits.[657]

Representatives from T4 and KdF were also frequent visitors to the center of operations in Lublin and the death camps. Dieter Allers (T4), who was the liaison between *Reinhardt*, the KdF and T4, occupied an office in Lublin, although he later denied this.[658] *SA-Oberführer* Werner Blankenburg was also a frequent visitor to Lublin and the death camps, where he frequently spoke to the SS staff.[659] Adolf Eichmann was in Belzec in early 1942 and in Treblinka in 1943.[660]

It was about the time of the Kołomyja transport that Belzec received a visit from the SS Technical Disinfecting Services in the persons of *SS-Oberconturmführer* Kurt Gerstein and *SS-Standartenführer* Prof. Wilhelm Pfannenstiel, a consultant hygienist from Berlin. Both men had been commissioned independently by the RSHA to carry out assessments of practical importance in respect of *Reinhardt.* Pfannenstiel was there to advise on sanitary conditions for a proposed new KZ that was to be built elsewhere. Pfannenstiel states quite definitely that his job was to improve sanitation and canalization in Majdanek and the city of Lublin. Gerstein's brief was more pragmatic. In Lublin both men met Globocnik, who briefed them about "a camp that was used to murder people of Jewish nationality." Globocnik instilled into both men that what they were going see was of the utmost secrecy and warned them that any failure to adhere to this warning meant automatic execution:[661] "this is one of the most secret things that there are, and even the most secret. Anyone, who speaks of it, will be shot immediately. ...Yesterday we silenced two babblers."[662] Globocnik stated that he was trying to solve two problems: to disinfect the mountain of lice-covered clothing, which had accumulated in the clothing stores of all three death camps; and to improve the efficiency of the gas chambers with an enhanced chemical agent. Globocnik assigned Oberhauser to show the "gentlemen" from Berlin around Belzec.

Gerstein had with him 260 kg of potassium cyanide pellets (prussic acid) when he entered Belzec camp. There are a number of versions by Gerstein and Pfannenstiel as to what happened next. Gerstein's accounts are based on his own records written in French and German, which have generally stood the test of time.[663] They describe in detail a transport believed to have arrived crammed with Jews from Hungary. Gerstein committed suicide after the war in French custody but among his papers was found a short reference note:

> At Belzec, it was dreadful to see the competition that was whipped up among the men and boys whose job it was to carry away the clothing. I still remember that little Jewish boy of three or four years of age who was made to hand out the bits of string with which the victims had to tie their shoes together: a child like that, harassed, all-unknowing of the frightful mind-machines created by Hitler and Wirth. I think of a little girl of five who dropped a little chain, which was picked up a few minutes later (a meter away from the gas chambers) by a little boy of three. He examined it with delight— and, a moment later, was thrown into the gas chamber.[664]

Closure of Sobibòr and Treblinka

After the Treblinka revolt on 2 August 1943, a nominal number of Jews were kept alive to dismantle the camp under the deputy commandant *SS-Untersturmführer* Kurt Franz (the former Belzec cook) and the Jewish Kapo, Karl Blau. But after the Sobibòr revolt on 14 October 1943, it was proposed, like Treblinka, to close the camp and destroy all incriminating evidence.

On 3 November, under the code name *"Erntefest"* (Harvest Festival), the total liquidation began of the 43,000 Jews in the camp at Majdanek and the labor camps of Lublin Airfield, Poniatowa, Trawniki and Dorohucza. They were shot during a six-day period. [665]

On 4 November 1943 further support SS personnel arrived from Treblinka to assist those already there in the demolition of the Sobibór camp. On 23 November *SS-Oberscharführer* Gustav Wagner, assisted by *SS-Scharführers* Jührs (Belzec) and Zierke (Belzec), together with the Ukrainian *Volksdeutsche* (Bodessa and Kaiser) decided to execute the remaining Jews in the camp.[666] To do this, and because the perimeter fences had been removed, they ordered the Jews to lie down in groups of five on the rails of the dismantled narrow gauge railway, and shot each one in the back of the neck. The bodies were cremated.[667] The SS garrison, having completed their task, prepared to follow the remainder of *Reinhardt* personnel to Trieste in northern Italy. The others had already left for Trieste on 20 September along with Globocnik, Stangl and Wirth.

Chapter 11. The Harvest Festival Massacres

In early 1943, the SS had set up in the General Government a number of industrial enterprises exclusively manned by Jewish slave labor. In Lublin, Globocnik was the overseer and main director of these enterprises, which made large profits for the SS and, of course, for a few senior SS dignitaries. To say there had been "creative" accounting is perhaps an understatement.

The *Reinhardt* Industries: Ostindustrie (Osti) and Deutsche Aursrüstungswerke (DAW)

One of the curious aspects of the Nazi State was the conspiratorial lengths to which the highest echelons of the SS went to establish their profit-making schemes. In the eastern territories "Ostinddustrie GmbH," abbreviated to "Osti" (Eastern Industries - Osti Pty Ltd.) was established in March 1943 with the aim of using Jewish slave labor. It was registered in Berlin within the confines of German company law, with nominated directors. In this case the entire executive board were bogus manufacturing officials made up of leading figures of the SS: Oswald Pohl (WVHA) as Chairman, Wilhelm Krüger (HSSPF Krakow) as deputy Chairman, Dr. Ferdinand von Sammern Frankenegg (SSPF Warsaw) and George Loener, a dealer in Jewish gold. Joining the board of directors was Engineer Odilo Globocnik (SSPF-Lublin), (According to a letter in Globocnik's BDC file, he did have the title "Engineer") and Dr. Max Horn, a dealer (SS-Hauptsturmführer RSHA).[668]

A second branch of OSTI was located in a very large camp at the old Lublin airfield. Here all manner of goods were produced under Globocnik's directorship: brushes of all kinds, shoes with wooden soles, and other articles made of wood. Globocnik himself was listed as Generaldirektor. This location was the heartland of *Reinhardt*. Here is where all the Jewish property was brought from the death camps, sorted and sent on at massive profits. The commandant since December 1942 was SS-Obersturmführer/ Kriminalkommissar Christian Wirth.

Unknown to the Jews at this time, the day of reckoning had arrived. Always fearing the worst about their own fate, when the day finally arrived, they were taken completely by surprise. Those manufacturing units employing Jews and aligned to *Reinhardt* were about to become extinct by order of Himmler.

Deutsche Ausrüstungswerke (DAW) – German Equipment Works, Lindenstrasse Camp, Lublin

Like several other camps, the *Deutsche Ausrüstungswerke (DAW - German Equipment Works)* at the Lindenstrasse camp in Lublin was still under Globocnik's control. The DAW was a firm employing exclusively Jewish slave labor and producing mainly wooden articles, which were made with the most modern machines. There were also various workshops for tailors, cobblers, saddlers, tanners and printers. The office staff was exclusively Jewish, guarded by Ukrainians who were posted around the camp perimeter. Inside the camp there was complete freedom of movement. The newly-appointed SSPF, Jakob Sporrenberg, had to obtain written authority from Globocnik's office, which was still functioning in Lublin, for permission to inspect the camp. It was arranged for a special guide to take Sporrenberg around the camp under escort.[669]

The Textile Factory in Poniatowa Labor Camp

Situated about 35 kilometers south-west of Lublin, Poniatowa was also one of Globocnik's business ventures, and as such, also came under the direct command of Wirth. In Poniatowa there were about 14,000 Jewish men, women and children, most of whom had been brought from the Warsaw Ghetto where they had been slave workers for Globocnik's associate director, Walter Caspar Többens. Representing security and in control of the camp were the commandant, SS-Hauptsturmfürer Gottlieb Hering, and SS-Oberscharführer Heinrich Gley from Belzec.

Trawniki Labor Camp

Trawniki, in addition to being the center for the training of the Ukrainians, also had a small industry operated by the firm of Schülz, under the direction of Globocnik, in which 8-10,000 Jews were employed manufacturing furs and other types of clothing. In late 1942, a brush factory, together with the Jewish workers, was transferred to Trawniki from the ghetto in Miedzyrzec Podlaska. The Jewish work complex consisted of workshops for tailors, furriers and broom makers. Among the arrivals from Warsaw were Dr. Emanuel Ringelblum and 33 members of the *Zydowska Organizacja Bojowa* (ZOB), the Jewish Fighting Organization. In May 1943 Jews from the Netherlands, Bialystok, Minsk and Smolensk arrived at Trawniki. In October 1943 the *Wehrmacht* factories were also transferred to Trawniki. After the Sobibor revolt on 14 October, it was proposed (unknown to the *Wehrmacht*), as at Treblinka,[670] to close the camp and destroy other incriminating evidence.[671]

Himmler had remained loyal to Globocnik ("his Globus"), extricating him from the many difficulties that he had brought upon himself by acrimonious relationships with authority. Towards the end of *Reinhardt,* however, their personal relationship was under severe strain; neither one of them had the stomach or the will to fight off the outside intrigues and pressures. Although Himmler remained sympathetic to his protégé, he could no longer avoid moving him from the General Government at the earliest opportunity. In March 1943, Himmler's brother-in-law, Richard Wendler, the civil governor in the Lublin District, had used his personal relationship with Himmler to urge him do something about Globocnik:

> Above all, I thank you for clearing the air regarding the SS-and Police Leader Lublin and trust you will transfer him somewhere else. This is the only noble and possible solution. I must even ask you today, to transfer Gruppenführer Globocnik within the shortest time to his new field of activity and to remove him from here.[672]

A planned transfer of his old friend to Kharkow never materialised, but when Italy capitulated to the Allies on 8 September 1943, and Northern Italy remained in German hands, Himmler seized the opportunity to transfer Globocnik as "HSSPF of the Adriatic Coast Region," effective from 13 September 1943. Meanwhile, *Reinhardt* was coming to a close.

On 13 September 1943, Globocnik was promoted SS- Gruppenführer and Generalleutnant der Polizei and a week later was transferred to Italy. He was replaced on 15 October by one of Himmler's most trusted SS and Police leaders, SS-Gruppenführer Jakub Sporrenberg.

Before Sporrenerg left for his new appointment in Lublin, Himmler warned him not to concern himself with the Jewish Question as this was in the hands of Globocnik, and for the foreseeable future would remain so. In the course of a long and detailed talk on policy, Himmler ordered Sporrenberg to concentrate his efforts on looking after the German settlers in Lublin; and further, that he expected the entire district to be Germanized by the end of 1944. Himmler also ordered him to build fortifications along the Bug River and along the 1941 Russo-German border.

On arrival in Lublin, Sporrenberg was coolly received by Globocnik (who had been called back to organize the Harvest Festival massacres) and his staff, who treated him with indifference. The headquarters staff of *Reinhardt* had remained loyal to Globocnik despite his removal as the SSPF. The hand-over of power from Globocnik to Sporrenberg was less than friendly. Globocnik contemptuously pointed out to Sporrenberg that his duties would never match what he and his men had achieved—which was an understatement. Leading this group of disgruntled senior staff now under Sporrenberg's command was SS-*Sturmbannführer* Hermann Höfle, SS-*Hauptsturmführer* Classen, and SS-*Obersturmführer* Bolten. His senior staff advised him quite bluntly to keep away from Globocnik's activities, as he was still acting on behalf of Himmler, and to direct his mind to partisan activity in the area.[673] According to Sporrenberg, before Globocnik left for Trieste, he had made arrangements that neither he (Sporrenberg) nor Governor Dr. Frank should have access to Majdanek KZ. Nethertheless, Sporrenberg succeeded in visiting the camp by stating to the commandant, SS-*Obersturmführer* Hermann Florstedt, that Himmler had authorized the visit. His controversial visit to Sobibor, as referred to earlier, was less successful. The commandant, SS-*Hauptsturmführer* Franz Reichleitner, although he had a much lower rank, bluntly refused Sporrenberg permission to enter the camp and referred him back to Globocnik or Himmler.

On 19 October, because of the deteriorating military situation in the East, General-Governor Dr. Hans Frank convened a special security conference in Krakow. Attending the conference was SS-*Oberführer* Bierkamp, Chief of the Security Service in Krakow, who had replaced the now disgraced Dr. Schöngarth, SS-*Obergruppenführer* F.W. Krüger (HSSPF), Major-General Hans Grünwald (*Schutzpolizei*), and SSPF Sporrenberg, who had replaced Globocnik.

Krüger showed them the following letter received from Himmler:

> To:
>
> Higher SS and Police Leader Obergruppenführer and General of the Police Krüger, Krakow:
>
> The Jews in the Lublin District have developed into a serious danger. This state of affairs must be cleared up once and for all. I have charged the "unit Globocnik" with the execution of this matter. The Higher SS and Police Leader East, and the SS and Police Leader Lublin, are requested to assist Globocnik with all resources at their disposal.
>
> (Signed) Heinrich Himmler[674]

According to Sporrenberg's account, which was recorded under interrogation after the war, those attending the conference were furious. Who had leaked this information to Himmler?[675] It was the consensus of those present that decisions had been made to finally eliminate all the Jews in the Lublin District. It was also the consensus of the conference that Himmler and Globocnik had worked this policy out between them. It is significant to note that although Globocnik and Wirth had been posted to Italy, they had been recalled to Lublin by Himmler for this operation, to take personal charge of events. Sporrenberg and his SS personnel in Lublin were sidelined, and according to Sporrenberg, were either treated with contempt or simply ignored. The leadership of Reinhardt had been resurrected and reformed for one last "operation."

The results were immediate. On 20 October 1943 several wagons arrived at Sobibor from Treblinka. An SS-unit and Jewish *Vorkommando* had arrived to dismantle the camp.[676] At Majdanek camp in Lublin, there was an influx of security personnel from Berlin, who, contrary to protocol, did not report their arrival to Sporrenberg. According to Sporrenberg (which must be treated as a defensive lie), unknown to him, anti-tank ditches were being dug in Majdanek. In the last days of October, 300 prisoners spent three days digging two-meter deep ditches that would be the places of execution. Each ditch was zigzag in shape, just like normal defense trenches, and extended for 100 meters. On 2 November loudspeakers were set up in the vicinity, and early the following morning all the preparations had been made for the operation, which was to be carried out under the code name "*Erntefest*" (Harvest Festival) operation.

According to Sporrenberg, he received from HSSPF Krüger a teleprinter message informing him that special-units of the *Feldkommando Stelle* (Field Command Post) of the RFSS consisting of 2,000 Waffen-SS and police regiments from East Prussia were to be used for "cordoning off" duties around Majdanek. In addition to these SS troops, a special *Kommando* of a 150 SS men had arrived from Auschwitz—the executioners.

SS-*Obersturmführer* Christian Wirth contemptuously informed Sporrenberg, who had a much higher rank, that he had orders signed by Himmler for organizing and commanding the total extermination of all Jews in the Lublin District. Wirth confirmed to Sporrenberg that this "action" would commence the following day. When Sporrenberg challenged Wirth on the basis that the orders were in fact addressed to Globocnik, Wirth stated that he was acting on Globocnik's behalf. Wirth showed Sporrenberg the orders and plans of the three camps and other places whose inmates were to be shot: Osti and DAW at the old Lublin airfield, DAW on Lindenstrasse in Lublin, and the labor camps at Poniatowa and Trawniki. Wirth handed the "order" to Sporrenberg:

1. On orders of the RFSS an operation called "*Erntefest*" will be carried out in the Lublin District, for which the cordoning-off troops under his command are to be used.

2. For this purpose, the units in question will be disposed and dispersed as shown on the plans.

3. The cordoning-off troops will remain posted until ordered to stand down and no person will be permitted to enter or exit the cordoned-off area.

4. In the case of the two camps at Lindenstrasse and the old airfield, the prisoners will be led out of the camps and taken to Majdanek under guard. At Majdanek the troops are to form a cordon round the camp while the operation is being carried out, and to remain in place until recalled.

5. The Commanders of the troops are to enter Majdanek on arrival and report to Wirth in order to establish contact and obtain information about when the troops are no longer needed.

6. On returning from Majdanek, the leaders are to report to the SSPF.

7. On the second day, the troops will surround the camps at Poniatowa and Trawniki at 06:00. The commanders will report to SS-Sturmbannführer Wirth.

The '*Erntefest*' (Harvest Festival) Massacres [677]

On the morning of 3 November under the code name "*Erntefest*" (Harvest Festival), the total liquidation of all Jewish labor in the Lublin district commenced. In total, 42,000 Jews were shot during a six-day period.[678]

Early that morning, the Jews reported for work as usual in the subsidiary labor camps in Lublin. It was only when they were led out of the camps in groups under strong SS guard and through the town towards Majdanek that they realized their end was near. As they entered the camp complex they were made to strip naked, hand over any valuables and cash, and form up in queues to await their turn to descend into the execution ditches.

The SS execution *Kommandos* were efficient: each Jew was beckoned forward, entered the ditch and lay on top the Jew previously shot. A short burst of gunfire and the next victim was called forward and the operation repeated—many thousands of times. Local Poles, who witnessed the "great march," saw a line of people stretching for several kilometers through and beyond the town, all marching in the direction of Majdanek. On that day, 18,000 Jews, men, women and children, were murdered.

Over several days, mass executions by shooting in Majdanek KZ and surrounding camps accounted for the murder of approximately 42,000 Jews.[679] The entire labor force of Többens and Schülz was massacred in this operation: Osti and DAW, 16,000; Poniatowa, 14,000; Trawniki, 12,000.

Poniatowa Massacres

In Poniatowa, Gottlieb Hering replicated Wirth's antics by appearing on horseback, accompanied by Gley. As this small entourage moved among the Jewish workers, Gley opened with his machine pistol, killing many of the Jewish workers.[680] Shootings, torture and cruelty were a daily occurrence in Poniatowa, but victim and oppressor alike were taken by surprise when on the 3 November the camp was cordoned off by regiments of SS and police. Like all the other camp commanders in the district, they were not informed of the impending "action." According to Gley:

> In November (3 November) 1943, I was called to see the commandant (Hering) who was with two police officers. Hering was informed that the camp was now surrounded and that orders had been received for the liquidation of all Jews, without exception. The Jews were ordered to assemble in different parts of the camp. Naked, they were led to execution ditches where they were shot.[681]

Once the executions commenced there was no escape. Two-hundred Jews who had remained unharmed were left alive. When they were ordered to cremate their brothers and sisters, many refused and were shot.[682] The shooting lasted several hours, until the last Jew lay dead in the ditches. According to German witnesses after the war, between 07:30 and 14:00 hrs, 14,000 Jews were shot in Poniatowa.[683]

On 5 November, the Trawniki camp was cordoned off and the Jews also murdered in ditches. Jews who refused to cremate the copses were shot and replaced by Jews from the Milejow camp near Lublin to carry out the cremations. They too were shot after completing the task.

The *"Erntefest"* massacres were completed between 3 and 5 November, 3,000 innocent victims killed every working hour. The 150-strong SS-execution squad from Auschwitz carried out the killings. Each man killed 280 people in 14 hours, or one person every 3 minutes. The 42,000 bodies were all buried within the camps.

This massacre did not go without reward for *Reinhardt*, as the economic assets were stripped from the bodies of the Jews lying dead in the ditches. Their mouths were stripped of gold and melted down. Some of the booty plundered from Jewish victims even found its way to the coffers of the T4 Central Office. In proceedings against Hans-Joachim Becker and Friedrich Robert Lorent in 1970, KTI witness Dr Albert Widmann testified that in one month alone he had to smelt dental gold and jewelry pieces in such quantity that he received from DEGUSSA[684] 27 kilograms of fine gold, of which he passed on a certain amount to T4.[685]

After the *"Erntefest"* massacres, Christian Wirth returned to Trieste; but a month later, in December 1943, Himmler ordered him back to Lublin to exhume and burn the corpses.[686]

Despite Sporrenberg's playing down to his interrogators of his own contribution to *"Erntefest,"* it is clear that he was one of Hitler's earliest and most fanatical supporters, who, by his efficiency, zeal and success quickly rose to high rank and important positions within the SS, the SD and Sipo.[687] The question of whether he opposed Himmler and his Jewish policies (as he maintained), is irrelevant, since jealously and corruption in high Nazi circles would turn today's friend into the most ruthless enemy of tomorrow, without his moral conceptions having undergone a change. Even if Sporrenberg to some extent disagreed with Himmler's orders and the methods adopted, he certainly lacked the moral courage to dissociate himself from his superiors. As an SD officer, his incrimination in the extermination of many thousands of Jews, including Polish POWs, is clear, and even if the main burden of killing 42,000 Jews rested on Himmler, Globocnik and Wirth, such a task could not have been carried out by a mere handful of men in 14 hours without the knowledge of SSPF Sporrenberg in Lublin.[688] *"Erntefest"* was the final act of *Reinhardt.* However, this was not the end of the SS blood-letting. Under the authority of SSPF Fritz Katzmann, on 19-20 November 1943 the remaining economic enterprises at the Janowska camp in Lviv were liquidated: 4,000 Jews were murdered.[689]

Reinhardt was a massive operation for the industrial killing of several million Jews from European countries by a few thousand Germans who worked for the SS and police. It is a sad reflection of events that what commenced with a virulent, nefarious, anti-Semetic and willful intent of the Nazis to murder the entire Jewish populations within their grasp, actually ended with some of the most ardent supporters of these measures regretting the consequences of their actions. SS-*Obergruppenführer* Wilhelm Krüger, the highest SS and Police official in Krakow and also Minister for Security in the General Government, admitted at a Government session on 31 May 1943 that the extermination was for the police one of the largest, most difficult and saddest tasks undertaken. It had to be completed because of Hitler's orders. And Governor General Dr. Hans Frank said at Nuremberg: "A thousand years will pass and Germany's guilt will not be washed away."

Chapter 12. Post Reinhardt

The old rice factory *(La Risiera)*, adjacent to the San Sabba crematorium in Trieste.[690]

Although Italy may appear to be far removed from Lublin and the *Reinhardt* death camps, the HHE continued to direct their attention to the Jewish Question. With the downfall of Mussolini on 25 July 1943 and the surrender of his satrap Marshal Badoglio to the Allies, Germany quickly entered the fray by occupying northern Italy and disarming all military forces. In early September 1943 vast numbers of German administrators and security forces entered the areas of occupation, just as they had in Poland in 1939 and Soviet territory in 1941, to maintain the status quo. On 25 September 1943 the HHE were again quick off the mark, outflanking their civilian cohorts and immediately proceeding with anti-Jewish measures as a priority over all other military objectives.[691]

It shows the emphasis and priorities of the HHE that the "Jewish Question" was still high on the agenda of Nazi policies. The HHE continued pulling the strings, so to speak, by installing their most experienced and well-proven anti-Semite operators in high positions: Dr. Otto Wächter, formally of Krakow and Governor of Galicia, was now chief of military administration; and Globocnik was installed as HSSPF, accompanied by a full contingent of the elite *Reinhardt* personnel.

Deployment of Personnel

Globocnik arrived in Trieste on 23 September 1943 to take up his appointment as the HSSPF and overseer of the "Einzatz" Trieste fortifications.[692] Accompanying him to Trieste was the old team from Lublin: Wirth, Stangl, Oberhauser and 120 other men, 10 of them from

Treblinka, a number of non-commissioned officers and five Volksdeutsche. Under Globocnik's leadership, the *Reinhardt* team were known as *"Einsatz R."* Upon arrival, the men were divided into four units: Christian Wirth held "R" until his death in May 1944. Dieter Allers, who had been transferred from T4/KdF to Trieste succeeded him.[693]

Globocnik installed several regional offices with the central base in Trieste: R I under Hering, in Fiume-Susak; R II under Reichleitner, in Undine; R III under Stangl. Another unit, R IV, was based in Metre, which was outside the Adriatic Coastland region. *Einsatz R*, under Wirth's overall command, was responsible for all Jewish measures and Italian and Yugoslav partisans.

A transit camp for Italian Jews and captured Italian and Yugoslav partisans was established in an abandoned rice mill ("La Risiera") in the San Sabba suburb of Trieste. It was operational from 30 October 1943 to 30 April 1944. San Sabba was established solely as a transit camp for deporting the last few Italian Jews to KZs in Germany, primarily to Auschwitz. That it became a "mini" death camp was due solely to Wirth, who had no orders to exterminate these Jews, only to deport them. San Sabba remained the HQ of the *Einsatz R* units under Dieter Allers right up until they withdrew across the border into Austria almost at the end of the war. Allers released the last few prisoners just before the retreat.

To emphasise the HHE's commitment to Jewish actions, T4 personnel who had returned to Berlin after *Reinhardt* closed were hastily recalled on Christmas Eve 1943, to report direct to Wirth in Italy.[694]

Einsatz R (Operation R) [695]

All the old familiar SS faces from Belzec, Sobibor and Treblinka were now ensconced together under the same proven police leadership.[696] Wirth and Hering had not lost their touch or commitment to the Jewish Question. The "R" staff continued to use the methods used in Poland: beating prisoners to death, torture and ordering young children to collect firewood to light the fires for their own cremation. The San Sabba crematorium was constructed in the inner courtyard of the mill, on Wirth's orders, by Erwin Lambert in early 1944. The staff introduced the necessary accoutrements for mass murder by establishing gas van facilities and crematoria.[697]

On 9 October, as the result of orders from the HHE, the SD, working independently of Einsatz R, commenced the rounding-up of Jews for resettlement and hand-over of Jewish property to Globocnik's coffers.[698] On the same day, these Jews were the first to be deported from Trieste to Auschwitz in a coordinated resettlement action originating from Milan in accordance with the SD in Italy. Many Jews who managed to avoid previous actions and resettlements were now caught up in the security sweeps by an even more determined enemy.[699]

According to Italian court documentation, Globocnik's units murdered over 3,000 people, including captured Italian and Yugoslav partisans and Jews, in the San Sabba camp alone. The records confirm that 22 deportation trains were organized in Trieste, sending Jews and political prisoners to Auschwitz, Ravensbrück and Bergen-Belsen. As in Poland, the old and the sick were weeded out and shot. These actions only terminated when the war front was approaching and defeat appeared imminent.[700] Even so, the Jews in Trieste fared far better than in other districts.[701]

Reinhardt Personnel Knew Too Much

Many of the T4/SS staff were convinced that the true reason for their transfer into this dangerous and partisan-infested district was a determined policy by Berlin to get rid of them. The question arose frequently among the men that because of the genocidal crimes they had carried out in *Reinhardt*, the HHE were mindful of their special knowledge that could tie them inextricably to the genocide and unravel the secrecy at some time in the future. It was accepted by some of those in authority that the war was already lost and it was only a matter of time before Germany would have to answer for her crimes.

Within this atmosphere of fear of possible retribution, the HHE may have considered a solution whereby these men could be placed in situations where their lives were likely to be lost more quickly. Rumors abounded among the old *Reinhardt* garrisons as to how their fate would eventually be decided. Stangl explained, "We were an embarrassment to the brass. They wanted to find ways to get rid of us."[702] Wirth had confided in a similar tone to his men in Treblinka in August 1942, "The Jews are here to be killed. The Ukrainians, after the job is done, will be killed too. What will happen to us we do not know. It could be that we, too, will die."[703] Globocnik had also made known his feelings, "I too, am no longer in it with all my heart. However, I am so deeply implicated in the matter that I have no choice—I must win, or perish with Hitler."[704] The rumors continued among the men for many months and were often the subject for discussion in the mess. The men felt deeply uneasy—and they were proved right. Josef Oberhauser stated, in answer to the Prosecution Counsel at the Munich court on 24 June 1963:

> It is right that the members of T4 cultivated the rumor that after the "final victory," or at some time when the military situation justified it, at the wish of the highest leader of the NSDAP (Hitler), we were to be sent on a "Strength through Joy" voyage.[705] The object of this pleasure trip was to gather all those with the unpleasant knowledge of the Jewish extermination operation and eliminate them. This rumor struck home and was naturally not good for morale. Wirth was interested enough to investigate the affair and to procure the certainty as to whether it was a rumor or an actual intention of the state leadership which had somehow leaked out.

Wirth had the opportunity to mention these fears when Blankenburg (KdF) came to see Globocnik. Without further ado, Wirth took hold of Blankenburg and reproached him with the rumor among the troops about the "Strength through Joy" voyage—and demanded an explanation. I (Oberhauser) personally heard this conversation. I stood immediately next to Wirth. This stunned Blankenburg. He fumed a glaring red, exactly as if one had confronted a murderer who believed until now he was undetected. His psychological reaction was unusual. He was unable to say anything and when he had pulled himself together, he muttered that he would go immediately to Reich Leader Bouhler and Reich Leader Bormann to bring a stop to this at the highest levels. In fact, one had the impression that he was completely in the picture, and that it was not a rumor but a secret intention of the NS-leadership, which through some kind of indiscretion had leaked out.

We never heard anything more about this subject. It is possible that Blankenburg had been directed to undermine the morale of the troops, but the rumor was never scotched.

Franz Suchomel (SS-*Scharführer* Treblinka), who was no friend of Oberhauser, corroborates this rumor; and although he thought it was unlikely, he says that "anything was possible."[706]

By December 1944 the rumors circulating about a possible "secret action" against the *Reinhardt* men had receded and were no longer the topic of conversation. Then suddenly, without warning, on 26 May 1944, and in quick succession, Wirth, Reichleitner, Schwarz, Gringers, and others from the *Einsatz R* units were dead, allegedly shot in partisan operations or killed in mysterious circumstances. Whether this was the case or not has never been clearly established. Wirth, by all accounts, had just disappeared from his place of duty and was "presumed dead," killed by partisans.

Stangl, who appears to have accepted the war's outcome, had slipped away to his native Austria, probably to mount a cover story for times gone by, but not before he had seen Wirth lying dead. In the Sereny interview, Stangl casually mentions seeing Wirth dead just before leaving Trieste: "I saw him dead. They said partisans killed him but we thought his own men had taken care of him."[707]

The assassinations of Reichleitner, Wirth and Schwarz by partisans are well documented in Ludwigsburg, and in the Ljubljana archives in Slovenia. There is a whole file on Globocnik's last days and suicide at the Public Record Office in London. Maj. Ken Hedley, who arrested Globocnik in the mountain chalet, and received very interesting information from former SS-*Stubafuherer* Ernst Lerch, was sent by Globocnik with an SS unit to hunt down Wirth's killers.

There were certainly a number of former KZ and death camp officers who either died in uncertain circumstances or just disappeared, "presumed dead."

Among them were the deaths in suspicious circumstances of Hering, Globocnik and Wilhelm Krüger (HSSPF Krakow) and many others.[708]

Wirth, Schwarz and Reichleitner all found their final resting place in the German cemetery on the hilltop town of Costermano on the slopes of Monte Baldo, between the eastern shore of Lake Garda and Verona, where they still remain. There was a long played out international dispute and protests, but oddly enough, the mayor and people of Costermano do not seem to care much about the scandal. Costermano is happily twinned with a town in Bavaria and regular cultural exchanges and holidays take place.

Although their names have been removed from the book of memory and the register of war dead and on the gravestones; once a year flowers are laid on the graves and unidentified visitors attend to pay homage. They have been observed giving the Nazi salute. The Italian Fascists openly hold ceremonies in the Costermano cemetery and pay homage at Wirth's grave.

Final Accounting

The *Führer's* Chancellery and the higher echelons in the *Reich* opened a special department designed especially to control the efficient manner of killing several million people. The Economics Ministry, the Reichsbank, and central institutions of the German Reich were involved in dividing up the spoils and in this manner all became accomplices in the killing process. Large German industrial establishments received Jewish materials for recycling which were distributed by the Economics Ministry. The Commercial Register in Berlin registered *Osti*, the above-mentioned fictional firm that was created by the Nazi hierarchy of the SS and Police to exploit Jews as slave labor.[709]

In Lublin, SS-Judge Konrad Morgan and SS-*Hauptsturmführer* Dr. Heinrich Wilhelm Weid from the SS-investigation squad of the RSHA scented blood as the whole complexity of Reinhardt had now been fully exposed. Wied was in Lublin in the summer of 1943 and knew about the activities of Wirth and Hering, very probably even before Morgan. Globocnik had read between the lines and immediately began a cover-up operation.[710]

Höß, a knowledgeable insider, considered the whole *Reinhardt* program in Lublin a center of corruption and theft where everyone so engaged was doing very well out of it.[711]

It was from his headquarters in Trieste that Globocnik confirmed in writing to Himmler (at the very time of the massacres occurring in Majdanek, 4 November 1943) that *Reinhardt* had been officially concluded on 19 October 1943, only five days after the revolt in Sobibor.

Globocnik's 38 page document, his final report for *Reinhardt*, confirms that *Reinhardt*—the extermination of several million Jews from different European countries—was a massive act of industrial killing. The report is divided into two separate sections with appendices, which contain a number of significant explanations and requests. The documents include details of the resettlement of Jews from the Lublin District, the retention of working[712] Jews for manufacture and furthermore, that he (Globocnik) had finally handed over the Jewish work camps to Oswald Pohl, who was in charge of all concentration camps. Attached as an appendix is a long and detailed list of various commodities and valuables that resulted from the Reinhardt operation. A specific schedule showed currency from 29 countries.[713]

In the same report, Globocnik reminded Himmler of his promise that for extraordinary achievements in fulfilling this work it would be possible to have the Iron Cross awarded to the men of *Reinhardt*. He requested permission to lodge special application forms and added that they had received such recognition for the liquidation of the Warsaw Ghetto, which was only a small part of the task that had been *Reinhardt*. Globocnik concluded with the words that he would be grateful if the *Reichsführer* recognized the hard work of his subordinates.[714]

Himmler's reply to Globocnik on 30 November 1943 was brief:

> Dear Globus.
>
> I acknowledge your letter of 11-4-43 and your report about the end of "Operation Reinhardt." In addition, I thank you for the attached files. I acknowledge your great and unique service in accomplishing "Operation Reinhardt" for the glory of the whole German Nation. My thanks and appreciation.
>
> Heil Hitler.
>
> Sincerely yours, H.H.

There was no mention of Iron Crosses or *Reinhardt* accounts in Himmler's reply.[715]

Medals and Promotions [716]

During Himmler's last visit to Lublin on 12 February 1943, he promoted Globocnik's *Reinhardt* leadership. All kinds of difficulties appear to have arisen regarding these promotions.[717] Further promotions of this team was frustrated by the RSHA; some were later confirmed while others were rejected. Wirth's promotion to SS-*Obersturmführer* was rejected by the RSHA Personnel Department, as Wirth had not held the intermediary rank of SS- *Hauptsturmführer*.[718] (Wirth had held the rank of SS *Obersturmführer* since October, 1939). Hering had been promoted to Police Inspector of the *Kriminalpolizei* and recommended for promotion to the SS-aligned rank of SS-*Hauptsturmführer*, which was rejected, as he had never been a member of the SS.[719] (Hering was later promoted to SS-*Hauptsturmführer* after Himmler's intervention with the SS Main Personnel Office in Berlin). However, SS-*Oberscharführer* Josef Oberhauser, who was a *bona fide* member of the SS, was promoted to SS-*Untersturmführer* in June 1943. The confusion continued when Globocnik tried to secure promotions for his police commandants, Reichleitner and Stangl, neither of whom held Orpo or SS ranks, and, as mere *Kriminalsekretäre*, were not qualified for the SS rank of *Obersturmführer*. [720]

It is interesting to note in this exchange that Globocnik confirmed that Stangl was not SS at all, but was a police officer working under cover: "Stangl is the best camp commander who was the most prominent individual in the whole action. While still in the Austrian police, he served as an under-cover SS man."[721] If Globocnik took this view about Stangl, and he should know, then the same view should apply to the majority of other personnel who were not SS, i.e. that they, too, were all working "under cover," carrying out their duties in mass murder and at the same time, by wearing the uniform of the SS, were also "impersonators." (They were entitled to wear SS-uniform for the duration of *Reinhardt* simply because that operation was run by the SS). Karl Frenzel (former *Scharführer* at Sobibor) formerly a carpenter in T4, where he progressed to "*Brenner*" (burner of corpses) stated, "I was not SS. There were only five SS. The rest were civilians in SS uniforms."[722] Even Rudolf Höß of Auschwitz referred to this group as Globocnik's "collection of misfits" and claimed that the men under him were out of control. [723]

These anomalies were to pervade *Reinhardt* to the end. These men, of whatever status, were looking for and indeed expected, that their commitment to and success in their tasks should be rewarded with advancement. The fact that some did not have the military background to command promotion was a continuing running sore for them. Globocnik entered the fray directly with Himmler and in addition to the promotions controversy, requested Iron Crosses for his team for their outstanding performance during the Warsaw Ghetto destruction, but again there was no response. [724] Himmler, probably reluctantly, and no doubt trying to distance himself from the corrupt side of Globocnik's Reinhardt activities, enforced the promotion issue but dallied on the issue of medals. [725]

Archival records regarding the promotions of personnel attached to SS-*Sonderkommandos* "*Einsatz Reinhard*" clearly show the ambiguities of membership of SS and police ranks.

With Wirth and Reichleitner dead and Stangl's flight to Austria, Globocnik stuck it out until mid-May 1945. In the general retreat of German forces, Globocnik teamed up with other fleeing *Reinhardt* personnel: *Gauleiter* Friedrich Rainer, Ernst Lerch, Hermann Höfle, Georg Michalsen and Karl Helletsberger. Globocnik disappeared for 10 days, whereabouts unknown even to his adjutants. He joined them later in the mountain chalet where they had been hiding.

At 11:00 on 31 May 1945, at Paternion, Globocnik, realising that the game was up, committed suicide by swallowing a potassium cyanide capsule. [726]

Maybe Globocnik had recalled Himmler's speech at Poznan and decided to take with him to the grave the knowledge about the genocide of the Jews.

Earlier, however, he had been unofficially exonerated by SS-*Gruppenführer* Maximlian von Herff, the Chief of the SS main personnel office, in May 1943:

> "Although Globocnik's unauthorized acts were named, they were not criticized, but excused and judged right, because they were successful."[727]

Chapter 13. Aftermath and Retribution

Globocnik, Wirth, Hering and Schwarz were long dead. The minions were either dead or already arraigned before German or Austrian courts, which more often than not, dwelt extensively upon the motivation and general outlook of the accused rather than attempting to establish individual culpability. Several were never sentenced by the courts, even after lengthy trials, or were released under various pretexts. Others simply vanished. About a dozen of the former SS staff of the Belzec death camp have never been traced.

Among the members of staff of *"Abteilung Höfle"* who had worked at the "Julius Schreck" barracks in Lublin, Albert Susitti and Josef Slany were reported "missing in action" in 1945; Amon Goeth was extradited to Poland and executed in Kraców in 1946 for crimes committed while commandant of the Plaszów camp. Kurt Claasen was also reported "missing in action" and officially declared dead by a magistrate's court in Otterndorf near Cuxhaven in 1953. Hermann Höfle committed suicide while on remand in a Vienna prison in 1961; the case against his deputy, Helmut Pohl, was discontinued. Georg Michalsen, arrested in 1961, spent three years in custody and was then released while the judicial enquiry into his wartime activities dragged on for another 11 years. He finally appeared in 1973 before a Hamburg court, which sentenced him to 14 years imprisonment. Two years later the sentence had still not been upheld. Ernst Lerch, Globocnik's closest adjutant, appeared many times before Austrian courts but never served a single day in prison. Karl Mahnke, in charge of the Jewish transports at Lublin station, was never traced after the war; and Willi Hausler, Wirth's chief clerk in the "Operation *Reinhardt*" inspectorate in Lublin, was never charged with any criminal offence as his job was not directly connected with the extermination of the Jews.

Hermann Worthoff, the "lord of life and death" in the Lublin ghetto, who had personally directed the round-ups for Belzec, was not arrested until 1970. He and five others were accused by a court in Wiesbaden, although Worthoff himself never appeared in the dock during the two-and-a-half year trial due to ill health. The case against him was eventually dropped.

The Belzec Trial in Germany of former SS personnel opened on 1 August 1963.

The former SS-NCOs from Belzec: Dubois, Fuchs, Gley, Jührs, Schluch, Unverhau, Zierke, Girtzig and Oberhauser, were arrested between 1959 and 1963 and underwent pre-trial interrogations and court hearings. After lengthy proceedings the court accepted their pleas in mitigation (with the exception of Oberhauser) and decided that a public trial was not warranted. All the accused (except Oberhauser) were therefore not "acquitted," but simply released without any public trial ever being held. Only Oberhauser was formally tried.

The crimes of genocide in Auschwitz and associated camps were well known during and immediately after the war. The crimes of genocide committed in the death camps at Belzec, Sobibór and Treblinka only began to emerge for the first time during the euthanasia trials of 1946-48.

1) Former *SS-Scharführer* Josef Hirtreiter, a locksmith, had been interrogated in Frankfurt on 6 July 1945 about the euthanasia center at Hadamar. He mentioned a camp near Malkinia (Treblinka) where the gassing of several thousand Jews had taken place. He named several Hadamar colleagues who had accompanied him there.

2) The most revealing evidence to rock the establishment and focus their minds, came during the Nuremberg proceedings on 8 August 1946, in the testimony of former *SS-Sturmbannführer* George Konrad Morgan, the former SS-Judge mentioned above in connection with the corruption investigations of the SS. Up until this point, only casual references had been made to the death camps, but now Morgan revealed to the court that the directives for the genocide came directly from Hitler's Chancellery, via T4.[728]

3) Further evidence of the death camps and the connection with euthanasia and the KdF emerged in 1947 during the investigation into chief physician Adolf Wahlmann and other Hadamar staff.

4) Heinrich Unverhau, who had been in charge of the sorting depot in the second phase at Belzec (cutting out the yellow stars from clothing after the victims had been gassed), was the first to be arrested and charged in 1948 in connection with the killing of patients at Grafeneck euthanasia center. It was during the course of the trial that information began to emerge about the *Reinhardt* death camps. Unverhau, after a lengthy hearing into the euthanasia allegations, was acquitted of all charges and released, as it was proved he had not been involved in the killings.[729] His testimony regarding the death camps was simply ignored by the court as being irrelevant to the Grafeneck Case.

5) Even then, the wheels of justice were slow to turn. It was only in 1959 that the West German government instigated a wide-ranging investigation into the *Reinhardt* death camps. Belzec was the first to be identified as a major killing center in the East. At the conclusion of these inquiries and in quick succession, the "Belzec 9" were arrested and underwent further interrogations. In August 1963, they were brought before examining magistrates regarding several counts pertaining to the murder of several hundred thousand Jews in Belzec.[730]

Although the defendants had made admissions, the defense case was a mixture of defensive lies, self exoneration concerning the actual killing and, not without some foundation, the mitigation that they were in fear of their very lives and the lives of their families should they not carry out the express orders of the Belzec camp commanders, Wirth and Hering. The defendants attempted to lessen their own involvement in the genocide, by suggesting that the "actions of destruction," could not have been carried out without the assistance of the Jews. They suggested to the court that the Jews carried out the whole operation: removed the victims from the transports, cut the hair of the females, removed the bodies from the gas chambers, extracted gold teeth, and buried the bodies in the pits they had previously prepared.[731] Fortunately, on this point the court was not persuaded;

To convict these men of the Belzec crimes there had to be direct evidence identifying them as *the* perpetrators of destruction. While there was circumstantial evidence or loose admissions by the accused, the main requirement, i.e. witnesses to events implicating individual defendants, was absent. The prosecution traced the Jews who had escaped from Belzec in 1942, but only two, Roman Robak (alias Rudolf Reder) and Sara Ritterbrand made written statements. When the pre-trial examination opened, Ritterbrand was too ill to attend court to give evidence. Robak, who had travelled from Toronto, Canada, was unable to positively identify any of the defendants in court. Robak had previously identified Oberhauser, Girtzig, Unverhau, and Schwarz from a photograph shown to him by the police.

To rebut the general defense offered, the prosecution relied on one principle: that the defendants were guilty of common participation, even though they may not have acted as instigators.

In principle, the individual in charge who gives the orders (Wirth/Hering) is solely responsible; yet he who carries out these orders must also share the responsibility if he knows the task in hand is unlawful.

The defense plea of "mitigating circumstances," i.e. "acting out of fear for life," was accepted by the examining magistrates [732] who decided not to proceed with a public trial. Only Oberhauser was ordered to stand trial because of his close association with Wirth throughout *Reinhardt.*

Immediately on leaving the court as free men, Zierke, Dubois, Fuchs, Jührs and Unverhau were re-arrested and held in custody on similar charges relating to Sobibór.[733]

In January 1965 Oberhauser appeared before the Munich Assize Court. Immediately, Oberhauser claimed to the court that he had already been sentenced to a term of imprisonment for the Belzec crimes at the Magdeburg court (East Germany) in 1948, where a Soviet Military Tribunal sentenced him to a term of 15 years imprisonment. When the Munich court investigated Oberhauser's claims, it was established that he had been tried and sentenced for crimes relating to "euthanasia" and not the Belzec crimes, as these were not known at the time. The trial continued.

Giving evidence against him were the co-defendants from the previous Belzec trial. In addition, and attending as a witness for the prosecution, was 73 year-old Wilhelm Pfannenstiel, former *SS-Standartenführer,* the consultant hygienist who had visited Belzec with Kurt Gerstein in August

1942; and Roman Robak (Reder), now 84 years-old. Neither witness was able to identify Oberhauser. Pfannenstiel, when describing to the court his visit to Belzec in August 1942, stated that it was the worst experience of his life. He confirmed to the court that he had seen the Jews operating the gas engines, a point picked-up in the closing speeches of the prosecution:

> The facts learned in this case show the extent of the conveyor belt killings. It is a mockery that Jewish people were forced to participate in the killings of their brothers in faith, while people like the accused get away with playing the gentlemen.[734]

In his defense, Oberhauser had refused to comment on any issue relating to the allegations, but prior statements made by him to the investigating officers were read to the court. Among the defensive answers to the officers' questions, Oberhauser made two relevant points:

> What Wirth ordered, I had to carry out. It would have not mattered to him to shoot even an SS man if he refused to carry out an order. As far as gassing of the old Jews was concerned, I could understand it, anything over and above that was too much for me. I thought to myself that there must be some other way of getting rid of the Jews.

A sentiment shared by Zierke and Fuchs.[735]

Because of Oberhauser's close association with Wirth and arrogant aloofness in Belzec, his colleagues took the opportunity to discredit him in court. They implicated him with the camp construction and the full gassing operations. *SS-Scharführer* Karl Schluch:

> If Oberhauser maintained that he did not participate in the extermination of the Jews in Belzec, or that he did not see the whole operation from beginning to end—from the unloading to the removal of the bodies— then I say, "Try another one!"
>
> Oberhauser not only knew the entire running of the extermination operation well but also took part in it. In my opinion, there is no doubt that Oberhauser was an authoritative person in the killing of the Jews in Belzec camp. The Belzec camp operated for only one reason, and for what Oberhauser did he was well promoted.[736]

One point that came over very strongly during the trial, and was corroborated by all the witnesses to Oberhauser's advantage, was that Wirth's law and discipline was fearful with no way of being challenged.

The prosecution were able to weaken Oberhauser's defense ploy of only being on the periphery of events in Belzec. He was convicted and sentenced to four years and six months imprisonment. After having served only half his sentence, he was released from prison and returned to Munich where he worked as a barman in a beer hall. He died in 1979.[737]

Josef Oberhauser was the only person ever convicted for the crime of murdering over 600,000 Jews in Belzec.

Sobibór trial - 20 December 1963 in Hagen[738]

1.	Zierke, Ernst (Belzec)[739]	Acquitted	
2.	Bolender, Kurt[740]	Suicide	Male nurse
3.	Dubois, Werner (Belzec)[741]	3 years imp.	
4.	Frenzel, Karl[742]	Life imp.	Builder
5.	Fuchs, Erich (Belzec[743])	4 years imp.	
6.	Ittner, Alfred[744]	4 years imp.	Male nurse
7.	Jührs, Robert (Belzec)[745]	Acquitted	
8.	Lachmann, Erich[746]	Acquitted	Police officer
9.	Lambert, Erwin [747]	Acquitted	Builder
10.	Schütt, Heinz-Hans[748]	Acquitted	Male nurse
11.	Unverhau, Heinrich (Bel)[749]	Acquitted	
12.	Wolf, Franz[750]	8 years imp.	Photographer

First Treblinka trial - 3 September 1965 in Düsseldorf

1.	Franz, Kurt	Life imp.	KZ/Cook
2.	Hirtreiter, Josef	Life imp.	Male nurse
3.	Küttner, Kurt	Died	Male nurse
4.	Horn, Otto Richard	Acquitted	Male nurse
5.	Lambert, Hermann	4 years	Builder
6.	Matthes, Arthur	Life imp.	Male nurse
7.	Mentz, Willy	Life imp.	Farm worker
8.	Münzberger, Gust	12 years	Cook
9.	Rum, Albert	3 years	Photographer
10.	Stadie, Otto	6 years	Male nurse
11.	Suchomel, Franz	7 years	Photographer

Second Treblinka Trial - 13 May 1970 in Düsseldorf [751]

Stangl, Franz Paul	Life	Police officer

Seven to nine-hundred thousand persons, predominantly Jews but also a number of Sinti and Roma, were killed in Treblinka.[752] According to the Stroop Report (Official German report on the Warsaw Ghetto Uprising), approximately 310,000 Jews were transported in freight trains from the Warsaw ghetto to Treblinka during the period from 22 July to 3 October 1942. Approximately 19,000 other Jews made the same journey during the period from January 1943 to mid-May 1943. During the period from 1 August 1942 to 23 August 1943, additional transports of Jews arrived by freight train at Treblinka from other Polish cities, including Kielce, Międzyrzec, Łuków, Włoszczowa, Sędziszów, Częstochowa, Szydłowiec, Łochów, Kozienice, Białystok, Sobibór Mazowiecki, Grodno and Radom.

Other Jews arrived at Treblinka in horse-drawn wagons and in trucks, as did the Gypsies, including some from countries other than Poland. In addition, Jews from Germany and other European countries, including Austria, Czechoslovakia, Bulgaria, Yugoslavia and Greece were transported to Treblinka, predominantly in passenger trains.

In the trials listed above where a total of 27 defendants appeared before West German courts, the following trades and political affiliation emerge: male nurses, 13; builders, 2; photographers, 2; KZ guards, 2; cooks, 1; mechanics/drivers, 2; and one farm worker. All were members of the Nazi Party and/or the SA; only one was a member of the SS.

In a random selection of a further 22 people who entered T4 with specific employment and Party status, and were later seconded to *Reinhardt* with the nominal rank of *SS-Scharführer*, the following picture emerges: male nurses, 12; driver/mechanics, 3; SS/KZ guards, 3; photographers, 3; metal worker, 1; farm worker, 1; builder, 1; and one cook. All 22 were either members of the Nazi Party and/or the SA. Four were members of the Nazi Party and/or the SA and SS.

Were these men—who had come from a disrupted society, were of average or below-average intelligence, and who had carried out the most horrendous crimes—natural-born killers and sadistic psychopaths who had been spurred on by blinded loyalty to their *Führer*, or were they caught up in the unstoppable merry-go-round of Nazi pseudo-political criminality when cold-blooded mass murder had ceased to touch them by its very repetitiveness? Was the Christian Wirth leadership central to this quandary, or is it out of absolute fear of the alternatives that the majority were unable to retreat or escape?

The answer, I suggest, can be found somewhere in the middle, in circumstances where each man was privy to his own thoughts and responsible for his own actions. After several years' exposure within the euthanasia program and *Reinhardt*, these more or less "ordinary" men manifested the effects of this conditioning accordingly in their daily behavior. However, as Browder and Browning have both emphasized, all of them, regardless, had in some way contributed significantly to the Third *Reich*.

Soviet Trials: *Trawnikimänner*[753]

When the tide of the war turned in the east, the Soviets were quick to exploit their military advances. To show the world that Soviet justice was paramount, hastily convened war crimes trials were held and summary justice was generously meted out to former German collaborators, usually finalized with a 25-year sentence in the Gulag, or a military firing squad.

Initially, these trials were held in public, but as Soviet westward gains consolidated their position, there was less emphasis on the "public" and more placed on trials held behind closed doors. As early as 1943, trials were held in Krasnodar (in July), and Kharkov (in October), when various grades of "collaborators" were dealt with. However, as the Great Patriotic War came to an end in 1945, the Soviet machinery of justice (some say in undue haste) unleashed a ferocious prosecution program. This purge came in two phases: between 1947 and 1952, and in the 1960s and 1970s. High on the list for retribution were the Soviet citizens who had been former guards in the death camps of Operation *Reinhardt*—the *Trawnikimänner*.

The Soviet State Trials of those who had not managed to seek refuge in the West were short and direct. On the day of conviction—there was no appeal—they were taken out and shot. The *"Wachmann"* Nikolay Petrovich Malagon, who served briefly in Belzec, and who had been interrogated by the Soviets in February 1945, has given us a general overview of the torture and cruelty inflicted on helpless people in the *Reinhardt* camps. Malagon only served in Belzec for five days when there was an attempted escape by his compatriots. All were arrested and returned to Trawniki. Malagon was later posted to Auschwitz and then Buchenwald KZ, from where he escaped in March 1945.[754] Of these guards who were hunted down and arrested by the Soviets and placed on trial in Kiev, few escaped the wrath of the mother country: B. Bielakow, M. Matwijenko, I. Nikifor, W. Podienko, F. Tichonowski, F. Schultz, J. Zajczew, and several others who had served in Belzec and Sobibór, were tried and executed. In 1965, at Kiev, a further 10 guards who had served in these camps were arrested, tried and executed by firing squad. In a third Kiev trial, another three Ukrainian guards met the same fate.[755] During the investigation in the USSR in connection with the Demjanjuk trial, it was found that many other guards had not been executed, but had served sentences of 10-15 years and were then released. They testified on Demjanjuk's behalf, that he had been in Sobibór, not Treblinka.

The history of the *Trawnikimänner* has yet to be told. The main archival sources remain with the Federal Security Service (AFSB) in Moscow. Other sources are held in various archives at *oblast* level throughout the former Soviet Union. Documents cited in this account were collected from various archival locations, but all originate from the United States Department of Justice and from Israel in connection with the criminal proceedings against Ivan (John) Demjanjuk. The former KGB archives in Vilnius, Lithuania, and in Prague, Czech Republic, all hold a vast amount of material relating to Soviet criminal proceedings against German collaborators. A lack of resources on behalf of the archivists has inhibited important indexing and filing of this material. So far we have only scratched the surface of this most important aspect of Holocaust research. David Rich's *Reinhardt's Footsoldiers* points the way, but it is a chapter of history just waiting to be explored and written.[756]

Psychology of the Perpetrators

The attitude of the majority of German perpetrators towards the Jews was unsympathetic, cruel and sometimes barbarous. On the other hand, as we know from the evidence, while the principle of murder, whether by shooting or by gas, was carried out efficiently, there was a quirk in the system: the timing and place of death was to be controlled by the murderers. Although the principle of a painless death for the victims of euthanasia was a consideration for the T4 bureaucrats, the practical day-to-day conduct of gassings in *Reinhardt* was anything but considerate. The psychological circumstances surrounding the victim during the course of the perpetrators' execution of their murderous policy was in many cases more terrifying than the act itself. The victim's cardinal affront to the perpetrators was taking the decision not to subject him/herself to the orderly progression of events, but to beat and defy the system by suicide. Nothing was more certain of inflaming the perpetrator than this, which very often set off a train of events that brought on even more brutality and death to otherwise helpless and innocent victims.[757]

The files are replete with descriptions of occasions such as this, not only concerning the conventionally recognized victims of German brutality, but also the Germans themselves, as occurred in diverse situations such as the cruel punishment meted out to officers engaged in the attempt on Hitler's life in July 1944.[758] For the crimes allegedly committed, execution was not enough to satisfy the persecutors who demanded torture of the most demeaning kind first. It was exactly the same for the victims in the death camps. In both cases there was no alternative. Realization of the inevitable consequences, with no hope of escape, concentrated the mind and in so doing, enabled the victim. Choosing the time and place to beat the hangman, rather than facing what lay before them, was a luxury. For those who chose this path, life was just not worth living. The luxury of choosing the final action was the same—for Jew and German alike.

For the answers as to why this phenomenon of German psychological brutality should be so, we must look to the individual perpetrators. As has been indicated elsewhere, the men holding the power in the *Einsatzgruppen*, the KZs and AR camps were all hardened ideological Nazis. They were authorized to act on their own responsibility and encouraged to dream up new ways of death and torture. This gave them a wide discretion as to how they were to be effective. Some responded by developing their methods through experimentation in the day-to-day killings. This does not necessarily mark them all down as wanton killers as described above, since many firmly believed they were doing their best while acting under orders. Certainly many of the *Einsatzgruppen* commanders carried out executions of innocent people, but in doing so, they also adhered to well recognized principles, such as the procedures laid down for properly convened, regulated firing squads. This concept of military honor, in the well-established code of shooting at "twelve paces" and the "*coup de grace*," given by the squad leader, deteriorated once mass murder of the Jews began to accelerate. This was evident in the methods implemented by the SD in east Galicia and even more so in the AR camps. Each SD commander interpreted his own conduct independently in carrying out these murders, based on the authority given to him at the outset of Barbarossa. This being the case, and given the numbers now involved, the theory no longer corresponded to the facts of the situation now facing them. The enormity of the shooting task had engulfed them.

Finally, what appears to me as completely surreal is the normality of lifestyle these men adopted immediately after the war by assimilating themselves into conventional society. Only a short time before, these men had committed the most gruesome crimes against humanity; and yet, they could talk across a table, their wives looking on with sympathetic interest, eye to eye with survivors from the death camps, discussing their problems over a cup of coffee.[759] Others mingled in society, some as builders, others as petrol pump attendants and in other low profile occupations, and carried on as though nothing had happened.

Two former Belzec SS guards were known to be still alive in Germany until recently: Robert Jührs, aged 86 and now totally blind, who lives in Frankfurt-am-Main; and Kurt Franz, aged 84—released in 1993 after 34 years in prison for crimes committed at Treblinka—who lived in Düsseldorf. He died in 1998.

Chapter 14. Archaeological Investigations[760]

Introduction

The investigation carried out at Belzec by leading archaeologists was historically unique, as no similar investigations had been carried out at the other two other exclusively designated death camps of Sobibór and Treblinka.[761] The magnitude of events in Belzec has never been fully described in historical literature until now. According to previous studies, which have always been inhibited by lack of eye-witness evidence, several hundred thousand Jews perished in Belzec.[762] The archaeological investigations confirm by overwhelming evidence that mass murder was committed here on an unprecedented scale and that there was a determined attempt to conceal the enormity of the crime. In this the Nazis failed.[763] The material unearthed at Belzec not only confirmed the crime but enabled historians to reconstruct the probable layout of the camp in the first and second phases by scientific analysis, for the first time.

Previous Investigations

The 1997 archaeological investigations at Belzec were initiated by an agreement between the Council for the Protection of Memory of Combat and Martyrdom (*Rada Ochrony Pamieci Walk I Meczenstwa – ROPWiM*) in Warsaw in association with the United States Holocaust Memorial Council and the United States Holocaust Memorial Museum in Washington, D.C. How Belzec was to be commemorated was the subject of a wide-ranging competition among artists who placed their suggestions before a selection committee. The successful contributors were a team of architects and artists led by Marcin Roszczyk, who intended "To honor the earth that harbored the ashes of the victims." It is within this definition that the archaeological investigations were commenced, to examine the topography of the former camp and locate mass grave areas before the erection of a suitable memorial commemorating the victims murdered in Belzec.

As a result of the work carried out by the archaeological team from Toruń University, and an historical assessment of the findings by the author, a clearer picture has emerged of how the camp was constructed, organized and functioned in both phases of its existence. Before looking at the most recent survey, some background regarding previous investigations may be helpful.

First Investigation, 1945 [764]

Very shortly after the end of the war, several War Crimes Investigation Commissions were established in Poland by the Soviet-backed civil authorities. At all locations in eastern Europe where Nazi atrocities had taken place, teams of specialist investigators descended to set up officially constituted boards of inquiry with powers to summon local people to attend and give evidence. On 10 October 1945, an Investigation Commission team lead by Judge Czesław Godzieszewski from the District Court in Zamosc entered Belzec and commenced investigations. In addition to hearing oral testimony from many inhabitants of Belzec village and its environs, the team of investigators carried out an on-site investigation at the camp. Nine pits were opened to confirm the existence of mass graves. The evidence found indicated that thousands of corpses had been cremated and any remaining bones crushed into small pieces. The human remains unearthed were re-interred in a specially built concrete crypt near the northeast corner of the camp.[765] Within hours of this simple ceremony to commemorate the victims, local villagers ransacked the grave area looking for treasure. This desecration of mass graves by local inhabitants continues to this day. Immediately after completion of the 1998 excavations, overnight, the excavation sites were penetrated and damaged by searches for Jewish gold. Similar acts of malicious damage have been recorded at Sobibór and Treblinka.

Second Investigation 1946

This was a continuation of the earlier investigation during which certain witnesses were re-interrogated. In view of the findings at Belzec, the Investigation Commission published a report on 11 April 1946,[766] which concluded that Belzec was the second death camp to have been built or adapted by the Nazis for the specific purpose of murdering Jews. The report cites the first camp in which mass murder took place as being at Chełmno, which operated between December 1941 and early 1943.[767] The Investigation Commission relied on the testimonies of eyewitnesses who had been employed in the construction of these camps, or who lived locally and had observed what was taking place.[768] One of the Belzec witnesses, Chaim Hirszman (mentioned earlier), had escaped from the transport taking the last few members of a Jewish "death brigade" from Belzec to Sobibór, where they were shot. He testified before a Lublin court on 19 March 1946 and was due to continue his testimony in court the following day, but was murdered, either by Polish anti-Semites or because of his connections with the NKVD, before he could do so.[769]

The Investigation Commission drew attention to the systematic destruction of the ghettos and the "resettlement" transports to the transit ghettos in Izbica and Piaski from towns within the Nazi-occupied territory of Poland then known as the *Generalgouvernement*. The Commission further noted "resettlement" transports from Western Europe to Belzec, and the inclusion in these transports of Polish Christians who had been engaged either in anti-Nazi activities or accused of assisting or hiding Jews. The Commission concluded that 1,000-1,500 Polish Christians were murdered in Belzec.[770] The final part of the report by the Belzec Investigation Commission dealt with winding-down activities: cremations, destruction of evidence, dismantling of the gas chambers, removal of fences, and the ground being plowed-up and planted with fir trees and lupines. The Commission verified from the evidence that a final inspection had been carried out at Belzec by a special SS Commission to ensure that everything had been done to cover up the enormity of the crimes perpetrated in the name of *Reinhardt*.[771]

Third Investigation, 1961

The Council declared that the former death camp at Belzec should be commemorated as a place of remembrance. In order to preserve the site as a memorial, extensive excavations were carried out. Approximately six hectares were levelled and fenced off (a reduction in the actual size of the original camp area) and marked out as the memorial site. A monument was erected above the crypt where the human remains found in the first investigation in 1945 had been interred.[772] Immediately behind the monument, four symbolic tombs cast in concrete were placed where the mass graves were believed (incorrectly) to be located.[773] On the north side of the camp, six large urns intended for eternal flames were positioned on a series of elevated terraces. Over the years, further landscaping has been carried out on parts of the former camp area adjoining the timber yard.

Fourth Investigation, 1997-2000[774]

The four phases of this most recent investigation were directed by Professor Andrzej Kola, director of the Archaeological Faculty at the Nicholas Copernicus University in Toruń, Poland. The principal investigating officers on site were Dr. Mieczysław Gora, Senior Curator of the Museum of Ethnology in Łódź, Poland, assisted by Dr. Wojciech Szulta and Dr. Ryszard Kaźmierczak. Unemployed males from Belzec village were engaged in all four phases of the most recent investigations to assist with the labor-intensive drilling.

Recent Investigations

The methodology of all four of the most recent investigations was similar: marking out the area to be examined to a fixed grid system at 5 m intervals (knots). Exploratory boreholes to a depth of 6 m were made,[775] obtaining core samples of the geological strata.[776] A total of 2,001 archaeological exploratory drillings were carried out and were instrumental in locating 33 mass graves of varying sizes. From these exploratory drillings, many graves were found to contain naked bodies in wax-fat transformation (complete), and carbonized human remains and ashes were also identified. The investigating personnel were divided into three teams, each working at a table to record data as soil samples were withdrawn and examined. Using a map of the area to a scale of 1:1,000, prepared by the District Cartographic Office in Zamosc, a Central Bench Mark (BM 2007) was utilized as the reference point from which the archaeologists worked. Positive data and negative findings were recorded before replacing the soil samples in the boreholes.

The team of archaeologists from Toruń University in Belzec In 1998.
As photographed by the author May 1998

Area of Mass Graves[777]

The most significant and unexpected evidence to emerge as a result of the 1997-99 investigations are the location of a large number of mass graves and the substantial quantity of camp structures found, (65) scattered throughout the area of the former death camp. Several of the structures correspond in approximate position with known buildings in the camp area: the undressing and barbers' barracks, workshops, warehouse, and bunker for the electricity generator; in Camp II, the barracks and kitchen for the Jewish "death brigade." The first priority of the archaeologists was to locate and map the mass graves.

During its first phase, Belzec was a temporary and experimental camp in which the procedures and logistics of mass extermination by gas and the burial of corpses were tried and tested. The camp structures and mass graves of the first phase in Belzec were concentrated along the northern fence, leaving the majority of the camp area unused but ready for utilization and expansion at a later date. The primitive, experimental gassing barrack and undressing barracks were also temporary structures replaced later by bigger and more solidly constructed buildings to accommodate the increased number of victims for the second and final phase in August 1942.

The two phases of the gassing operations may be identified by the arrangement of the mass graves and camp structures between the graves. Thus, the apparent proliferation of small wooden structures between the graves of the first phase may have been temporary barracks for the Jews of the "death brigade," employed in digging the mass graves, and shelters for the guards. Three of the smallest wooden structures arranged at intervals around the western and southern part of the grave field from the first period suggest watchtowers overlooking the grave-digging area. The structures in the southern half of the camp area date from the second period.

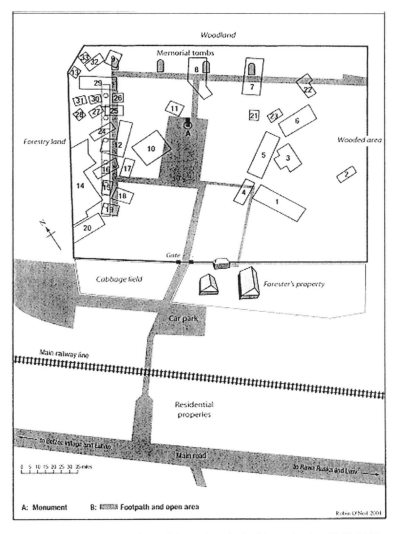

The memorial area at the time of the archaeological investigation 1998-2000.

The mass graves numbered as they appear on the plan above are located looking into the camp from the main gate, with the forester's property on the right. On the right, the graves marked 1-6 are grouped together. These were the graves located by investigators in the first phase (1997), and believed to be the last series of graves dug in late 1942.

Graves 12 and 14-20, situated along the north fence, are in accordance with statements by witnesses with respect to the period of February-May 1942.[778]

These graves probably contain the remains of the Jews from the Lublin and Lvov Districts deported to Belzec camp between mid-March and mid-April 1942, and the remains of early transports from the Lvov ghetto and transit ghettos at Izbica and Piaski. It is also very probable that the remains of German Jews deported from the *Reich* in April through May 1942 are located here.

Graves 10, 25, 27, 28, 32, and 33 all contain a layer of lime covering decomposed human remains. It is probable that these graves also date from these early transports when the local authorities complained about the health hazard caused by the smell of decomposing corpses in open graves. Chloride of lime was spread over the six still open mass graves identified above in an effort to avoid epidemics breaking out. Evidence of the subsequent failed attempt at cremating corpses in graves may be found in the small graves near the north fence: 27, 28 and 32, in each of which a layer of burnt human remains and pieces of carbonized wood were found. The bottom of each of these graves is lined with a layer of burnt human fat.

The preparation and digging of these graves would appear to have been arranged on an *ad hoc* basis with the early graves located in the northeastern part of the camp. Many graves were close together and when the exhumation and cremation work commenced, the sides of the graves would have collapsed, thereby rendering any subsequent accurate record of grave sizes difficult. This suggests a hurried sealing of the ground, together with the destruction of any identifiable border, which in turn made the archaeologists' work more difficult and their findings less precise. In addition, as part of the attempt to destroy the evidence, a mechanical excavator had been used to remove the top layer of soil and remove the corpses, and then refill the pits with the cremated human remains and ash. The use of this equipment rendered the archaeologists' task even more demanding.

Mechanical excavator in Treblinka that had previously been used in Belzec.

It has been suggested that some of the smallest graves (e.g. Nos.: 13, 27, 28, 32 and 33) could have been the execution pits in which the old, sick and infirm Jews were shot during the first phase, while graves 2, 21 and 23 could be the execution pits from the second phase.[779] The smaller graves correspond with sketches and written descriptions of the camp layout during the second phase (July-December 1942), as provided by members of the former SS garrison.[780]

From the evidence uncovered by the 1997-98 investigations, the camp SS could not possibly have destroyed all traces of the extermination camp. Their purpose was to disguise the enormity of the numbers buried in Belzec. In the clean-up operation after the burning of the corpses, the cremated human remains, as well as the remnants of the burnt-down wooden barracks and demolished solid structures, were simply dumped into the pits and covered over. Solidly constructed cellars beneath certain buildings were also used as refuse pits into which were thrown glass and metal objects, which could not be completely destroyed by fire. The cellars, just like the graves, were simply filled in with soil.

Mass Graves numbered 1-33 are in the order of discovery.

Location and first period 1997: Graves 1- 6 [781]

Grave pit No. 1: Located in northwestern part of the camp. Dimensions of the grave were determined as 40 m x 12 m and more than 4.80 m deep, filled with bodies in wax-fat transformation, and a mixture of burnt human bones and charcoal. Beneath this deep stratum lay a several-centimeters-thick layer of foul-smelling water, beneath which were found unburnt corpses compressed by the weight of soil to a layer 20 cm thick. The drill core brought to the surface putrid pieces of human remains, including pieces of skull with skin and tufts of hair attached, and unidentifiable lumps of greyish, fatty, human tissue. The bottom of the grave was lined with a layer of evil smelling black (burnt) human fat, resembling black soap. As no evidence of fabric was brought to the surface, it may be assumed that the corpses are naked. The conclusion was drawn that the preservation of the corpses was due to the fact that they lay virtually hermetically sealed between the layer of the water above and the layer of solidified fat below. Underneath this the natural, dry and compressed sand, through which no air could penetrate, resulted in their partial mummification.

Grave pit No. 2: Located in northeastern part of the camp. Dimensions of the grave were determined as 14 m x 6 m x 2 m deep, containing a layer of unburnt corpses and a mixture of cremated substances.

Grave pit No. 3: Located in the southern part of the camp. This was the first mass grave, the location of which was positively identified from a Luftwaffe aerial photograph taken in 1944. It appears as a T-shaped white patch and has the appearance of being one of the largest graves in the camp. Dimensions of the grave were determined as 16 m x 15 m x 5 m deep. Contained a mixture of carbonized wood, fragments of burnt human bones, pieces of skulls with skin and tufts of hair still attached, lumps of greyish human fat, and fragments of unburned human bones. The bottom layer consisted of putrid, waxy human fat.

Grave pit No. 4: Located immediately to the south. Dimensions of the grave determined as 16 m x 6 m. At a depth of 2.30 m drilling was suspended due to contact with bodies in wax-fat transformation. Contained cremated remains. From below the water layer, the drill core brought to the surface pieces of unburned human bones, including pieces of skulls with skin and hair still adhering and lumps of foul smelling greasy fat, indicating the presence of unburned corpses.

Grave pit No. 5: Located in the southwestern part of the camp and formed from the left-hand bar of the T-shaped arrangement of graves 3, 5 and 6. Dimensions of the grave determined as 32 m x 10 m x 4.50 m deep. Contained pieces of burnt human bones so densely packed together that the drill could not penetrate further.

Grave pit No. 6: Located in south-central part of the camp. Dimensions determined as 30 m x 10 m x 4 m deep. Contained carbonized wood and fragments of burnt human bones. At the eastern end of the grave, the ground is covered with grey sand containing a mixture of crushed pieces of burnt and unburned fragments of human bones.[782]

13. 10: Investigations at the Ramp (1)

The focus of the investigation moved away from the grave area to where the "resettlement transports" had terminated inside the camp, the "ramp." Here the Jews disembarked from the wagons to be addressed by the camp command before moving on to the undressing barracks and the gas chambers. The archaeological team carried out four excavations and located what is believed to be the end of the railway spur line. The investigating team selected a 75 m. long section at the southwestern end of the site where the former railway siding(s) emerged between two earth banks 8 to 10 m apart. The terrain at this location is forested and uneven, rising steeply to the east.

13. 11: Four Excavations

1. At right angles to the line of the Ramp, which concluded that the rail-link did not extend this far.

2. Located 15 m northwest of excavation No. 1, measuring 14 m x 1 m and 1 m deep. There were positive findings: traces of a standard gauge railway track-bed; and a layer of crushed brick and cinders (ballast) covered with black grease. A second track-bed was found running parallel and to the east of the first. Six samples of oil were taken for analysis.

3. Excavations were carried out parallel to excavations 1 and 2, and 30 m northwest of excavation 2. Further indications of track-beds in parallel were found. (These findings are crucial to our understanding of the *modus operandi* during the second phase of the camp, from August 1942).

4. The fourth excavation was located 15 m northwest of excavation 3 and measured 8.5 m x 1 m x 2 m deep. Further evidence of the twin track system was found.

Investigations with Metal Detector (2)

With the use of a metal detector, a sweep was made of the Ramp area, which produced important results.[783] The most significant find was the lid of a silver cigarette case bearing on the inside the inscription: *Max Munk, Wien 27.*[784] In all probability, the cigarette case belonged to a Max Munk, born in Vienna in 1892, and deported to Theresienstadt via Prague on 17 December 1941 on transport "N." From Theresienstadt, a Max Munk was deported on transport 'Ag' to the transit ghetto in Piaski, near Lublin, on 1 April 1942.[785] Max Munk would have been one of the early victims of Belzec. This cigarette case is the first evidence that Jews from Vienna had ended up in Belzec.[786]

Second Period 1998 and Location of Mass Graves 7 - 33[787]

The second archaeological investigation at Belzec to locate mass graves commenced on 28 April 1998, and continued without interruption until 4

June 1998. The author was present throughout and carried out a daily video and photographic record of proceedings and findings. The procedures during the survey were the same as in the October investigation. During the period April-June 1998, further exploratory boreholes were made, which located 27 mass graves, of which the dimensions and contents were determined. A number of camp structures were also located, recorded and excavated.

The location and number of graves found corroborate both the testimonies and plans made by Rudolf Reder in 1945, Chaim Hirszman in 1946 and the Report of the Polish War Crimes Investigation Commission of 1945-46.

The author interviewed a survivor from the Plaszów KZ, Joseph Bau, in Tel-Aviv. At the time, Belzec was of secondary interest, but during the interview, Bau related how he had met Rudolf Reder in Kraków in 1945, and, with the information given by Reder, drafted plans of Belzec showing the location of mass graves, gas chambers and other buildings. Bau produced for the author the original sketches of Belzec made by Reder.

Even before work commenced, a cursory examination beyond the outer perimeter of the northeastern part of the camp indicated the presence of human bone fragments on an exposed sand escarpment.[788]

At the conclusion of the investigations, it was established that the camp was one large patchwork of mass graves and camp structures. By determining the size, position and soil content of these graves, the investigators were able to establish the probable configuration of the camp buildings in both phases of the camp's operations. Graves numbered **12** and **14**, which appear to be the largest and probably those identified by the Polish War Crimes Investigation Commission in 1945, enabled the historians to pinpoint details of the early transports into the camp during phase one.[789] There is no way of determining with certainty exactly where the first victims came from. We know only that they were probably either from the transit ghettos in Piaski or Izbica, or from Lvov or Lublin.[790] It was also difficult to determine exactly where the first graves were dug in the first phase of the camp's existence. We know only that they were in the northwestern part of the camp. Max Munk from Vienna probably lies here.

The finding of lime in the sample soil cores extracted from graves **9, 12, 14, 15, 17, 22, 24, 25, 29, 31, 32** and **33**, located towards the top left corner (i.e. northwest corner) may corroborate the description by Franz Stangl of when the pits were overflowing with corpses. The unusually warm spring of 1942 necessitated truckloads of lime being brought into the camp to avoid a possible epidemic.

The sizes of graves, particularly in the northwestern corner, indicate hurriedly excavated pits to deal with exhumed corpses during the second phase when extensive attempts were made to destroy the evidence. In graves **13, 27, 28, 32** and **33** this was particularly evident.[791] It was also seen that some graves had not been opened and the contents burnt. Here, the team found evidence of unburnt, mummified bodies. It was established that six graves, probably from the first phase, and three graves, probably from the second phase, had not been emptied. It was concluded that the nature of this task was so gruesome, and had become so unacceptable, that collusion not to disinter these corpses, and thus not to complete the undertaking as ordered, probably occurred (without authorization) between the SS and members of the Jewish "death brigade" engaged in this horrific duty.

Mass Grave Locations: 7 – 33

Grave pit No. 7: initially located in October 1997, this grave is near where symbolic tomb No. **4** was situated at the eastern-central part of the camp. The dimensions of the grave (in a shape closely resembling a trapezoid) were determined as 13 m x 14 m, and a depth of 4.50 m. The symbolic tomb lies just to the right (south) of the grave. The grave contained carbonized pieces of wood and fragments of burnt human bones mixed with dark grey ash.

Grave pit No. 8: located at the southwestern part of the camp. Dimensions were determined as 28 m x 10 m x 4 m. The grave contained burnt pieces of human bones and fragments of carbonized wood.

Grave pit No. 9: located immediately behind symbolic tomb No. **1**, next to the northeast fence. Dimensions determined as 10 m x 8 m x 3, 80 m. It contained burnt human remains and pieces of carbonized wood mixed with grey sand.

(Surface soil/sand in the vicinity of graves **7, 8** and **9** was grey in color, suggesting large quantities of crushed pieces of human bone).

Grave pit No. 10: one of the biggest graves; located in the northern-central part of the camp. Dimensions determined as 24 m x 18 m x 5 m, containing a thick layer of human fat, unburned human remains and pieces of unburned large human bones. The drill core brought to the surface several lumps of foul smelling fatty tissue still in a state of decomposition, mixed with greasy lime.

Grave pit No. 11: located at northeastern corner of the camp. Dimensions determined as 9 m x 5 m x 1 90 m, containing a few fragments of burnt human bones mixed with innumerable small pieces of carbonized wood.

Grave pit No. 12: located immediately to the north of grave No. **10**; an "L-shaped" grave with the foot measuring 20 m, lying to the west. The stem was 28 m in length, pointing north. A small number of pieces of unburned human bones were found at a depth of 3 m, mixed with grey sand and innumerable small fragments of carbonized wood. This layer extended to a depth of 4.4 m.

Grave pit No. 13: located next to the western fence. Dimensions of the grave (trapezoid in shape), were determined as 12.50 m x 11.00 m x 4.80 m. deep. It contained a mixture of burnt human remains and pieces of carbonized wood mixed with grey sand.

Grave pit No. 14: the largest grave in the camp, it extended beyond the north fence into the area of the adjacent timber yard. The section within the fence is an irregular zigzag on the south side, measuring 37 m x 10 m at its widest point east to west, and 8 m wide at its narrowest; it is 5 m deep. It contained burnt pieces of human bones and fragments of carbonized wood mixed with grey, sandy soil to a depth of 5 m. Originally, grave No. **14** could have measured ca. 70 m. x 30 m.

(According to witnesses the first and largest mass grave (No. **14**) was dug by members of the Soviet guard unit while the camp was under construction. It took six weeks to complete the task.[792])

Grave pit No. 15: another small grave measuring 13.50 m x 6.50 m, with a depth of 4.50 m, it was situated adjacent to the south side of grave No. **14**. It contained a mixture of pieces of burnt human bone fragments, carbonized wood, and grey sand.

Grave pit No. 16: located adjacent to grave No. **14** and immediately east of grave No. **15**. Measuring 18.50 m x 9.50 m, it contained a mixture of burnt fragments of human bones and carbonized wood to a depth of 4.00 m.

Grave pit No. 17: situated next to and south of graves **12 and 16**, measures 17 m x 7 m 50 cm x 4 m, and contained a mixture of pieces of burnt human bones, carbonized wood, and grey sand.

Grave pit No. 18: situated next to the southern edge of grave No. **15** and measuring 16 m x 9 m x 4 m, contained the same mixture of burnt pieces of human bones, carbonized wood and grey sand.

Grave pit No. 19: located within the area formed by graves **14, 15, 18** and **20**, and close to the southwestern corner of grave 14, measuring 12 m x 12 m and containing a mixture of grey sand, burnt pieces of human bones, and carbonized wood to a depth of 4 m.

Grave pit No. 20: in the form of a long trench at the western end of grave No. **14**, is the last of the graves at the northern end of the group and of 18 along the north fence. In the same manner as its neighbor, grave No. **14**, it also extends beyond the north fence into the area of the adjacent timber yard. The section within the fence measures 26 m x 11 m x 5 m. At a depth of 4 m a dental bridge with four false teeth was found.

Grave pit No. 21: located centrally. Dimensions determined as 5 m sq and situated in the forested southern part of the memorial area, midway between graves **5** and **7**. It is unexpectedly shallow, being only 1.70 m deep and containing pieces of burnt human bones and fragments of carbonized wood mixed with grey sand.

Grave pit No. 22: located in the eastern part of the camp in the shape of an inverted "L," close to grave No. **6**. Measuring 27 m on the long (east) side and 10 m on the south side, containing pieces of burnt human bones and fragments of carbonized wood mixed with grey sand to a depth of 3.50 m.

Grave pit No. 23: one of the smaller graves, measuring 16 m x 8.50 m x 4.20 m and located between graves 6 and 21; it contained burnt human remains.

Grave pit No. 24: a narrow trench measuring 20 m x 5.50 m x 5 m., located at the north fence and next to the eastern corner of grave No. **14**, it contained burnt human remains.

Grave pit No. 25: located immediately to the east of graves **12** and **14**. Dimensions determined as 12 m x 5 m. Contained a mixture of burnt human remains, including corpses and skeletons, to a depth of 4 m. Below this level, there was a 1 m deep layer of waxy fat and greasy lime. A foul odor was released when the drill penetrated the layer of corpses and the drill core withdrew lumps of decaying fatty tissue and large pieces of bone.

Grave pit No. 26: another small grave, measuring 13 m x 7 m x 4.20 m, and located immediately next to the eastern edge of grave No. **25**. It contained a mixture of burnt human remains.

(Note: The soil above and around graves **25** and **26** is covered with a layer of innumerable small fragments of burnt human bones and small pieces of carbonized wood)

Grave pit No. 27: measuring 18.50 m x 6 m x 6 m, and situated close to the north end of grave No. **25**. It contained burnt and unburned human remains: the top layer consists of burnt human bones and carbonized wood beneath which there is a layer of grey, waxy lime. The bottom of the grave contains completely decomposed human remains mixed with putrid smelling greasy human fat.

Grave pit No. 28: one of the smallest graves, measuring 6 m x 6 m x 5 m, located between grave **27** and the north fence. It contained burned human remains beneath which there is a layer of grey greasy lime. The bottom of the grave is lined with putrid smelling, greasy human fat.

Grave pit No. 29: measuring 25 m x 9 m x 4.50 in the form of a long trench and located just to the northeast of grave **26**. Its eastern corner is immediately in front of symbolic tomb No. **1**. It contained pieces of burnt human bones mixed with fragments of carbonized wood and grey sand.

Grave pit No. 30: located in the north angle between graves **26 and 29** and measuring 5 m x 6 m. It contained pieces of burnt human bones and fragments of carbonized wood mixed with grey sand to a depth of 2.70 m.

Grave pit No. 31: similar in size to grave No. **30**, measuring 9 m x 4 m x 2.60 m. Situated next to the north fence between graves **28** and **29**, this grave also contained a mixture of burnt pieces of human bones, fragments of carbonized wood and grey sand.

Grave pit No. 32: situated close to the north corner of the memorial site between graves **9** and **13**, and measuring 15 m x 5 m. It contained a mixture of burnt human bones and carbonized wood mixed with grey sand, beneath which there is a layer of grey, greasy lime and a foul smelling layer of human fat containing decomposing human remains. The drill core brought to the surface pieces of skull with skin and tufts of hair still attached. At the bottom of the grave, at a depth of 4.10 m, lay a large number of unburned human bones. The path to the small gate near the north corner of the memorial area passes over the southern end of the grave.

Grave pit No. 33: a small, shallow grave measuring only 9 m x 5 m x 3 m, located in the extreme northeastern corner of the memorial site. It contained tiny fragments of burnt human bones mixed with small pieces of carbonized wood and grey sand.

Further Investigations with Metal Detector

Carried out by the author, these produced a miscellaneous collection of enamel kitchenware and assorted scrap metal. Further sweeps of the area located a metal door to a kitchen stove and assorted pre-war Polish coins. The only item of interest was another silver cigarette case with no inscription.

Ramp Area (2)

Continuing investigations at the Ramp were carried over from the 1997 survey. In the 1940 and 1944 aerial maps the two rail tracks are clearly shown entering the death camp.[793] These tracks were not built specifically for operations within the camp but were there because the area on which the camp was built had been a pre-war logging area.[794] This was undoubtedly one of the main reasons the death camp was built at this location. This evidence also confirms that the "Otto line" was built subsequent to May 1940, as there is no photographic evidence to show its existence before that date.[795]

In the first phase of Belzec, no more than 20 train cars could be accommodated at any time because the uneven ground rises steeply at the southern end of the terrain, which made any further extension of the tracks impossible. The second ramp, constructed initially to handle the bigger transports from Kraków which commenced on 3 June, was the same length as the first and could also only accommodate 20 train cars at a time.

Close examination of the 1944 aerial photograph, and the ground scarring, clearly indicates this. The *Luftwaffe* aerial photo taken in May 1944 shows that the spur line had been partly removed, probably when the camp was decommissioned and destroyed.[796] The archaeologists corroborated the extent and termination of the rail tracks within the camp but came to their conclusions from a different direction.

Examination of the 1944 aerial photographs indicates the presence of freight cars on a siding just outside the former camp entrance. Further examination and measurement show that it was possible to accommodate 20 cars plus the locomotive on ramp "A" (first phase) and at least 20 cars on the second ramp (constructed for phase 2 in August 1942). This confirms that it was possible to accommodate at least 40 train cars inside the camp: 20 on Ramp "A," with another 20 on ramp "B," waiting while the victims on Ramp "A" were being "processed."

By August 1942, the handling of "goods" (Jews) had developed into a well-organized and smoothly functioning killing machine. This, I would suggest, is the reason why Belzec in its short life span as compared with Treblinka and Sobibór was so successful in murdering so many people. Another reason was that a maximum number of train cars could be accommodated on the ramps simultaneously with less shunting back and forth between station and camp, as was the case in the other two death camps. These conclusions were drawn in collaboration with my colleague Michael Tregenza and are mainly supported by the findings of the official archaeological report.

Conclusions [797]

The total surface of the mass graves is estimated at 21,000 cubic meters.[798] At least a dozen graves still contain unburnt, partially mummified or decomposing corpses today. Exactly why the SS did not empty all the graves and destroy their contents is not known; they were in no hurry to leave the area as the entire SS-garrison was redistributed to other camps in the Lublin District for at least five months after the liquidation of Belzec. However, that all the corpses were not disinterred and destroyed may be due to the following:

a) Six of the graves not emptied date from the first phase and contain decomposing corpses under a layer of lime; the corpses would have been in such an appalling state of disintegration that even the SS were reluctant to attempt disinterment.

b) Three of the graves incompletely emptied date from the second phase and are among the largest in the camp (with the exception of grave 14); removal of their entire decomposing contents presented a daunting task.

Perhaps after five months of supervising the gruesome work of exhuming and cremating the hundreds of thousands of rotting remains, day and night, the SS had simply had enough—and against orders, abandoned the task. The opened and partly emptied graves were refilled with the fragments of burnt human bones and pieces of carbonized wood from the bone mill, mixed with sand.

From the wealth of evidence uncovered by the 1997-98 investigations it is obvious that the camp SS did not by any means erase all traces of the extermination camp, as previously believed. The majority of the wooden barracks were burnt down and the carbonized wood broken into fragments; solid structures were demolished and the bricks, stones and concrete or cement broken into pieces and buried. Solidly constructed cellars beneath certain buildings were used as refuse pits into which were thrown items of glass and metal that could not be completely destroyed by fire. The cellars were then simply filled in with soil. Other articles of glass and metal were buried among the remains of burnt wooden barracks. At the Ramp, the wooden support posts and planks retaining the sandy soil of the two platforms —the negative images of which were uncovered during the 1997 investigation —were also removed and most likely burnt.

It has long been thought that only one railway siding existed at the Ramp and that it was later extended further into the camp to accommodate the longer transports of the second phase. However, the construction of such an extension would not have been possible due to the forested and uneven terrain at the southwestern end of the camp. *Luftwaffe* aerial photographs of Belzec taken in 1940 and 1944 clearly show that two parallel tracks existed on the camp area. Witnesses also mention the existence of two tracks during the second phase.[799]

SS-Oberscharführer Heinrich Gley, who supervised the daytime shift at the cremation pyres, has testified about the cremations: "The whole procedure during the burning of the exhumed corpses was so inhuman, so unaesthetic, and the stench so horrifying that people today who are used to living everyday lives cannot possibly imagine what it was like."[800]

It was apparent from the large amounts of engine oil and grease found on the track beds in 1997 that locomotives entered the camp and did not always remain outside the camp gate, having shunted the wagons from behind as stated by many witnesses.

The number of watchtowers around the camp perimeter was probably larger than claimed by witnesses. The original number of three towers at the corners (with the exception of the northwestern corner by the main gate) and one in the camp itself, must have been increased during the reorganization/rebuilding of the camp in June-July 1942, prior to the increased extermination activity that began on 1 August, with the employment of 1,000 "work Jews" in the camp. Evidence of three small wooden structures at 55 m intervals along the eastern fence indicate the probable position of such additional watchtowers.

In the autumn of 1942 there was increased partisan activity in the Belzec area, which necessitated extra security precautions by the camp SS and Soviet guard unit. One such measure was the construction of a concrete bunker at the southeastern corner of the camp, on the highest point of the terrain. It would also have been logical and effective to have had a watchtower above the bunker, affording a clear all-around view and field of fire over the entire camp area and its environs.

Belzec was a temporary, experimental operation where the procedures and logistics of mass extermination by gas and the burial of corpses were tried and tested, initially on the Jews of the Lublin ghetto, before being applied at the Sobibór and Treblinka extermination camps. It can also be seen that the original camp structures and mass graves of the first phase were concentrated along the northern fence, leaving the majority of the camp area empty and unused but ready for utilization and expansion at a later date. The primitive, experimental gassing barrack and undressing barracks were also temporary structures replaced later by bigger and more solidly constructed buildings to accommodate the increased number of victims.

That the original camp area was much bigger than the present day memorial area is not in doubt, but the exact extent of the camp remains unknown to this day. Determining the exact dimensions presents certain problems:

1. Locating the line and direction of the northern boundary has been rendered especially difficult by the complete obliteration of the original terrain;

2. The southern boundary lies in a densely forested area and extends at least 50 m beyond the present day fence;

3. The southwestern part of the area of the former camp has been buried beneath a railway embankment, constructed in the late 1960s to accommodate a set of sidings.

Only the topography of the eastern boundary, along the top of the ridge above the road to the hamlet of Szalenik, has remained virtually unchanged.

The main gate was located immediately to the south of the 1940 anti-tank ditch and rampart destroyed in 1970 and within a few meters of the main Lublin-Lvov railway line. With the aid of the *Luftwaffe* aerial photographs, surveying equipment, and local knowledge, it should be possible to locate its position with accuracy.

The concrete foundations, or part thereof, of the original gassing barrack, could still lie beneath the rough grass verge between the forester's field, to the left of the former entrance gate to the memorial area, and the paved road that ran alongside the main road, at a point about half-way between the path to the entrance gate and the north end of the allotment field. The forester has mentioned to the author that on occasions he has damaged farm machinery on a concrete structure near the east end of his field, suggesting an obstruction that could be the walls of the pit in which the gassing engine was placed, 30 m from the gassing barrack.

The lack of any clear evidence to date locating the second gassing building is intriguing. It may well be the case that the SS deliberately destroyed and removed all evidence of the most incriminating structure in the camp. On examination of the arrangement of all the mass graves and camp structures located during the 1997-98 investigations, one area stands out as the most likely site of this building: an area devoid of any graves or structures near the northeastern corner of the camp. Today it is a few meters in front of symbolic tomb No. 2.

From the probable position of the second gassing building described above, and the position and angle of the undressing barracks during the second phase, it should be possible to plot the most likely route of "*die Schleuse.*"

There is much discrepancy about the number of cremation pyres. Witnesses mention one to four, while the SS at their trial in Munich 1963-64 admitted to only two being used, each one measuring 5 m x 5 m. The first was constructed in mid-November 1942, and the second during the first week of December, but the SS were not asked where the pyres were located in the camp and they did not offer the information.

According to SS testimonies, at least 500,000 corpses were cremated on these two pyres between November 1942 and March 1943.

It may be possible during future investigations at Belzec to estimate at least an approximate number of corpses once contained in the 33 mass graves, based on the known number of corpses exhumed from mass graves at other sites such as Katyn, Kharkhov, Miednoje, etc. and the contents and cubic capacity of these graves.

Chapter 15. Statistics

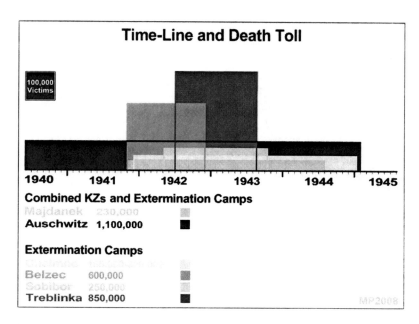

Time-Line and Death Toll

100,000 Victims

1940   1941   1942   1943   1944   1945

Combined KZs and Extermination Camps
Majdanek   230,000
Auschwitz   1,100,000

Extermination Camps
Chelmno   1,000,000 (est.)
Belzec   600,000
Sobibor   250,000
Treblinka   850,000

MP2008

Introduction

Of the estimated six million Jews murdered in the Holocaust, the dedicated death camps accounted for about *1.7 million.* This reassessment is focussed on the Jews deported from within the *Generalgouvernment* (incorporating the Districts of Galicia and Lublin), who were transported to Belzec, Sobibór and Treblinka between March 1942 and October 1943.

One of the most fundamental and controversial issues in the history of the death camps is the imprecise number of their victims. The exact number of Jews who were killed in Belżec will never be fully established because the decisions and facts relating to the extermination were rarely committed to paper. History has not been helped by the obliteration of all traces of the camp in 1943, and in addition, the standing orders for evidential destruction from the *Reichsführer SS.* [801]

The catchment area for deportations to Belzec was extensive. Deportation trains to the camp arrived from the towns and villages of Chrzanów and Żywiec, Kraków and Bochnia in the west, to Tarnopol in the east; and Kołomyja and Stanisławów in the south; from the environs of Lublin, to the cities of Western Europe.

Although my focus has been directed to Belzec, I have also touched on resettlement transports to Sobibór, Treblinka, Chełmno and Auschwitz. Sobibór is of particular interest, being geographically close to Belzec and often used as the main back-up murder site.

In view of the genocide perpetrated in the death camps, it is not surprising that the Nazis made extraordinary efforts to cover up their crimes and destroy the evidence. Aside from the destruction of corpses in the mass graves, the *Reichsführer-SS*, Himmler, also ordered the destruction of all documentation that might become a source of information concerning *Reinhardt* and the involvement of the RSHA. The "destruction order" was no doubt issued to evade all legal or moral accountability in the event of Germany losing the war. According to Rudolf Höß, reassigned in the meantime from Auschwitz to head Amt D1 of the RSHA, orders went out to senior police commanders and to Globocnik for the destruction of all records connected with the activities of *Reinhardt*.[802] Nevertheless, despite the attempted cover-ups, some documentary evidence did survive, if only of secondary importance. No Nazi documents of significance survived with regard to Belzec, except recently discovered German Police Decodes, which were declassified by the British government in 1997.[803]

The intercepted radio telegram ("the document") is in two parts marked *"Geheime Reichssache"* (Secret State Matter), and consists of messages from Lublin, *Generalgouvernment*, dated 11 January 1943.[804] The communication from the *Reinhardt* headquarters in Lublin, sent by the executive head of *Reinhardt*, *SS-Sturmbannführer* Hermann Höfle (who had previously been Globocnik's chief-of-staff) gives, in the first part, a statistical return of the total number of victims received in *Reinhardt* camps for a two-week period; in the second part, the total number of victims who entered the individual death camps, including Majdanek, for the calendar year 1942.[805] The importance of this "document" should not be underestimated; and in the absence of any other German documentary evidence, it must be considered of some historical value and be taken into consideration in any future reassessment of the numbers of victims.[806]

The postwar investigations carried out by the Main Commission for the Investigation of Nazi Crimes in Poland had much difficulty in establishing the Belzec chronology due to this absence of documentation. The only other Nazi statistical documentation dealing with "numbers" and appearing reasonably reliable are the section of the Korherr Report of 1943 specifically dealing with *Reinhardt* and the Katzmann Report to HSSPF Krüger of 30 June 1943, where mention is made of the census of 1931. This census counted 502,000 Jews in Galicia (Lvov alone had a population of 160,000 Jews).[807] SSPF Katzmann also took great pride in and boasted about the murder of 434,329 Jews. He emphasized the mood and spirit of his men and the great burden they had to endure during these extraordinary "operations," which he said were commendable. *(Er herausstrich mit dem Mord von 434,329 Juden, und betonte die Stimmung und Geist seiner Männer, und der Last, den seine Männer während dieser aussergewöhnlichen Handlungen aushalten mussten, war empfehlenswert).*[808] These statistics, however, do not focus on Belzec *per se;* the best source of direct evidence comes from employees of the railway network at the material time, when the transports were flowing into Belzec. From their testimonies, the numbers of transports and their frequency of arrival at Belzec can be seen to have created a pattern of systematic destruction. It is from the Polish rail employees, particularly the locomotive drivers who drove the trains into the death camps, that assessments have been drawn. Although German train crews took over the transports for the final entry into the camp, Polish railwaymen were able to observe from the periphery, and very occasionally gained access to the camp, where they noted numbers and procedures. Railway freight listings of the "*Ostbahn*" were an essential record whereby the railway authorities claimed payment for the transports from the SS. The railway authorities were concerned that payments for these "special transports" were not being made according to the SS contract and consequently admonished their staff, and instructed them to record independently all movements of "special freight."[809] The railway authorities therefore became an important source for reconstructing a picture of the deportations. Evidence from the perpetrators— T4 and guard personnel who were indicted and prosecuted after the war— was also useful but should be assessed with great care.

Records of Victims

Jews from the Galician District deported to the *Reinhardt* camps were not registered but were killed *en mass* immediately after arrival and, as far as can be established, no lists or camp correspondence were kept. It is improbable that no records at all were kept of the deportations, as normally a weekly return of numbers was sent to the HHE. The Witte/Tyas "new document" suggests just this. Thus, although "numbers" were indeed counted off at the place of departure, e.g. Kołomyja 8,205, there is no evidence to show that on entry into Belzec a further calculation was made, apart from the records kept during the exhumation and cremation operation. Even then the uncertainty of any accurate calculations being made at the time has been demonstrated by the archaeological investigations, during the course of which it was discovered that some of the mass graves located contained bodies in wax fat transformation (usually at the bottom part of the ditches), over which there are layers of human ashes and charcoal.[810] Some complete bodies were therefore overlooked by the burning brigade.

The only certainty is that Jews entering the camps were not afforded the luxury of a personal identity or selection, as practiced in Auschwitz and elsewhere. We are on much firmer ground when assessing numbers deported from western European cities, as lists compiled by convoy commanders at the points of embarkation were sent to the camp political division at the RSHA. Outside of the *Generalgouvernement*, death transports were not usually designated for a particular death camp, but rather to transit camps (Izbica and Piaski), before joining the queue for Belzec, Sobibór or

Treblinka. In the main, Jewry from the Galician District went directly to Belzec; it was only later that some transports were directed first to the transit camps.

Reinhardt Camps

In Majdanek it took several days to murder a thousand Jews; in Chełmno, 1,000 could be murdered in a day; in the *Reinhardt* death camps, on average, 10,000 were murdered every day—at each camp!

The dedicated death camps and their areas of operation for Jewish "resettlement" transports within the *Generalgouvernement* and annexed areas consisted of Chełmno-on-Ner (Warthegau), Belzec (Lublin District and Galicia), Sobibór (Lublin District), Treblinka (Warsaw/Radom Districts), and Maly Trostinets, near Minsk. Chełmno and Maly Trostinets are set apart as individual death camps as they used shootings and gas vans for their murderous work. All these camps were located close to major rail communications, and to say that these camps were all isolated and camouflaged is not strictly correct. Chełmno, Belzec and Sobibór were very close to villages. Belzec and Chełmno actually adjoined the local community, and the comings and goings of Jewish transports were *the* topic of local gossip.[811] When this fact was realized, the Nazis reorganized both the mode of transport and "resettlement" actions so that they would be out of public view. Belzec was adjacent to the railway station and directly opposite village dwellings. Like Chełmno, the camp was the within sight and walking distance of the local population. Treblinka was isolated, tucked away in deep woodland and away from prying eyes—but only one kilometer from the village of Wółka Okrąglik!

The hybrid concentration camps such as Auschwitz, and to a lesser extent Majdanek, combined labor and mass murder. They had gassing facilities and were utilized alongside the dedicated death camps. The camps of Janowska (Lvov), Płaszów (Kraków), Poniatówa and Trawniki (Lublin), although designated as concentration camps, also had facilities for mass shootings. The inclusion of these concentration camps was basically to accommodate a "free for all" killing policy and to deal with the overflow of proposed victims of the death camps. When it was decided in July 1942, that *all* Jews, regardless of labor requirements, were to receive "special treatment," every facility available was used for this purpose.[812]

Auschwitz KZ became the main murder center for Jews, Poles, Gypsies and Soviet citizens throughout the war (1940-1945). The *Reinhardt* "death camps" were used specifically for solving the "Jewish Question." When they closed down,[813] Auschwitz remained the principal site for mass elimination by gassing. In the main this consisted of the extermination of the remaining Jews in the *Generalgouvernement*, as well as Jews destined for "special treatment" from outside the *Reich*, in particular Hungary and the Łodz ghetto.

Victims per Railway Car

Immediately after the war, the various commissions investigating the number of victims murdered in the death camps could only estimate figures, which were based on an average of 100 persons transported per railway car. If we take the Kołomyja transport of 10 September 1942, we know that 51 freight cars were made available and that 8,205 victims were counted off, with so many to a wagon—165 on average. The Bill of Lading says just this, which fact is corroborated by the report of the security personnel who loaded and escorted the train from Kołomyja to Belzec. The original reports, submitted by the escorting security personnel of the Kołomyja transport, have survived for scrutiny.[814] Even so, apart from this written evidence, we have no other documentation from the railway authorities to verify or corroborate that this capacity was the norm. To add to the difficulties of any analysis, Belzec railway station was blown up and all records destroyed in July 1944, when a lone Soviet aircraft dropped a single bomb on an ammunition train parked in the railway sidings.[815]

The estimate of the Polish War Crimes Investigation Commission of 100 persons per railway wagon arriving at Belzec, if anything, is not too high, but too low. Taking into account all the available evidence from witnesses, and from all sources, we arrive at a much higher average of persons per wagon. As Belzec was primarily for Galician Jews, we may perhaps downgrade the importance of the larger western freight wagons. The important factor here was that other European Jews were brought to Belzec either in freight wagons or in passenger coaches, unlike the Galician Jews, who only came in wagons crammed to capacity. The excess numbers in these latter wagons may be attributed to a number of factors, including the many children clinging close between the knees of their parents and the emaciated condition of the adults, both thereby creating room for more victims. For Galician Jewry, there is reason to think that transports in general exceeded the nominal average calculated by others.

A final complication when tracing "special transports" to their ultimate destination is that the transit ghettos (except Piaski and Izbica), were destroyed when the last Jews left. Beyond these transit ghettos in the Lublin District, major towns in Galicia, such as Kołomyja, Stanisławów, etc., were used as central collecting points for the surrounding areas. The lack of information regarding smaller communities is mainly due to the Nazi policy of removing populations of less than 500 people to the nearest larger town. Yad Vashem has compounded these difficulties by deciding not to register Jewish communities of less than 500. In my view, for the historian and other interested parties, this was a major historical blunder.

Polish War Crimes Investigation Commission in Belzec

According to the evidence given to the Polish War Crimes Commission by Alojzy Berezowski, the Polish stationmaster at Belzec, the camp opened in mid-March 1942 and ran continuously, except for part of May and June (the reconstruction period), until October 1942. From then on, he states that there was a gradual reduction in transport activity. During the resettlement period from March to October 1942, one to three transports arrived in Belzec daily, averaging 40 wagons per transport and 100 persons per wagon. From October 1942, the transports were cut to one or two per week until they finally ceased altogether in early December.

Each transport consisted of 15 to 60 wagons (there are reports of 70 to 80 wagons in the second phase), the average being about 40. The numbers of victims transported were marked in chalk on the outside of some of the wagons, varying from 100 to 130. The witness Berezowski stated to the Commission that railway deportation documents were handed over by the escorting security supervisor to Rudolf Göckel, the German stationmaster on duty at Belzec.[816] However, it sometimes happened that they were given to a member of the Polish railway staff, so it was occasionally possible to obtain accurate information about the number of people and wagons entering the camp.

Based on this information the Commission concluded that from 18 March to the beginning of May, and from the beginning of July to the end of September 1942 (a period of 133 days), on average, one transport of 4,000 people (40 wagons containg 100 people each) arrived at the camp each day. Simple multiplication arrived at a figure of approximately 530,000 people during the period of mid-March to the end of September 1942. In the final stage of the murder operation, at least two transports per day entered the camp.

Number of Victims

Taking into consideration all the evidence available to them at that time (1945-46), the Commission concluded that the total number of victims murdered in the Belzec death camp was *not less* than 600,000 people. Eugeniusz Szrojt concludes 600,000 victims;[817] Raul Hilberg, 550,000.[818] Yitzhak Arad arrived at a figure of 414,000, but estimated 600,000 as the actual lowest figure.[819] My own estimates were loosely determined at 600,000; but I eventually conceded, due to the lack of clear evidence, that it was necessary to fall back on the Report of the Polish War Crimes Investigation Commission and abandon the "numbers task" as unachievable.[820]

By treating the resettlement transports from the Galician District to Belzec individually, we are able to establish a clear pattern of deportations throughout the *Generalgouvernment*. The calculation method is, as stated, inhibited by the lack of documentation relating to transports of persons (Jews) deported to the camp. The only evidence of non-Jews murdered at Bełzec mentions approximately 1,500 non-Jewish Poles sent to the camp for execution because of anti-Nazi activity or assisting/hiding Jews. In Lvov, a special "operation" was directed against non-Jewish Poles who were seized in the streets, stores and public places. A transport consisting entirely of non-Jewish Poles was sent to Belzec, where they shared the same fate as their Jewish compatriots. This occurred on just one occasion.[821]

When the Polish scholar Franciszek Piper calculated the numbers killed in Auschwitz, he was on much firmer ground; he was able to draw on numerous sources where lists of deportees were made. These lists were either of individuals destined for Auschwitz from elsewhere, or were those transferred from Auschwitz to other places. This documentation survived the war and enabled Piper (and researchers before him) to arrive at reasonably accurate conclusions.

An overview of the deportations for Belzec shows that during a matter of selected days, complete geographical pockets of the Jewish community were targeted and transported. For example, we see that Stryj and district was "actioned" on 5-6 September, followed immediately by Kołomyja and district between 7-10 September 1942. Office-bound bureaucrats had devised a co-ordinated, systematic method of destruction. There is one incontrovertible fact: although we may never know the exact numbers, the tragedy of the genocide is not in dispute.[822]

Notes

[1] A German Government was established in Krakow under Dr. Hans Frank (the Governor) who was legally entitled, based upon a law of the Fuhrer from 12 October 1939, to fulfill the civil authority of those parts of Poland that at first did not belong to the Soviet Union or were not attached to the German Reich. The entire area was called the General Government.

[2] See Chapter 1, page 23.

Chapter 1

[3] Browder, *Enforcers*, 35-48. In 1934, there were a number of organizations targeted by the security services: Marxists, reactionaries, foreigners, Freemasons, cults and religious organizations (including Jews).

[4] Rupert Butler: *The Gestapo, London*, 1992, 51. Typewriters always seemed to be in short supply and during "operations" officers left their posts, not to join in, but to seize any typewriters that may have been left over.

[5] Author: In recent times, police forces outside Germany have sought radical solutions to solve policing problems: leadership by means of direct entry to supervisory positions, amalgamations, police academies of excellence, senior command courses, special squads to deal with particular issues (terrorism, drugs, major crime, special branch, etc.).

[6] The HHE organized and supervised these changes from the newly-established RSHA Amt V, under the direction of Arthur Nebe.

[7] In most Holocaust literature there is an overuse of the word "Gestapo" (Geheime Staatspolizei = Secret State Police). The early Prussian version under Goering was the GESTAPA (Geheime Staats Polizeamt). The later Gestapo had offices all over the Reich). In popular parlance, however, it is applied to all police institutions created since 1933. See: Paechter, Nazi Usage, 79. The organization of the Sipo-SD in Galicia, of the BdS and KdS replicated the five departments of the RSHA: Personnel, Administration, Intelligence, Secret State Police, and Criminal Police. Department IV dealt with Jewish matters.

[8] The SD laid a heavy emphasis on pursuing ideological and racial enemies. In total, the SD establishment was only about 3,000 strong. The Sicherheitspolizei (Sipo = Kripo +Gestapo) establishment was much higher: 60,000. In the Reich Sipo-SD was collectively termed "Inspektor der Sicherheitspolizei und des Sicherheitsdienstes" (IdS), but in the occupied territories "Befehlshaber der Sicherheitspolizei und des Sicherheitsdienstes" (BdS). The SD preserved its independent identity at all times.

[9] Rupert Butler, *The Gestapo*, Allen, London, 1992, 51

[10] The Trial of German Major War Criminals, HMSO, London 1946. IMT, Speeches, 19.

[11] Sipo-SD training academies were established in 1935 when they came under Zentralamt II (Personnel Office), Hauptabteilung III (Training, education and recruitment of the Sicherheitshauptamt). With the amalgamation of all security services in 1936, they crossed the corridor to the RSHA.

[12] The SD had its own organization with an independent headquarters with posts established throughout the Reich and in the occupied territories. It included a membership of 3-4,000 professionals assisted by thousands of honorary members, known as "V"-men ("Vertrauensmänner" = confidential agent/informer), and by spies in other lands. The Abwehr, headed by Admiral Wilhelm Canaris, was the

military intelligence branch and did not become amalgamated with the SD until towards the end of the war when Canaris was executed, allegedly involved in the 20 July 1944 bomb plot against Hitler.

[13] Sereny, *Stangl*, 30-37. I suggest we treat Stangl's explanations with scepticism.

[14] Ibid.

[15] O'Neil, The Rabka Sipo-SD School, in which the persona of commandant SS-Untersturmführer Wilhelm Rosenbaum is fully exposed. (Publication by Yad Vashem Holocaust Studies pending).

[16] Browder, *Enforcers*, 57. Among the earliest members of the Sipo und SD, 20 percent came from the lower ranks of the civil service.

[17] "Carrying" a uniform is a police phrase which, in this meaning, reflects a professional, hard working officer. On the other hand, it can also mean "uniform carrier," an officer who wears a uniform, and draws his pay, and does little work.

[18] After ignoring the Concordat with the Holy See, signed in July 1933 in Rome, the Nazi Party carried out a long and persistent persecution of the Catholic Church, its priesthood and congregation members, including police officers.

[19] Sereny, *Stangl*, 37.

[20] Browder, *Enforcers*, 212.

[21] Andrew Ezergalis: *The Holocaust in Latvia*, Washington, DC, 1996, 146.

[22] Other police secondments for "special duties" to the Führer: Fritz Tauscher (Sonnenstein), Franz Schemmel, Jacob Wöger (Grafenek), Hermann Holzschuh (Grafenek and Bernburg), Franz Hirsch (Brandenburg and Bernburg), Franz Reichleitner (Hartheim) and Arthur Dachsel.

[23] Only Dr. Eberl (T4), who was temporarily in charge of Treblinka, was outside this police cadre. Dr. Eberl could not agree with Wirth's practices and because of this, he was considered an outsider. He was later ousted by Globocnik and Wirth.

[24] TAL/ZStL, Belzec Case: Statement of Karl Werner Dubois, 16 September 1961. He was killed by Polish partisans on 29 March 1943 near the village of Tarnawatka on the road to Zamosc.

[25] An appraisal of Christian Wirth and Gottleib Hering in collaboration with my colleague Michael Tregenza. See: Tregenza, Michael, "Belzec Death Camp," in: *Wiener Library Bulletin*, vol. XXX, London 1977. "Christian Wirth a pierwsza faza Akcji Reinhard," in: *Zeszyty Majdanka*, vol. XXVI, Lublin 1992.

[26] BDC/YV 862: Christian Wirth: Police Constable in the city police - CID (Kriminalpolizei/Kripo) - Nazi Party (NSDAP) - SA (Sturmabteilungen). Post -1936 (Himmler reorganization of the police service when SS membership was compulsory): Sicherheitsdienst (SD 1936) - SS (1939). RSHA (Reichssicherheitshauptamt) - SD Academy (Berlin-Charlottenburg) Kriminalkommissar - T-4 - Reinhardt (December 1941-September 43). In the death camps, Wirth (promoted 1.1.43) continued to wear his green police uniform of Major der Schützpolizei and Kriminalrat of the Kriminalpolizei of the Stuttgart police (with the SD silver corded insignia on his left sleeve), but on occasions, he took to wearing the grey uniform of the Waffen-SS with the equivalent rank of SS-Obersturmführer.

[27] PRO, File No: WO/208/4209: British Intelligence Report of the interrogation of Fritz Bleich, 2 April 1945.

[28] Although most applicants considered entry into the Kripo as a promotion, this was not the case. A constable is a constable whether in the uniformed branch or the

242

investigation branch. Quite simply it was a sideways move. This perception remains today, much to the annoyance of uniformed officers.

[29] Sereny, *Stangl*, 30-37.

[30] Ibid. I found this interview by Sereny with Stangl very persuasive. It reflects a true situation based on language usage and police jargon.

[31] Ibid.

[32] Schutzpolizei (Schupo) consisted of two groups: the Schupo, who were heavily armed and housed in barracks, were engaged for crowd control (especially strikes and demonstrations) and the suppression of revolutionary uprisings. The Schupo were the regular uniformed urban police force. The remainder were assigned to urban districts for routine patrol and police work. In the countryside were uniformed Gendarmerie or Landjägerei, separate from Schupo. The remainder of the State police served in plain clothes. Units of detectives (Kriminalpolizei) were assigned to the cities and administrative police (VerwaltungStanisławowspolizei) performing regulatory roles, see: activities of the Ordnungspolizei and Schutzpolizei in the town of Kołomyja between the 7 - 10 September 1942, in: Tuvia Friedmann: "Police Battalion 24/Company 7, September 1942." See also: YVA/ZStL: Collection UdSSR, vol. 410, "Reports," Haifa 1957. See: " Schupo-Kriegsverbrecher vor dem Wiener Volksgericht: Schutzpolizei Dienstabteilung in Boryslaw," in: Institute of Documentation in Israel, Haifa 1995. (3 vols. Boryslaw, Kołomyja, Stryj).

[33] Sereny, *Stangl*, 56.

[34] Ibid., 81. According to Dieter Allers, Stangl's recruitment to T4 was probably on recommendation by fellow Austrian contacts. For Brack, see: BDC/YV 496.

[35] Sereny, *Stangl*, 55.

[36] Ibid.,, 49; recollections of Stangl, 80-81; recollections of Dieter Allers re: mode of recruitment.

[37] Ibid., 52.

[38] Stangl's appointment was consistent with the times: no written orders were given, no paraphernalia, just a chat on a garden seat overlooking Lublin, talking with Globocnik at the rear of the SS-Standortverwaltung building.

[39] See Longerich, *Ermordung*, 339.

[40] Ibid. For overview of Stangl's interrogation and questioning at his subsequent trial in Germany, 367-8.

[41] Samuel Willenberg, *Revolt in Treblinka*, New York 1989, 96.

[42] Friedlander, *Origins*, 206.

Chapter 2

[43] Acknowledgement to Michael Peters.

[44] T4. The "Gemeinnützige Stiftung für Anstaltspflege" (Charitable Foundation for Institutional Care), was the camouflage organization to hide the involvement of the Kdf. The first managing director was Dr. Gerhard Bohne, replaced at the beginning of 1941 by SA-Obersturmbannführer and O'Reg Rat Dietrich Allers, while the senior consultant psychiatrists were Prof. Dr Heyde and Prof Dr. Nitsche. The "Stiftung" had limited authority only over all mental homes in the whole of Greater Germany. Some of the buildings had been partially converted into "Stammanstalten" (extermination centers) over which the "Stiftung" maintained full control. They were: Grafeneck (CMO Dr. Schumann), Brandenburg/Havel (CMO Dr. Schmalenbach) Bernburg/Saale (CMO Dr. Eberl) Hartheim nr. Linz/Donau (CMO Dr. Renno), Sonnenstein at Pirna/Elbe (CMO) Hadamar/Lahn (CMO *the Gemn.*

Kranken. – abbreviated to "Gekra" t was the org. that transported patients from their home institutes to the killing centers. An additional justification for equating "Ahnenerbe" with the "Stiftung" is the fact that experiments on KZ inmates were carried out under the aegis of the "Stiftung" (14f13).

[45] See Weindling, *Nazi Medicine*, 250

[46] Ibid., 225.

[47] H.E.A.R.T: *Euthanasia*: I am grateful to Melvyn Conroy for imparting to the author his contribution to the research project on Euthanasia: The quotation is from Michael Burleigh, *The Third Reich*, 356. See also, James Knowlson, *Damned to Fame,* London 1996, 297. Burleigh goes on to comment: "Rarely can such an unprepossessing group of people have so much to say about fitness and purity."

[48] Weindling, *Nazi Medicine,* 256: Viktor Brack commissioned the well-known author and Nazi sympathizer, Hellmuth Unger, to prepare a film script to win over public support for a euthanasia program.

[49] Ibid., 251.

[50] Knauer was not the real name. Acknowledgement to Paul Weindling who cites the "Benzenhöfer papers," which delve into this error.

[51] Lifton, R. Jay, *The Nazi Doctors*, New York 1986, 50, n.3.

[52] Reichsleiter Bouhler und Dr. med. Brandt sind unter Verantwortung beauftragt, die Befugnisse namentlich zu bestimmender Ärzte so zu erweitern, dass nach menschlichen Ermessen unheilbar Kranken bei kritischster Beurteilung ihres Krankheitszustandes der Gnadentod gewährt werden kann.

[53] Friedlander, *Origins*, 191.

[54] Blatt, 24.

[55] Blatt, 115. SS-Scharführer Frenzel (Sobibór) in conversation with Blatt after the war stated: "*I was not SS, I was ordered there. There were only five SS, the rest of us were all civilians.*"

[56] Sereny, 55.

[57] Ibid., 197.

[58] Blatt, 39.

[59] Blatt, 40.

[60] ZStL, 151/59-6-1192: statement of Karl Frenzel 18 April 1962. In one Ukrainian/Jewish transaction when they were caught red-handed, three Jews were shot and the two Ukrainians also shot.

[61] "Bełżec Nine" refers to the nine Bełżec personnel who were investigated post war.

[62] Friedlander, 237.

[63] Ibid., 236.

[64] Ibid.

[65] Ibid.

[66] Bełżec Verdict. General overview of the documentation available.

[67] Bełżec Verdict (Oberhauser).

[68] Sereny, 82.

[69] IMT: testimony of Viktor Brack.

[70] Everyone was in some way implicated in theft or corruption. At the top, Globocnik and his camp commanders were all quietly looking after their own interests. The lower echelons, the Scharführers, were more open with their acquisitions by sending parcels of acquired goods to their families via T4. Kurt Bolender in Sobibór took gold dental bridges and gold teeth home when on leave (Mrs. Bolender, Sobibór

Verdict). Although Wirth knew all this, he overlooked it in respect of his own men, but the Ukrainians didn't fare as well. In the drinking bars of Bełżec and Tomaszow-Lubelski, paper money was often smudged with blood or some other substance.

[71] See Oberhauser testimonies for 12 December 1962, 26 February 1960, and 20 April 1960. The two earlier testimonies, if placed alongside the later one of 12 December, 1962, reveal discrepancies which point to a manipulation of the facts: that for the period up until August 1942 (the period when he was at Bełżec) he tries to imply that this was the lowest period of Jewish resettlement when only small murders were carried out in a single gas chamber, which of course was not the case. Oberhauser was a loner and never really mixed with the rest of the SS, and was never trusted by them. He was chained and wholly subservient to Wirth, and would remain so.

[72] Ibid., 83. The reference that no training was necessary is odd, but when you consider what Wirth was like, that he led by example and goaded his men exactly to his requirements, Suchomel's statement is understandable.

[73] Having read their full antecedent history, this is the view to which I have come.

Chapter 3

[74] See: *Tagebuch*, 402-410: entries for 11, 15, 20 September 1941. For biography of Dr Hans Frank see: Joachim Fest, *The Face of the Third Reich*, London 1972, 325.

[75] Himmler would have had to put someone in Krakow as HSSPF to supervise the SSPFs in the other Districts of the Generalgouvernment. Krüger, by all accounts, was the one best suited to the job.

[76] See: Sandkühler, *Endlösung*, 86.

[77] On Globocnik, see: Sandkühler, *Endlösung*, 130-134: Himmler's authorization to Globocnik to set up the network of camps in the "eastern territories." Several biographic studies about Globocnik have been written, some published, others not. Extensive works about the intermediate leaders are rare. Party membership 1 March 31, provisional membership card, 22 April 1931 issued on 6 September 1932; membership No. 442,939.

[78] PRO, File No. UK: HW 16/5: Radio decodes November 1939 and October 1940 refer to Globocnik's relations with the Nazi civil authorities concerning his problems within "General Plan Ost." I am grateful to Steven Tyas for this information.

[79] Madajczyk, *Sonderlaboratorium*.

[80] Joseph Poprzeczny and Carolyn Simmonds, Origins of Nazi Plans for Eastern Settlement and Extermination. Power and Freedom in Modern Politics, in: Jeremy Moon and Bruce Stone (eds.), University of Western Australia Press 2002, 190-2. See Poprzeczny, Essay, in which he quotes Robert Koehl, *RKFDV - German Settlement and Population Policy 1939-45*, Harvard University Press 1957, pp. 71, 83-84, 147-148. Koehl points out that in 1941, the year of the invasion of the Soviet Union, Meyer-Hetling was "released from the routine practicality of property confiscation measures to take on the great task of planning Germany's—and Himmler's—European empire. Throughout the first five months of anxious German preparation for the last clean sweep, January - May 1942, Meyer-Hetling and his academic colleagues worked to prepare a new 'General Plan East', to embrace the choicest areas of European Russia." Significantly, Meyer-Hetling was one of the 14 defendants at Nuremberg in Case VIII, also known as the RuSHA Case (Rasse-und Siedlungshsauptamt = Race and Settlement Head Office).

[81] Tomasz Piesakowski: *The Fate of Poles in the USSR 1939-1989*, London 1990, 50-54.

[82] Poprzeczny, *Essay*. See also: Zajdlerow: *Dark Side of the Moon*, John Coutovidis and Thomas Lane, London 1989. This is a fine personal recollection detailing the *modus operandi* of Soviet expulsion in East Galicia.

[83] Ibid.

[84] Ibid.

[85] Burleigh: *Third Reich*, 446.

[86] Zamosc is an old town that gives the name to four Polish counties: Zamosc, Biłgoraj, Sobibór and Hrubieszów.

[87] Klukowski, *Diary*.

[88] Ibid.

[89] Ibid., 276. According to the 2nd edition [1959] of Klukowski's Diary, there is no such incident recorded for the month of April 1943. Besides, Globocnik could hardly be referred to as "low-ranking German official"; he was the senior and most powerful SS/Police officer in Lublin District!

[90] Ibid., 240.

[91] Ibid.

[92] Burleigh, *Third Reich*, 454.

[93] Pucher, *Globocnik*.

[94] Ibid. Between 8 November 1937 and 23 January 1938, the exhibition had been in Munich where 412,300 visitors attended (over 5,000 per day). The exhibition moved on to Berlin on 12 November 1938, at the height of anti-Jewish demonstrations. See Kershaw, *Hitler*, 337, photo 10-11.

[95] Ibid., 42

[96] TAL/ZStL, File No. 208 AR-Z 268/59: Case against Johannes Müller et al. (Lublin Gestapo Case). Testimony of Max Runhof, 1 September 1961.

[97] Ibid.

[98] Breitman, *Genocide*, 103.

[99] Porrzeczny, *Essay*.

[100] Ibid., 16. See: *Dienstkalender*, 261-3, entry for 31 July 1940.

[101] In October 1940, 7,500 Jews were deported from Baden and the Saar in Germany to concentration camps in southern France; most were later sent to Poland.

[102] See Longerich, *Unwritten Order*, 57.

[103] Ibid., 59.

[104] Browning, *Nazi Policy*, 37.

[105] Ibid., 38-9. See also: Longerich, *Unwritten Order*, 80.

[106] Ibid., 35.

[107] Ibid., 39.

[108] Ibid., 55.

[109] Ibid. Cited in: Witte, *Two Decisions Concerning the Final Solution*, 333-336.

[110] See: Longerich, *Unwritten Order*, 109.

[111] Ibid., 114.

Chapter 4

[112] See: Yehoshua Büchler, "Kommandostab Reichsführer-SS - Himmler's Personal Murder Brigade, 1941" in: *Holocaust and Genocide Studies*, 1 (1986), 11-25. On the

17 August 1938, Himmler had segregated part of the SS for his own personal needs in cases of State and wartime emergency. The "Verfugungsstruppe" (Readiness or Disposal Troops) - the forerunner of the Waffen-SS - were at the disposal of the Wehrmacht in wartime, but only with the personal authorization of the Reichsführer-SS and Chief of the German police, Himmler. By September 1939, this SS-Division consisted of over 25,000 men.

[113] After HSSPF Krüger had submitted his report and recommendations to Frank about the "Selbstschütz," it was agreed (perhaps as a compromise) to set-up a similar but more closely supervised auxiliary security force, which would keep everyone happy and further placate Globocnik in the process. This new unit, the Sonderdienst, was transferred to the authority of the SSPF in Lublin where Jewish "operations" were concentrated. However, there was one subtle change; the real authority was now held by the civilian government in Kraków, not Globocnik in Lublin. With the removal of the "Selbstschütz," the continued persecution and murder was now continued under a different name.

[114] Once operations commenced, formations of Schützmannschaften were recruited from local Volksdeutsche, ethnic German personnel who acted under the direct orders of German commanders. The "Schuma," as they were known, were mainly employed on traffic duties with very limited powers of authority, and, for example, could only direct motor vehicles and enforce traffic regulations. They had no powers over ethnic Germans as such, but when acting in emergency military situations, they had the same rights and duties as the German police.

[115] TAL/ZStL: No. 1/4544/47 Juc. KI/Si, collection UdSSR, vol. 410, 509-10: Operations in Kołomyja by the Schützpolizei. Generally known as "Schupo," they were recruited and organized within the German police forces in the Reich and sent to the cities of East Galicia where they initially acted as metropolitan police officers engaged in normal policing duties. However, they soon became enmeshed in Jewish "operations" and were particularly evident in the Galician towns of Stanisławów and Kołomyja. There were also other Einsatzgruppen in Poland in 1939, which carried out atrocities and mass executions by shooting in the same way as in Russia after the invasion in 1941. These operations were directed against the intelligentsia, clergy, and known opponents.

[116] Suitable candidates from Austria, Czechoslovakia, Slovak Republic and Ukraine, who also included many Volksdeutsche, were recruited into the *Reichsprotektorat* for this purpose. Many women were also used as police and guard auxiliaries in the KZs and ghettos.

[117] This was the case in the early days of the war, but when the manpower resources diminished these principles vanished.

[118] The SS "Totenkopf" troops from the KZs were utilized because they were Himmler's élite who had been entrusted before the war with guarding "enemies of the State." It was now to be their task to rid Europe of the "danger to the Reich" of Jews – the Jewish exterminations were a matter only for the SS/Police under Heydrich/Himmler. Their leaders, the police officers, were also SS-officers under Himmler's command.

[119] In late 1941 and well into 1943, there was a close liaison between the Lublin *Reinhardt* office and the Rabka SD Academy. There was a constant exchange of personnel, by "Jewish experts" from both establishments.

[120] Globocnik was the key security manager in eastern Poland and was already directing the Sipo-SD, Ordnungspolizei, Schützpolizei, rural Gendarmerie, the Polish Police and Ukrainian auxiliary units.

[121] See Burleigh, *Third Reich*, 640.

[122] Black, *Rehearsal,* 204-226. Emergence of this force appeared on 23 November 1939 in Janów County.

[123] Paechter, *Nazi Deutsch*, 49.

[124] Ibid.

[125] Frank had issued decrees on 26 October 1939 and 24 January 1940, authorizing the seizure of labor and property for the benefit of the Reich. The main warehouse was at Ulica Chopin Street 27 in Lublin where confiscated Jewish property sorted and stored. The warehouse came under the authority of SS-Hauptsturmführer Höfle. Working under the direction of Globocnik was SS- Standartenführer Walter Gunst, who was later dismissed for corruption and replaced by Hermann Dolp. Dolp, a habitual drunkard, was commandant of Lipowa Street camp in Lublin and then overall commander of the Belzec labor camp complex.

[126] Black, *Rehearsal*, 218.

[127] Ibid., 220: The brutal killings in Józefów on 14 April 1940, where 150 Poles (not Jews) lay dead in a field, shocked the Nazi leadership. The day before these killings, it was alleged that Poles had killed a German family. The investigation by the Polish police and German gendarmerie concluded the motive for these murders was robbery. Globocnik overruled requests for restraint and let his Selbstschütz off their leashes. These marauders surrounded the village and selected all males of 20-70 years of age, then shot them down. It did not stop here…. in the same locality, 27 farms and 71 other buildings were destroyed. In a further action on 3 May 1940, SS units assisted by the Selbstschütz shot several Jews (including an 80-year-old blind woman) and destroyed a small ghetto. The ghetto survivors of this operation were sent to the much larger ghetto nearby of Majdan Tartarski. On 16 June 1940, further atrocities occurred in the village of Radawiec, near Lublin, where 27 Poles and Jews were shot

[128] SS Troops (Waffen SS): Originated in the so-called "Leibstandarte."

[129] Among those he retained: SS- Hauptsturmführer Karl Streibel and SS-Sturmbannführer Anton Binner.

[130] See: www. Nizkor Project: *Operation Reinhard,* location Belzec, which quotes Commanding General, Eighth Service Command, ASF Dallas, to Provost Marshall, dated 21 May 1945, account of POW Willi Kempf. NA RG 153, entry 143, box 571, folder 19-99.

[131] Breitman, *Genocide,* 198-201.

[132] Soviet trial source material comes from three main sources: 1) Russian, 2) Ukrainian and 3) Baltic archives of the former Soviet KGB which contain prosecution files of the Trawniki men. German documentation re: Trawniki camp administration records in GstA Hamburg. The author obtained quality source information from a number of external sources: Yad Vashem, Washington D.C., Majdanek Camp Museum and the Tregenza Archives in Lublin.

[133] Soviet troops who were captured or had surrendered were not given the status of POWs because Stalin had not signed the relevant international Conventions, hence their appalling maltreatment and murder in the "cages" in which they were held.

[134] Ghettos: Hrubieszów, Izbica, Łęczna, Łomaza, Międzyrzec, Piaski and Włodawa.

[135] The Nazis only tolerated the German-Ukrainian alliance for collaboration purposes, molded to Nazi requirements for the time being, and not considered an immediate threat. The Ukrainians were to remain an expendable commodity in the future.

[136] USDC, Nikolay Petrovich Malagon, Protocol, 00887 18 March 1978.

[137] Lord Russell of Liverpool: *Scourge of the Swastika*, Cassell, London 1954, 51-52. Several months before Barbarossa, Lieut-Gen. Reinecke of the OKW ordered that all Soviet troops captured or who surrendered were be kept in open-air "cages" surrounded only by barbed wire, and further to shoot "without warning" any prisoner attempting to escape. To feed Soviet prisoners was "misconceived humanitarianism."

[138] Post-mortems carried out on several Soviet prisoners in Lvov showed the stomach contents to consist of grass, worms, etc.

[139] Ibid. "Operational Order" No. 8 of the Chief of the Sipo and SD, dated 17 June 1941 in Berlin clearly sets out the *modus operandi* for the summary execution of all Soviet prisoners. The follow-up Orders, Nos. 9 and 14, confirm the manner in which these executions were to be carried out. See: IMT, Speeches, 155. The number of "volunteers" was minimal compared to the several million prisoners held by the Germans; Streibel mentions a maximum of 5,000 throughout the war. It was largely a matter of finding men who were still reasonably healthy despite the privations.

[140] Eichmann Trial Reports, vol. 2, session 39, 713: witness Musmanno. After the Kiev battle, over 600,000 Soviets were taken prisoner. Under code name "Operation Zepplin," many (mostly Ukrainian) were recruited to the KZ system; many others were shot out of hand by the EG under the direction of Brig. Gen. Neumann, Commander of EG "B." In Belarus, 700,000 Soviet prisoners were shot out of hand.

[141] BDC: No. 834: Personal file of Karl Streibel sent to the author by Yad Vashem. Streibel was commandant of the SS Training Camp at Trawniki (1941-1944) and then commander of SS-Battalion Streibel (1944-1945). See Zentralestelle Ludwigsburg 208 AR 643-71 for trial records and judgment.

[142] Hilberg, *Destruction,* vol. 3, 899: Chełm (Stalag 325) in Lublin District. Rovno, 200 miles east of Lublin, was the main collecting center for Soviet prisoners. In September 1942, Streibel visited Treblinka to see how his guards were performing. See: TAL/GstA Düsseldorf, File No. 8 Js 10904/59, vol. 19a (1969), 5030.

[143] PMML: Aleksei Nikolaevich Kolgushkin: Protocol, 0012724, September 1980. See also Nikolay Petrovich Malagon, Protocol, 00889, 18 March 1978, which corroborates induction procedures. Over 90,000 died in the two Chełm camps alone in a few months.

[144] Rich, *Footsoldiers*, 690.

[145] Ibid.

[146] Ibid.

[147] Ibid. Personal description requested at Trawniki: Warrant No, full name, father's name, date and place of birth, nationality, citizenship, occupation, marital status, children, wife's maiden name, mothers maiden name, military service, type, service rank, military service, remarks, languages known, special skills, height, facial form, hair, eyes, special markings (USDC, Protocol, 00285, Statement of Ivan Marchenko, 11 January 1941).

[148] Ibid. Kharkovsky, Protocol, 00087, 11 September 1980. See also: TAL/*Streibel Case*, vol. 19, 5030. Statement of Karl Streibel, 4 September 1969.

[149] Hilberg, *Destruction*, Vol. 3, 899 n. 23. See also Tagebuch, 428-430: the stand made by Globocnik on the Gendarmerie 17 October, 1941; For further comment see: on his poor handling of the Sonderdienst recruiting 8 April 1941; his conflict with Zoerner 20 May 1942; remarks of Frank made against Globocnik 16 July 1941.

[150] Goldhagen, *Executioners*, 224.

[151] Rich, *Footsoldiers*, 690/1.

[152] Michael Janczak, a German police officer, was drafted to Trawniki to train these prisoners of war mainly from the Baltic's and Ukraine. He corroborates the training procedures and postings to Reinhardt camps. See: TAL/*Sobibór Case,* Kurt Bolender and others, vol. 5, 915-916.

[153] Ibid.

[154] The word "wachman" (guard) or plural, "wachmänner" (guards) is used throughout. In Russian it is written "vachman" (plural "vachmaenner"), a transliteration from the German.

[155] USDC, Protocol, 00089: Statement of Kharkovski.

[156] Hiwis: "Hilfswilliger" (volunteer), subordinates who performed the unpleasant work. "Blacks" – so-called because of their SS-"Totenkopf" style uniforms.

[157] USDC, Protocol, 00109: Statement of Yakov Limentevich Savenko, 11 September 1980. At the end of 1942, Savenko was employed on building maintenance in Trawniki when his group were taken out of the camp to the forest to dig a pit. A transport with 30 Jews were brought to the site by the SS and shot in the pit. Savenko and his group returned to Trawniki and carried on working.

[158] Ibid., Protocol, 00107: Sevenko, 11 September 1980.

[159] This is why we see the same personnel appearing in different post war trials and facing completely separate indictments relating to Belzec, Treblinka and Sobibór.

[160] USDC, Protocol, 00887, Statement of Nikolai Petrovich Malagon, 18 March 1978.

[161] Trawnikmänner did not guard the Reinhardt buildings or Globocnik's HQ as SSPF-Lublin. This part of Lublin was strictly for German SS/Police personnel only.

[162] Among these Soviets were Ukrainians, Soviets, Latvians and Mongolians. The Volksdeutsche were a special breed and relied on by the SS to "work the camp": Schneider, Kaiser and Siviert, among others.

[163] Josef Oberhauser, on his transfer from T4, was attached to *Reinhardt* in Lublin working directly under SS-Hauptsturmführer Höfle. SS-Hauptscharführer Schwarz was later appointed. Schwarz had overall responsibility for the Ukr. Guards, especially in matters of discipline. Wirth appointed individual SS-NCOs as their instructors, including Franz. TAL/Belzec Case: Statement of Kurt Franz, 14 September 1961.

[164] Not accounting for Feix's crimes in Belzec, he moved on to even greater crimes in the Budzyń forced labor camp near Kraśnik and in the surrounding area. After the war Feix was indicted on 15 counts of the most barbarous acts committed on camp prisoners and the civilian population. TAL/ZStL, File No. 208 AR-Z 384/61: Case Against Bruno Muttersbach.

[165] See: phase two map.

[166] USDC, Protocol, 00893, Malagon, 18 March 1978.

[167] Ibid: 00338-40, Nina Dmitriyevna Shiyenko, 3 May 1951: "he (Ivan Ivanovich Marchenko) wore a black uniform of the German 'SS' forces; on his belt in a holster he carried a weapon."

250

[168] USDC, Melania Yefimovna Nezdiyminoha: Protocol: Statement 3 May 1951. Nezdiyminoha worked in the Treblinka kitchen and was a close friend of Ivan Ivanovich Marchenko, the operator of the gassing engine in Treblinka. See also: Protocol, 00351: Statement of Maria Korobka, 19 May 1951.

[169] PRO, File No. WO/208/4673: Interrogation of George Konrad Morgan. In the summer of 1943, Morgan was sent by Himmler to Lublin to investigate corruption between the SS-guards and Jewish prisoners. (See: TAL/Belzec verdict: Statement of Heinrich Unverhau, 21 July 1960).

[170] USDC, Protcol, 00423: 21 February 1945.

[171] Ibid.

[172] Ibid.

[173] USDC, Protocol, 00715: Statement of Aleksander Ivanovich Yeger, 16 April 1948.

[174] Ibid. 00458: Statement of Skydan, 16 February 1950: "Oberwachman Robertus and others, whose names I do not recall, once hacked with axes members of a work crew." Robertus was later attacked by the Jewish Sonderkommando who cut his throat at the entrance of the gas chambers. The repercussions were immediate—they were all were shot. (Ibid. Protocol, 00827: Statement of Ananiy Griegoryevich Kuzminsky, 20 March 1965). See also: Rich, *Footsoldiers*, 694.

[175] Ibid.

[176] USDC, Protocol, 00827: Statement of Ananily Grigoryevich Kuzminsky, 20 March 1965. On another occasion, a work-Jew assaulted a Ukrainian guard and knocked him to the ground in front of the assembled Jewish work force.

[177] TAL/OKBZ: Statement of Mieczysław Niedużuk, 17 October 1945.

[178] Ibid.

[179] Rich, *Footsoldiers*, 693. This is not as unusual as locally brewed vodka was and still is the staple alcoholic drink in Poland and Ukraine to this day (2002). Vodka brewed in Ukraine is the biggest smuggling operation on the Polish/Ukraine border town of Hrebenna. On 9 November 2002, in Belzec the author was accosted by a "vodka mule" (a woman walking the streets who had entered Poland from Ukraine carrying packs of homemade vodka ready to dispense at 15 zloty a measure to casual customers walking the streets). It is well known in the locality that unwelcome visitors are plied with the "special vodka" (corrupted) to cause the maximum damage to the buyer, some of whom have ended up in a hospital or have even died from alcoholic poisoning.

[180] Belzec had a mixed population of Ukrainian and Polish inhabitants who were employed in the camp and in local commodity suppliers of goods for the camp. Many local women who resided in the houses outside the camp were employed for domestic work: laundry, cleaning, mending. The Ukrainian guard were resident in barracks which were also cleaned by local women. Sarah Ritterbrand (nee Beer) was removed from a death transport on arrival at Belzec, despite the fact she had a 4-year-old daughter with her. Ritterbrand's brother, Moshe Hellman, lived under a false identity in Belzec and worked in the local bakery. Hellman was later shot at the camp in front of his sister after having spirited the child out of the camp in a breadbasket. Mother and daughter were to survive the war.

[181] Hilberg, *Documents,* 212.

[182] Klee, Dressen, Riess, *Days,* 230. For biography, see: Longerich, *Ermordung,* 369.

[183] Ibid. TAL/OKBZ, Statement of Maria Wlasiuk, 21 February 1946. Wlasiuk was killed in Lublin just before the liberation in a "hit-and-run accident" by the Lublin AK. They knew he had been a guard in Belzec.

[184] Polin, *Belzec*, 270. One of the very few corroborative statements that the Lvov Jews knew what was in store for them.

[185] TAL/OKBZ, Statement Mieczyslaw Kudyba, 14 October 1945. TAL/ZStL, Statement of Robert Jührs 7 January 1963.

[186] Höß, *Auschwitz*, 260.

[187] Richard Rashke, *Escape from Sobibór*, London 1995, 204.

[188] Blatt, 87.

[189] TAL/ZStL, 208 AR-Z 340/59 (*Treblinka Case*): Statement of Franz Stangl, 26 June 1966.

[190] Ibid., *Belzec Case*, Statement Heinrich Unverhau, 21 July 1960.

[191] Ibid. Statement of Unverhau, 2 June 1960.

[192] Ibid. Statement of Karl Werner Dubois, 16 September 1963.

[193] Ibid. Statement of Heinrich Gley, 7 January 1963. See also statements: 8 May 1961, 23 and 25 November 1963, 7 January 1963, and 6 February 1962. See also statement of Kurt Franz, 14 September 1961.

[194] Ibid., *Sobibór Case*: Statement of Karl Frenzel, 18 April 1962. See also: *Blatt, Sobibór*, 41

[195] Ibid.

[196] Ibid., 42: Statement of Franz Stangl, 27 June 1967.

[197] Ibid. Statement of Franz Suchomel.

[198] TAL/ZStL, File No. 208 AR-Z 230/59: Statement of Franz Stangl, 27.6.1967).

[199] Photograph by courtesy of Regional Museum, Sobibór Lubelski to the author. See also: Kola, *Belzec,* 67-68: "The Jews from the staff near the wooden buildings in the northern part of the camp." See also background to figure 3.

[200] Ibid. Based on the testimonies of Reder and Kozak. See photograph p, 1 chapter 5: Kurt Franz walking past the sheds as shown in 1 and 2 above.

[201] Ibid.

[202] Polin, *Belzec,* 273.

[203] Tadeusz Pankiewicz, *The Kraków Ghetto Pharmacy,* New York 1987, 48. As happened to the president of the Judenrat, Dr Artur Rosenzweig in Kraków, June 1942.

[204] Żydowski Instytut Historyczny, Warsaw, File 102/46: Interview by Jan She with Rudolf Reder. See also TAL/ZStL, *Belzec Case*: Statement of Professor Wilhelm Pfannenstiel, 6 June 1950.

[205] Polin, *Belzec,* 277.

[206] USDC, Protocol, 00369: Statement of Nikolay Yegorovich Shalayev, 3 May 1951. Shalayev refers to his fellow Ukrainian: "Ivan Marchenko, two Germans and two Jews at the motor which produced the exhaust gas which fed into the chambers of the gas chamber." See also: Statement 20 December 1951: "The Jews re-fuelled and turned on the motors which fed the exhaust gas into the gas chambers."

[207] It is most unlikely that any SS-man would be treated by a Jewish doctor—it was a criminal offense. I know of only one case: Dubois in Sobibór after the revolt as a matter of life or death—he had an axe in his head and a bullet in a lung.

[208] Ibid.

[209] TAL/ZStL, *Belzec Case*: Statement of Werner Dubois, 16 September 1961.

[210] Polin, *Belzec,* 281.

[211] Ibid.

[212] TAL/OKBZ: Statement of Chaim Hirszmann, 19 March 1946. Hirszmann states that the children were under the age of three years and recalls how the earth moved until they suffocated. See: Tregenza, *Belzec,* 13.

[213] Ibid. One of the lessons learned here was that corpse carrying was time wasting. With the much improved and larger second phase gas-chambers which were murdering 10-15,000 Jews per day in each camp, Wirth improved the system at Sobibór and Treblinka with the installation of a narrow-gauge track which carried not only the corpses but also those Jews too old or sick who were off-loaded at the "Lazarett" (killing pit).

[214] Ibid. The eight "dentists," young Jews taken off the transports, occupied and shared a separate barrack in Camp II with a doctor and a pharmacist. After the day's work they collected all the gold teeth, melted them down into gold ingots 1 centimeter thick, 50 centimeters wide, and 20 centimeters long. Other valuables were collected daily and removed to the admin office in Belzec. See also: TAL/ZStL, *Belzec Case*: Statement of Werner Dubois 15 September 1961.

[215] Ibid.

[216] Ibid.

Chapter 5.

[217] *Dienstkalender:* See also: PRO (Tyas), HW 16/32: message transmitted 5 September 1941, where Globocnik uses his new title.

[218] BDC/YV, Globocnik's SS file sent to the author by Yad Vashem.

[219] See Longerich for an overview: *Politik der Vernichtung: Eine Gesamtdarstellung der nationalsozial- istischen Judenverfolgung*, Munich, 1998, 577–86 and 448, 457, 465, as cited by Browning in: *Nazi Policy*, 170-171.

[220] See: Franciszek Piper, Auschwitz: How Many Perished Jews, Poles, Gypsies..., Oświęcim 1996, 33.

[221] Sandkühler, *Endlösung*, 126 n. 48.

[222] However, see evidence of Georg Konrad Morgan at Nuremberg, re: Himmler's verbal orders to Höß and Wirth, and evidence of Dieter Wisleceny who claims to have seen a written order from Himmler to Eichmann.

[223] Browning, *Nazi Policy*, 26-27. For general background see: Browning, *Fateful Months*, 86-121.

[224] Ibid., 76 who also brings to notice the work of Christian Gerlach in this regard ("Die Bedeutung der deutschen Ernährungspolitik für die Beschleunigung des Mords an den Juden 1942" in: *Krieg, Ernährung Völkermord,* Hamburg 1998, 167-257).

[225] Bogdan Musial: *The Origins of 'Operation Reinhard*, 116-18.

[226] Pohl, *Judenpolitik*, 97-106.

[227] Witte, *Two Decisions*, 318-45.

[228] Aly, *Endlösung*, 97-106.

[229] Philippe Burrin, *Hitler and the Jews*, London 1994, 127; see particularly notes 37-39.

[230] Ibid.

[231] This refers to Brack's letter of 23 June 1942 about sending additional T4 personnel for the accelerated operations due to begin on 1 August.

[232] TAL/IMT: Statement of Viktor Brack, 15 September 1946. That last sentence is, of course, wishful thinking on Brack's part. See the Nuremberg interrogation in which the interrogator "loses his cool" calls Brack a liar and reduces him to tears.

[233] They came under Globocnik's direct orders, but formally remained employees of the T4 organization. Officials in the Tiergartenstraße managed all personnel issues for the new Reinhardt recruits, including salary and benefits. A special courier from the T4 Central Office came to Lublin every week with special payment and mail for the former euthanasia functionaries.

[234] TAL/ZStL, Belzec Case: Statement of Josef Oberhauser. Oberhausr had to say this to distance himself from "inside knowledge." Why was he in Lublin collecting more building materials for Belzec if not for expanding the camp? Is it believable that he, as Wirth's right-hand man and constant companion, knew nothing, as he claims? He himself admits to being present at meetings between Wirth, Brack and/or Blankenburg.

[235] Ibid.

[236] Browning, *Path*, 115.

[237] See Burrin, *Hitler and the Jews*, 125.

[238] Sandkühler, *Endlösung*, 159.

[239] Ibid.

[240] See Browning, *Nazi Policy*, 28/41

[241] Burrin, *Hitler and the Jews*, 127, n. 29.

[242] Browning, *Nazi Policy*, 43.

[243] See: Kershaw, *Hitler*, chapter 10, note 103 (962, for remarks re: Eichmann's visit).

[244] YVA: Eichmann Trial: Transcript. Interrogation notes by Captain Avner Less (Israeli Police), 30 May 1960, tape No. 5, 172.

[245] Ibid.

[246] Rudolf Höß, *Auschwitz*, 206.

[247] Hilberg, *Documents*, See also Rudolf Höß, *Auschwitz*, 164.

[248] See: *Himmler Diary, p. 186 and n.17)*. Globocnik was probably informed verbally by Himmler during a conference in Lublin on 20 July 1941. Oswald Pohl and Hans Kammler were in Lublin on the same day.

[249] Gassing experiments had already been conducted at Novinki and Mogilev in September 1941, by Dr. Widmann, the KdF's expert on gassing for T4.

[250] Pucher, *Globocnik.*

[251] For a summary of Wannsee see Longerich, *Unwritten Order*, 95-98.

[252] Browning, *Path,* 140. Two distinct methods of operating separated Chełmno and Belzec: Chełmno used gas vans operating from an adapted building; Belzec were constructed from scratch and improvised as the work progressed. Even so, Belzec gassings were not far behind Chełmno.

[253] The gas van in Belzec was used during February 1942, and the experimental gassings in the first gas chambers at the beginning of March). The actual beginning of the Reinhardt exterminations was 17 March 1942 in Belzec. The experiments were not considered a part of the extermination operation, according to Oberhauser.

[254] Abraham I. Katsh (ed.), *Scroll of Agony: The Warsaw Diary of Chaim A. Kaplan,* Indianapolis 1999.

[255] See Weindling, *Nazi Medicine*, 253.

[256] See Browning, *Nazi Policy*, 29: n 11 (Longerich's assessment on this point).

[257] Phillippe Burrin, *Hitler and the Jews,* 127. See also Yahil, *Holocaust*, 310.

[257] Ibid.

[258] Rudolf Höß, *Holocaust*, 147-206.

[259] See: Patricia Heberer, "Continuity in Killing Operations," *Conference* "Aktion Reinhardt": Der Völkermord an den Juden im Generalgouvernment, Lublin, Poland, 8 November 2002. Hans Bodo Gorgass, quoted in: Klee, *Euthanasie,* 418.

[260] Pohl, *Judenpolitik*, 101-2.

[261] Heberer, *Conference.* See: Verfahren gegen Adolf Wahlmann u. a. Testimony of Lydia Thomas, 25 February 1947, 59). Fritz Todt was killed in an airplane crash after visiting Hitler's Wolfsschanze headquarters on 8 February 1942.

[262] TAL/IMT: Statement of Viktor Brack, 15 September 1946, Nuremberg.

[263] The security and police personnel at Chełmno consisted of: 10-15 SD and about 80 Ordnungspolizei. Within a 24-hour period, there were on average 12 Orpo men, assisted by a few Polish prisoners and approximately 60 work Jews, 20 of whom were always chained when unloading the bodies from the gas vans. The Poles were allowed Jewish women for entertainment. As in the Reinhardt camps, the Germans were given extra pay and rations and allowed to take Jewish property.

[264] Ibid. At about this time (late summer 1941), Wirth had confided to a T4 doctor that he had been transferred to a new installation in the Lublin area.

[265] Klee, *Euthanasie* (NS-Staat), 372-3. In 1948, a close friend of Pauline Kneissler told post-war investigators that Kneissler had revealed she had "(given) injections at a reserve military hospital in Russia, from which soldiers died painlessly."

[266] Ibid.

267 See: Brack's meeting with Himmler at 12:00 hours on Sunday, 14 December 1941, and comments by Witter et al., re: a possible discussion point: *Diensttagebach Himmler*, 290 n. 48.

268 Heberer, *Conference*. See: Testimony of Viktor Brack, Nuremberg Medical Trial, quoted in Arad, *Belzec,* 17. As discussed, Brack appears to have been against the extermination of the Jews as he kept making alternative proposals: Madagascar and mass sterilization; he finally resigned from the KdF in the summer of 1942 because he was not in complete agreement with the extermination policy.

269 See Heberal: *Conference.* Dr. Alfred Wetzel, Reich Ministry for the Eastern Territories, to Heinrich Lohse, Reichskommissar Ostland, re: The Solution of the Jewish Question ("Gaskammer Brief") reprinted in: Jeremy Noakes and Geoffrey Pridham (eds.), *Nazism 1919-1945*, vol. III. Foreign Policy, War, and Racial Extermination: A Documentary Reader, University of Exeter Press 1991/1995, 1144.

270 Ibid. Wetzel wrote: "In the present situation, there are no objections to getting rid of Jews who are unable to work with the Brack remedy. Incidents such as those that took place during the shooting of Jews in Vilna, according to the report I have received, can hardly be tolerated, in view of the fact that the executions took place in public; and the new procedures will ensure that such incidents will no longer be possible. On the other hand Jews who are fit for work will be transported further east for use as labor. It is clear that men and women in this latter group must be kept apart from one another. Please report to me about any further measures you may take."

271 Witte et al., *Der Dienstkalender*, 290.

272 For a further assessment concerning the date when Belzec was constructed see: Browning, *Fateful Months,* 30-31.

273 See: Heberer, *'Exitus Heute' in Hadamar: The Hadamar Facility and 'Euthanasia' in Nazi Germany.* (Ph.D. Dissertation, University of Maryland at College Park, 2001).

274 Arad, *Belzec,* 18.

275 Ibid.

276 TAL/ZStL, *Belzec Case*: Statement of George Wippern, 21 September 1967. ZStL, File No. 147 Js 7/72, vol. 73: Verfahren gegen Dr. Ludwig Hahn u. a. Testimony of August Wilhelm Miete, 23 April 1964, Düsseldorf, 14110-14119; Klee, *"Von der 'T4' zur Judenvernichtung,"* 147.

277 TAL/ZStL, *Belzec Case*: Statement of Josef Oberhauser, 12 December 1962.

278 Blatt, Sobibór, 24.

279 TAL/ZStL, *Belzec Case*: Statement of Kurt Franz, 14 September 1962.

280 Friedlander, *Origins,* 298.

281 The first Jews arrived in the camp between December 1941 and March 1942. Over 2,000 Jewish males were sent from the Lublin ghetto, which at the same time was sending the first transports to Belzec extermination camp. On the implementation of Reinhardt, further transports of Jews arrived from western European countries. Jews were now being transported from all over into the Lublin transit camps, waiting their turn to be sent to the exterminations camps at Belzec and Sobibór. Those fit for work were sent to other ghettos in the district from where in time they also would go to the death camps. Many thousands were held in Majdanek for labor.

282 See Weindling, *Epidemics and Genocide*, 314.

283 By the autumn of 1942, three medium size gas chambers, a mortuary and crematoria were built. The gas chambers, similar in principle to those at Auschwitz, utilized

Zyklon B gassing techniques. This killing complex was established in one unit with a 12 meter high chimney at the far end of the camp.

[284] PRO, File No. WO 309/1217: Interrogation of Höß, 14 May 1946. See also Höß, *Auschwitz*, 206.

[285] It is inconceivable (or most unlikely) that senior SS officials outside Reinhardt were unaware of the situation and what was being perpetrated in the East.

[286] PRO, File No. WO 208/4673: Statement of Jakub Sporrenberg, 25 February 1946. Another incident occurred in the spring of 1942, when a drunken sergeant who had been sent by Globocnik with a message approached Stangl, the newly installed commandant of Sobibór. Stangl was affronted at the manner in which he was spoken to. The sergeant passed the message: "If the Jews did not work properly just bump them off and get some others." (Sereny, *Stangl,* 110).

[287] Sereny, *Stangl*, 201.

[288] TAL/ZStL, *Belzec Case*: Statement of Josef Oberhauser, 13 March 1962. Oberhauser was the closest to Wirth, but even this did not protect him from Wirth's wrath, which happened on a number of occasions (my bracket).

[289] Ibid. Statement of Josef Oberhauser, 13 December 1962.

[290] Ibid. Opening remarks by prosecuting counsel at the Belzec trial. The only Belzec trial was Oberhauser's in January 1965. All the others underwent interrogations by Kripo officers and pretrial hearings before magistrates. The presiding magistrate ruled that a public court hearing was "not necessary" as all the accused had successfully argued their defense, namely, that they had been forced to act "under extreme duress," i.e. dire threats by Wirth.

[291] Ibid. Statement of Heinrich Gley, 7 January 1963.

[292] Tregenza, *Belzec, 2*.

[293] Klee, Dressen, Riess, *Days*, 201.

[294] PRO, File No. WO/218/4673: Statement of George Konrad Morgan, 8 August 1946.

[295] Goldhagen, *Executioners*, 379-381, 590, n.3-4.

[296] Friedlander, *Origins*, 235-6.

[297] Ibid., 85.

[298] TR10/1154: *Krüger Verdict*: Statement to the court, 22 May 1963.

[299] See Longerich, *Unwritten Order*, 87.

[300] Ibid.

[301] Ibid.

[302] For an overview of the killings in Nadworna and Stanisławow, see: Dieter Pohl, "Hans Krüger and the Murder of the Jews in the Stanisławow Region (Galicia)," in: *Yad Vashem Studies,* vol. XXVI, Jerusalem 1998, 139-151, 239-264. Sandkühler, *Endlösung*, 148-165: Burleigh, *Hitler*, 614: Longerich, *Unwritten Order*, 85.

[303] Ibid., 82.

[304] See Klee, Dressen, Riess, *Days*, 80.

[305] Ibid. This was a real prospect: See: Commander of the SD in Riga, 80. See also: SS-Scharführer and Kriminalassistant in Kołomyja, 78.

[306] PRO, File No. WO 235/631, dated 5.3.1946, ref: BAOR/15418/124/130/JAG.

[307] Ibid.

[308] TAL/ZStL, *Belzec Case*: Statement of Friedrich Lorent, 4 May 1961.

[309] When Dr. Choronzhitzki committed suicide in Treblinka, extensive efforts were made by the SS to revive him in order to execute him at their bidding, not his. See: Samuel Willenberg, *Revolt in Treblinka*, Warsaw 1991, 136.

[310] Klee, Dressen, Riess, *Days,* 243.

[311] Henri Roques, *The Confessions of Kurt Gerstein.* Institute for Historical Review, Costa Mesa 1989, 77-49. (Hereafter: Roques, *Gerstein).*

[312] Arad, *Belzec,* 224.

[313] Ibid.

[314] TAL, Franz Suchomel, *Christian Wirth* (private report), Altötting 1972. (Hereafter; Suchomel, *Wirth).* Kainer had fallen foul of Wirth earlier at the Hadamar T4 killing institution and served a short sentence in a concentration camp on Wirth's orders. Another T4 employee, SS-Scharführer Heinrich Matthes, former male nurse at Hadamar mental institution, replaced him. Kainer shot himself in the head and died the same day. SS- Oberscharführer Heinrich Unverhau states that when he realised what was going on in T4—the gassing of mental patients—he objected but was threatened with KZ. This was no idle threat: Wirth had already sent two male nurses (Kaiser and Arudt) to KZ-Sachsenhausen for six weeks. Both men were, however, reinstated in T4.

[315] Ibid. See: TAL, Suchomel, *Wirth.*

[316] Ibid.

[317] Gustav Wagner: allegedly murdered by Sobibór Jewish prisoner.

[318] Hilberg, *Documents,* 212.

[319] *Krüger Verdict:* Statement of Hans Krüger, 8 January 1962.

[320] Ibid.

[321] Sereny, *Stangl,* 224.

[322] Ibid. This may have been the transport Robert Jührs was ordered to supervise at the Ramp as his description corresponds in date and facts.

[323] TAL/ZStL, *Belzec Case:* Statement of Heinrich Gley, 7 January 1963. See also: Statement of Robert, 11 October 1961. In the first phase, the pit where the sick were shot was a short distance from the Ramp. In the second phase, the pit was inside Camp II.

[324] Ibid. Statement of Robert Jührs, 11 October 1961. See also: Ibid., Statement Heinrich Gley, 7 January 1963.

[325] Ibid. Statement of Heinrich Unverhau, 21 July 1960.

[326] Ibid. Statement of Werner Dubois, 15 September 1971.

[327] Ibid. See statement of Karl Schluch: "for me, as a 'little man', it was in no way possible to get away from there. If I never once made any such attempt, it was solely because I feared for my own life ... I was a witness when Wirth, in front of the assemble garrison, aimed a pistol at Unverhau because he had attempted to justify his attempt to get away in Berlin."

[328] Ibid. Statement of Heinrich Unverhau, 10 July 1961 and 8 January 1963.

[329] Ibid. Statement of Erich Fuchs. The Scharführers who saved Fuchs were Erwin Fichtner and Johann Niemann.

[330] Ibid. Similar incidents had occurred with Kurt Franz (later commandant of Treblinka), and Scharführer Fritz Kraschewski, who was transferred to Auschwitz.

[331] Ibid.

[332] Ibid. Statement of Josef Oberhauser.

[333] Ibid. Statements of SS-Scharführers Erwin Lambert and Otto Horn.

[334] Ibid. See: Sobibór Trial press report in: *Süddeutscher Zeitung,* 20 January 1965.

[335] Ibid. Statement of Franz Suchomel.

[336] Ibid.

[337] Ibid. Statement of Heinrich Gley 23, January 1961. He was almost certainly shot by firing squad in Lublin Castle.

[338] Ibid. Statement of Franz Suchomel, 12 February 1963.

Chapter 6

[339] Arbeitserziehungslager (Workers educational labor camp), Zwangsarbeitslager (forced labor camp), Straflager (Penal camp), Judenlager/Durchgangslager (Jewish transit camp/death camp), Gefaengnisse (Prisons), Internierungslager (Civilian internment camp), Kriegsgefangenenlager (Prisoner-of-war camps), Konzentrationslager (Concentration camp), Strafgefangenenlager (Penal camp for POWs), Vernichtungslager (Extermination camp) and Ghettos. Hartheim is listed as a death camp, which was situated 30 kilometers west of Linz and served the Mauthausen KZ. 2,700 inmates from Gusen were gassed there. In addition, 1,500 civilians were cremated there 1939-1945.

[340] For an overview of SS Concentration camps in the Greater Reich, see: Orth, *Camps SS*, 306-336.

[341] Szymon Datner: *War Crimes in Poland: Genocide 1939-1945*, Warsaw 1962, 47 for overview of the camp system in Poland.

[342] Paechter, *Nazi Deutsch*, 128.

[343] Dienstkalender, 146.

[344] Ibid., 327.

[345] Ibid., 457. See also: Longerich, *Unwritten Order*, 97.

[346] *Tagebuch*, 588, as cited in: Browning, *Nazi Policy*, 79.

[347] The three main protagonists who were the founders of the German camp system were Theodor Eicke, Richard Glücks and Oswald Pohl.

[348] Herbert, *Labor and Extermination*, 172-4.

[349] 7 zloty was paid for each Pole, 5 zloty for each male Jew and 3 zloty for female Jews; it was therefore advantageous to employ Jews at the lower rate. As the Jews were incarcerated in SS camps, their living costs were much lower (2 zloty) per Jew.

[350] It is interesting to note that the term "East" is continually used when referring to Jews transported beyond the Bug River; as the resettlement progressed, this term took on other connotations relating to the death camps.

[351] MG, *Map*, 48-60 (47-56).

[352] On 22 April 1940, Globocnik set up a "Jewish Office" (Judenreferat) under SS-Obersturmführer Dr. Karl Hofbauer to coordinate and administer this forced labor. SS-Standartenführer Willi Stemmler was appointed by Globocnik to supervise these camps (later SS-Sturmbannführer Hermann Dolp). The Jewish Council in Lublin were additionally ordered to pay all costs.

[353] BDC/YV No: 684.

[354] See: E. Dziadosz, J. Marszałek, "Wiezienia i obozy w dystrykcie lubelskim w latatch 1939-44," in: *Zeszyty Majdanka*, vol. 3, Lublin 1969, 60-66. See also: Tregenza, *Belzec- Das Vergessene*, 246.

[355] 1,140 Gypsies, men, women and children, of whom a small proportion were sent to work.

[356] The SS ensured the good behaviour of the Jews by keeping family records: any escape and their families would suffer reprisals. Globocnik referred to this special unit of guards as "SS unreliables" (Hilberg, *Destruction*, vol. 1, n. 241).

[357] On 10 September 1940, the Kreishauptmann for Zamosc County reported that conditions in these camps were very primitive. (The camps were located on the Narol road within the village community environs). The Gypsies were located at Moraczewski farm complex. One photograph shows the proclaimed King of the Gypsies, Jan Kwiek, talking to German guards at the gate of the camp. Several photographs of Jews and Gypsies taken in the Belzec labor camps are incorrectly captioned in several archives and publications as having being taken in the Belzec death camp. See: photographic collection in the Regional Museum in Sobibór-Lubelski Archive and Yad Vashem in Jerusalem. See also: Tregenza, *Belzec - Das Vergessene*, 241.

[358] Klukowski, *Diary*, 119.

[359] The "Otto Line" was 10 m wide and 6 m deep, zigzag, and stretched for many miles. Other photographs show Jews working on the "Otto line" in Belzec, many of whom had been deported from Warsaw. Adam Czerniaków, Chairman of the Warsaw Judenrat, refers in his diary to seeking information about the Jews who had been sent to the Belzec labor camp.

[360] BDC/YV: No. 28. Personal file of SS-Sturmbannführer Hermann Dolp. In Belzec village today, there are still witnesses who remembered Dolp and his methods of extracting food and property from the Belzec residents outside of the camps. They also remember Dolp's favorite pastime of forcing Jews to submerge themselves in the local pond for two minutes; he ordered the guards to shoot anyone who resurfaced before that time.

[361] See Sandkühler, *Endlösung*, 132-42.

[362] Browning, *Nazi Policy*, 63.

[363] Statement of Chaim Lejst in: *From Suche-Lipie to Sobibór*, Warsaw 1946. Lejst lived with the Gypsy King, Jan Kwiek, in the Jewish/Gypsy camp on the Moraczewski farm in Belzec. A male, who had escaped from the death camp in March 1942, entered the labor camp and informed them of the massacres taking place there. (* There was no labor camp in Belzec or vicinity during the existence of the death camp 1942-43).

[364] Gilbert, *Holocaust*, 286. Gilbert refers: "the first site (death camp), had been a labor camp." My brackets. See also Arad, *Belzec*, who has the same opinion. In my view, both authors are mistaken. Burleigh, *Third Reich*, 640, draws a similar conclusion. See also: TAL/OBKZ, Statement of Tadeusz Misziewicz. See also: Mieczysław Wieliczko: "In Memoriam": an appreciation of Dr Józef Marzałek's research, *Labor Camps in the Generalgouvernment in the Years 1939-1945*. Lublin 1998, 191.

[365] (* TAL/OKBL,File No. Ds. 1604/45 – Zamosc (The Death Camp at Belzec): Statement by Stanislaw Kozak, 14.10.1945. See also: Szrojt, *Oboz zaglady w Belzcu*, 35.

[366] Pohl, *Ostgalizien*, 348-55.

[367] Kershaw, *Hitler*, 483.

[368] See Burleigh, *Third Reich*, 640.

[369] Browning, *Fateful Months*, 30-31. Breitman, *Architect*, 200.

[370] Witte, *Diensttagebuch*, 233 n. 35. "18:00 – 20:00: Besprechung m. SS-Ogruf Krüger u. SS-Brif. Globocnik."

[371] A title he was to be branded with by the Jews of Plaszów KZ: recollections by two survivors, Victor Dortheimer (London) and Josef Bau (Israel). See: O'Neil, *Oskar Schindler*, MA Thesis, University College, London 1996. Goeth was the most

prolific ghetto clearer in the Generalgouvernment: Kraków, Bochnia Tarnów, Lublin, to name but a few.

[372] Ibid.

[373] Sandkühler, *Endlösung*, 11.

[374] Klukowski, *Diary*, 197.

Chapter 7

[375] Longerich, *Unwritten Order*, 81-2.

[376] Ibid. See also: Browning, *Nazi Policy*, 41-47. Gerlach, *Grundsatzentscheidung,* 9, 43 (cited by Browning).

[377] Ibid., Browning, *Nazi Policy*, 45.

[378] Ibid., 46

[379] Ibid. Construction of Belzec, Sobibór and Treblinka was directed and supervised from the Zentral bauleitung der Waffen-SS und Polizei (Central Construction Office of the Waffen-SS and Police at Bernhardiner Strasse 9, now Ulica Bernardynska 9) in Lublin, which had a branch office in Zamosc, 40 km from Belzec. The officer with overall responsibility was SS-Hauptsturmführer Richard Thomalla, a former building contractor from Silesia.

[380] SS-Oberscharführer Gottfried Schwarz held the post of deputy commandant of Belzec from the end of 1941 until May 1943 when the camp was dismantled under his supervision. In 1943 Himmler promoted him to the rank of SS-Untersturmführer (see Polin, *Belzec*, 284, n. 23).

[381] Hilberg, *Destruction,* vol. 3, 875 n. 27. See also: TAL/OKBZ, Statement of Stanislaw Kozak, 14 October 1945. This practice has not changed; during the 1997-1998 archaeological survey of the camp conducted by a team of archaeologists from Toruń University, local labor was employed for the manual labor of digging and drilling at the rate of $1 per hour.

[382] TLA/ZStL, *Belzec Case:* Statement of Heinrich Unverhau. From the end of July 1942, Unverhau supervised the warehouse in the old locomotive shed near Belzec station in which the clothing and belongings of the victims were sorted by a "work brigade" of German-speaking Jews.

[383] TAL/OKBZ: Statement of Ludwig Obalek, 10 October 1945.

[384] Ibid. Statement of Michał Kuśmierczak, 16 October 1945.

[385] Ibid. Statement of Edward Ferens, 14 October 45. See also: Statements of 19 May 1945 and 20 March 1946. See also: Szrojt, *Belzec*, 35. Chruściewicz, *Sprawozdanie,* 128.

[386] TAL/OKBZ, Statement of Stanislaw Kozak, 14 October 1945. See also: Szrojt, *Belžec*, 40, fig. 2.

[387] See: TAL/ZStL, Der Leitende Oberstaatsanwalt beim Landgericht, Hamburg: File No. 45 Js 27/61. Sobibór was a variant of Belzec to the northeast, adjacent to the Chelm-Włodawa railway line and was commissioned on 3 May 1942, under Commandant Franz Stangl. Shortly after Sobibór's commission, Dr Irmfried Eberl also arrived in Sobibór prior to taking over as commandant of a third constructed death camp, Treblinka 2. Treblinka I, the labor camp, was commanded by van Eupen.

[388] Klee, Dressen and Riess, *Days,* 228: Statement of Josef Oberhauser.

[389] See: Kola, *Belzec,* 28. It was the opinion of the investigators on-site that this grave could well be double the size.

[390] Ibid., 67, for an alternative view. Lime was spread on the decomposing corpses in the graves in an attempt to at least lessen the possibility of an epidemic. The argument about the line of the narrow gauge railway depends entirely of the site of the first gas chambers.

[391] TAL/OKBZ: Statement of Kazimierz Czerniak, 18 October 1945. Further testimonies relating to the construction of the camp and the gassing facilities can be found in the testimonies of: Edward Luczynski, 15.10. 1945; Michael Kusmierczak, 16.10.1945; Eustachy Ukrainski, 11.10.1945; Jan Busse, 23.5.1945; Marie Własink, 21.2.1945; Jan Glab, 16.10.1945; Edward Ferens, 20.3.1945; and Eugeniusz Goch, 14.10.1945. For overview of the witness Ukraiński (inhabitant of Belzec), see: Longerich, *Ermordung,* 360-362

[392] Ibid.

[393] Ibid.

[394] These wooden doors that opened outwards to remove the bodies from the chambers caused some difficulty in the gassing operations due to sealing problems. To overcome this, piles of sand were kept outside the doors to secure the gaps.

[395] It will be shown later that recently discovered Luftwaffe aerial photographs show a second rail link into the camp, thus doubling the number of wagons from 20 to 40.

[396] Witte, *Diensttagebuch,* eentry for 14 March 1942: 10:00: SS-Ogruf. Krüger, SS-Oberf. Schöngarth, 379, n. 42.

[397] Browning, *Nazi Policy,* 57.

[398] Sandkühler, *Endlösung,* 11.

[399] PRO, File No. FO 371/50971/85681: Foreign Office papers dated 16 March 1945: Copy of German document found in an SD office in Romanian and believed to be a Jewish report dated 12 November 1944, which had been intercepted by the SD.

[400] TAL/OKBZ: Statement of Alojzy Bereszowski, 5 November 1945. See also: Statement of Viktor Skowronek, 16 October 1945.

[401] According to Longerich (*Politik,* 513), the decision to exterminate (vernichtet) most of the Jews of the Districts of Lublin and Galicia had probably been taken at the beginning of March 1942.

[402] TAL/JHIW: Statement of Chaim Hirszman, 19 March 1946.

[403] Ibid.

[404] TAL/OKBZ: Statement of Stanislaw Kozak, 14 October 1945.

[405] TAL/ZStL, Belzec Case: Statements of Heinrich Gley, 10 May 1961; Heinrich Unverhau, 10 July 1961; Hans Girtzig, 18 July 1961; Robert Jührs, 11 October 1961; and Karl Schluch, 11 November 1961.

[406] Orth, *Camps SS,* 310.

[407] Sereny, *Stangl,* 82.

[408] TAL/ZStL, Belzec Case: Statement of Josef Oberhauser.

[409] TAL/ZStL, File No. 208 AR-Z 251/59 (Sobibór Case): Statement by Erich Bauer, 10.12.1962). Sobibór Case: Statement by Erich Fuchs, 8 April 1963.

[410] Klee, Dressen, Riess, *Days,* 230.

[411] Ibid., 234: Statement of Oskar Diegelmann, 12 December 1961. Diegelmann was Reichsbsahnober- inspektor (Senior Inspector of the Reich Railways) at Lublin station. See also: TAL/ZStL, 208 AR-Z 80/60: Case against Rudolf Göckel.

[412] Blatt, *Sobibór,* 52.

[413] Ibid.

[414] Ibid. Statement of Abraham Margulies.

[415] TAL/Novitch, *Sobibór*: Statements of Moshe Bahir and Eda Lichtman.

[416] Ibid.

[417] Ibid. See also: TAL/ZStL, Sobibór Case: Statement of Erich Bauer.

[418] Ibid.

[419] Ibid.

[420] TAL/ZStL, Belzec Case: Statements; Josef Oberhauser, Werner Dubois, Erich Fuchs, Heinrich Gley, Robert Jührs, Karl Schluch, Heinrich Unverhau and Ernst Zierk—all former members of the Belzec death camp garrison. See: Statement of Josef Oberhauser, 12 December 1962, Munich.

[421] Ibid.

[422] Ibid. Globocnik had sent Oberhauser from Lublin to Belzec to find out about Wirth's apparent absence from the camp.

[423] Ibid. See also: YVA 04/32. Main sources: Investigation by Jewish Committees in 1945 - Tuviah Friedmann (*Documents*), Director of the Institute of Documentation, Haifa, Israel. Friedmann investigated the Kołomyja murders and personally interviewed the surviving witnesses, including the testimonies of the brothers Moshe and Joseph Schliesser in Vienna in the summer of 1947. Friedmann was the driving force that culminated in the eventual prosecution of several of those mentioned, albeit the sentences bore no relation to the crimes committed.

[424] Generaldirektion der Ostbahn (Gedob): General Management of Eastern Railways. Gedob worked very closely with the "Otto" program (Operation Todt - "OT") in the reconstruction of bridges and modernization of over 600 km of track on the East-West line. Initiated in Krakow in November 1939, Gedob operated the expropriated Polskie Koleje Pañstwowe (PKP) - Polish State Railway, under the auspices of the Reichsbahn, which in turn came under the Reich Ministry of Transport. The Gedob headquarters in Kraków was headed by Reichsbahnrat Dr. Peicher, with branch offices in Warsaw, Lublin and Radom, and from the summer of 1941 in Lvov, and employed a staff of over 70,000. The Jewish deportation trains came under Department V (Operations), headed by Erwin Massute.

[425] Lanzmann, *Shoah,* 132-145: interviews with Raul Hilberg and with Walter Stier, head of Reichsbahn Abteilung 33 (Reich Railways, Department 33) These centers controlled all traffic (military, civilian and goods) and were the lynchpin of all Jewish Resettlement Trains (special trains) ordered by the Sipo-SD. They operated in a building adjacent to HSSPF Odilo Globocnik's Reinhardt Headquarters, located at 14 Finkstrasse (1942)— today 14 Niecala Street—and the local unemployment centers in Lublin.

[426] Ibid. In a typical Fahrplananonordnung (Timetable Order) at Yad Vashem, nowhere does the word "Geheim" ("Secret") appear. Hilberg also draws attention to this and concludes that classifying these documents as secret would only have drawn attention to them.

[427] Lanzmann, *Shoah,* 138. The "Mittel Europäische Reisburo" (Central European Travel Agency), an agency one might find on the high street of any town

[428] Raul Hilberg, *German Railroads - Jewish Souls,* London 1976, 60-76.

[429] Ibid. There was no budget for destruction; the Jews themselves paid for their own extermination!

[430] The only occasions on which the railway authorities lost out on a payment was for the Jews transported to Auschwitz from Salonika in Greece, because the Reichsbahn only accepted RM. The commanding officer where the transports were initiated

(Salonika) was responsible for transport payment, and although the SD in Greece had Jewish money, Greek Drachmas, this was a currency neither acceptable nor exchangeable. This could only be overcome if the SD conveyed RM from Greece to Germany, which in wartime was difficult. Hilberg in: Lanzmann, *Shoah*, 144.

[431] Robert Kuwalek, "Transit Ghettos in the Lublin District." *Conference.*

[432] Ibid. Kiełbón, "Deportation of Jews to the Lublin District."

[433] Ibid.

[434] Longerich, *Unwritten Order*, 101.

[435] Pucher, *Globocnik.*

[436] TAL/ZStL AR-Z 74/60: Statement of George Michalsen.

[437] Ibid.

[438] Sandküher, *Endlösung*, 11.

[439] Klukowski, *Diary*, 191.

[440] PRO, File No. F0 371/50971/85681: German document found in SD office in Romania and believed to be a Jewish report seized by the Germans. The document found its way to the British Foreign Office, 16 March 1945.

[441] Ibid. The transport of the dead Jews with the living confirmed their thoughts that they were destined for death and economic reasons (bodies for soaps and fertilizers). The ghettos were set up about two weeks after the August deportations.

[442] Longerich, *Unwritten Order*, 102.

[443] Pucher, *Globocnik.*

[444] Sandkühler, *Endlösung*, 212

[445] The later transports in autumn became notorious for loading the victims naked into the wagons, which were sometimes strewn with lime. This policy allowed the victims to be taken directly from the wagons into the gas chambers.

[446] Margaret Rubel, unpublished paper to the author re: deportations to Belzec, 1998.

[447] Szrojt, *Belzec*, 31-45; see also: Chrościewicz, *Sprawozdanie*, 127-130.

[448] Polin, *Belzec*, 272 n. 5. Göckel was the railway intermediary with the camp administration. (*Göckel was arrested by the Soviet NKVD in E. Germany in 1947 at the request of the Polish authorities and extradited to Poland. He was tried and sentenced but released in 1950 during an amnesty.)

[449] TAL/OKBZ: Statement of Mieczysław Kudyba, 14 October 1945.

[450] By the time Sobibór and Treblinka were in operation, Wirth enhanced the reception areas and procedures. Wirth's idea to do this was formed in Belzec in his overall deception policy. As we know, bogus ticket offices were installed in Sobibór and Treblinka.

[451] Höß, *Auschwitz*, 169.

[452] Lillian Siegfried to the author, 16 September 2002: "My husband's parents, two brothers and two sisters were deported from Jaslo to Belzec. One brother jumped off the train and after nine concentration camps survived the war. The rest were murdered in Belzec."

[453] Polin, *Belzec*, 276.

[454] Roques, *Gerstein*, 77-78.

[455] Klee, Dressen and Riess, *Days*, 238-241: Statements of Professor Wilhelm Pfannenstiel and Kurt Gerstein.

[456] Polin, *Belzec*, 276. Unaccompanied children were normally taken to the pits and shot or clubbed, or just flung on top of those already in the gassing rooms.

[457] Rich, *Footsoldiers*, 695.

264

[458] TAL/ZStL, Belzec Case: Statements of Werner Dubois 15 September 1971, Karl Schluch, 10 November 1961.

[459] Höß, *Auschwitz*, 170.

[460] Sereny, *Stangl*, 111.

[461] See: Kora (analysis of soil content on-site), 63.

[462] TAL/ZStL, Belzec Case: Statement of Josef Oberhauser, 12 December 1962.

[463] Arad, *Belzec*, 72 (Statement of Josef Oberhauser): Arad refers to Wirth's immediate higher authority (Globocnik or T4). This is just one part of the uniqueness of Reinhardt.

[464] The dates of Wirth's exit from Belzec have never been confirmed and are contradicted by a number of other sources.

[465] In early April the decision had been made to kill ALL Jews, with the exception of a few kept for labor; that was the reason for Wirth's recall to Berlin and orders to extend and improve the camp. The original purpose of the camp, to kill the non-working Jews of Lublin, had virtually been accomplished.

[466] Kola, *Belzec*, 68.

[467] Klee, Dressen, Riess, *Days*, 228. See also: TAL/ZStL, Belzec Case: Statement of Josef Oberhauser, 14 December 1962.

[468] Christopher Browning also picks up a similar point. See: Browning, "Beyond Warsaw and Łódź; Perpetrating the Holocaust in Poland" 75-90 (Part 1, 4) in: James S. Pacy and Alan P. Wertheimer, *Perspectives of the Holocaust Essays in Honour of Raul Hilberg*, Oxford 1995.

[469] Sereny, *Stangl*, 113.

[470] Ibid.

Chapter 9

[471] Klee, Dressen, Riess, *Days*, 226-7.

[472] Pohl, *Judenpolitik*, 129-131. Jews of economic value were separated and held in KZ camps.

[473] This was a very strict rule introduced by Wirth and continued until the camp was dismantled. There were exceptions of course; Rudolf Reder as senior maintenance worker was allowed, but he was closely supervised.

[474] Kola, *Belzec*, 69.

[475] One of the most controversial elements in the Holocaust literature concerns the number of persons who could fit in the various gas chamber compartments. The so-called "Revisionists" and "Exterminationists" have been arguing their theories for years. In support of their particular view, a number of "papers" have emerged discussing the number of persons who were able to fit into the Gerstein suggested area ratios. The point that is crucial to our understanding to events as to 'numbers' has been the basis of accounting hourly and daily rates of murder. Without delving too deeply into the literature at this point, it is perhaps of interest to note briefly the pros and cons. The literature states 750 persons per gas chamber with an area of 25 sq m. During the first phase in Belzec there were three gas chambers, and in the second phase six gas chambers. Consequently, according to Gerstein, 2,250 and 6,000 persons were capable of being gassed in one "action". In some kind of curious agreement and meeting of minds, the "Revisionists" and the "Exterminationists" agreed that Gerstein's ration was impossible. This would have been the end of the matter except for one thing: in a commendable "paper" on this issue, Charles D.

Proven published his experimental findings in 1996, "Kurt Gerstein and The Capacity of the Gas Chamber at Belzec." In short, Proven concludes that by extensive experiments with live people, Gerstein was right; it was possible to fit 7-800 people into 25 sq m room. See also Polin, *Belzec*, 274 n. 9; Hilberg, *Destruction*, vol. 3, 879. See Kola: 69: "Each of those 6 gas chambers of that building killed 750 persons at once." Kola quotes note 35 which is missing from the report.

[476] TAL/ZStL, Sobibór Case, Statement of Erwin Lambert, 2 October 1962.

[477] Ibid. File No. 45 Js 27/61. In Sobibór, the capacity was increased to over 1,200. Another important technical change was the introduction of a narrow-gauge rail link, which ran from the railway platform to the mass graves in Camp II. Previously horse drawn carts had been used. Similar improvements were also carried out at Treblinka where the number of chambers was increased from three to ten.

[478] Ibid.

[479] TAL/ZStL, File No. 208 AR-Z 252/59 (Belzec Case): Statement by Hans Girtzig, 2.5.1960.

[480] Ibid. From the batch of about 10 men sent to Belzec, only one, Hans Girtzig, was a *bona fide* member of the SS; the rest were male nurses from the T4 euthanasia centers. Girtzig had been trained as a Quartermaster before secondment to Grafeneck at the end of 1939. In Belzec he was in charge of the kitchen/canteen for the Ukrainian guards.

[481] TAL/ZStL, Belzec Case: Statements of Hans Girtzig, 2 May 1960 and 18 July 1961.

[482] Pohl, *Ostgalizien*, 339.

[483] TAL/ZStL, *Belzec Case*

[484] Ibid. Statement of Kurt Franz 14 September 1961.

[485] TAL/Franz Suchomel, Christian Wirth, (Private report), *Altötting* 1972. See also: Lanzmann, *Shoah*, 62-63).

[486] Ibid. Statement Robert Jührs, 11 October 1961.

[487] Hilberg, *Destruction*, vol. 2, 491.

[488] Ibid.

[489] TAL/IMT Doc. NO-5574.

[490] YVA, 04/4-2.

[491] Hilberg, *Documents*, 134.

[492] Ibid.

[493] Ibid.

[494] See: *Tagebuch*, 507-509; also cited in: Browning, *Nazi Policy*, 76.

[495] Ibid.

[496] PRO, (Tyas): HW16/21.

[497] Ibid.

[498] Ibid. Message transmitted on 24 August 1942 re: intended deportation of 200,000 Romanian Jews to begin in late 1942. According to Tyas, the Romanian Jews were to be sent to Trawniki for selection and the remainder sent to Belzec.

[499] Tyas quotes: *Dokumente über Methoden der Judenverfolgung im Ausland*, submitted by the United Restitution Organization in Frankfurt-am-Main, 1959, 75-76.

[500] For an overview of the Kołomyja deportations, see: Sandkühler, *Endlösung*, 242-49: Longerich, *Ermordung*, 216-21.

[501] David Kahane, *The Lvov Ghetto Diary*, London 1990, 16.

[502] Ibid.

[503] Sandkühler, *Endlösung*, 179.

[504] Bibliography, see: Sandkühler, *Endlösung*, 439-442.

[505] The established selection policy of the SD varied: The old and sick were now being shot *in situ* as they had enough Jews of all categories to make up the numbers. All the ghettos were now divided and marked A, B, or C. This was the policy in the Generalgouvernment.

[506] Sandkühler, *Endlösung*, 243.

[507] Ibid.

[508] Sandküler, *Extermination Policies,* 121.

[509] To ease the workload in Belzec many of the transports were emptied at Janowska. Thousands of Jews were stripped naked and all their baggage taken. They were either taken to other camps or shot locally. The remainder loaded naked onto the transport for Belzec. This carefully worked plan saved much time.

[510] This once again demonstrates this well tried procedure occurring all over the occupied territories: fill the ghetto from communities in the immediate vicinity; selection of the weakest for killing; removal from the ghetto; replenish from other localities; repeat and repeat until there were no Jews left.

[511] Krakowski, *Diary*, xi.

[512] Ibid, 191.

[513] Klukowski, *Diary,* 210.

[514] Ibid, 219.

[515] Sandkührer, *Endlösung*, 179.

[516] Lanzmann, *Shoah*, 132.

[517] On 1.8.41, the German authorities established the civil administration in the town: Volkmann appointed Kreishauptmann (Chief of District). See: R-37; Michael took over the Labor Office; Dr Jordon, Landwirtschsftsrat (Head of Supply Department) and Lt. Hertl as head of a detachment of Schützpolizei (Resident City Police) (Regular uniformed German police), see: R-73, and Hohlmann as Stadthauptmann (Town Commissioner). Jewish Affairs in Kołomyja were directed by a triumvirate: Leideritz, Volkmann and Hohlmann. For bibliography details, see: Sandkühler, *Endlösung*; Pohl, *Ostgalizien.*

[518] ARHQ - Reinhardt operations room for resettlement, Lublin.

[519] HSSPF (Kraków) Krüger/SSPF Katzmann (Lvov) 5th District, were responsible for all SS-SD, Police detachments (Ordnungspolizei, etc.).

[520] Friedmann, *Documents,* mentions that 51 freight units were ordered for this transport.

[521] YVA-ll/7/b: The Judenrat in the occupied areas was ordered by the Sipo-SD to keep statistics recording personal details of all men, women, and children in the ghettos. It was no different in Kołomyja and the Judenrat were able to supply the SD with exact numbers of Jews likely to be required for the resettlement transport of Jews. In the Kraków ghetto, for example, these statistics show charts and graphs of the Jewish population in the ghetto divided into ages, sex and employment. Copies of the original documents were given to the author by Joseph Bau (Tel-Aviv). Bau was responsible for this duty in Plaszów KZ.

[522] Ibid. Including the villages and vicinities of Pistyń; Jabłonów; Jabłowice; Żabie. Michael (Kołomyja Labor Office), initiated resettlement proceedings in this region by ordering the Judenrat to assemble its Jews. Five hundred assembled and were immediately arrested by SS-Untersturmführer Frost and Hauptscharführer

Weissmann and local Gendarmerie. The Ukrainian police hunted and shot many Jews in their bunkers. Sixty-six selected Jews were allowed to remain in Kosów to work, while the remainder were forced to march 35 km to the prison in Kołomyja and joined the transport for Belzec on 10.9.1942. Jews who escaped this round-up and were caught later were also sent to Kolomiyja prison. On another occasion (late September 42), the Kosów Jews were taken to the Scheparowce forest and shot in pits. (YV 03: Report dated 5.6.45 - LL/1).

[523] Ibid. The Horodenka resettlement operation was carried out in much the same way as in Kosów (see above); 1,600 Jews were rounded up in this period by the Sipo-SD and local Gendamerie and loaded onto rail transports, transferred to Kołomyja to join the "resettlement" transport for Belzec at 20:50. The principle security personnel in Horodenka were Petsch, the Landeskommissar (Local Commissioner), and Koenig and Kraemer of the Sipo-SD. The Jews rounded up later were either shot on the spot, or transferred to Kołomyja or the pits of Scheparowce.

[524] Ibid. The above principles applied in Kuty. On 8.9.42, all Jews in possession of the "A Stamp" were ordered by the Judenrat to assemble but only 600 actually turned up—over 200 had fled to the Romanian border or had gone into hiding. The assembled Jews were arrested by the Sipo-SD, SS-Hauptsturmführer Schwenker and SS-Sturmscharführer Frost of the Jewish Department and members of the local Gendarmerie, and forced march the 50 km to Kołomyja for the transport to Belzec at 20:50.

[525] Ibid. One thousand Jews were rounded up to join the same transport as the Horodenka Jews to Belzec. Fifteen Jews were selected to remain in Sniatyn to work. The stragglers and those in hiding were all subsequently shot or removed for liquidation in Scheparowce forest. A very few escaped to Rumania or Slovakia.

[526] Ibid. The SD drew on their experience with "resettlement" operations when the Jews of Stryj were "resettled" between 3-5 September 1942 (R. 1952).

[527] Ibid. The Schützpolizei in Kołomyja was a separate unit and acted independently of other police support units. The police unit in Kołomyja came together in a variety of circumstances: Kleinbauer had been a serving police officer in the Vienna police when he was ordered to Kołomyja on 6.10.1941; Schipany had seen service with the Schupo in Wieliczka, Częstsochowa, Kraków, Tarnów and Lvov, when he was transferred to Kołomyja; Pernek arrived via Kost in October 1941. The Reinforcements of 7./24 police detachment, who had been engaged in Jewish resettlement in Skole, Stryj and Chodorów during the period 3-5 September 1942, arrived in Kołomyja in time for the operation of the 7.9.42. A special Ukrainian Auxiliary Police and the Jewish Order Police also assisted the SD-Sipo as well as the Schutzpolizei.

[528] Ibid. They were divided up into two groups, A and B. There was an officer section, a quartermaster section and the police station personnel: Lt. Hertl (commander), Witmann (deputy), Wittich, Doppler, Gross and Kleinbauer; sergeants Layer, Pernek, Kneissl, Hofstetter and Steiner: corporals Gallhart, Straka; constables Gall, Harko, Kroegner, Layer, Mauritz, Reisenthaler, Ruprechtsofer, Stanka Schipany, and Uitz.

[529] Friedman, *Documents,* vol. 410, 508-520: report by Schutzpolizei Leutnant der Reserve und Kompanieführer Westermann, Polizeibataillon 13 (Polizeiregiment 24), to the Kommandeur der Ordnungspolizei in the Galician District. In the original report of Lt. Westermann, it shows Diary No. 64/42 (g). Looking at other similar

reports, I concluded that this was occasion No. 64 on which Westermann had been engaged in "resettlement" duties in the Galician District.

[530] Ibid. Statement of Franz Schipany, 4 September 1947.

[531] Ibid. *Diary.* 1a-1526-42.

[532] Ibid.

[533] Ibid. The "resettlement" described is clearly shown as 7-10 September 1942, a transport of 30 freight wagons. The report clearly shows that 4,769 Jews were loaded on 7.9.42, which was completed at 19:00 and departed for Belzec. The report continues directly to the 8-9 September, with details of the sweep in the districts of Kuty, Kosów, Horodenka, Zapłatów and Sniatyn where 20 wagons were loaded with Jews with 180-200 per wagon (minimum = 3,780 Jews). A further 1,500 Jews were forced marched to Kołomyja from Kuty and Kosów (50 kms and 35 kms respectively) and loaded onto the wagons already in the sidings. The 20 wagons that were loaded with a total of 3,780 Jews in Horodenka and Sniatyn were coupled to the 30 wagons still in the siding at Kołomyja, which I conclude was the same transport referred to for 7 September, and that this transport had not moved but waited for the Sniatyn and Horodenka wagons. I conclude that we are not talking about two separate transports to Belzec (7 and 10 September), but a single transport of 51 wagons that left Kołomyja on 10 September. If this is the case, and I think it is, the 3,780 Jews loaded on 7 September had remained in the wagons for three days without food or water. See also: Statement of Alois Steiner on 3.9.1947.

[534] Ninety-five percent of all resettlement traffic from the Galician District was by freight wagon. During the resettlements from the Reich sphere of interest (Germany, Holland France, etc.), from early spring to July 1942, Jews were sent "to the east" in regular 3rd Class passenger cars with wooden benches. This was all part of the Nazi deception plans. The luggage of the Jews was usually stored in freight wagons that adjoined the transport. The only instances of people being transported from the Reich in freight wagons were the handicapped, insane, etc., who came under T4 administration and in the main, went directly to Piaski and Sobibór, or Izbica and Belzec.

[535] Friedman, *Documents.* 180-200 Jews, men, women and children, loaded per freight wagon. Ordinary rail passenger cars were seen in Belzec in late 1942. The author interviewed (with interpreter) a Ukrainian lady in Belzec June 1998 who lives in a dwelling directly opposite Belzec rail station. She recalled that in 1942, her family, peering through the net curtains of their dwelling, saw such a passenger train waiting in a siding at Belzec. She referred to fat men smoking cigars, standing up and looking out of the window, women were knitting and children were seen, as though excited at finally arriving at their new home. All would have been gassed in a matter of hours. The house of this witness is 50 m from the railway line, and the author stood in the same position to confirm her line of vision.

[536] The Jewish (Public) Order Service and the rail construction gang of Kołomyja carried out the regulation sealing of the Kołomyja transport.

[537] Friedman, *Documents:* Report of Lt. Westermann to the KdO in Galicia, 14 September 1942. See my remarks re: numbers of dead on arrival at Belzec.

[538] Painting by the author, 1998.

[539] Ibid. The "resettlement" train was handed over to Zugwachtmann. d. Schützpolizei Jacklein of the escort guard by Hauptwachtmeister Zitzmann.

[540] Many of the transports to Belzec, Sobibór and Treblinka had chloride of lime spread in the wagons before departure, which caused the skin to peel from the passengers' bodies. Many were asphyxiated *en-route* by this method. At Sobibór SS-Frenzel met a transport from Majdanek and poured chloride of lime on the heads of the Jewish prisoners, which resulted in horrific injuries.

[541] The Soviet transports before Barbarossa treated the deportees reasonably by giving the prisoners food and water. See: personal memoir of Zoë Zajdlerowa, *The Dark Side of the Moon*, London, 1989. The Kołomyja transport had no such luxuries. There are many reports where families taken for execution and ordered to strip naked, fathers, grandfathers and uncles, suffering with shame to appear naked before their families, refused and preferred to be shot rather than remove their clothes.

[542] In the Kołomyja transport, and after the first breakouts had occurred, the Jews were questioned when the train stopped at Stanisławów. They stated to the security services that they had been allowed by the loading guards to retain the tools of their trades, explaining that they would need them at their future destination for work.

[543] Friedmann, *Documents*.

[544] Ibid. The escorting SS could not specify the numbers that had escaped. Nonetheless, it can be assumed that at least two thirds of the escaping Jews were shot or rendered harmless in some other way.

[545] Miscellaneous report dated January 1958, "The Organization of former Jewish residents of Kołomyja," sent to the author by Ben Nauchan (USA). See also: Friedmann, *Documents,* 410, 994-96, 498, 500-501. Report of No. 5 Company, RPB 133, PR 24, 7-11 - 12.12.1942. Shortly after the "resettlement" and ghetto clearing operations in the Kołomyja and Stanislawów districts, Reserve Police Battalion 133, of which Lt. Westermann and his unit were attached, concentrated on the rounding up and shooting of the "jumpers" from the Belzec transports. From their reports, which have survived, we find that between 1 November - 12 December 1942, they killed 481 Jews in "anti-partisan operations," i.e. "Jew hunts" at this crucial location, the crossroads for "resettlement" in the Galician and Lublin Districts.

[546] Ibid. In Kołomyja, selections of these workers had been sifted from the masses and loaded separately for delivery to the Janowska slave labor camp in Lvov.

[547] Ibid. Reference to the wife of Leideritz. See: Yad Vashem, 0-4/32: report dated 3.9.1962 - Report of Jewish Commission dated 13.5.1945: "Murder of the Jews in Kołomyja." It was not unusual for wives and girlfriends to attend, and even take part in Jewish operations. This was a regular occurrence in the Rabka Sipo-SD Academy, when the women associates of the SD climbed on to the roof of the Academy to watch executions taking place. See also: Browning, *Ordinary Men*, 132. Wives and girlfriends also attended ghetto clearance operations to watch their menfolk at work.

[548] Deportations to Belzec: February - March 1942.

Chapter 10

[549] (TAL/OKBL, File No. 1604/45 – Zamosc (Belzec Investigation): Statement of Andrzej Jonko, 10.10.1945. Jonko is still alive and well in Lublin.

[550] Ibid.

[551] YVA: Interviewed by the Israeli Police on 23 June 1960. Ref. No. 280. File, 13. 142/4BP.

[552] Interviewed by the author. See also: press report in: *The Express*, 3 April 2000.

[553] Polin, *Belzec*, 272.

[554] Hilberg *Destruction,* vol. 3: Statement of Stefan Kirsz, 15.10.1945.

[555] The number of Jews found dead on arrival in Belzec was a daily occurrence. In the final operation in clearing the Tarnów ghetto in early September 1943, 10,000 Jews were rounded up and transported to Auschwitz. On arrival, only 400 remained alive, and they were immediately gassed. See: Trial of Amon Goeth: Opening remarks by Prosecuting Counsel Dr Tadeusz Cyprian. Another example in: TAL/IMT, Doc. No. 1553-PS: Statement of Kurt Gerstein: "In 10 minutes, the first train will arrive! A few minutes later the first train came from Lemberg (Lvov): 45 cars, containing 6,700 persons, 1,450 of whom were already dead on their arrival."

[556] Friedmann, Documents: Report of Lt. Westermann: "Die immer grosser werdende Panik unter den Juden, hervorgerufen durch starke Hitze, Uberfullung der Wagons und den Leichengestank - es befanden sich beim Ausladen der Wagons etwa 2,000 Juden tot im Zuge - Machten den Transport fast undurchfuhrbar Um 18:45 Uhr kam der Transportzug in Belzec." Both Longerich (*Ermordung,* 220), and Sandkühler (*Endlösung,* 247) have followed (the) Hilberg (*Sonderzüge nach Auschwitz,* Mainz, 194-197), quoting 200 "dead on arrival' when it should read 2,000."

[557] On this date, the planning for the fate of the Jews in the Lvov region was being discussed at a conference chaired by Himmler at his residence. Attending (Besprechung mit): SS-Brigadeführers Katzmann, Globocnik Wächter and SS-Sturmbannführer Losacker. See: Witte, *Diensttagebach,* entry for Monday, 17 August 1942, 18:30 hours, 521.

[558] Ibid. See also: Polin, *Belzec,* 273 n. 8.

[559] Kola, *Belzec,* 11.

[560] Polin, *Belzec,* 276. According to Reder, this was the decisive moment for the women; the deception had worked—until now!

[561] TAL/ZStL, *Belzec Case*: Statement of Heinrich Gley, 23 November 1961. See also: Polin, *Belzec,* 276 n. 12.

[562] Ibid.

[563] Ibid. Statement of Robert, Jührs 11 October 1961.

[564] Zugführers were the overseers of the Jewish "work Jews" in the camp including the "death brigade." They did not wear uniforms or camp insignia. These men (all Jewish) ran the camp under SS supervision (see: Figure 2).

[565] Polin, *Belzec,* 277 n. 13. See also: TAL/ZStL, *Belzec Case*: Statement of Wilhelm Pfannenstiel, 6 June 1950.

[566] Ibid. Although having close contact with the workings of the system, he is unable to state with certainty how these people were murdered: "From the engine, pipes with a diameter of 1" led into each chamber. The open end of each pipe opened into each chamber. Whether these pipes let gas into the chambers, extracted the air from the chambers, or pumped air into the chambers, I do not know. I never detected any smell. The corpses showed no signs of unnatural discoloration. They all looked like living people with their eyes open."

[567] Ibid. The mechanical excavator used to dig the graves was brought in from Treblinka: see TAL/ZStL, Belzec Case: Statement of Robert Jührs, 11 October 1961.

[568] Kola, *Belzec,* The area of examination between grave 29 and grave 26 to the NE was covered with a layer of innumerable fragments of burnt and crushed bones mixed with grey sand. Graves 12, 15, 16, 19, 24-26 and 29 lie partly beneath the six-grass topped tiers bearing the urns. Graves No. 1-5 were probably the last graves to be dug that contain unburned and mummified corpses. Why these corpses were not

destroyed and burnt is not known; the investigators formed the view that perhaps the burning Kommando had had enough by then. Graves 10, 25, 27, 28, 32 and 33 containing evidence of lime content, probably relating to the warm spring of 1942 when the pits over-flowed with decomposing corpses. Complaints from the civic authorities persuaded the Nazis to spread lime over these graves. Graves 14 and 20 extend beyond the present day fence, confirming our supposition that the camp was much larger.

[569] Hillberg, *Destruction,* vol. 3, 963.

[570] Ibid. 975: Statement by Kurt Gerstein, 26 April 1945, PS-1553. Pfannenstiel admitted that he was in Belzec, but denied making this remark, See: TAL/ZStL, Belzec Case: Statements of Wilhelm Pfannenstiel, 6 June 1950, and November 9, 1952.

[571] Ibid. Described by former SS-Oberscharführer Werner Dubois, in interrogation document, dated 15 September 1971: "These graves were massive and were left open for several days before they were sprinkled with lime and covered. At the final closing, the corpses always protruded above ground level, but after a few days the contents would sink to ground level."

[572] Hilberg, *Documents,* 135.

[573] See Polin, *Belzec,* 273.

[574] Tregenza, *Wirth,* n. 170;

[575] TAL/JHIW: Chaim Hirszman's recollections of Belzec were recorded by his second wife, Pola, in 1946.

[576] Ibid.

[577] Heberer, *Conference*: August Miete, 1964-1965 Treblinka Trial proceedings, quoted in Arad, *Belzec,* 122.

[578] Klee, Dressen, Riess, *Days,* 245: Statement of Willi Mentz.

[579] For descriptions of an execution pit and method of shooting see: TAL/ZStL, Belzec Case, 1554, Heinrich Gley, 24 November 1961/Munster; 1484: Robert Jührs, 12 October 1961/Frankfurt-am-Main. Both Gley and Jührs were assigned to execution duty. It is not conceivable that only one such execution pit existed in the camp, as these witnesses state.

[580] Ibid. Heinz Schmidt, a Latvian Volksdeutsche guard in Belzec, shot several Jews every day at the mass graves. See: TAL/*Belzec Case*: Interrogation document and statement of Robert Jührs, 11 October 1961. In Sobibór, SS-Scharführer Paul Bredow set himself a target of shooting 50 Jews a day. It was his "hobby" approved by Wirth.

[581] Sereny, *Stangl,* 207.

[582] Ibid. This incident upset Gitta Sereny so much that she nearly abandoned the project. It is not known what happened to Singer, but according to Suchomel, after the revolt the Blaus remained at their posts. Those Jews who had not engaged in the revolt were to be shot. According to Suchomel, he advised the Blaus what was to happen and suggested the alternative of poison. That same day both took poison; "It was better that way," said Suchomel.

[583] Klukowski, *Diary,* 225.

[584] The President Garfinkiel survived by escaping with his wife first to Izbica and then to Warsaw. After the war he lived in West Germany under the name "Garwin."

[585] The band consisted of six Jewish musicians who played continuously every day between the gas chambers and the mass graves.

[586] Polin, *Belzec,* 283/4.

[587] TAL/ZStL, *Belzec Case*: Statement of Roman Robak (Rudolf Reder) 8 August 1960. See also: Polin, *Belzec,* 280.

[588] Polin, *Belzec,* 284. The transport referred to by Reder may well have been the Kołomyja transport of mid-September 1942.

[589] Polin, *Belzec,* 282.

[590] Ibid., 280

[591] Ibid., 282.

[592] Ibid., 280. It was not unusual for as many as 30-40 work-Jews to be shot each day. Reder is our only reliable witness to these happenings in Belzec. Many of the former SS who were interviewed after the war broadly outlined what happened here, but fell far short of any detail, which is in no way surprising.

[593] Blatt, *Sobibór,* 50.

[594] Interview by author in Vilnius, November 1996, with Dimitri Gelpernas, deputy partisan leader in Kovno, who cites: "Masines zudynes Lietuvoje 1941-1944, " *Dokumentu rinkinys,* 11 Dalis, Vilnius 1973, 377-379.

[595] Hilberg, *Destruction,* vol. 3, 977.

[596] Although Blobel was charged with the task of exhuming the corpses and burning them, it is evident that the "order" was more widespread and that in individual camps the destruction was to commence forthwith on the commandant's own responsibility. This is common sense, as Blobel himself could in no way complete this task single-handed. Thus, in June 1942, independent of Blobel, the exhumation of the bodies, cremation and bone crushing commenced in the Janowska camp. Blobel's remit was probably to find the best and most economical way forward which would form the basis of procedures throughout the occupied areas. For an in-depth review of how this was carried out and the practical difficulties experienced, see: Leon W. Wells, *The Death Brigade: The Janowska Road,* Macmillan 1963). (Hereafter: Wells, *Janowska*).

[597] Hilberg, *Destruction,* vol. 3, 977.

[598] PRO (Tyas): HW 16/21.

[599] Alex Faitelson, *The Escape from the IX Fort,* Kaunas 1998, 42. (Hereafter: Faitelson, *Escape*).

[600] Wells, *Janowska, 43.*

[601] Faitelson, *Escape,* 18. He cites: *Kż Niurenbergski prozess, (T. I),* vol. I, Moscow 1952, 496.

[602] Ibid. Faitelson identified both his parents at the IX fort: in Belzec, Chaim Hirszman identified his wife among a pile of bodies outside the gas chambers, and in Vilna, Szloma Gol recognised his brother.

[603] Investigations carried out by the author at Rabka.

[604] PRO (Tyas): HW 16/69: Message transmitted 27 February 1944.

[605] TAL/ZStL, Belzec Case: Statement by Josef Oberhauser, In addition to Hackenholt, SS-NCOs Jührs, Unverhau and Girtzig assisted with this work, supervised by Tauscher and Gley. Another British Intelligence decoded message intercept shows that a few months previously (September), SS-Untersturmführer Johann Oppermann from Globocnik's headquarters in Lublin was in Holland buying two mechanical excavators (Eimerbagger). Whether these were machines used in the 1005 program is not known but in any event, it is unlikely they were used outside Reinhardt. One further unexplained decode message which particularly refers to Belzec appears on

12 September (same period) referring to a worker transport from Lublin via Dębica to Belzec. In the same decode reference is made to bringing materials and equipment on uncovered wagons from Warsaw to Lublin. Further, there is a reprimand from Globocnik to the railway authorities in the name of the Reichsführer-SS concerning these arrangements which is not fully explained. Dębica is between Warsaw and Lublin so there must have been an important purpose in this diversion. We simply do not know what was behind these messages, only that this was the height of the deportation period. See: PRO (Tyas): HW 16/21.

[606] Ibid.

[607] TAL/ZStL, *Belzec Case:* Statement of Heinrich Gley, 6 February 1962. See: Chróściewicz, *Sprawozdanie*, 97-129

[608] Sobibór had sorted out their cremation procedures and sent Herbert Floss who was the Reinhardt cremation expert who organized the exhumations/cremations in all three camps.

[609] Hillberg, *Destruction*, vol. 3, 977.

[610] TAL/OKBZ: Statements by witnesses: Mieczysław Kudyba (mentions 1-3 pyres), Stanisław Kozak and Alojzy Berezowski (2-3), Eugeniusz Goch and Edward Ferens (3), Edward Łuczyński, Maria Daniel and Jan Głąb (3-4).The archaeological investigations found only three.

[611] At Vilna, 68,000 corpses were counted by two of the Jews in the pit who were ordered by the Germans to keep count. See: IMT, *Speeches*, 45. This practice was also carried out in the Reinhardt camps.

[612] TAL/ZStL, Belzec Case: Statement of Heinrich Gley, 7 January 1963. The dimensions of the pyres are also by Gley.

[613] Author's interview Gelpernus, as above n. 823. See also: Faitson, *Escape,* 42.

[614] Ibid. See: TAL/ZStL, Belzec Case: Statements of Heinrich Gley and Robert Jührs, 11 October 1961.

[615] Ibid.

[616] Ibid.

[617] In May 1998 in Belzec, the author met Professor Borowski, a tree specialist, who was living just outside the village at the time of the cremations and could clearly remember the smoke and stench that permeated in the area. He also recalled a transport arriving from Rawa Ruska which contained several hundred POWs of mixed nationality who were taken into the camp. (This "legend," repeated in several books, has been discredited. The POWs from the Rawa Ruska camp, mostly Italians, were shot in a nearby forest; the graves were found about four years ago.)

[618] Kola, *Belzec*, 21. Three Jews of the "death brigade" escaped from Belzec during the cremation period: Birder, Bracht and Velser. All three emigrated to Israel after the war and in 1961 wrote testimonies for the Belzec investigation conducted by the ZStL. The last gassings at Belzec took place in early December 1942.

[619] In Margaret Rubel's translation of Reder's booklet (Polin, *Belzec*, 288, n. 34), she states that burning of the corpses began after the last transports entered the camp. This appears contrary to the evidence.

[620] My assessment is confirmed. See: Höß, *Auschwitz,* 212: "In addition the ashes were to be disposed of in such a way that it would be impossible to calculate the number of corpses burnt."

[621] Hilberg, *Destruction,* vol. 3, 977.

[622] Ibid.

[623] Polin, *Belzec*, 289.

[624] Ibid.

[625] Sandkühler, *Endlösung*, 195.

[626] TAL/JHIW: Statement of Hirszman, 19 March 1946.

[627] He refers to SS-Scharführers Dubois and Jührs, a Ukrainian detachment and about 350 Jewish workers.

[628] KZ - Trawniki, Budzyń, or Lublin.

[629] TAL/OKBZ: Statement of Tadeusz Dujanowicz, 17 October 1945. (* The fir saplings were bought from Dujanowicz, the chief forester in Sobibór, and taken from a wooded valley outside the town). Initially the SS requested 1 m high firs, but were advised to plant smaller ones due to the softness of the ground. The lupines were specifically planted with the firs in order to stabilize the soil and provide nitrogen to the firs. In the spring of 1998, these firs were over 20 feet high (their maturity), and the lupines (mauve) were in abundance in the area below the present day monument. Lupines were particularly suited for Belzec as they required well drained, light, sandy soil and flourish in sun or shade. These plants were also planted when Sobibór and Treblinka were liquidated. They can still be seen today.

[630] TAL/JHIW: Report by Hirszman, 19 March 1946.

[631] TAL/ZStL, File No. 208 AR-Z 252/59: Case Against Josef Oberhauser et al. (Belzec Case): Statement by Heinrich Gley, 8.5.1961).

[632] Blatt, *Sobibór*, 56.

[633] TAL/JHIW: Statement of Leon Feldhandler. See also: Blatt, *Sobibór*, 56.

[634] Ibid. Statement of Hirszman, 19 March 1946: The escorting SS-NCO on this transport was SS-Scharführer Paul Groth. Blatt, *Sobibór*, 56.

[635] Ibid., 60.

[636] Ibid.

[637] (TAL/OKBL, File No. 1604/45 – Zamosc (Belzec Investigation: Statement of Mieczyslaw Nieduzak, 17.10.1945).This happened in the 1997 and 1998 survey. Within hours of our leaving, certain local inhabitants plundered our excavation sites and large holes were made in the exposed constructions. This was also a common occurrence elsewhere.

[638] Hilberg, *Destruction*, vol. 3, 979.

[639] (TAL/OKBL: Statement of Mieczyslaw Kudyba).

[640] Ibid. The subsequent fate of the two women is not known, but they almost certainly died during a later round-up. Their story was published after the war in a booklet about the fate of the Jews of Zolkiew: Gerson Taffet, *Zagłada Żydów Żółkiewskich*, Łódź 1946, 29. See also: Arad, *Belzec*, 264.

[641] Ibid. Statement Eugeniusz Goch, 14 October 1945. See also: TAL/ZStL 208 AR-Z 268/59: The Case against Schubert et al (Lublin Gestapo Case): Statement of Mieczyslaw Garfinkiel, Chairman of the Zamosc Judenrat. Tregenza, *Belzec*, 12.

[642] Tadeusz Pankiewicz, *The Kraków Ghetto Pharmacy* , New York 1987, 60. Arad, *Belzec*, 208, mentions Bachner but refers to the October deportations. I think he is mistaken.

[643] Trial notes and indictment of Amon Leopold Goeth. Although only hearsay, in 1995 I interviewed Sofia Stern (wife of Yitzhak Stern, collaborator with Oskar Schindler in Kraków) when she stated that Schindler, on hearing Bachner's story, went to Belzec to verify the details but was turned back by the SS-guards at Sobibór Lubelski.

[644] Yaffa Eliach, "A Sip of Coffee," in: *Hasidic Tales of the Holocaust,* New York 1982, 114-6.

[645] TAL/JHIW: Three Poles of the *(AKW ?)* right-wing "WiN" underground organization went to Hirszman's residence and shot him.

[646] Ibid. TAL/OKBZ: Statements of Edward Łuczyński, 15 October 1945 and Mieczysław Kudyba, 14 October 1945. Herc escaped from the transport and went to Kraków. After the war, he returned to Belzec where he met Luczynski. (Herc junior retuned to Belzec after the war; Herc senior was a Zugführer killed in the camp).

[647] TAL/Belzec Case: Statement of Sarah Ritterband (née Beer).

[648] There is some doubt that the Ritterbrand story is true.

[649] Polin, *Belzec*, 279 n. 15.

[650] Tregenza, *Belzec*, 23.

[651] *Diensttagebuch*, 310-311 n. 26.

[652] According to Arad (*Belzec*, 165-9), Himmler never went to Belzec. See also: Polin, *Belzec* 287 n. 30.

[653] Ibid. See TAL/OKBZ: Statement of Eustachy Ukrainski, 13 October 1945. See also: Dr Janusz Peter ("Kordian"), *Tomaszowskie za Okupacji,* Sobibór-Lubelski 1999.

[654] Polin, *Belzec,* 287. For biographical details re: Katzmann see: Sandkühler, *Endlösung,* 426; Pohl, *Ostgalizien,* 416.

[655] TAL/ZStL, *Belzec Case:* Statement of Josef Oberhauser.

[656] Blatt, *Sobibór,* 11. See also TAL/ZStL, *Sobibór Case*: Statements of Kurt Bolender and Karl Frenzel. TAL/Indictment against Erich Bauer, Count No. 4 of the Indictment. For testimonies, see: Miriam Novitch, Sobibór – Martyrdom and Revolt: Documents and Testimonies, Holocaust Library, New York 1980; 64: Abraham Margulies; 108: *Hershel Zuckerman;* 156: *Moshe Bahir).*

[657] Ibid. Despite information to the contrary, Himmler was never in Belzec on 16 August as claimed by Reder *et al.* On this date he was in Vinnista in the Ukraine. 1-4 October 1942 he was in Berlin; 4 October, flight from Berlin to Kraków, then to Zhitomir, and on 7 October to his Ukrainian HQ at Hegerwald; 10 October, flight to Munich; 10-15 October he was in Italy; 18-22 October, back in Zhitomir; 22-26 at the Führer's "Wolfsschanze" HQ in Rastenburg; 27 October, back to Zhitomir and a journey through the Ukraine until 2 November.

[658] PRO: WO File No. 208/4673 (Interrogation of Globocnik's staff).

[659] TAL/ZStL, Sobibór Case: Statement of Franz Suchomel.

[660] Blatt, *Sobibór,* 11.

[661] Ibid. Statement of Kurt Gerstein, 19 July 1946. See also: Hilberg, *Destruction,* vol. 2, 964, 975.

[662] Roques, *Gerstein,* 28.

[663] After the war, Gerstein was totally confused about what he actually delivered to Belzec. Not once does he mention "Zyklon B." Gerstein mentions "a leak on the road from the lorry ahead," which indicates pure hydrocyanic acid in liquid form in glass carboys packed in wicker baskets, the only way it can be stored. But how was Gerstein going to kill Jews in gas chambers with liquid acid? Pfannenstiel's testimonies are far more accurate concerning this visit to Belzec. Gerstein's "Reports" are now generally accepted as being a compilation of several visits to Belzec; Pfannenstiel denies ever witnessing the scenes described by Gerstein.

[664] Ibid.

[665] PRO/FO371/42790: Report from the Jewish National Committee Warsaw, dated 15 November 1943.

[666] Blatt, *Sobibór*, 90/1.

[667] Ibid., 91.

Chapter 11

[668] Stanislaw Piotrowski, *Misja Odila Globocnika: Sprawozdania o Wynikach Finansowych Zaglady Zydw w Polsce*, Panstwowy Institut Wydawniczy, Warsaw 1949. This document was lodged at the International Military Tribunal at Nuremberg in the report of Odilo Globocnik and refers to the financial outcomes of the extermination of the Jews in the General Government. Document sent to the author in translated form by Joseph Poprzeczny, Australia 1998.

[669] Ibid.

[670] After the Treblinka revolt in August 1943, a nominal number of Jews were kept alive to dismantle the camp under the directions of their Jewish Kapo, Karl Blau, and SS-Untersturmführer Kurt Franz..

[671] Pohl, *Extermination Policies*, 90. See also: *Judenpolitik*, 171.

[672] Pucher, *Globocnik*,

[673] Ibid.

[674] Ibid.

[675] Ibid. Although Sporrenberg gives a full and detailed account, it must be treated with care; the information is so detailed, however, that some credence can be afforded to it.

[676] Blatt, *Sobibor*, 90. The Treblinka revolt was not fully reported to Berlin, as there were no German fatalities. Sobibor was a different matter as many SS troops died in the revolt. On receiving the report, Himmler ordered the destruction of the camp and removal of all traces of mass murder. At the Sobibor trials, a freight document was produced in evidence showing that wagons numbered: 22757, 130789, 19796, 22536 and 70136 had left Treblinka for Sobibor on 20 October 1943. See also statement of Francziszek Zabecki, stationmaster at Treblinka, who reported the incident to the Polish underground.

[677] Browning, *Ordinary Men*, 135, refers to "Erntefest" as the "single largest killing operation against Jews" undertaken by Germans during the war, eclipsing even Babi Yar. See also: Grabitz and Schefler, *Die Spüren*. For the 3-4 November 1943 liquidations of Jewish labor camps in Trawniki, Poniatowa and Majdanek, see: Sandkühler, *Endlösung*, 270.

[678] PRO/FO371/42790: Report from the Jewish National Committee Warsaw, dated 15 November 1943.

[679] Ibid. See also: Pohl, *Judenpolitik*, 172-3.

[680] TAL/JHIW: Document No. 965: Statement of Ester Rubinstein

[681] Arad, *Belzec*, 366 (slightly edited).

[682] Ibid, 367.

[683] Longerich, *Ermordung*, 229.

[684] See: Heberer: "Deutsche Gold-und Silber-Sheide-Anstalt," known as DEGUSSA, this was the largest German smeltery for precious metals, which participated in the smelting of dental gold plundered from Nazi victims.

[685] *(Ibid?)* Becker/Lorent proceedings, 1970, quoted in Arad, *Belzec*, 148.

[686] PRO, File No. WO 208/4673.

[687] The roles of Sporrenberg and Globocnik in issuing the orders for "Erntefest" have never been clearly established. See Longerich, *Ermordung*, 229.

[688] PRO, File No. 208/4673: Interrogation Protocols, 25 February 1946.

[689] Pohl, *Ostgalizien,* Conclusion.

[690] See: Heberer. Adolfo Scapelli and Enzo Collotti, San Sabba: Istruttoria e processo per il Lager della Risiera, Associazione nazionale ex deportati politici nei campi di sterminio nazisti, Milan 1995.

[691] The RSHA sent a circular to all stations instructing that "all Jews of listed nationalities could now be included in deportation measures," see: Hilberg, Destruction, vol. 2, 669.

[692] Construction project in the Po valley where 500,000 Italian workers were used as forced labor.

[693] Rückerl, NS-Prozesse, 75.

[694] TAL/ZStL, Belzec Case: Statement of Heinrich Gley, 4 December 1961.

[695] "R" as in "Reinhardt", the name also stands for the "program" of this unit. According to Pucher "R" may be identical to "special account R" which existed before Heydrich's death and into which flowed donations from the "circle of friends of the Reichsführer-SS."

[696] San Sabba personnel: (Globocnik?), Wirth, Hering, (Reitlinger?), Stangl. (Reichleitner and Stangl were not members of San Sabba Staff – they led their own "R" units). Plus 18-20 SS from Sobibor and Treblinka. There were nine from Belzec: Oberhaser, Franz, Hackenholt, Tauscher, Dubois, Gley, Jührs, Girtzig and Barbl.

[697] The gassing location was a large garage that was converted by SS-Scharführer Erwin Lambert (T4), the master builder who had constructed the gas chambers at T4 and in Reinhardt. As in Belzec, exhaust gasses were used. See Friedlander, *Origins*, 215. (Lambert also constructed the San Sabba crematorium).

[698] Pucher. That Globocnik's "R" units were engaged and in command of Jewish operations is shown by preserved arrest certificates that show the letter heading of the SD/Sipo had been crossed out and "R I" inserted by hand. Unit "R" in San Sabba stored all Jewish property.

[699] The Italian public have a long tradition in protecting their Jews and this was the case when the Nazi security forces began their Jewish operations. Even the Fascist element advised the Jews to leave and seek safety.

[700] For an overview of Jewish resettlement polices, see: Hilberg, *Destruction*, vol. 2, 665-678, and Susan Zuccotti, *The Italians and The Holocaust*, New York 1987, 133. See also: Blatt, *Sobibor*, 94.

[701] The Donati Chart, in: Hilberg, *Destruction*, vol. 2, 678 n. 74.

[702] Ibid., 134.

[703] TAL/ZStL, Belzec Case: Statement of Josef Oberhauser, 12 February 1963, Munich. See also: Statement of Franz Suchomel, 12 February 1963, and Blatt, *Sobibor*, 95.

[704] Tregenza, *Wirth*, 51.

[705] Ibid. "Strength through Joy" was introduced in 1936 when the Nazis arranged special excursions for the "volk" (subsidised travel).

[706] TAL/ZStL, Treblinka Case: Statement of Franz Suchomel, 12 February 1963.

[707] Sereny, *Stangl*, 262: Stangl always maintained that Wirth's pugnacious character had been his undoing: "They said that the partisans killed him, but we believed that his own men did him in (ihn erledigt hätten)." See also Blatt, *Sobibor*, 95.

[708] Michael Elkins, *Forged in Fury*, London 1996, 185-6. Elkins (now deceased) was a well-respected journalist but in the individual details fails to definitively source his information. Other personnel claimed to have been disposed of by "DIN": SS-Brigadier General Dr. Wilhelm Albert (SD Chief in Lodz), SS-Major Dr. Wilhelm Altenloch (SD Chief in Bialystok), SS-Hauptsturmführer Hans Aumeier (Commandant, Camp I in Auschwitz), SS-Major Hans Bothmann (Commander at Chelmno), SS-Colonel Dr. Hans Geschke (SD Chief Hungary), Paul Giesler Gauleiter Munich), SS-Lieutenant General Richard Glücks, Inspector General of KZs, SS-Brigadier General Dr. Ernst Grawitz (Chief Medical Officer Ravensbrük), SS-Colonel Albert Hohlfelder (Sterilization program), SS-Lieutenant Kurt Mussfeld (Majdanek and Auschwitz), SS-Major Adalbert Neubauer (AR), and SS-Major Karl Puetz (SD Chief in Rovno). Further corroboration has now come to notice, see *The Times* newspaper 27 April 2000, 15: 125 "Nazis believed to have been executed by a team of 35 Jewish soldiers."

[709] Piotrowski, Misja.

[710] Ibid.

[711] Ibid., 261.

[712] Working Jews/work Jews discussed in Götz Aly, Endlösung, 263-268.

[713] Piotrowski, Misja.

[714] Ibid.

[715] Blatt, *Sobibor*, 92. SS-Obersturmbannführer Konrad Morgan had already commenced his investigations into Reinhardt. (My brackets.)

[716] BDC/YV 862: Wirth's personal file sent to the author by Yad Vashem. The initial promotions are shown on document dated 19 August 1943 "Feld-Kommandostelle" (Field Headquarters), Personalhauptamt, Berlin, "Bei seinem letzten Besuch in Lublin am 12. 2. 1943 hat der Reichsführer-SS die Beförderung von....."After Himmler's visit to Treblinka in 1943, he came away impressed with the dedication of his Reinhardt personnel and decided to promote the camp commanders and several non-commissioned officers. Globocnik had already submitted a list recommending certain promotions to the head of personnel (RSHA) listing 28 of these men. For some reason the report was lost. In a follow-up report of 23 May 1943, Globocnik made a further request: "to explain the whole matter, I would like to add the following. The above-mentioned: Wirth, Hering, Reichleitner and Stangl are the commanders who were at the forefront of the action in 'Operation Reinhard.'" The RSHA stated that there were "obstacles" to their promotion. After much pressure, the following promotions took place: Wirth - Sturmbannführer, the camp commanders, Hering, Reichleitner and Stangl to Hauptsturmführer. The three deputy commanders: Schwarz (Belzec), Niemann (Sobibor), and Franz (Treblinka) were promoted to SS-Untersturmführer See also: Arad, *Belzec*, 168.

[717] BDC/YV 862.

[718] Ibid.

[719] Ibid. See also: Hilberg, *Destruction*, vol, 3, 897, n. 18.

[720] BDC/YV 862: Letter from Globocnik (Sonderkommando "Einsatz Reinhard") to the RSHA, re: promotions for his men who had distinguished themselves (file from SS-Oberführer Dr. Katz, dated 21.4.1943).

[721] Ibid. Stangl had temporary service with the Ordnungspolizei and appears to have had difficulty establishing his rank and status in the SS Personnel Main Office. See: Hilberg, Documents, 204.

[722] Blatt, *Sobibor*, 115: Thomas Blatt in conversation with former SS-Scharhührer Karl Frenzel in Hagen in 1983.

[723] Rudolf Höß: Auschwitz, 262.

[724] Reitlinger, Final Solution, 296.

[725] Ibid. Himmler had long suspected that Globocnik had been pilfering Jewish assets but had ignored his protégé's corrupt practices. When the RSHA auditors descended on Lublin in late 1943, they confirmed Himmler's suspicions. He had not learned any lessons from his mixing-up of Party funds as Gauleiter in Vienna.

[726] This seems the most plausible account of Globocnik's demise.

[727] Pucher, *Globocnik.*

[728] PRO, File No. WO/208/4673: Interrogation of George Konrad Morgan, 8 August 1946.

[729] Blatt, *Sobibór*, 95

[730] Josef Oberhauser: Procuring materials for destruction; received transports into the camp; close collaboration and conspiring with Christian Wirth, knowing well that Belzec, Sobibór and Treblinka were camps for the murder of Jews. That he assisted in the murder of approximately 450,000 Jews. Werner Dubois: Procuring materials for the camp gassing barracks; being party to the murder of 360,000 Jews. Erich Fuchs: Assisting in the construction of the gas chambers and party to the murder of 150,000 Jews. Heinrich Gley: Being party to the murder of 170,000 Jews. Robert Jührs, Karl Schluch, Heinrich Unverhau and Ernst Zierke all being party to the murder of 360,000 Jews.

[731] TAL/ZStL, Belzec Case: Official communiqué of the court in Munich announcing suspension of the pre-trial Belzec hearings.

[732] Ibid. Certified copy of the court conviction.

[733] Ibid.

[734] Ibid. Opening statement of the prosecution.

[735] TAL/*Belzec Case*: Statements of Oberhauser, Zierke and Fuchs.

[736] TAL/ZStL, File No. 208 AR-Z 252/59: Case Against Josef Oberhauser et al. (BelzecCase): statement of Karl Schluch, 11 November 1961. This comes from the earlier court hearings, not from Oberhauser's trial. In fact, thanks to the court testimony of Oberhauser's former colleagues from Belzec, he came off in rather a good light. They would not, dare not, say anything incriminating against him in court.

[737] In 1976, Oberhauser was among a number of former SS personnel, including Dieter Allers, who were tried *in absentia* by an Italian Court in Trieste for crimes committed in the San Sabba camp. Oberhauser and Allers were both sentenced to life imprisonment. After his release Oberhauser returned to Munich where he worked in a beer hall and was a subject in Claude Lanzman's film *Shoah*. See Lanzmann, *Shoah*, 63. (* *Neither Allers nor Oberhauser served any sentence for San Sabba*).

[738] TAL/ZStL, File No. 208, AR-Z 251/59: Sobibór Case. The Sobibór trial commenced on 6 September 1965 and concluded on 20 December 1966. SS-Gruppenführer Jakob Sporrenberg's report to the HSSPF Kraków gave details of the revolt. See also: Blatt, *Sobibór*, 86. Of a total of 17 SS staff and approximately 120 guards at Sobibór, 10 SS-NCOs, 2 Volksdeutsche and 8 Ukrainians were killed in the revolt. (2 of the SS-NCOs had previously served at Belzec).

[739] Accused of participating in the mass murder of 30 Jews.

[740] Accused of participating in the mass murder of 86,000, and personally murdering 360 Jews. Committed suicide while on remand in prison.

[741] Accused of participating in the mass murder of 43,000, and 15,000 Jews.

[742] Accused of personally killing 42 Jews and participating in mass murder of 250,000, and 150,000 Jews.

[743] Accused of participating in the mass murder of 3,600, and 76,000 Jews.

[744] Accused of participating in the mass murder of 57,000, and 68,000 Jews

[745] Accused of mass murder of 30 Jews.

[746] Accused of participation in the mass murder of 150,000 Jews.

[747] Accused of participation in the mass murder of an unknown number of Jews.

[748] Accused of participation in the mass murder of 86,000 Jews.

[749] Accused of participation in the mass murder of 72,000 Jews.

[750] Accused of participating in the mass murder of 115,000, and 39,000 Jews.

[751] Passed on 22 December 1970 in the trial of Franz Stangl at the Court of Assizes, in: TAL/Düsseldorf: Az-Lg X1-148/69 S, 111 ff.

[752] Like Belzec and Sobibór, it has not been possible to establish the exact number of people transported to Treblinka. Calculations are based on a formula that has formed the basis of subsequent assessments: 60 wagons per transport, each containing 100 persons (6,000). Where people were transported in ordinary passenger carriages, these estimates may be halved. See: expert opinion submitted to the court by Dr Helmut Kraunsnick, Director of the Institute for Contemporary History (Institut für Zeitgeschichte) in Munich. The Belzec calculations were 40 wagons x 100 people.

[753] For an overview of the Trawniki Men, see: Rich, *Reinhardt's Foot Soldiers*, 688-701.

[754] Malagon Protocol, 00268, 18 March 1978.

[755] Blatt, *Sobibór*, 99. By the time *Reinhardt* was dissolved, it is estimated that 80 percent of the close-knit SS and guard personnel had served in all three-death camps. More importantly, throughout its existence, *Reinhardt* had one senior command administration for security personnel, and although not the most senior, Christian Wirth was the binding force and improviser of the procedures in all three camps. We can therefore be reasonably confident that what was happening in Belzec, was also happening in Treblinka and Sobibór.

[756] Rich, David A., *Reinhard's Foot Soldiers*: Soviet Trophy Documents and Investigative Records as Sources, in: John K. Roth & Elizabeth Maxwell (eds.), *Remembering for the Future: the Holocaust in an Age of Genocide*, vol. 1 (History), Basingstoke 2001.

[757] Ibid.

[758] Most of the personnel were caught up in the purge, and there were several thousand who were summarily shot with little or no judicial proceedings. A handful was allowed to shoot themselves. Only Rommel was given the choice of taking poison, thereby ensuring that his honor was upheld. The principals were humiliated before the People's Court and then subjected to a cruel hanging. So we may draw the conclusions that it wasn't only in the camps that the principle existed of making the condemned suffer in a manner of the State or the executioner's choosing; it was there constantly and endemic in Nazi psychology.

[759] Thomas (Toivi) Blatt, Sobibór USA, 1998: in discussion with Karl August Frenzel, late of T4 and Sobibór.

[760] Associate scholars have carried out all Polish translations for the author.

[761] In May of 2000, the author met Dr. Gora at Sobibór where he was engaged in a similar examination of the – area of Camp III, the extermination compound.

[762] Edited by the Main Commission for the Investigation of Nazi Crimes in Poland (Główna Komisja Badania Zbrodni Hitlerowskich w Polsce) and The Council of Protection of Memory of Combat and Martyrdom (Rada Ochrony Pamięci Walk i Męczeństwa - ROPWiM), in an encyclopaedic information book: - Obozy hitlerowskie na ziemiach polskich 1939-45, Warsaw 1979, p. 94 - the number of victims of Belzec camp is estimated at about 600,000.

[763] Ibid.

[764] See "The Council of Protection of Memory of Combat and Martyrdom (ROPWiM)" in Warsaw: (a) Reports of the investigation at the site of the former death camp in Belzec between 10-13 October 1945; (b) excavations within the cemetery area of the former death camp; reports of findings by the medical team in attendance during the course of these investigations. See: Kola, *Belzec*, 6, n. 3.

[765] Believed to be the site of the second phase gas chambers.

[766] The Main Commission for the Investigation of German Crimes in Poland (Warsaw, 1947).

[767] Chełmno, in central Poland near Łódź (Warthegau), was not specially built but adapted at an abandoned country mansion which was utilized as a receiving establishment for Jews. The gassings in Chełmno were carried out in gas vans that collected the Jews from the mansion and drove them to the Rzuchów forest (4 km away), during which time 90 people were killed per journey with the exhaust fumes pumped into the sealed rear compartments of the vehicles.

[768] The same evidence that was available to the Investigation Commission has been referred to in this research. All relevant statements kindly made available by TAL/OKBZ.

[769] Ibid.

[770] TAL/OKBZ: Testimonies of: Stefan Kirsz, 20 February, 1946: "On eight occasions wagonloads of Poles were brought into Belzec. They told me that they had been arrested because of their anti-German political activities, or for assisting Jews." Kirsz was a train driver from Rawa Ruska station engaged in bringing transports into the camp from the direction of Lvov, and on occasions saw what was going on inside the camp.

[771] The camp officially closed on 8 May 1943, when the SS-garrison was dispersed to other camps. (The majority had been disbanded prior to this. The last few SS-men left Belzec on that date—Schwarz, Tauscher and Dubois.) See: TAL/OKBZ: Statement of Tadeusz Misiewicz, the booking clerk at Belzec railway station, 15 October 1945.

[772] The area of remembrance was designed by Henryk Jabłuszewski; the main monument was later adorned with a sculpture by S. Strzyzynski and J. Olejnicki which depicts two emaciated human figures, one supporting the other.

[773] The Polish investigations showed that only two of these symbolic tombs were near mass graves. (Nos. 7 and 8).

[774] Kola, *Belzec*. All technical date as recorded by Dr Mieczysław Góra, on-site leader of the 1997-99 investigations.

[775] The Kola team had knowledge of similar findings in Miednoje (Belarus), Kharkov (Ukraine) and Katyn (Russia), using the same drilling methods.

[776] Each drill-hole was given a consecutive identification reference number.

[777] Collated from material formed on-site, and from the Kola Report.

[778] The early transports consisted of 8-15 wagons with an average of 100 Jews with their luggage per wagon. (TAL: Statement Heinrich Gley, 7 January 1963).

[779] This is the opinion of Tregenza. I take the view that no special grave was used for this purpose and that the first available open pit was utilized for these executions.

[780] See: TAL/ZStL, File No.: AR-Z 252/59: The Case against Josef Oberhauser et al. Statements of Heinrich Gley, 10 May 1961; Heinrich Unverhau, 10 July 1961; Hans Girtzig, 18 July 1961; Kurt Franz, 14 September 1961; Robert Jührs, 11 October 1961; Karl Schluch, 11 November 1961.

[781] The author was not present at these 1997-2000 investigations and is grateful to Dr Mieczysław Góra and my colleague Michael Tregenza for imparting the results for this period.

[782] Additional exploratory drillings were made near the four symbolic tombs close to the east fence in an area where the Luftwaffe aerial photograph also indicated the presence of mass graves. Because several of the mass graves located and investigated in October 1997 were found to be deeper than 5 m, the length of the drills in the 1998 investigation were increased from 5 m to 6 m. The location of three graves was confirmed in the area of symbolic tombs 1, 3 and 4. Their dimensions and depths were not determined at this time.

[783] Items found: 1 paraffin-fuelled railway signalling lamp, metal parts of a gas mask, 2 metal spoons, 1 pre-war Polish coin (10 groszy, minted 1923), 1 live round of rifle ammunition, 4 spent rifle cartridge cases, 1 small aluminium screw, 1 cylindrical aluminium tube (length: 4.5 cm, diameter: 1.8 cm, with a label in Polish listing the pharmaceutical ingredients), a piece of metal pipe (length; 45 cm, diameter: 1.8 cm), a .needle from a hypodermic syringe, the lower part of a round aluminium tin (diameter: 8 cm). 3 iron keys, 3 iron railway staples, several lengths of barbed wire, 3 large nails, a round copper identity disc, and 1 brass hook for a railway wagon locking bar.

[784] Ibid., 76

[785] Peter Witte, who had read my account, sent this information to the author.

[786] In addition to the possible movements of a Jew named Munk, the author has traced a Rabbi Schlesinger in Stamford Hill, London, who knew a Max Munk in Vienna and may be related to him.

[788] Collected by the author on site.

[789] TAL/OKBZ: Statements by Belzec villagers 1945-46.

[790] See: Appendix. See also: Leni Yahil, *Holocaust,* 323-9 for overview.

[791] By the time it was decided to exhume and burn the corpses some considerable time had elapsed. This allowed the corpses to settle and compact. With the exhumations, and despite the cremations, the considerable amount of cremated human remains together with material from the demolished camp structures was perhaps too much to be buried in the opened graves. This is probably why small graves were hurriedly dug for disposal purposes.

[792] TAL/OKBZ, File No.: Ds. 1604/45: Zamosc (The Death Camp in Belzec). Statements by Belzec's villagers 1945-46.

[793] Ibid., 65. See also: Hilberg, *Documents*, 209: notes by a German non-commissioned officer, Wilhelm Cornides, diary entry for 31 August 1942: "A double track led into the camp. One track branched off from the main line; the other ran over a turntable

from the camp to a row of sheds." The second track was probably the line used by the Jewish work brigades for removing property from the unloading area in Camp I to the property sheds. Wagons were used for this purpose and pushed by the Jews.

[794] The logging path and rail tracks can be seen in the 1940 and 1944 Luftwaffe aerial photographs. See also: Kola, *Belzec,* 42.

[795] See: Kola, *Belzec,* 6 and 8.

[796] Ibid., 42-3, 65

[797] Conclusions made in collaboration with Michael Tregenza, the Torun team, and the cartographer, Billy Rutherford.

[798] Earlier reports by the author (*East European Jewish Affairs*) concerning the total cubic capacity were unfortunately erroneous through mistranslation and misinformation.

[799] For descriptions of an execution pit and method of shooting see: ZStL, file No.: AR-Z 252/59: The Case Against Josef Oberhauser et al, p. 1554: Heinrich Gley, 24 November 1961/Munster; p. 1484: Robert Jührs, 12 October 1961/Frankfurt-am-Main. Both Gley and Jührs were assigned to execution duty. It is inconceivable that only one such execution pit existed in the camp, as these witnesses state.

[800] Ibid.: Heinrich Gley, 24 November 1961/Munster; p. 1487.

[801] See: Piper, *Auschwitz,* 9, who quotes *Wspomnienia Rudolfa Hoßa - Komendanta obozu oświęcimskiego,* Warsaw 1965, 18, 204; T. Cyprian, J. Cyprian and Sawicki, *Sprawy polskie,* 438-439.

[802] Ibid.

[803] Witte/Tyas, *New Document,* 468-486. Tyas discovered the "document" while trawling through radio messages intercepted and decoded by British Intelligence. The "document" has been generously made available to scholars by Tyas since 1997. See also: Richard Breitman, *Official Secrets: What the Nazis Planned, What the British and Americans Knew,* London 1999, 236-245.

[804] Ibid., 468.

[805] Ibid., 470. See Witte/Tyas, 471: "Until recently it has been accepted by historians that only these three (Belzec, Sobibór, Treblinka) extermination camps belonged to *Einsatz Reinhardt.* This surely is not the case as it is also well known that during the Höß-Himmler discussion in mid-summer 1941, Himmler mentioned to Höß that Auschwitz was to be used for the overflow of victims, since the killing facilities in the east would not be able to cope. Whether Höß was referring to the death camps or the sites of shooting executions is not known. Although part of the mass killing process, they were never part of *Reinhardt,* as we know it. It has long been accepted that all camps with gassing facilities were used (Auschwitz/Majdanek). See autobiographical notes of Rudolf Höß: "Himmler": "The existing extermination camps in the East are not in a position to carry out the large *Aktionen* which are anticipated. I have therefore earmarked Auschwitz for this purpose." (See: Höß, *Commandant of Auschwitz,* London 1961, 206).

[806] For an overview of intercepted messages during this short period (in addition to Witte/Tyas), see: PRO, *Most Secret* - HW 16 - 23; ZIP/GPDD 355a 13.1.43. The author has been aware of this document since 1998 (via Tregenza), but had come to the provisional conclusion that the "numbers" may have referred to bodies removed and burnt. Having studied the Witte/Tyas conclusions I am persuaded this was not the case.

[807] Friedmann, *Documents*: "Police Battalion 24/Company 7 September 1942". ZtLS: Collection UdSSR, Vol. 410, Stanisławów Reports (Haifa 1957).

[808] Ibid., See also: Sandkühler, *Endlösung*, 9.

[809] Hilberg, *Destruction*, vol. 3, 1203.

[810] Kola, *Belzec*, 40.

[811] Yahil, *Holocaust*, 320-2 for an overview of Chełmno.

[812] Piper, *Auschwitz*, 20 n. 59, concludes that this may be interpreted as Himmler referring to the Einsatzgruppen operations in the east after Barbarossa. I take the view that he was not only referring to Einsatzgruppen but also to the unknown capacity of the death camps and the large numbers of victims that had to be dealt with. Piper's reference: "Einsatzgruppen," in: *Wspomnienia Höß*, 193. See also: Höß, *Commandant*, 234.

[813] Chełmno closed April 1943, Belzec May 1943 (gassings stopped December 1942), Treblinka September 1942, Sobibór October 1943. After the last mass executions in Majdanek in November 1943, (Erntefest Aktion), Auschwitz was the only center of mass murder.

[814] Ibid. As quoted by Friedmann in: *Documents*.

[815] See: Tregenza, *Belzec - Das vergessene*, 254-5.

[816] After Belzec closed down Göckel was transferred to Treblinka. See: Polin, *Belzec*, 272 n. 5.

[817] Szrojt, *Belzec*, 44.

[818] Raul Hilberg, *Die Vernichtung der europäischen Juden*, Frankfurt-am-Main 1990, 1299.

[819] See: *Arad Belzec*, 127.

[820] O'Neil, "Belzec - The Forgotten Death Camp," in: *East European Jewish Affairs*, 28 February 1998, 49-62. See also: Pohl-Witte, "The Number of Victims of Belzec Extermination Camp: A Faulty Reassessment," in: *East European Jewish Affairs*, 31 January 2001, 19. See also: Witte/Tyas, *New Document*, 481 n. 15, where Witte is a little disingenuous in citing that my own research was based on Gilbert's outdated maps, when in fact Gilbert was used more as corroboration of the research findings of Tatiana Berenstein et al. Gilbert's map references were used as primary sources mainly for "operations" outside Reinhardt deportations. It was always appreciated that Gilbert's research was inhibited due to the restricted access to East European archives at that time.

[821] PRO, File No. FO 371/50971/85681. British Intelligence report dated 16 March 1945.

[822] In view of the Witte/Tyas findings, when assessing my own estimates of the "numbers" murdered in Belzec, I am persuaded to provisionally concede, and take into account their conclusions. I have maintained throughout my own research that my purpose was to record statistics from many sources and thus expose the enormous calamity of the Jewish people. The "numbers game" is fraught with difficulties.

Appendix

Maps and Plans

What makes the *Reinhardt* death camps unique in comparison with concentration/death (hybrid) camps like Auschwitz and Majdanek was that the latter were not overtly secret—whereas the *Reinhardt* camps were, as far as was possible, camouflaged to conceal their real purpose. There were reasons for this, among them that non-*Reinhardt* camps were acknowledged labor camps known to the persons being deported there, whereas the purpose of the *Reinhardt* camps as killing centers had to remain secret in order to avoid mass hysteria breaking out among the victims well before entry. The majority of Jews from outside of Poland had no idea of the real purpose of these camps until it was too late.

When the death camps were finally liquidated, much effort was made to eliminate every trace of their existence by removing all structures and other evidence of their former purpose. To perpetuate this cover-up, farm buildings were erected, a caretaker farm worker installed, and the camp area planted with trees.

According to witnesses' reports during the existence of the camp it was impossible to see its true purpose as all views were obscured by high camouflaged fences. Belzec camp went through different stages of layout and construction, with features added and fencing changed. There are few plans of Belzec published today that reflect a reasonably accurate representation of the appearance of the camp and the way in which it functioned. The archaeological report by Prof. Andrzej Kola is the key to a probable reconstruction of Belzec; but before arriving at his conclusions, it may be helpful to plot the initial sequences of the former camp area through examining aerial photographs of the terrain taken by the *Luftwaffe* during the war. The author has made a significant contribution to the historiography of Belzec by analysing these enhanced aerial photographs, as follows:

1940 Luftwaffe aerial photograph. [1] **Note: "Otto Line" not yet constructed.**

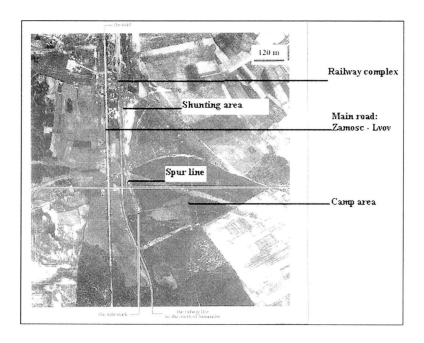

The above aerial photograph above was taken in May 1940 when the Belzec labor camps were being established in the village. It shows the pre-war logging path cutting through the site of the future death camp, toward the start of the railway spur that was eventually utilized for transports. The forest area (top right) has been cleared of trees.

Considerable care was taken when locating Belzec and the follow-on camps of Sobibor and Treblinka. Belzec occupied a crucial geographical position, as it was situated 400 meters from the central rail marshalling yard and was on the direct route from the most heavily populated Jewish catchment areas of the Lublin District [2] and east and west Galicia. [3]

Belzec was far away to the east, situated in the forgotten lands on the (former) Polish-Russian border. The proposed camp site was located just on the edge of the village, not hidden away from prying eyes, but only 100 meters from the main road and 400 meters from the railway station. Directly to the west of the camp the railway line from Lublin ran through Belzec to Rawa Ruska and Lvov via Zamosc and Zwierzyniec. (The road running in parallel stretched from Warsaw to Lvov via Zamosc and Sobibor Lubelski, Belzec, and Rawa Ruska). [4]

The 1944 Luftwaffe aerial photograph is shown below.

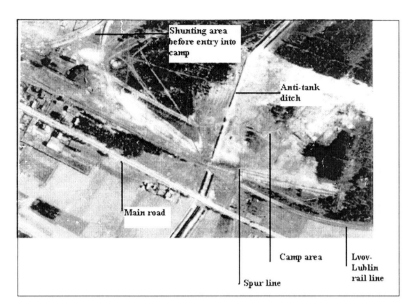

The Luftwaffe aerial photo (1944) shows the location of the death camp. (The breach in the anti-tank ditch is a bomb crater.) The nearest houses in the village were at least 400 m away. There were isolated cottages to the east. Witnesses still living in Belzec village testify that they suffered from the smoke and stench produced by the open air cremation of the corpses on pyres.

When reports filtered through to the West in early 1942 that Jews were being sent east for work, it was not known that these journeys terminated at a death camp. In the towns within a radius of 50 kilometers of Belzec, from which came reports of the transports traversing their district at night, the inhabitants were never sure of the real purpose of Belzec. All manner of rumors circulated, and even when the first escapees returned home and reported what they had seen, they were not believed.

Belzec's camouflage was assisted by the on-going work on the fortification ramparts, which had been under construction since 1940. It was well known and accepted within the Jewish communities that Jewish labor was feeding these construction sites.

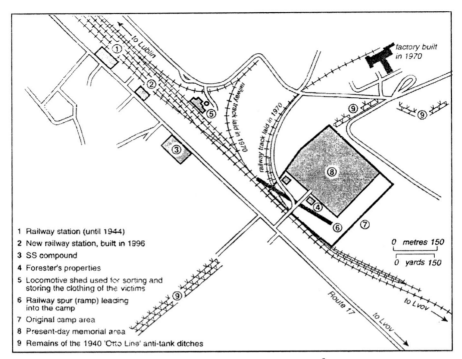

1 Railway station (until 1944)
2 New railway station, built in 1996
3 SS compound
4 Forester's properties
5 Locomotive shed used for sorting and
storing the clothing of the victims
6 Railway spur (ramp) leading
into the camp
7 Original camp area
8 Present-day memorial area
9 Remains of the 1940 'Otto Line' anti-tank ditches

Belzec Village 2001 (Martin Gilbert)[5]

Mapping of Belzec (detail)

The entire camp area was relatively small and compact, rising slightly away from the road line, (the top of the ridge was 10 meters above the road and lower camp area, Camp I) and measured approximately 275 meters. x 265 meters, much larger than the present day enclosed memorial area.[6]

Mapping Belzec death camp in the first and second stages of its operation has for years been a matter of some guesswork. Although previous maps have been drawn from documented sources,[7] it was not until the Andrzej Kola archaeological investigations of 1997-99 that indisputable evidence of the scale of mass murder emerged.[8] Kola's precise location of mass graves 1-33 leaves no room for speculation in this area. Even so, despite the immense importance of these findings, Kola did not attempt to reconstruct the camp as it may have appeared in the first and second phases of its operations. It has been left for the historians to take on this task. Now, for the first time, a reconstruction can show how this camp may have operated, based not only on documentary and witness testimony, but also on Kola's archaeological findings.

Until Kola, our understanding of how Belzec functioned was based on the recollections of two survivors, local witnesses, and the testimonies of several former SS guards who had served there. It was not until after the war (1945) that a preliminary investigation was carried out. Mass graves were opened and the contents forensically analysed. It was at this stage that it was suspected that Belzec had functioned in two phases: March – June and July – December 1942.[9] A general idea of how the camp was probably constructed has been presented by only two cartographers to date: Szrojt (1947)[10] and Billy Rutherford, in co-operation with the author (2002). Szrojt made a carefully calculated reconstruction based on the testimony of local witnesses. Sztrojt's plan is extremely basic, whereas that of Rutherford/O'Neil (the latter being present during much of the archaeological investigation 1997-99), is based on archaeological data per the Kola findings. Kola's map, although based on the best available information, does not interpret or make the best use of this information by presenting a reconstruction of Belzec in phases one and two. All other mappings of Belzec, including Reder's, whose map was drawn by the artist Joseph Bau, are inadequate for historical purposes. Rudolf Reder (the eyewitness survivor) was the one man who could have passed on a more precise map of Belzec, but he did not do so. All other maps, plans and drawings are, in my view, totally unreliable.

1944 *Luftwaffe* Aerial Photograph: Triangular Area to the Left of the Marked 'Otto Line'

This aerial photograph taken in 1944 shows ground scarring at the site of the former death camp. The two ramps are also evident in the photograph. See below for the area of the present day sawmill, the triangular area.

2002: O'Neil/Rutherford re construction

Aerial map 1944

Aerial map 1944
**Area of the locomotive shed. See triangular area (above) and the suggested route (below)
for removal of property to the property sorting sheds.**

Layout

The camp layout during the second phase (July-December 1942) was given in written evidence, together with sketches, by members of the former SS-garrison, and further corroborated by witnesses in 1945-46.[11]

The following three photographs provide the location of the barracks in this area, all of which show a downward slope towards the outer perimeter fence (not camouflaged) surrounding the area. The huts face southwest. There were seven in all, three single barracks with two double sheds at either end. The double barrack scheme was also adopted at Sobibor and later at Treblinka, although built on a far larger scale as the standard *Pferdestahl* (horse stable) type.

A: Rudi Kamm

B: Kurt Franz (right)

C: Rudi Kamm

The 1944 aerial photograph shows the perimeter of the sorting area in Belzec described by Rudolf Reder as being to the south of the camp. Yet no structures of any sort were located in this area; the terrain does not allow for building as it is too uneven and is covered by pre-war forest.

The photographs (above) show a different picture. The section depicted shows seven sorting sheds located to the north of the extermination area and beyond the Otto Line anti-tank ditch, within a triangular space. On the right of the photographs one can see a sand depression in the foreground of the hut entrances. This depression was caused by the recently filled-in section of the former anti-tank trench, which was patted down before construction began. The sheds partially sit in this former ditch. The primary entrance allowed these structures to be viewed from the main Lvov-Lublin line.

To the west of the scarring left by these huts (see 1944 map) there are three barracks in an inverted U-shape. The larger barracks to the left and right were the accommodation barracks for the Ukrainian guards, with a sick-bay, dentist and barber in the right-hand barrack. The kitchen and canteen were in the top barrack, which connected to the other two. As can be seen from the photographs, this area was completely cleared of grass/vegetation, trees, etc, although nearly one year later the aerial photograph shows it has now been seeded, and planted with trees and bushes. A building was located in the extreme eastern part of the sorting yard. It can be partially seen in the background behind the SS man's cap in photograph "A" above.

It is believed that an additional spur line connected the undressing area with the sorting warehouse turntable located just outside the camp. It was previously thought that an open wagon, without an engine, was used for this purpose. I find this improbable, as it would have taken many men, perhaps 100, to push and pull one of these wagons to the warehouse and then back again. Given the loaded transports entering the camp and their turn-around times, added to the total policing that would have had to have been in force *en route* to the warehouse (outside of the camp confines) such a cumbersome system would have compromised security.

A unit of 20-30 Ukrainian guards was assigned to the security of the locomotive shed and environs. There is a photograph of this guard unit sitting on the sand bank above the railway line from the sorting yard to the locomotive shed. It suggests the alternative answer that a separate narrow gauge link was established (going the back way) direct to the sorting sheds.

Spur Lines into the Camp

The branch line leading into the camp had to be kept in continuous operation; regularly arriving trains, some of which were 50 to 60 wagons in length, meant that a number of wagons would be kept waiting until the "processing" of the first deportees had been completed. Then these waiting wagons in turn were shunted onto spur lines in the reception area. It was essential that this traffic was precisely coordinated because the main railway line carrying important war freight, as well as military and civilian traffic, was only a matter of meters away. The wife of a railway policeman, who was sharing a carriage with other passengers on a train passing through Belzec, drew attention to the odor: "*Jetzt kommt es schon* (Now it comes)." A strong sweetish smell greeted them. "*Sie stinken ja schon* (They are stinking already)." Her husband commented, "*Ach, Quatsch, das ist ja das Gas* (Oh, nonsense, that's the gas for sure)."[12]

In the first phase at Belzec, the wagons entering the site used only the eastern siding on which 10 to 15 wagons at a time could be accommodated, depending on their size. Initially, as there was no raised ramp, many broken limbs and other injuries occurred among the Jews when the wagons were unloaded. A refinement of this system was adopted in constructing two ramps (A and B) in the second phase of the camp in July 1942. (The ramps in the second phase were banks of sand shored up with timber and topped with asphalt). This innovation, introduced by Commandant Wirth, made disembarkation easier, thus resulting in fewer injuries while at the same time speeding up the "processing" and making life easier for the camp personnel. Now only the elderly, sick, and impaired, or those who were "difficult" were detained in the holding pen to be taken to the currently available pit for "special treatment."

On-site inspection by the author in 2002, and close scrutiny of ground scarring in the 1944 aerial photograph, suggest a track directly linking the sorting area with the warehouse locomotive area. This would appear to be a logical route for transporting mounds of property (the back way) from the undressing barracks by dump truck or narrow gauge rail-link to the turntable and warehouse. It is of note that Sobibor used such a method, perhaps learned from Belzec. The camp leadership were constantly looking for ways to improve their methodology, given the huge pressure of the many thousands of people milling around the receiving area and the necessity to clear the sector before the next transport arrived. By these methods valuable time was saved.

To gauge the number of people in these transports and to place my theory in perspective, consider that some transports consisted of 60 to 80 wagons. This presents an awesome picture of the turmoil that may have surrounded entry. (Only one transport consisted of 80 wagons; the average was 50 to 60). Close scrutiny of the 1944 photographs shows a post-extermination period train consisting of 25 wagons parked by the former site of the camp. From this, we can estimate the number of wagons that could be fitted onto ramps A and B.

Our estimate is that from July 1942, a total of 40 wagons—20 on each ramp—could be accommodated. By multiplying the number of wagons we can assess the total length of the Belzec transports.[13]

It had long been thought that only one railway siding existed at the ramp and that it was later extended farther into the camp to accommodate the longer transports of the second phase. However, the construction of such an extension would not have been possible due to the forested and uneven terrain at the end of the camp. *Luftwaffe* aerial photographs of Belzec taken in 1940 and 1944 clearly show that two parallel tracks existed on the camp area. Witnesses also mention the existence of two tracks during the second phase. (The two railway sidings dated from before the First World War, and were used to transport timber from the logging path to the railway station). It is also apparent from the large amounts of engine oil and grease found on the track-beds in 1997 that locomotives entered the camp and did not always remain outside the camp gate, having shunted the wagons in from behind, as stated by many witnesses.

The Ramps

A section of the 1944 aerial photographs shows wagons (see below, numbered 1-9) on the rail line, which coincidentally helps us gauge the number of wagons that it was possible to accommodate on the ramps in 1942. This section should be read in conjunction with the Belzec map of the second phase.

Camp Entrance (below) Showing Sand Mound, Fence (Camp I) and Main Gate

Above: Overview showing guard hut and sand mound. Arrows to the left indicate a section of the defunct 'Otto Line.' Arrows to the right indicate demarcation of the reception area and Camp I. Right: (The arrows to the right, pointing upwards, indicate the slope for vehicles to the top of the ramp).

The guardhouse was located in the zone separating the grave area and the camp buildings that served to receive the transports and organize initial activities, prior to directing the victims to the gas chamber. (The gatehouse was immediately adjacent to the main gate, close to the northwest corner of the camp. The fence beyond separated the main—eastern—ramp from the rest of Camp I). The *Volksdeutsche* playing the mandolin was named Kunz. The figure immediately to his right is probably T4/SS, or possibly a Jewish *Kapo*. Behind these figures a jagged line of high uneven posts is evident. That they are of contrasting heights (due to sand based foundations) indicates a separation between Camps I and II.

A further sketch of the camp and second stage gas chambers has come to the author's notice and is probably the most reliable of all versions, including that of the author.

The following is the statement of the defendant Karl A. Schluch (former *SS Scharfuhrer*), about his duty in Belzec. Schluch indicated his recollection of the death camp by sketches:

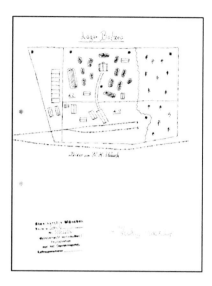

Belzec Phase 2 - 387 / F / III

They sent me to the camp at Belzec, June 1942. The situation there was worse than I had thought. Most of us hated this job but the fear of Wirth was greater. He ordered me for duty at the ramp and in the "tube." This job I had to do until December 1942. In this month the gassing was finished. Then I supervised the digging out and burning of about 520,000 corpses. In June 1943 I left the camp and was sent to the Poniatowa labor camp. My job was to lead the victims through the "tube" to the gas chamber building. I had to carry a whip but I never used it. Also I had to calm the victims down and tell them that they had to take a bath. I can't say anything about the first gas chamber because when I came to the camp there was only the new building.

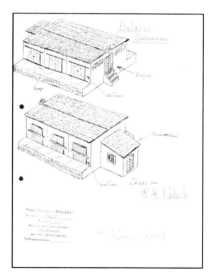

Gas Chamber Phase 2

A low house with a flat roof, in the center a corridor, left and right three gas chambers, each one for holding about 200 people. On the outside were big doors and concrete ramps ran along the length of the building, 80 cm high and 2 m wide. Over the entrance door was a big yellow Star of David; left and right of the door were signs with the inscription: "Stiftung Hackenholt" and "Bade und Inhalationsräume." The outer doors were used to remove the corpses; they were wooden and could be lifted up. At first iron sliding doors were used, but these did not close hermetically and were replaced by lift-up doors. The engine house was built at the rear gable side. Inside were two big diesel engines; their exhaust was led by pipes into the chambers. The corpses were brought to the pits. The pits were dug around the gas chamber building. They had different dimensions; some were about 50 m long, 25 m wide and 10 m deep.

Number of Victims

I decided to deal with the individual resettlement transports, Jewish communities and geographical detail separately. This gave me a certain freedom when dealing with matters I considered of background interest to the destruction of these communities prior to, and subsequent to, deportations to Belzec.

To achieve some consistency when referring to a particular ghetto or town, I used the conclusions (where applicable) and spelling shown by Martin Gilbert as my final reference. The resettlement numbers referred to cannot be relied upon due to inadequate evidential material. The scholars differ when assessing numbers of Jews deported, but in general they basically agree and I have used a certain amount of common sense when recording these variances.

There may be an overlap where one month merges into the next when figures vary from the source material. I have taken this into account in the final analysis of the document. A final complication when tracing individual transports to their ultimate end was the fact that the transit ghettos, Izbica, Piaski, and Krasnik, were some of the central collection points before the onward journey, thus eradicating any positive embarkation conclusion. Beyond these transit camps in the Lublin region, major towns such as Kolomyja, Stanislawow etc. would be the central collecting points from surrounding districts. The lack of information regarding smaller town communities is mainly due to the Nazi policy of removing populations of less than 500 to the nearest town.

My calculations and conclusions, which can never be definitive, are based on a collective of previously researched information, the established bedrock of analysis over a number of years. Each contributor has approached this task independently on the basis of the information available. By drawing together known sources, cross referencing and analysis, I concur in the main conclusions and findings with a few minor reassessments. In addition, I have added other sources gathered from elsewhere, primarily on the resettlement transports and other activities to the Belzec extermination camp between 17 March 1942—when the first rail transports commenced—and the last transports into the camp in December, 1942. No fewer than 500,000 Jews perished in this camp.

I have avoided showing "totals" after each list. This is because I know that double counting, errors and other inaccuracies cannot fail to have been made. Generally, my purpose is to show the enormous scale of Nazi genocidal activity under the auspices of *Aktion Reinhardt*.

Tables 1 - 24[14]

Table 1: March 1942[15]

	Town	Deported	Numbers
1	Belzec	25. 2. 42	500[16]
2	Bilgoraj	25. 3. 42	2500[17]
3	Biskupice	30. 3. 42	850[18]
4	Cieszanow	1. 3. 42	hundreds[19]
5	Drohobycz	24. 3. 42	1500[20]
6	Dubienka	17. 3. 42	843[21]
7	Hrubieszow	17. 3. 42	1343[22]
8	Izbica	17. 3. 42	2200[23]
9	Kazimierz Dolny	30. 3. 42	2000[24]
10	Komarow Osada	23. 3. 42	hundreds[25]
11	Lublin	17-31 -3.	11600[26]
12	Lubycza Krol*	17. 3 42	100[27]
13	Lviv	20. 3. 42	15000[28]
14	Mielec	1. 3. 42	4500[29]
15	Mosty Male	17. 3. 42	100[30]
16	Opole Lubelskie.	31. 3. 42	3000[31]
17	Piaski	30. 3. 42	3400[32]
18	Rawa Ruska	20. 3. 42	1500[33]
19	Rohatyn	20. 3. 42	2000[34]
20	Rzeszow	30. 3. 42	2000[35]
21	Siennica Rozana.	24. 3. 42	272[36]
22	Stanislawow	31. 3. 42	6000[37]
23	Tomaszow Lub	25. 2. 42	100[38]
24	Trawniki	1. 3. 42	600[39]
25	Truskawiec	? 3. 42	100[40]
26	WawolnicaOpole	1. 3. 42	1500[41]
27	Zolkiew	15. 3. 42	700[42]

Table 2: April 1942[43]

	Town	Deported	Numbers
1	Bilgoraj	4. 4. 42	500[44]
2	Chelm	11. 4. 42	hundreds[45]
3	Czieszanow	1. 4. 42	5000[46]
4	Izbica Lub.	8. 4. 42	2400[47]
5	Kolomyja District	22-4. 4. 42	8150[48]
6	Kolomyja		(1000)
7	Horodenka	4. 4. 42	(1500)

8	Kosow	22-4. 4. 42	(1000)
9	Kuty	22-24	(950)
10	Peczenizyn	22-24	(1000)
11	Sniatyn	22-24	(1000)
12	Tlumacz	3. 4. 42	(1300)[49]
13	Zablotow	22-24	(400)
14	Krasniczyn	13. 4. 41	1000[50]
15	Krasnik	12. 4. 42	2500[51]
16	Krasnystaw	13. 4. 42	1000[52]
17	Lubaczow	28/30. 42	2000[53]
18	Lubartow	9. 4. 42	800[54]
19	Lublin	3-30 4. 42	20000[55]
20	Lviv	23-9. 4. 42	5000[56]
21	Piaski	10. 4. 42	4200[57]
22	Radomysl nad Sanem	12. 4. 42	384[58]
23	Skalat	23. 4. 42	600[59]
24	Stanislawow	01. 4. 42	2500[60]
25	Zamosc	11. 4. 42	3000[61]
26	Rejowiec	13. 4. 42	2400[62]

Table 3: May 1942

	Town	Deported	Numbers
1	Baranow.	8. 5. 42	1500[63]
2	Belz	20. 5. 42	1500[64]
3	Bilgoraj	18. 5. 42	1000[65]
4	Czieszanow	24. 5. 42	1300[66]
5	Germany	27. 5. 42	2252[67]
6	Janow Lubelski	27. 5. 42	4500[68]
7	Komarow-Osada	23. 5. 42	1500[69]
8	Laszczow	22. 5. 42	350[70]
9	Opole Lub	5. 5. 42	hundreds[71]
10	Szczebrzeszyn	1-8. 5 42	280[72]
11	Tyszowce	22. 5. 42	1000[73]
12	Zamosc	27. 5. 42	1600[74]

Table 4: June 1942.[75]

Town		Deported	Numbers
13	Czortkow	6. 6. 42	1100[76]
14	Kolomyja	21. 6. 42	3000[77]
15	Gwozdziec	1-4. 6. 42	
16	Kosow		
17	Kuty		
18	Obertyn		
19	Zablotow		
20	Kopyczynce		1100[78]
21	Krakow	1-8. 6. 42	10000[79]
22	Lviv	24-6. 6. 42	5000[80]
23	Niemirow	19. 6. 42	500[81]
24	Olkusz	11-19. 6.42	3000[82]
25	Tarnow	11-18. 6.42	11500[83]
26	Dabrowa Tarnowska	11. 6.42	450[84]

Table 5: July 1942[85]

Town		Deported	Numbers
1	Bircza	27. 7. 42	1000[86]
2	Chyrow	29. 7. 42	900[87]
3	Debica	21-5. 7.42	12000[88]
4	Baranow	21. 7. 42	
5	Pilzno	21. 7. 42	
6	Radomysl Wilk.	21. 7. 42	
7	Ropczyce		
8	Rozwadow		
9	Sedziszlow		
10	Stalowawola		
11	Dobromil	27. 7. 42	1700[89]
12	Dukla Frysztak	29. 7. 42	3000[90]
13	Kopyczynce	29. 7. 42	hundreds[91]
14	Niebylec	7. 7. 42	hundreds
15	Miechow	7. 7. 42	hundreds[92]
16	Niemerow	29. 7. 42	800[93]
17	Przemysl	27. 7. 42	13000[94]
18	Przeworsk	1. 7. 42	hundreds
19	Rawa-Ruska	27. 7. 42	hundreds
20	Ryglica	7-22. 7 42	400[95]

21	Rzeszow	7-18. 7.42	22000[96]
22	Blaszowa	7. 7. 42	
23	Czudec		
24	Glogow	7. 7. 42	
25	Jawornik Polski.		
26	Kolbuszowa		
27	Niebylec	7. 7. 42	
28	Sokolow	7. 7. 42	
29	Strzyzow	7. 7. 42	
30	Tyczyn		
31	Sasow	15. 7. 42	1000[97]
32	Szczebrzeszyn	9. 7. 42	400[98]
33	Tarnobrzeg	21-5.7 42	12000[99]
34	Tarnow	24-5.7 43	1800[100]
35	Tluste	27. 7. 42	300[101]
36	Uhnow	27. 7. 42	1000[102]
37	Warsaw	22. 7. 42	hundreds[103]

Table 6: August 1942 [104]

Town	Deported.	Numbers
1 Biecz	16. 8. 42	700[105]
2 Bilgoraj	9. 8. 42	500[106]
3 Blizyn	1. 8. 42	hundreds[107]
4 Bobowa	16. 8. 42	hundreds[108]
5 Bochnia	25. 8. 42	6000[109]
6 Bobrka	12. 8. 42	1260[110]
7 Bolechow	3-6. 8. 42	2000[111]
8 Boryslaw	6-8. 8. 42	2000[112]
9 Brzeszow	10. 8. 42	hundreds[113]
10 Brzuchowice	26. 8. 42	250[114]
11 Chorostkow	28. 8. 42	1500[115]
12 Chyrow	27. 8. 42	900[116]
13 Czortkow	28. 8. 42	2800[117]
14 Czernelica	28. 8. 42	hundreds[118]
15 Dolina	26. 8. 42	3000[119]
16 Drohobycz	12. 6.43	5000[120]
17 Dukla Frysztak	8. 42	hundreds[121]
18 Garbatka	18. 8. 42	1100[122]
19 Glogow	18. 8. 43	500[123]
20 Gorlice	14-16. 8.42	700[124]
21 Goraj	21. 8. 42	800[125]
22 Grodek Jagiellonsk	13. 8. 42	2500[126]

23	Jasienica Rosienia.	10. 8. 42	hundreds[127]
24	Jaslo	16-20. 8.42	16000[128]
25	Bezdziedza		
26	Jedlica		
27	Kolaczyce		
28	Olpiny		
29	Jezierna	28. 8. 42	300[129]
30	Korczyna	10. 8. 42	hundreds[130]
31	Krosno	10-15. 8.42	5000[131]
32	Domaradz		
33	Dukla		
34	Golcowa		
35	Gwoznica		
36	Komancz		
37	Markowiec		
38	Niebieszczany		
39	Nowotaniec		
40	Orzechowk		
41	Pielnia		
42	Tokarnia		
43	Wesola		
44	Wola Janienicka		
45	Zmigrod	21. 8. 42	12000[132]
46	Lancut		
47	Lezajsk		
48	Zolynia		
49	Radymno	24. 8. 42	hundreds
50	Limanowa		50000[133]
51	Lviv	10-22. 8.42	
52	Bobrka		
53	Strzeliska		
54	Mikolajow		
55	Szczerzec		1200[134]
56	Mikulince	28-31. 8. 42	16000[135]
57	Nowy Sacz		
58	Grybow	24-28. 8.42	
59	Krynica Zdroj		
60	Labowa		
61	Lacko		
62	Piwiniczna	28-30. 8. 42	3000[136]
63	Nowy Targ		
64	Czarny Dunajec		
65	Czortszyn		
66	Krosienko	10. 8. 42	300[137]
67	Rabka	29. 8. 42	472[138]
68	Olesko	3. 8. 42	12500[139]
69	Przemysl		500[140]
70	Rymanow		1000[141]
71	Rzeszow	15. 8. 42	4000[142]

72	Sambor	29. 8. 42	100[143]
73	Sasow	6. 8. 42	200[144]
74	Schodnica	31. 8. 42	600[145]
75	Skalat	28. 8. 42	2000[146]
76	Skawina	12. 8. 42	1000[147]
77	Stanislawow	5-6. 8. 42	1500[148]
78	Stary Sambor.	17. 8. 42	700[149]
79	Stary Sącz	4. 8. 42	150[150]
80	Stebnik	12. 8. 42	1252[151]
81	Strzeliska Nowy	12. 8. 42	270[152]
82	Strzylka	9. 8. 42	400[153]
83	Szczebrzeszyn	9. 8. 42	1000[154]
84	Tarnogrod	28-31. 8.42	4000[155]
85	Tarnopol	28. 8. 42	9000[156]
86	Tarnow	26. 8. 42	300[157]
87	Tluste	31. 8. 42	hundreds[158]
88	Trembowla	17. 8. 42	3000[159]
89	Truskawiec	21. 8. 42	5000[160]
90	Turka	27. 8. 42	8000[161]
91	Wieliczka	11-13. 8.42	500[162]
92	Zamosc	29. 8. 42	4000[163]
93	Zaslaw	31. 8. 42	5000[164]
94	Zbaraz	31. 8. 42	1300[165]
95	Zborow	30. 8. 42	2700[166]
96	Zloczow	10. 8. 42	1000[167]
97	Zolkiewka	10. 8. 42	300[168]
98	Zwierzyniec		

Table 7: September 1942 [169]

	Town	Deported	Numbers
1	Baligrod	10-15. 9.42	13000[170]
2	Sanok	10. 9. 42	
3	Lesko	9. 9. 42	(2000)
4	Zagorz	9. 9. 42	
5	Bilgoraj	9. 9. 42	5000[171]
6	Boroszczow	27. 9. 42	800[172]
7	Brody	19. 9. 42	3000[173]
8	Brzesko	10. 9. 42	?

9	Brzezany	20. 9. 42	7150[174]
10	BialyKam	22. 9. 42	(350)[175]
11	Bolszowce	20. 9. 42	(1000)[176]
12	Buczącz	03. 9. 42	(1000[177]
13	Bukaczowce	22. 9. 42	(200)[178]
14	Burstyn	22. 9. 42	(200)[179]
15	Kozowa	22. 9. 42	(1000)[180]
16	Narajow	21. 9. 42	(1400)[181]
17	Podhajce	21. 9. 42	(1000)[182]
18	Rohatyn	22. 9. 42	(1000)[183]
19	Czortkow	26-30. 9.42	1500[184]
20	Chorostow	26-30. 9.42	1200[185]
21	Husiatyn	26-30. 9.42	
22	Suchystaw		
23	Oryszkowice		
24	Jezierzany		900[186]
25	Kopyczynce	26-30. 9.42	1000[187]
26	Korolowka	26. 9. 42	700[188]
27	Mielnica	26-30. 9.42	2000[189]
28	Probuzna	26-30. 9.42	1500[190]
29	Zaleszczyki	20-26. 9.42	2000[191]
30	Skala Podlaska	25-27. 9.42	1500[192]
31	Dabrowa Tarnow	13. 9. 42	1176[193]
32	Goraj	14-21. 9.42	700[194]
33	Gorlice	14. 9. 42	700[195]
34	Kalusz	15. 9. 42	4600[196]
35	Kolomyja	7-10. 9. 42	15000[197]
36	Horodenka		(800)
37	Jablonow		(600)
38	Kosow		(800)
39	Kuty		(100)
40	Pistyn		(100)
41	Roznow		(100)
42	Zablotow		(2000)
43	Kamionk Strumi.	15. 9. 42	1500[198]
44	Sokal	15. 9. 42	1400[199]
45	Sniatyn	17. 9. 42	2500[200]
46	Zabie	7. 9. 42	1000[201]
47	Kopyczynce	15. 9. 42	hundreds[202]
48	Krakow	10-18. 9.42	12000[203]
49	Dabrową Tarn.	10-18. 9.42	(hundreds)
50	Brzesko	10. 9. 42	(500)
51	Zabno	10. 9. 42	(hundreds)
52	Tuchow	10. 9. 42	(3000)
53	Zakliczyn	10. 9. 42	(hundreds)
54	Lublin	02. 9. 42	2000[204]
55	Lviv	11. 9. 42	1000[205]
56	Miechow	3-7. 9. 42	10000[206]

57	Dzialoszyce		(8300)
58	Proszowice		(hundreds)
59	Skalbmierz		(hundreds)
60	Slomnik		(hundreds)
61	Wolbrom	7. 9. 42	(1000)
62	Piaski	- 9. 42	thousands[207]
63	Pomorzany	23-30. 9.42	1000[208]
64	Przemyslany	9. 9. 41	2500[209]
65	Rabka	3. 9. 42	hundreds[210]
66	Sambor	9. 9. 42	2000[211]
67	Skalat	21-22. 9.42	3000[212]
68	Stanislawow	12. 9. 42	5000[213]
69	Stryj District	1. 9. 42	3000[214]
70	Bolechow	3-5. 9. 42	2000[215]
71	Chodorow	4-5. 9. 42	2000[216]
72	Brzozdowce	3-5. 9. 42	300[217]
73	Mikolajow	4. 9. 42	500[218]
74	Rozdol	4-5. 9 42	1000[219]
75	Skole	2-4. 9. 42	2000[220]
76	Zydaczow	4-5. 9. 42	500[221]
77	Zurawno	4-5. 9. 42	500[222]
78	Tarnopol	30. 9. 42	1000[223]
79	Tarnow	6-18. 9.42	4000[224]
80	Ustrzyki Dolne	15. 9. 42	1500[225]
81	Zamosc	6. 9. 42	400[226]
82	Zbaraz	1. 9. 42	hundreds[227]
83	Zborow	23-30. 9.42	1000[228]
84	Zydanow	5. 9. 42	500[229]

Table 8: October 1942[230]

	Town	Deported	Numbers
1	Annopol	1-14. 10.42	1943[231]
2	Belzyce	1-14. 10.43	3000[232]
3	Bilgoraj	15-31.1042	500[233]
4	Bolechow	15-31.1042	400[234]
5	Bolszowce	26-30.1042	1000[235]
6	Brzezany	10. 10. 42	4000[236]
7	Buczacz	12-7.10 43	1500[237]
8	Bukaczowice	26. 10. 42	300[238]
9	Bursztyn	10. 10. 42	4000[239]
10	Bychawa	11. 10. 42	3000[240]
11	Chodorow	18. 10. 42	350[241]

12	Chorostkow	19. 10. 42	2200[242]
13	Czortkow	3-5. 10. 42	2800[243]
14	Drohobycz	23-9. 10.42	2300[244]
15	Boryslaw	10. 10. 42	1500[245]
16	Sambor	17-22.1042	4000[246]
17	Dzierkowice	1-14. 10.42	146[247]
18	Firlej	1-14. 10.42	317[248]
19	Grodek Jagiellons.	14. 10. 42	450[249]
20	Grzymalow	14. 10. 42	200[250]
21	Jablonow	3-13. 10.42	hundreds[251]
22	Kamionka Strumil.	28. 10. 42	500[252]
23	Kolomyja	3-13. 10.42	4500[253]
24	Konskowola	1-14. 10.42	2000[254]
25	Koropce	8. 10. 42	1000[255]
26	Kosow	3-13. 10.42	hundreds[256]
27	Krakow	28. 10. 42	6000[257]
28	Krasnik	15. 10. 42	
29	Krasnystaw		thousands[258]
30	Krowica	15-31.1042	10000[259]
31	Kuty	10. 10. 42	hundreds[260]
32	Leczna	3-13. 10.42	hundreds[261]
33	Lopatyn	23. 10. 42	1000[262]
34	Lubaczow	22-3.10.42	400[263]
35	Lubartow	10. 10. 42	2000[264]
36	Lubycza Krolewsk	1-14. 10.42	4500[265]
37	Modliborzyce	10. 10. 42	1000[266]
38	Mosciska	1-14. 10.42	2500[267]
39	Opole Lubelskie	10. 10. 42	2000[268]
40	Mosty Wielkie	14. 10. 42	3000[269]
41	Oleszyce	22-4. 10.42	1000[270]
42	Pistyn	10. 10. 42	hundreds[271]
43	Podhajce	3-13. 10.42	hundreds[272]
44	Podwoloczyska	30. 10. 42	1500[273]
45	Pomorszany	22-4. 10.42	1000[274]
46	Radomysl nad San.	22-4. 10.42	hundreds[275]
47	Radziechow	29. 10. 42	hundreds
48	Sadowa Wisnia	22-4. 10.42	1000[276]
49	Sandomierz	10. 10·42	500[277]
50	Skalat	29. 10. 42	3230[278]
51	Sniatyn	21-2. 10.42	3000[279]
52	Sokal	3-13. 10.42	hundreds[280]
53	Stryj	22-8. 10.42	2500[281]
54	Szczebrzeszyn	18. 10. 42	2000[282]
55	Tarnopol	20-1. 10.42	1000[283]
56	Tartakow	5-7. 10. 42	750[284]
57	Tluste	22-4. 10.42	900[285]
58	Turek	5. 10. 42	1000[286]
59	Ulhnow	10. 42	hundreds[287]
60	Urzedow	15-31.10.42	1500[288]

61	Witkow Nowy	1-14. 10.42	500[289]
62	Zablotow	22-4. 10.42	1000[290]
63	Zakrzowek	3-13. 10.42	hundreds[291]
64	Zamosc	1-14. 10.42	1176[292]
65	Zawichost	15-30 142	4000[293]
66	Zbaraz	15-31 1042	5000[294]
67	Zwierzyniec	21.10.42	1000[295]

Table 9: November 1942

	Town	Deported	Numbers
1	Budzanow	-	2000[296]
2	Bilgoraj	2-9. 11. 42	4000[297]
3	Bochnia	10. 11. 42	570[298]
4	Bolechow	20-3. 11.42	300[299]
5	Borszczow	26-7. 11.42	800[300]
6	Boryslaw	5. 11. 42	600[301]
7	Brody	2. 11. 42	250[302]
8	Brzezany	4. 11. 42	1000[303]
9	Brzesko	15. 11. 42	2500[304]
10	Buczacz	27. 11. 42	2750[305]
11	Budzanow	5. 11. 42	hundreds[306]
12	Drohobycz	9. 11. 42	1000[307]
13	Frampo l	1-6. 11. 42	600[308]
14	Janow-Lubelski.	November	300[309]
15	Janow		300[310]
16	Jawarow	7. 11. 42	1500[311]
17	Jozefow	2. 11. 42	600[312]
18	Komarno	1-6. 11. 42	2000[313]
19	Komarow Osada	10. 11. 42	1000[314]
20	Kolbuszowa	15. 11. 42	2500[315]
21	Kosow	1. 11. 42	2500[316]
22	Kozlowa	8. 11. 42	hundreds[317]
23	Krasnik	1. 11. 42	3000[318]
24	Krzeszow	2. 11. 42	2500[319]
25	Kulikow	25. 11. 42	500[320]
26	Lviv	18. 11. 42	10000[321]
27	Mikulince		2000[322]
28	Modliborzy	Oct/Nov.	1300[323]
29	Mosciska	28. 11. 42	2500[324]
30	Oleszynce		1000[325]
31	Przemysl	18. 11. 42	4000[326]
32	Rudki	7. 11. 42	800[327]
33	Rzeszow	10. 11. 42	2000[328]
34	Sasow	25. 11. 42	400[329]

35	Skalat	9. 11. 42	1100[330]
36	Sasow		hundreds
37	Stryj	11. 11. 42	1500[331]
38	Szeczebrzeszyn	20. 11. 42	2000[332]
39	Szczerzec	2930.11.42	600[333]
40	Tarnogrod	2-3. 11. 42	3000[334]
41	Tarnopol	8. 11. 42	2500[335]
42	Tarnow	15. 11. 42	5000[336]
43	Tlumacz	27. 11. 42	2000[337]
44	Trembowla	5. 11. 42	1400[338]
45	Tuchow	15. 11. 42	1000[339]
46	Zaklikow	1-3. 11. 42	2000[340]
47	Zakliczyn	10-15.1142	500[341]
48	Zakrzowek	1. 10. 42	hundreds[342]
49	Zamosc	15. 11. 42	4000[343]
50	Zbaraz	8. 11. 42	1000[344]
51	Zabno	15. 11. 42	1000[345]
52	Zloczow	2-3. 11. 42	2500[346]
53	Zolkiew	22-3. 11.42	2500[347]
54	Zwierzyniec	Nov, 42	hundreds[348]

Table 10: December 1942 [349]

	Town	Deported	Numbers
1	Bolszowice	7-12. 12.42	hundreds[350]
2	Brzezany	4-5. 12. 42	1500[351]
3	Bukaczowce	7-12. 12.42	hundreds[352]
4	Burstyn	7-12. 12.42	hundreds[353]
5	Czortkow	7-12. 12.42	1000+[354]
6	Borszczowce	7-12. 12.42	hundreds[355]
7	Buczacz	7-12. 12 42	hundreds[356]
8	Kopyczynce	7-12. 12.42	hundreds[357]
9	Krosno	4. 12. 42	600[358]
10	Narajow	4-5. 12. 42	500[359]
11	Przemyslany	5. 12. 42	3000[360]
12	Rawa Ruska	7-11. 12.42	2500[361]
13	Lubycza Krolewsk		700[362]
14	Magierow		hundreds[363]
15	Niemirow		1000[364]
16	Potylicz		300[365]
17	Uhnow		hundreds[366]
18	Rohatyn	8. 12. 42	1250[367]
19	Tomaszow Lub.	12. 12. 42	hundreds[368]

Table 11: Deportations Post Closure of Belzec

After Belzec closed to receiving transports, the murders continued at the other killing sites and concentration camps. The murder of Jews was accomplished by shooting, liquidation of camps, ghettos and resettlement actions. From the districts of the Generalgouvernment (GG) and elsewhere, the following data has been collated:

January 1943	Numbers	Actions
Chelm	hundreds[369]	Sobibor
Grodek Jag.	1300[370]	Shooting
Izbica	750[371]	Sobibor
Jaryczow Nowy	2500[372]	Shooting
Kamionka Strum.	hundreds[373]	Shooting
Krakow	400[374]	Auschwitz
Lubaczow	2000[375]	Shooting
Lviv (Janowska)	15000[376]	Shooting
Sanok	hundreds[377]	Ausch/Shooting
Stanislawow	1000[378]	Shooting
February		
Boryslaw	1200[379]	Shooting
Buczacz	2000[380]	Shooting
Chelm	300[381]	Sobibor
Chodorow	200[382]	Shooting
Kolomyja	1500[383]	Shooting
Mosty Wielkie	hundreds[384]	Shooting
Stanislawow	10000[385]	Shooting
Stryj	2000[386]	Shooting
Tluste	40[387]	Shooting
Zamosc	417[388]	Auschwitz
March		
Debica	hundreds[389]	Shooting
Krakow	4000[390]	Auschwitz
Lviv (Janowska)	1500[391]	Sobibor
Sambor	900[392]	Shooting
Szebnie	hundreds[393]	Transferred
Zolkiew	2000[394]	Shooting
April		
Brzezany	2000[395]	Shooting
Borszczow	800[396]	Shooting
Budzyn FLC	71[397]	Shooting
Izbica	200[398]	Sobibor
Jaworow	3489[399]	Shooting

Komarno	500[400]	Shooting
Krakowiec	529[401]	Shooting
Leczna	200[402]	Sobibor
Mosciska	2328[403]	Sobibor
Plebanowka	2245[404]	Shooting
Sadowa Wisnia	25[405]	Sobibor
Szklo	53[406]	Sobibor
Wielkie Oczy	547[407]	Sobibor
Komarno	500[408]	Shooting
Kopyczynce	600[409]	Shooting
Kozowa	1000[410]	Shooting
Leszniow	100[411]	Shooting
Lviv (Janowska)	hundreds[412]	Shooting
Przemysl	100[413]	Shooting
Rudki	1700[414]	Shooting
Sambor	1000[415]	Shooting
Skalat	750[416]	Shooting
Wlodawa	2000[417]	Sobibor
Zloczkow	5000[418]	Shooting
Zolkiew	hundreds[419]	Shooting

May

Baranow	1500[420]	Sobibor
Belzyce FLC	500[421]	Shooting
Brody	2500[422]	Shooting/Sob.
Busk	1000[423]	Shooting/Janow
Debica	200[424]	Shooting
Drohobycz	hundreds[425]	Shooting
Lviv (Janowska)	thousands[426]	Sobibor
Przemyslamy	hundreds[427]	Shooting
Skalat	660[428]	Shooting
Sokal	2500[429]	Shooting
Stryj	1000[430]	Shooting
Tluste	3000[431]	Shooting
Wlodawa	150[432]	Sobibor

June[433]

Belzec	306[434]	Sobibor/Shot
Boroszczow	700[435]	Shooting
Boryslaw	700[436]	Auschwitz
Brzezany	hundreds[437]	Shooting
Buczacz	1800[438]	Shooting
Czortkow	thousands[439]	Shooting
Debica	250[440]	Shooting
Drohobycz	hundreds[441]	Shooting
Kozowa	400[442]	Shooting/Plasz
Lviv (Janowska)	13000[443]	Sobibor
Olesko	hundreds[444]	Shooting
Podhajce	300[445]	Shooting

Podwoloczyska	hundreds[446]	Shooting
Przemyslany	hundreds[447]	Shooting
Rawa Ruska	1000[448]	Shooting
Skalat	hundreds[449]	Shooting
Rohatyn	1000[450]	Shooting
Skala Podolska	800[451]	Shooting
Stryj	hundreds[452]	Shooting
Sambor	hundreds[453]	Shooting
Tarnopol	4000[454]	Shooting
Trembowla	900[455]	Shooting
Tluste	1000[456]	Shooting
Wlodawa	1000[457]	Sobibor
Zbaraz	hundreds[458]	Shooting

July

Boryslaw	hundreds[459]	Auschwitz
Bolechow	300[460]	Shooting
Jaryczow Nowy	hundreds[461]	Shooting
Jezierzna	hundreds[462]	Shooting
Kamionka Strum.	5000[463]	Shooting
Lviv (Janowska)	thousands[464]	Sobibor
Skalat	400[465]	Shooting
Winniki	hundreds[466]	Shooting
Zloczow	hundreds[467]	Shooting

August

Bochnia	3000[468]	Auschwitz
Borszczow	360[469]	Shooting
Bialystok	hundreds[470]	Sobibor
Debica	2000[471]	Sobibor
Drohobycz	hundreds[472]	Shooting
Jaktorow	1000[473]	Shooting
Lackie Wielkie	1000[474]	Shooting
Sasow	1000[475]	Shooting

September

Bochnia	7000[476]	Auschwitz
Bialystock	hundreds[477]	Sobibor
Dorohucza	hundreds[478]	Sobibor
Tarnow	5000[479]	Auschwitz
Przemysl	3500[480]	Auschwitz
Dabrowa Tarnow.	1300[481]	Auschwitz

October

| Lviv (Janowska) | 2000[482] | Auschwitz |
| Treblinka | 100[483] | Sobibor |

312

November

Borki	50[484]	Shooting
Czortkow	200[485]	Shooting
Drohobycz	200[486]	Shooting
Krychow	1500[487]	Shooting
Lviv (Janowska)	thousands[488]	Shooting
Lublin	2500[489]	Shooting
Majdanek	18000[490]	Shooting
Poniatowa	14000[491]	Shooting
Dorohucza	thousands	Shooting
Old Airfield	thousands	Shooting
Rzeszow	1000[492]	Auschwitz
Szebnie	3300[493]	Auschwitz
Trawniki	8000[494]	Shooting

December

Boryslaw	700[495]	Auschwitz
Buczacz	300[496]	Shooting
Drohobycz	200[497]	Shooting

Table 12: Final Sweep of Galicia 1943

February

Trzebnia	200	Auschwitz

March

Boryslaw	600[498]	Shooting

April

Drohobycz	600[499]	Auschwitz

June

Boryslaw	700[500]	Auschwitz

July

Boryslaw	hundreds[501]	Auschwitz
Tarnow	3000[502]	Auschwitz

August

Galicia	9[503]	Auschwitz

Table 13: Deportations within GG to Sobibor 1942

Town	Date	Numbers
Barnow	May 8	1500
Konskowla	May 8	hundreds
Belzyce[504]	June 2	1000
Belzyce/Bychawa	October 30	7000
Biala	Oct/Nov	4800
Biala Podlaska	June 10-13	6000
Chelm	May 21-23	2300
Chelm	May 25-30	1500
Chelm	July 31	300
Chelm	October 27-28	3000
Chelm	November 6	10000
Cycow	June 1	hundreds
Cycow	May 25-30	500
Czemierniki	Oct/Nov	1000
Demblin-Irena	May 6	2500
Dubecznow	June 10-13	hundreds
Dubecznow	December 23	650
Dubienka	June 2	2670
Pulawy	June 5	hundreds
Opole Lub.	June 5	hundreds
Duchaczow	October 1-5	150
Gorzkow	May 13-14	2000
Grabowce	June 8	1200
Hrubieszow	June 1-2	3049
Hrubieszow	June 7-9	500
Hrubiesow	October 28	2000
Izbica	October 8	1500
Izbica	November 2	1750
Izbica[505]	May 15	400
Komarow	May 3	2000
Komorow	Oct/Nov	600
Krasniczyn	May 25-30	hundreds
Krasniczyn	June 6	800
Krasnystaw	May 14-15	3400
Krychow (labour C)	Mid April	250
Krzywowierzba	June 10-13	hundreds
Leczna	October 23	3000
Lubartow	April 9	hundreds
Lubartow	October 11	3000
Lukow	October	7000
Lukow	November	3000
Lysobyki	May 25-30	500
Majdanek KZ	June 29	5000
Markuszowa	May 9	1500
Michow	May 10	2500

Miedzyrzec	August	11000
Olchowiec	June 10-13	hundreds
Opole Lubelski	May 5	2000
Opole	May 12	2000
Parczew	August	5000
Pawlowa	June 10-13	hundreds
Radzyn	October	2000
Piaski-Izbica	October 22-30	5000
Pulawy	May 12	2500
Radzyn	Oct/Nov	2000
Rejowiec	August 10	2000
Rejowiec	October 10	2400
Rudnik	May 25-30	hundreds
Rycywol	September 8	2000
Ryki	May 7	2500
Sawin	June 10-13	hundreds
Siedliszcze	May 18	630
Siedliszcze	October 22	500
Slawatycze	June 10-13	1000
Staw	December 22	800
Turobin	May 12	2000
Uchanie	June 10	1650
Ustrzyki	September 6	hundreds
Wawolnica	May 25-30	500
Wlodawa	May 23	1200
Wlodawa	July 24	hundreds (children)
Wlodawa	October 24	5000
Wlodowa	October 30	500
Wohyn	Oct/Nov	800
Wojslowice	October 12	1200
Wysokie	May 25-30	1000
Zamosc	May 15-16	5000
Zolkiewka	May 12	2000
Zolkiewka	August 10	1000

Table 14: Deportations within GG to Sobibor 1943

Izbica	January	750
Belzec[506]	June 26	306[507]
Bialystok	August	hundreds
Bialystok	September 29	hundreds
Chelm	January	hundreds
Chelm	February	300
Debica	August 8	2000
Dorohucza	September 10	hundreds
Izbica	April 28	200
Leczna	April 29	200
Lviv (Janowska)	May 22	thousands
Lviv (Janowska)[508]	July 4	thousands
Miedzrzec	May	3000
Treblinka[509]	October 20	100
Wlodawa	April 30	2000
Wlodawa	May 1-7	150

Table 15: Deportations outside GG to Sobibor 1943[510]

Holland	March 5-6	1105
France	March 6	71
France	March 11	hundreds
Holland	March 13	1105
France	March 18	hundreds
Holland	March 20	964
Holland	March 26	1250
Germany	March 31	hundreds
Holland	April 2	1255
Holland	April 9	2020
Holland	April 16	1204
Germany (Berlin)	April 21	938
Holland	April 23	1166
France	April 25	2000
Holland	April 30	1204
Holland	May 7	1187
Holland	May 14	1187
Holland	May 21	2511
Holland	May 28	2862
Holland	June 4	3006
Holland (Children)	June 8	1266
Holland	June 11	3017
Holland	July 2	3397
Holland	July 9	2417

Holland	July 16	1988
Holland	July 23	2209
Lida (Sov. Union)[511]	September 18-19	2700
Minsk	September 18-23	6000
Vilnius	September 23-24	5000

Table 16: Deportations within GG to Treblinka 1941-3

Town	Date deported
Bedkow	1. 9. 42
Biala Podlaska	10. 6. 42
Biala Rawska	22. 10. 42
Bialobrzegi	1. 10. 42
Bialystock[512]	10. 11. 42
Bialystock	16. 9. 41
Bielski Podlask	2. 11. 42
Bocki	2. 11. 42
Bogusze-Sam	10. 11. 42
Busko-Zdroj	1. 10. 42
Checiny	13. 9. 42
Chmielnik	1. 10. 42
Ciechanowiec	15. 10. 42
Ciepielow	15. 10. 42
Czestochowa	21. 9. 42
Cmielow	1. 10. 42
Deblin-Irena	6. 5. 42
Dobre	15. 9. 42
Drzewica	1. 10. 42
Gielniow	1. 10. 42
Gniewoszow	29. 9. 42
Grodno	18. 11. 42
Iwaniski	15. 10. 42
Ilza	15. 10. 42
Jadow	19. 8. 42
Janow	10. 11. 42
Jasionowka	25. 1. 43
Jedrzejow	16. 9. 42
Kaluszyn[513]	1. 12. 42
Kaluszyn	15. 9. 42
Kielce	20. 8. 42
Klimontow	30. 10. 42
Lviv	22. 10. 42
Kobylnica[514]	1. 10. 42

Kock	1. 8. 42
Koluszki	22. 10. 42
Koniecpol	7. 10. 42
Konskie	3. 11. 42
Kosow Lacki[515]	19. 12. 42
Kosow Lacki	22. 9. 42
Kozienice	27. 9. 42
Kolbiel	15. 9. 42
Krynki	10. 11. 42
Kunow	30. 10. 42
Latowicz	14. 10. 42
Legionowow	19. 8. 42[516]
Lipsko	15. 10. 42
Laskarzew	27. 9. 42
Losice	22. 8. 42
Lukow	5. 10. 42
Miedzyrzec[517]	1. 5. 43
Miedzyrzec	25. 8. 42
Minsk	21. 8. 42
Mazowie	
Mordy	22. 8. 42
Mrozy	15. 9. 42
Nowe Miast[518]	22. 10. 42
Nowy Korczyn	2. 10. 42
Opatow	20. 10. 42
Opoczno	22. 10. 42
Osiek	25. 10. 42
Ostrowiec	11. 10. 42
Otwock	19. 8. 42
Ozarow	30. 10. 42
Parczew	19. 8. 42
Parysow	2. 10. 42
Pinczow	1. 10. 42
Piotrkow Tryb.	15. 10. 42
Przedborz	9. 10. 42
Przysucha	27. 10. 42
Radom[519]	4. 8. 42
Radom [520]	19. 2. 42
Radomsko[521]	6. 1. 43
Radomsko	10. 10. 42
Radoszyce	3. 11. 42
Radzymin	19. 8. 42
Radzyn Pod.	1. 10. 42
Rawa Maz.[522]	31. 10. 42
Ryki	7. 5. 42
Siedlce	22. 8. 42
Siemiatycze	2. 11. 42
Siennica	15. 9. 42
Sienno	15. 10. 42

Skarzysko[523]	21. 9. 42
Sobienie-Jez	2. 10. 42
Sobolew	2. 10. 42
Solkolka	10. 11. 42
Sokolow Pod.	22. 9. 42
Stanislawow	15. 9. 42
Starachowice	15. 10. 42
Staszow	7. 11. 42
Sterdyn	22. 9. 42
Stoczek	22. 9. 42
Stopnica	1. 10. 42
Suchedinow	21. 9. 42
Suchowola	10. 11. 42
Sulejow	15. 10. 42
Szczekociny	16. 9. 42
Szydlowiec	13. 1. 43
Taczyn	27. 1. 42
Tarlow	15. 10. 42
Tomaszow. M	22. 10. 42
Ujazd	31. 1. 43
Warsaw 1.[524]	19. 8. 42
Warsaw 2.[525]	19. 8. 42
Wegrow	22. 9. 42
Wodzislaw	16. 9. 42
Wolomin	19. 8. 42
Wloszczowa	16. 9. 42
Zwolen	29. 9. 42
Zarki	6. 10. 42
Zelechow	2. 10. 42

Table 17: Deportations within GG to Auschwitz 1941-3

Ghetto	Date Deported
Andrychow	12. 11. 43
Augustow	2. 11. 42
Bedzin	5. 5. 42
Bialystock	16. 9. 41
Bochnia	25. 8. 42
Chrzanow	1. 6. 42
Ciechanow	6. 11. 42
Czeladz	1. 5. 43
Dabrowa	5. 5. 42
Grodno	18. 11. 42
Jasionowka	25. 1. 43
Krakow	1. 6. 42

Klobuck	22. 6. 42
Makow Maz.	6. 12. 42
Mlawa	6. 12. 42
Olkusz	2. 6. 42
Pruzana	30. 1. 43
Przemysl	27. 7. 42
Plonsk	1. 11. 42
Radom 1.	19. 2. 42
Rzeszow	1. 11. 43
Solkolka	10. 11. 42
Sosnowiec 1.	12. 5. 42
Sosnowiec 2.	1. 5. 42
Modrzejow	20. 6. 42
Sucha Beskidz	8. 5. 43
Tarnow	11. 6. 42
Wadowice	10. 8. 43
Wolkowysk	30. 1. 43
Zambrow	13. 1. 43
Zawiercie	5. 5. 42

Table 18: Deportations to Chelmno 1941-2

Town	Date deported
Belchatow	1. 8. 42
Brzesc [526]	1. 10. 41
Brzeziny	14. 5. 42
Dabie	14. 12. 41
Gabin	1. 4. 42
Gostynin	7. 4. 42
Grabow	1. 4. 42
Izbica Kujawsk	14. 1. 42
Kobylnica	1. 12. 41
Kowale- pansk	10. 12. 42
Kozminek	1. 3. 42
Kolo	8. 12. 41
Krosniewice	2. 3. 42
Kutno	1. 3. 42
Lutomiersk	1. 7. 42
Lututow	11. 8. 42
Lask	28. 8. 42
Leczyca	10. 4. 42
Lodz	7. 12. 41
Nowiny Brd.	1. 11. 42
Ozorkow	1. 3. 42
Pabianice	17. 5. 42

Piatek	22. 4. 42
Poddebice	1. 3. 42
Prazka	1. 8. 42
Sanniki	17. 4. 42
Sieradz	1. 12. 41
Szadek	1. 8. 42
Sluzewo	1. 5. 42
Warsaw	22. 7. 42
Warta	24. 8. 42
Wielun	22. 8. 42
Wieruszow	21. 8. 42
Wloclawek	30. 9. 41
Zdunska Wola	22. 8. 42
Zelow	1. 9. 42
Zloczew	1. 5. 42
Zyrardow	1. 2. 41

Table 19: Liquidation of Ghettos 1941-3[527]

Town	Date deported	Status.
Belzyce	May 43	Majdanek KZ
Bialopole	?	Shooting
Bobowa	16. 8. 42	Shooting
Bogoria	?	Shooting
Chodel	?	Unknown
Czernice	?	Unknown
Drobin	?	Unknown
Gora Kalwaria	1. 2. 41	Shooting
Grodziec	9. 3. 41	Shooting
Jozefow	July	Shooting
Kamionka	1. 10. 42	Shooting
Kosin	?	Unknown
Kolaczyce	?	Unknown
Konskowla	Oct	Shooting
Krasnobrod	1. 3. 43	Shooting
Kurow	1. 11. 42	Shooting
Lomazy	?	Shooting
Lukow	?	Shooting
Majdanek	3-4 Nov	Shooting
Nowy Dwor	?	Unknown
Nowy Zmigrod	?	Shooting
Ostrow Lub.	1. 10. 42	Unknown
Parczew	Oct.	Shooting
Pionki	1. 8. 42	Unknown
Polaniec	1. 10. 42	Unknown

Poniatowa	3-4 Nov	Shooting
Radogoszcz	?	Unknown
Rakow	1. 10. 42	Unknown
Rzepiennik Str	11. 8. 42	Shooting
Rzgow	1. 3. 41	Shooting
Serockomla	1. 12. 40	Shooting
Sieniawa	25. 8. 42	Shooting
Sobolew	?	Unknown
Sobota	1. 1. 40	Unknown
Stawiski	1. 11. 42	Shooting
Talcyn/Kock	Sept.	Shooting
Tomaszow Lub	25. 2. 42	Shooting
Trawniki	1. 3. 42	Unknown
Tluszcz	1. 5. 42	Shooting
Ulanow	1. 10. 42	Unknown
Warsaw 1[528]	?	Unknown
Warsaw 2.[529]	?	Shooting
Warsaw 3.	1. 3. 42	Shooting
Wasowa	1. 5. 42	Unknown
Wisznice	17. 6. 42	Shooting
Wolanow	1. 7. 42	Unknown
Zagorow	1. 10. 41	Shooting

Table 20: Deportations from Germany[530]

Date of Deportation	# of Person	Country/City of Departure
11. 03. 1942	1001	Terezin
13. 03. 1942	1003	Germany
17. 03. 1942	1000	Terezin
19. 03. 1942	800-1000-	Germany
25. 03. 1942	955	Germany (Probably Aachen, Koblenz, Kassel
27. 03. 1942	1008	Germany (Bamberg, Fürth, Würzburg and 426 from Nürnberg). A part was sent to Krasniczyn. Austria (Wien)
09. 04. 1942	998	Germany (Duisburg, Düsseldorf, Essen,
22. 04. 1942	942	Krefeld, Mönchengladbach, Oberhausen, Wuppertal). Germany (Stuttgart, Baden-Württenberg

		region).
26. 04. 1942	628	Teresin and from selection in Lublin
27. 04. 1942	600	Germany (Bamberg, Fürth, Nürnberg, Schweinfurt, Würzburg). A part was sent to Krasniczyn.
28. 04. 1942	700-800	Germany (Frankfürt/M) via Lublin, where 154 men were sent to Majdanek.
		Austria (Wien)
		Austria (Wien).
08. 05. 1942	784	Germany (Frankfürt/M, Wiesbaden) via Lublin where 122 men were taken to Majdanek
12. 05. 1942	1001	Slovakia (Spisska Nova Ves) via Lublin
15. 05. 1942	1006	Slovakia (Poprad) via Lublin
24. 05. 1942	835	Austria (Wien)
		Germany
29. 05. 1942	1052	Germany (Aachen, Duisburg, Düsselforf, Essen, Koblenz, Köln, Krefeld, Mönchengladbach).
30. 05. 1942	1000	Germany (Frankfurt/M, Wiesbaden) via
05. 06. 1942	1003	Lublin, where 188 men were taken to
13. 06. 1942	1003	Majdanek.
15. 06. 1942	1066	
15. 06. 1942	947	

Table 21: Deportations from Theresienstadt[531]

Transport	Date of Deportation	Destination	# of Persons
By	26.10.1942	Auschwitz	1866
Cq	20.1.1943	Auschwitz	2000
Cr	23.1.1943	Auschwitz	2000
Cs	26.1.1943	Auschwitz	1000
Ct	29.1.1943	Auschwitz	1000

Cu	1.2.1943	Auschwitz	1001
Dl	6.9.1943	Auschwitz	2479
Dm	6.9.1943	Auschwitz	2528
Dn - Kindertransport	5.10.1943	Auschwitz	1196
Dn/a	5.10.1943	Auschwitz	53
Dr	15.12.1943	Auschwitz	2504
Ds	18.12.1943	Auschwitz	2503
Dx	20.3.1944	Auschwitz	45
Dz	15.5.1944	Auschwitz	2503
Ea	16.5.1944	Auschwitz	2500
Eb	18.5.1944	Auschwitz	2500
Eh	1.7.1944	Auschwitz	10
Ek	28.9.1944	Auschwitz	2499
El	29.9.1944	Auschwitz	1500
Em	1.10.1944	Auschwitz	1500
En	4.10.1944	Auschwitz	1500
Eo	6.10.1944	Auschwitz	1550
Ep	9.10.1944	Auschwitz	1600
Eq	12.10.1944	Auschwitz	1500
Er	16.10.1944	Auschwitz	1500
Es	19.10.1944	Auschwitz	1500
Et	23.10.1944	Auschwitz	1715
Ev	28.10.1944	Auschwitz	2038
AAy	28.7.1942	Baranovici	1000
Rum	17.5.1944	Bergen-Belsen	5
Eg	4.7.1944	Bergen-Belsen	15
Ej	27.9.1944	Bergen-Belsen	20

Aa	11.3.1942	Izbica	1001
Ab	17.3.1942	Izbica	1000
Aq	27.4.1942	Izbica	1000
AAx	14.7.1942	Klein Trostinetz	1000
AAz	4.8.1942	Klein Trostinetz	1000
Bc	25.8.1942	Klein Trostinetz	1000
Bk	8.9.1942	Klein Trostinetz	1000
Bn	22.9.1942	Klein Trostinetz	1000
Al	23.4.1942	Lublin	1000
Ay	17.5.1942	Lublin	1000
Az	25.5.1942	Lublin	1000
Ax	9.5.1942	Ossowa	1000
Ag	1.4.1942	Piaski	1000
Be	1.9.1942	Raasika	1000
Ap	18.4.1942	Rejowiec	1000
O	9.1.1942	Riga	1000
P	15.1.1942	Riga	1000
Bb	20.8.1942	Riga	1000
AAk	12.6.1942	Trawniki	1000
Bo	19.9.1942	Treblinka	2000
Bp	21.9.1942	Treblinka	2020
Bq	23.9.1942	Treblinka	1980
Br	26.9.1942	Treblinka	2004
Bs	29.9.1942	Treblinka	2000

Bt	5.10.1942	Treblinka	1000
Bu	8.10.1942	Treblinka	1000
Bv	15.10.1942	Treblinka	1998
Bw	19.10.1942	Treblinka	1984
Bx	22.10.1942	Treblinka	2018
AAi	13.6.1942	unbekannt	1000
An	25.4.1942	Warschau	1000
Ar	28.4.1942	Zamosc	1000
As	30.4.1942	Zamosc	1000

Table 22: Rank Structures
SS, Wehrmacht and British Equivalents

SS – Rank	Wehrmacht	British Army
Reichsführer SS	General of the Army	Field marshal
SS-Oberstgruppenführer	Generaloberst	General
SS-Obergruppenführer	General der Infanterie	Lieutenant General
SS-Gruppenführer	Generalleutnant	Major General
SS-Brigadeführer	Generalmajor	Brigadier
SS-Oberführer	Oberstl	-
SS-Standartenführer	Oberst	Colonel
SS-Obersturmbannführer	Oberstleutnant	Lieutenant Colonel
SS-Sturmbannführer	Major	Major
SS-Hauptsturmführer	Hauptmann	Captain
SS-Obersturmführer	Oberleutnant	Lieutenant
SS-Untersturmführer	Leutnant	Second Lieutenant
SS-Hauptscharführer	Stabsfeldwebel	Sergeant Major
SS-Oberscharführer	Hauptfeldwebel	Quarter master Sergeant
SS-Scharführer	Unterfeldwebel	Staff Sergeant
SS-Unterscharführer	Unteroffizier	Sergeant
SS-Rottenführer	Gefreiter	Corporal
SS-Sturmann	Obergrenadier	Lance Corporal
SS-Mann	Grenadier	Private

Uniformed and non-uniformed German Police Ranks - Equivalents

Sipo (security police)	Ordnungspolizei (uniform)	SS (including Waffen SS)
Reichskriminaldirektor	Generalleutnant	Gruppenführer
Kriminaldirigent	Generalmajor	Brigadeführer
Regierungs-und Kriminaldirekto	Oberst	Stndartenführer; Oberführer
Oberregierungs-und Kriminalrat	Oberstleutnant	Obersturmbannführer
Regierungs-und Kriminalrat	Major	Sturmbannführer
Kriminalkommissar	Hauptmann	Hauptsturmführer
Kriminalinspektor	Oberleutnant	Obersturmführer
Kriminalobersekretar	Leutnant	Untersturmführer
Kriminalsekretar	Meister	Sturmscharführer
Kriminaloberassistent	Hauptwachtmeister	Hauptscharführer
Kriminalassistent	Zugwachtmeister	Oberscharführer

Table 23: Personnel who served in Aktion Reinhardt Camps

NAME	SS Rank	T4 Service
Arndt, Kurt	SS- Scharführer	Hadamar/T
Bär, Rudi	SS-Scharführer	Bernburg/T
Bärbl, Heinrich	SS-Rottenführer	Hartheim/B/S
Bauch, Ernst	SS-Rottenführer	Bernburg
Bauer, Hermann Erich	SS-Oberscharführer	S.
Baumann, Max	SS-Scharführer	B.
Becher, Werner	SS-Unterscharführer	Sonnenstein/S
Beckmann, Rudolf	SS-Oberscharführer	Hartheim/ S
Beulich, Max	SS-Scharführer	Sonnenstein.
Bielas, Max	SS-Scharführer	Bernburg/Brandenburg/T
Blauroch,	SS-Scharführer	Sonnenstein/S
Boelitz, Kurt	SS- Scharführer	T.
Bolender, Kurt	SS-Oberscharführer	Bran/Had/Hart/Sonn/S.
Bootz, Helmut	SS- Scharführer	Bernburg/Grafeneck/T/S.
Börner, Gerhardt	SS-Scharführer	Sonnenstein/S
Borowski, Werner	SS-Untersturmführer	Bernburg/T/B.
Bredow, Paul	SS-Scharführer	Grafeneck/Hartheim/S/T.
Bree, Max	SS-Scharführer	Grafeneck/Hadamar/S/T.
Cook	SS-Scharführer	Hartheim/Treblinka
Daschel, Arthur	SS-Oberwachtmeister	Sonnenstein/B/S.
Dietz, Erich	SS- Scharfuhrer	Sonnenstein/S.
+*Dubois, Werner	SS-Oberscharführer	Bernburg/Hadamar/B/S.
Eberl, Irmfried (Dr).	Obersturmführer	Bernburg/Brandenburg
Eisold, Johannes	SS-Scharführer	Sonnenstein/T.
Feix, Reinhold	SS-Untesturmführer	Trawniki/B.
Felfe, Hermann	SS- Scharführer	Grafeneck/Sonnenstein/T.
Fereleng, Gustav	SS-Unterscharführer	T4. B.

Fettke, Erich	SS-Unterscharführer	T4. S.
Fichtner, Erwin	SS-Scharführer	Bernburg/B.
Floss, Herbert	SS-Scharführer	Bernburg/B/S/T.
Forker, Albert	SS- Scharführer	Sonnenstein/S/T.
**Franz, Kurt Hubert	SS-Untersturmführer	Brand/Graf/Sonn/B/T.
+Frenzel, Karl	SS-Oberscharführer	Bernburg/Graf/Hadamar/S.
Friedel,	SS-Schaführer	T4. B/S.
+*Fuchs, Erich	SS-Unterscharführer	Bernburg/Bran/B/S/T.
Gaulstich, Friedrich	SS-Unterscharführer	T4. S.
Gentz, Ernst	SS-Scharführer	T4 T/S.
Getzinger, Anton	SS-Oberscharführer	Hartheim/S.
*Girtzig, Hans	SS-Scharführer	Grafeneck/Hartheim/B/S.
*Gley, Heinrich	SS-Oberscharführer	Grafeneck/Sonnenstein/B.
Gomerski, Hubert	SS-Oberscharführer	Hadamar/S.
Goetzinger, Anton	SS-Oberscharführer	Hartheim/S.
Graetschus, Siegfried	SS-Oberscharführer	Bernburg/T/S.
Gringers, Max (Karl)	SS-Scharführer	Hartheim/B.
Grömer, Josef (Ferdl)	SS-Sturmmann	Hartheim/ S.
Grossmann, Willi	SS-Scharführer	Hadamar/Sonnenstein/T.
Groth, Paul	SS-Unterscharführer	Hartheim/B/S.
Hackel, Emil	SS- Scharfuhrer	Sonnenstein/S.
Hackenholt, Lorenz	SS-Hauptscharführer.	Grafeneck/Sonnenstein/B/S/T.
Haunstein	SS- Scharführer	Sonnenstein/ S.
Hengst, August	SS- Scharführer	Bernburg/Brandenburg/T.
Hering, Gottleib	SS-Hauptsturmführer	Bern/Brand/Hart/Sonn/B.
Herman, Erwin	SS-Scharführer	T4. S.
Hiller, Richard	SS-Unterscharführer	T4.
Hirsch, Fritz	SS-Scharführer	Hartheim/B.
Hirtreiter, Josef	SS-Scharführer	Hadamar/T/S.
Hödl, Franz	SS-Unterscharführer	Hartheim/S.
**Horn, Otto	SS-Scharführer	Sonnenstein/S.
Irrmann, Fritz	SS-Scharführer	T4/B.
+Ittner, Alfred	SS-Oberscharführer	T4-HQ Berlin/S
+*Jührs, Robert	SS-Unterscharführer	Hadamar/ B/S.
Kainer, Erwin	SS- Scharführer	Hadamar/T
Kaiser, Aleksy	SS-Oberscharführer	T4. S.
Kamm, Rudolf	SS-Scharführer	Sonnenstein/B/S.
Kielminsky, Otto	SS-Scharführer	T4. S.
Klier, Johann (Josef)	SS-Unterscharführer	Hadamar/S.
Kloss, Walter	SS-Scharführer	Sonnenstein/B.
Konrad, Josef (Fritz)	SS-Scharführer	Grafeneck/Sonnenstein/S.
Kraschewski, Fritz	SS-Scharführer	Grafeneck/Hadamar/B.
Kramer, Johann	SS-Rottenführer	T4. S.
**Küttner, Karl 'Kiwi'	SS-Oberschaführer	T4. T.
+Lachmann, Erich	SS-Scharführer	T4. S.
**Lambert, Erwin	SS-Unterscharführer	Bern/Had/Hart/Sonn/S/T.
Lindenmüller, Alfons	SS-Hauptscharführer	T4. T.
Löffler, Albert	SS-Unterscharführer	T4. T/M.
Ludwig, Karl Emilr	SS-Scharführer	T4-HQ

**Matthes, Heinrich	SS-Scharführer	Berlin/Sobibor/Treblinka.
		Sonnenstein/Treblinka/Sobibor.
Mätzig, Willi	SS-Scharführer	Bernburg/Brand/Treblinka/Sob.
**Mentz, Willi.	SS-Scharführer	Grafenesck/Hadamar/Treb./Sob.
Michalsen, Georg	SS-Scharführer	T4. Sobibor.
Michel, Hermann	SS-Oberscharführer	Grafeneck/Hartheim/Sobibor
**Miete, August	SS-Scharführer	Grafeneck/Hadamar/Treblinka
Möller, Max	SS- Unterscharführer	T4. Treblinka
Müller, Adolf (Karl)	SS-Scharführer	T4. Sobibor.
**Münzberger, Gustav	SS-Scharführer	Sonnenstein/Treblinka
Niemann, Johann	SS-Untersturmführer	Bernburg/Belzec/Sobibor.
(Josef)		
Nowak, Walter (Anton)	SS-Scharführer	Sonnenstein/Sobibor.
*Oberhauser, Josef	SS-Oberscharführer	Bern/Brand/Graf/Sonn/Belzec.
Pflanzer Alexander	SS-Unterschaführer	T4. Sobibor.
Poul	SS-Scharführer	T4. Sobibor
Pötzinger, Karl	SS-Scharführer	Bernburg/Brand/Treb/Sobibor..
Rehwald, Fritz	SS-Unterscharführer	Bern/Had/Hart/Sonn/Sobibor.
Richter, Kurt (Karl)	SS-Scharführer	Hartheim/Sonnenstein/Sob/Treb.
Reichtleitner, Franz	SS-Hauptsturmführer	Hartheim/Sobibor.
Rost, Paul	SS-Scharführer	Hartheim/Sonnenstein/Sob/Treb.
**Rum, Franz Albert	SS-Scharführer	T4-HQ
		Berlin/Treblinka/Sobibor.
Ryba, Walter	SS-Unterscharführer	T4. Killed/Sobibor revolt
Schafer, Herbert	SS-Scharführer	Sonnenstein/Sobibor.
Schemmel, Franz	SS-Scharführer	Hartheim/Sonnenstein/Sob/Treb.
Schiffner, Karl	SS-Scharführer	Sonnenstein/Belzec/Sobibor/Treb.
*Schluch, Karl	SS-Scharführer	
Schmidt, Fritz	SS- Scharführer	Grafeneck/Hadamar/Belzec.
Schreiber, Klaus	SS-Unterscharführer	Bernburg/Sonnenstein/Treblinka.
Schulz, Erich	SS- Scharfuhrer	T4. Sobibor.
Schumacher, Ernst	SS-Unterscharführer	Graf/Had/Sonn/Sob/Trebinka.
		T4. Sobibor
+**Schütt, Heinz-Hans	SS-Scharführer	Grafeneck/Hadamar/Sobibor.
Schwarz, Gottried	SS-Untersturmführer	Bernburg/Grafeneck/ Belzec.
Sidow	SS-Scharführer	T4. Treblinka.
Stadie, Otto	SS-Scharführer	Bernburg/Treblinka.
Stangl, Franz Paul	SS-Hauptsturmführer	Bernburg/Hartheim/Sob/Treb.
Steffl, Thomas	SS-Scharführer	T4-HQ Berlin/Sobibor.
Steubel, Karl	SS-Scharführer	T4. Killed/Sobibor revolt
Sporleder	SS-Scharführer	T4. Sobibor
**Suchomel, Franz	SS-Scharführer	Hadamar/Treblinka/Sobibor.
Szpilny, Heinrich	SS-Scharführer	T4. Sobibor.
Tauscher, Fritz	SS-Oberscharführer	Brand/Hart/Sonn/Belzec.
Thomalla, Richard	SS-Hauptsturmführer	(Builder) Belzec/Sob/Treblinka.
+*Unverhau, Heinrich	SS-Oberscharführer	Grafeneck/Hadamar/Belzec/Sob.
Valaster, Erich Josef	SS-Scharführer	Hartheim/Belzec/Sobibor.
Vey, Kurt	SS- Scharfuhrer	Sonnenstein/Belzec/Sobibor.
Wagner, Gustav Franz	SS-Oberscharführer	Hartheim/Sobibor.

Wallerang, Bernard	SS-Scharführer	T4. Sobibor.
Weiss, Bruno	SS-Hauptscharführer	T4. Sobibor.
Wendland, Willi	SS-Scharführer	T4. S.
Werner, Kurt	SS-Scharführer	T4. Sobibor.
Widemann, Albert	SS-Obersturmbannführer	T4. Belzec.
Wirth, Christian	SS-Sturmbannführer	Brand/Graf/Had/Hart/S/B/T.
+Wolf, Franz	SS-Unterscharführer	Hadamar/Sobibor.
Wolf, Josef	SS-Unterscharführer	T4. Sobibor.
Zanker, Hans	SS-Scharführer	Sonnenstein/Belzec/Treblinka.
+*Zierk, Ernst	SS-Unterscharführer	Graf/Had/Sonn/Belzec/Sobibor.

*Prosecuted for crimes in Belzec: +Prosecuted for crimes at Sobibor: ** Prosecuted for crimes in Treblinka. Staff at all three "AR" camps was interchangeable.

Note: T4-euthanasia practitioner: B-Belzec: S- Sobibor: T-Treblinka: KZ-concentration camp guard: PO- Police Officer: WSS- Waffen. Euthanasia centers sometimes abbreviated.

Table 24: Community Towns Subjected to Deportation to Belzec[532]

1. Annopol	2. Badzanow	3. Baligrod
4. Baranow**	5. Belz	6. Belzec
7. Belzyce	8. Bezdziedza	9. Biala
10. Bialy Kamień	11. Biecz**	12. Bilgoraj
13. Bircza	14. Biskupice,	15. Blazowa
16. Blizyn	17. Bobowa**	18. Bobrka
19. Bochnia**	20. Bolechow	21. Bolszowce
22. Bororodczany	23. Boroszczow	24. Boryslaw
25. Brody	26. Brzesko	27. Brzeszow
28. Brzezany**	29. Brzozdowce	30. Brzozow
31. Brzuchowice	32. Buczacz,	33. Budzanow
34. Bukaczowce	35. Bursztyn	36. Busk
37. Buszcza	38. Bychawa	39. Chelm
40. Chocim	41. Chodel	42. Chodorow
43. Chorostkow	44. Chrzanow	45. Chyrow
46. Czeczersk	47. Czieszanow**	48. Czarny Dunajec
49. Czernelica	50. Czorsztyn	51. Czortkow
52. Czudec	53. Dabrowa Tarnow**	54. Delatyn
55. Dalnicz	56. Debica*	57. Dobczyce
58. Dobromil	59. Dobrowa-Tarno**	60. Dolina
61. Domaradz	62. Drohobycz	63. Drybin
64. Dubienka**	65. Dukla*	66. Dukla Frysztak*

67. Dynow	68. Dzialoszyce**	69. Dzwinogrod
70. Firlej **	71. Frampol**	72. Garbatka**
73. Gdow	74. Gdowca	75. Glogow* **
76. Golcowa	77. Goraj	78. Gorlice **
79. Grodek Jagiellonski	80. Grabow	81. Grodek
82. Grodzisko	83. Grzymalow	84. Gwozdziec
85. Gwoznica	86. Halicz	87. Horodlo
88. Horodenka	89. Horyniec**	90. Hrubieszow **
91. Husiatyn	92. Huszlew	93. Izbica
94. Jablonow	95. Janow	96. Janow Lubelski,**
97. Jaryczow	98. Jaroslaw**	99. Jasiennica Ros**
100. Jaslo**	101. Jawornik Polski	102. Jaworow
103. Jaworzec	104. Jedlica	105. Jezierna
106. Jezierzany	107. Jordanow**	108. Jozefow* **
109. Kalusz**	110. Kamien	111. Kamionka Strumi**
112. Karolowka	113. Kazimierz Dolny	114. Kazimierz Wisla**
115. Klodno	116. Knihiczyn	117. Kock
118. Kolaczyce	119. Kolbuszowa	120. Kolomyja **
121. Komancz	122. Komarow	123. Komarow Osada**
124. Konskowola**	125. Kopyczynce**	126. Kopylow
127. Korczyna**	128. Korolowka	129. Koropce
130. Kosow**	131. Kozlowa	132. Kozowa
133. Krakow * **	134. Krasiczyn	135. Krasnik**
136. Krasnystaw	137. Kroscienko**	138. Krosno*
139. Krownica	140. Kruhow	141. Krynica Zdroj
142. Krystnopol	143. Krzeszow	144. Kulikow
145. Kurow	146. Kuty	147. Labowa
148. Lack	149. Lesko**	150. Lezajsk**
151. Limanowa*	152. Lubaczow **	153. Lubartow**
154. Lublin **	155. Lubycza Krolewska	156. Lviv* **
157. Lancut**	158. Laszczow**	159. Leczyn
160. Lopatyn	161. Losice	162. Magierow
163. Majdan Gorny	164. Makow **	165. Markowiec
166. Maryampol	167. Medenica gm	168. Medrzechow
169. Michalowice	170. Michow**	171. Miechow**
172. Miedzyrzec Pod.	173. Mielec*	174. Mielnica
175. Mikolajow	176. Mikulince	177. Modliborzyce **
178. Monasterzyska	179. Mosciska	180. Mosty Male

181. Mosty Wielkie	182. Muszyna	183. Myslenice
184. Myslowice	185. Narajow	186. Narol
187. Niebieszczany	188. Niebylec	189. Niemirow
190. Niepolomice**	191. Niewiarow	192. Nowotaniec
193. Nowa Gora	194. Nowy Sacz**	195. Nowy Targ*
196. Nowy Wisnicz	197. Obertyn	198. Olesko
199. Oleszynce**	200. Olkusz	201. Olpiny
202. Opole Lubelski	203. Orchowek	204. Orzechowka
205. Orzyszkowice	206. Osada	207. Ostrow
208. Peczeniczyn	209. Piaski	210. Pieczychwosty
211. Pielnia	212. Pilzno**	213. Pistyn
214. Piwniczna	215. Podbor	216. Podhajce
217. Podwoloczyska	218. Pomorzany	219. Potylicz
220. Probuzna	221. Proszowice	222. Przeclaw
223. Przemysl**	224. Przemyslany	225. Przworsk
226. Pulawy	227. Rabka**	228. Radomysl - Wielki
229. Radymno**	230. Radziechow **	231. Radzyn
232. Rawa Ruska	233. Rejowiec	234. Rohatyn
235. Ropczyce	236. Rozdol	237. Roznow
238. Rozwadow*	239. Rudki	240. Ryglica
241. Rymanow**	242. Rzeczyca	243. Rzeszow**
244. Sadowa- Wisznia	245. Sambor	246. Sandomierz**
247. Sanok **	248. Sasow	249. Schodnica
250. Sedziszow**	251. Siedlce	252. Siedliska
253. Siedliszcze	254. Siennica Rozana	255. Skala Podlaska**
256. Skalat	257. Skalbmierz	258. Skawina
259. Skole	260. Skotniki	261. Slomnik
262. Sniatyn	263. Sokal	264. Sokolow
265. Stalowawola	266. Stanislawlow **	267. Stara Slupia
268. Stary Sacz	269. Stary Sambor	270. Stebnik
271. Steniatyn	272. Strusow	273. Stryj
274. Strzeliska Nowe	275. Strzylka	276. Strzyzow
277. Suchystaw	278. Swierze	279. Szczucin
280. Szczawnica	281. Szczebrzeszyn **	282. Szczerzec
283. Tarnobrzeg**	284. Tarnogrod **	285. Tarnopol **
286. Tarnow **	287. Tarnowka	288. Tartakow
289. Tarutino	290. Tlumacz	291. Tluste
292. Tokarnia	293. Tomaszow**	294. Lubelski.
295. Trawniki	296. Trembowla **	297. Truskawiec
298. Tuchow**	299. Turka**	300. Turobib
301. Tyczyn	302. Tyszowce*	303. Uchanie
304. Uhnow	305. Ulanow	306. Urzędow

307. Ustrzyki Dolne	308. Wawolnica**	309. Wesola**
310. Wieliczka*	311. Wielopole-Skrz.**	312. Wisnicz
313. Witkow Nowy	314. Wlodawa	315. Wola Janienicka
316. Wolbrom	317. Zabia	318. Zablotow
319. Zabno**	320. Zagorz	321. Zakliczyn
322. Zaklikow	323. Zakrzowek	324. Zalesie
325. Zaleszczyk	326. Zamosc **	327. Zarnowiec
328. Zaslaw	329. Zator	330. Zawichost**
331. Zbaraz	332. Zborow	333. Zeldec
334. Zloczow	335. Zmigrod	336. Zolkiew
337. Zolkiewka**	338. Zolynia	339. Zurawno
340. Zwierzyniec	341. Zydanow	342. Zydaczow

Bibliography

Arad, Yitzhak, *Belzec, Sobibor, Treblinka: The Operation Reinhard Death Camps*, New York (rev. ed.) 1999.

Berenstein, T, "Eksterminacja ludnosci zydowskiej w dystrykcie Galicja 1941-43," in: *Biuletyn Zydowskiego Instytutu Historycznego*, No 61, Warsaw, January - March 1967.

Black, Peter R., "Rehearsal for Reinhardt? Odilo Globocnik and the Lublin Selbstschutz," in: *Central European History*, vol. 25, No. 2, 1992, pp. 204-226.

Blatt, Thomas, *Sobibor: The Forgotten Revolt. A Survivor's Report*, Issaquah, WA 1998.

Breitman, Richard, *The Architect of Genocide: Himmler and the Final Solution*, New York 1991.

----------, *Official Secrets: What the Nazis Planned, What the British and Americans knew*, London 1999.

Browder, George C., *Hitler's Enforcers*, London 1996.

Browning, Christopher R., *The Path to Genocide: Essays on the Launching of the Final Solution*, New York, 1992.

----------, "Beyond Warsaw and Lodz: Perpetrating the Holocaust in Poland," in: James S. Pacy and Alan P. Wertheimer (eds.), *Perspectives of the Holocaust. Essays in Honour of Raul Hilberg*, Oxford 1995.

----------, *Fateful Months: Essays on the Emergence of the Final Solution*, New York 1985.

----------, *Ordinary Men: Reserve Police Battalion 101 and the Final Solution in Poland*, New York, 1991.

----------, "A Final Decision for the Final Solution? The Reigner Telegram Reconsidered," in: *Holocaust and Genocide Studies 10* (Spring 1966).

----------, *The Final Solution and the German Foreign Office*, Cambridge 1978.

---------, *Nazi Policy, Jewish Workers, German Killers*, Cambridge 2000.

Büchler, Yehoshua, "Kommandostab Reichsführer-SS. Himmler's Personal Murder Brigade 1941," in: *Holocaust and Genocide Studies 1*, 1986.

Burleigh, Michael, *Death and Deliverance: Euthanasia in Germany 1900-1945*, Cambridge 1994.

----------, *The Third Reich*, London 2000.

Burrin, Philippe, *Hitler and the Jews*, New York 1994.

Chrosciewicz, T., "Sprawozdanie o wynikach dochodzeń w sprawie obozu zaglady w Belzcu," in: *Biuletyn Glownej Komisji Badania Zbrodni Hitlerowskich w Polsce*, vol. XIII, Warsaw 1960.

Chroust, Peter/Pross, Christian, *Cleansing the Fatherland: Nazi Medicine and Racial Hygiene*: (transl. by Belinda Cooper), London 1994.

Elkins, Michael, *Forged in Fury*, London 1982.

Ezergalis, Andrew, *Nuremberg Laws* (unpublished lecture), Weiner Library, London, 1997.

Feuchtwanger, E.J., *The Holocaust in Latvia 1941-1944*, Riga 1996.

Friedlander, Henry, *The Origins of Nazi Genocide: From Euthanasia to the Final Solution*, London 1995.

Fröhlich, E., (ed.), *Die Tagebücher von Joseph Goebbels*, Munich 1987.

Gerlach, Christian: Die Wannsee-Konferenz, das Schicksal der deutschen Juden und Hitlers Grundsatzentscheidung, alle Juden Europas zu ermordern, in: *Werkstattgeschichte 18* (1997), 7-44;

----------, The Wannsee Conference, the Fate of German Jews, and Hitler's Decision in Principle to Exterminate All European Jews, in: *Journal of Modern History 12*, 1998, 759-812.

Gilbert, Martin. *Atlas of the Holocaust*, London 1993.

----------, *Holocaust Journey: Travelling in Search of the Past*, London, 1997.

----------, *The Holocaust: The Jewish Tragedy*, London 1987.

Golhagen, Daniel Jonah. *Hitler's Willing Executioners: Ordinary Germans and the Holocaust*, London, 1997.

Götz, Aly, "Jewish Resettlement," in: Ulrich Herbert (ed.), *Reflections on the Political Prehistory of the Holocaust*, Oxford 2000, pp. 53-82.

----------, *National Socialist Extermination Policy and the Extermination of the European Jews*, London 1999.

Grabitz, Helga and Wolfgang Schefler, *Die letze Spüren ghetto Warschau. SS-Arbeitslager Trawniki, Action Entefest*, Berlin 1988.

Heberer, Patricia "Targeting the 'Unfit' and Radical Public Health Strategies in Nazi Germany," in: Donna Ryan and Stan Schuchman (eds.), *Deaf People in Hitler's Europe:1933-1945*, Washington, D.C., Gallaudet University Press, 2002.

----------. "'Exitus Heute' in Hadamar: The Hadamar Facility and 'Euthanasia,'" in: *Nazi Germany* (PhD Dissertation, University of Maryland at College Park 2001.

Hohenstein, Alexander, *Wartheländisches Tagebuch aus den Jahren 1941/42*, Stuttgart 1961.

Höß, Rudolf, *Commandant of Auschwitz*, London 1961.

Hilberg, Raul, *The Destruction of the European Jews* (3 vols.), Chicago 1961 (rev. ed), New York 1985.

----------, *Documents of Destruction. Germany and Jewry 1933 -1945,* London 1977.

Kershaw, Ian. *Hitler 1936-1945*, vol. II – "Nemisis," London 2000.

Klee, Ernst. *Euthanasie im NS-Staat:Die Vernichtung "lebensunwertes Lebens,"* Fischer Taschenbuch Verlag, Frankfurt-am-Main 1986.

----------,"Von der 'T4' zur Judenvernichtung: Die 'Aktion Reinhard' in den Vernichtungslagern Belzec, Sobibor und Treblinka," in: Götz Aly, *Aktion T4 1939-1945: Die "Euthanasie"-Zentrale in der Tiergartenstraße 4,* Edition Hentrich, Berlin 1987), 147-152;

----------, *Was sie taten - was sie wurden. Ärzte, Juristen und andere Beteiligte am Kranken- und Judenmord,* Frankfurt-am-MainMain 1986.

Klee, Ernst. Dressen, Willi. Riess, Volker (eds.), *Those were the Days: The Holocaust as seen by the Perpetrators and Bystanders,* London 1991.

Klemperer, Victor, *I Shall Bear Witness: The Diaries of Victor Klemperer 1933-41* vol. I (abridged and translated by Martin Chalmers), London 1998.

----------, *To the Bitter End: The Diaries of Victor Klemperer 1942-1945*, vol. II (abridged and translated by Martin Chalmers), London 1999.

Klukowski, Zygmunt, *Diary from the Years of Occupation 1939-1944* (transl. from the Polish by George Klukowski, Andrew Klukowski and Helen Klukowski May (eds.), Chicago 1993.

Kola, Andrzej, *Belzec: The Nazi Camp for Jews in the Light of Archaeological Sources:Excavations 1997-1999,* Warsaw 2000.

Lanzmann, Claude, *Shoah: An Oral History of the Holocaust,* New York 1985.

Longerich, Peter, "Die Eskalation der NS-Juedenverfolgung zur 'Endlösung': Herbst 1939 bis sommer 1942," in: *Politik der Vernichtung:Eine Gesamtdarstellung der Nationalsozialistische Judenverfolgung,* Munich 1998.

----------, (in association with Dieter Pohl), *Die Ermordung der europäischen Juden:Eine umfassende Dokumentation des Holocaust 1941-1945*, Munich 1989.

----------, *The Unwritten Order: Hitler's Role in the Final Solution,* London 2001.

----------, *Politik der Vernichtung:Eine Gesamtdarstellung der nationalsozialistischen Judenverfolgung,* Munich 1998.

(*Author?), *Lwiwska zaliznicja, Istorija I suczasnist,* L'viv 1996.

336

Madajczyk, Czeslaw, *Zamojszczyzna - Sonderlaboratorium SS: Zbior documentow poskich i niemieckich z okresu okupacji hitlerowskie*, Warsaw 1977.

McFarland-Icke, *Nurses in Nazi Germany: Moral Choice in History*, New Jersey 1999.

O'Neil, Robin, "Belzec: A Reassessment of the Number of Victims," in: *East European Jewish Affairs*, vol. 29, Nos -1-2 (Summer-Winter) 1999.

----------, "Belzec - the Forgotten Death Camp," in: *East European Jewish Affairs*, vol. 28, No. 2 (Winter) 1998-9.

----------, *The Belzec Death Camp and the Origins of Jewish Genocide in Galicia* (unpublished PhD Thesis).

"Opening and Closing Speeches of the Chief Prosecutors Sitting at Nuremberg 1945-1946," in: International Military Tribunal: The Trial of German War Criminals. (2 vols.), London 1946.

Paechter, Heinz, *Nazi Deutsch*, New York 1944.

Pankiewicz, Tadeusz, *The Krakow Ghetto Pharmacy*, New York 1987.

Peter, Janusz, ("Kordian"), "W Belzcu podczas okupacji", in: *Tomaszowskie za okupacji*, Tomaszow Lubelski 1991.

Piesakowski, Tomasz; *The Fate of Poles in the USSR, 1939-1989*, London 1990.

Pohl, Dieter, *Nationalsozialistische Judenverfolgung in Ostgalizien 1941-1944*. Munich 1996.

----------, *Von der 'Judenpolitik' zum Judenmord: Der Distrikt Lublin des Generalgouvernments 1939-1944*, Frankfurt-am-Main 1993.

----------, *Nationalsozialistische Juden verfogung in Ostgalizien. Organisation und Durchführung eines staatlichen Massenverbrechens*, Munich 1996.

----------, "Hans Krüger and the Murder of the Jews in the Stanislawow Region (Galicia)," in: *Yad Vashem Studies XXVI*, Jerusalem 1997.

Polonsky, Antony, "Belzec: Rudolf Reder," in: *Polin - Studies in Polish Jewry*, vol. 13, (2000).

Poprzeczny, Joseph, *Origins of Nazi Plans for Eastern Settlement and Extermination*, n.d., Melbourne 1999.

Poprzeczny, Joseph and Carolyn Simmonds, "Origins of Nazi Plans for Eastern Settlement and Extermination," in: Jeremy Moon and Bruce Stone (eds.), *Power and Freedom in Modern Politics*, University of Western Australia Press 2002.

Präger, W. and W. Jacomeyer (eds.), *Das Diensttagebuch des deutschen Generalgouverneurs in Polen 1939-1943*, Stuttgart 1975.

Provan, Charles D., *Kurt Gerstein and the Capacity of the Gas Chamber at Belzec*, (unpublished article), Monongahela (USA) 1996.

Pucher, Siegfried J., "... in der Bewegung führend tätig," Odilo Globocnik-Kämpfer für den 'Anschluss,' *Vollstrecker des Holocaust*, Klagenfurt/Celovec 1997.

Reder, Rudolf, *"Belzec,"* Zydowski Instytut Historyczny, Krakow 1945, English transl. in: *Polin - Studies in Polish Jewry*, vol. 13, London 2000.

Rich, David A., "Reinhard's Foot Soldiers: Soviet Trophy Documents and Investigative Records as Sources," in: John K. Roth and Elizabeth Maxwell (eds.), *Remembering for the Future: the Holocaust in an Age of Genocide*, vol. 1 (History), Basingstoke 2001.

Roques, Henri, *The 'Confessions' of Kurt Gerstein*, Cosa Mesa (USA) 1989.

Rückerl, Adalbert, *NS-Vernichtungslager im Spiegel Deutschstrafprozesse,: Belzc, Sobibor, Treblinka, Chelmno*, Munich, 1977.

Sandkühler, Thomas, "Anti-Jewish Policy, and the Murder of the Jews in District of Galicia 1941-1942," in: *National Socialist Extermination Policy*, Oxford 2000.

----------, *Endlösung in Galitzien. Judenmord in Ostpolen und die Rettungsinitiativen von Berthold Beitz*, Bonn 1996.

Sereny, Gitta, *Into the Darkness: An Examination of Conscience*, London 1974.

Szrojt, Eugeniusz, "Oboz zaglady w Belzcu," in: *Biuletyn Glowej Komisji Badania Zbrodni Niemieckich w Polsce*, vol. III, Warsaw1947.

Thompson, Larry Vern, *Nazi Administrative Conflict: The Struggle for Executive Power in the General Government of Poland 1939-1943* (Doctoral Thesis), University of Wisconsin 1967.

Tregenza, Michael, "Belzec Death Camp," in: *Wiener Library Bulletin*, vol. XXX, London 1977.

----------, "Christian Wirth a pierwsza faza Akcji Reinhard," in: *Zeszyty Majdanka*, vol. XXVI, Lublin 1992.

----------, "Report on the Archaeological Investigation at the Site of the Former Nazi Extermination Camp in Belzec, Poland, 1997-1999," (unpublished report), Lublin 1999.

----------, "Belzec - Das vergessene Lager des Holocaust," in: Ingrid Wojak and Peter Hayes/Fritz Bauer Institut (eds.), *"Arisierung im Nationalsozialismus. Volksgemeinschaft, Raub und Gedächtnis,"* Jahrbuch 2000, New York/(Frankfurt-am-Main 2000.

Wells, Leon W., *The Death Brigade: The Janowska Road*, New York 1978.

Witte, Peter, "Two Decisions Concerning the 'Final Solution of the Jewish Question': Deportations to Lodz and the Mass Murder in Chelmno," in: *Holocaust and Genocide Studies*, 9/3, London/Jersusalem 1995.

----------, "A New Document on the Deportation and Murder of Jews during 'Einsatz Reinhardt' 1942," in: *Holocaust and Genocide Studies*, vol. 15, London/Jerusalem 2001.

----------, *Der Dienstkalender Heinrich Himmler 1941/2*, Hamburg 1999.

Zajdlerowa, Zoë, *The Dark Side of the Moon*, (John Coutouvidis and Thomas Lane, eds.), London 1989.

Secondary Sources

Abel, Theodore, *Why Hitler Came to Power*, Cambridge (Mass.) 1986.

Adelson, Alan, and Lapides, Robert, *Lodz Ghetto: Inside a Community Under Siege*, London 1989.

----------, Krakowski, Schmuel and Spektor, Schmuel, (eds.), *The Einsatzgruppen Reports: Selections from the Dispatches of the 'Nazi Death Squads' Campaign Against the Jews, July 1941- January 1943*, New York 1989.

----------, Gutman, Yisrael, Margaliot, Abraham (eds.), *Documents of the Holocaust,* Jerusalem 1981.

Arendt, Hannah, *The Banality of Evil: Eichmann in Jerusalem*, New York 1963.

Bankier, David, *The Germans and the Final Solution*, Oxford 1992.

Belzec (brochure), Warsaw 1967.

Blumenthal, Nachman (ed.), "Belzec," in: *Dokumenty i Materialy z Czasow Okupacji Niemieckiej w Polsce*, vol. I (Obozy), Lodz 1946.

Broszat, Martin, "Sozial Motivation und Führer-Bindung des Nationalsocialiismus," in: *Vierteljahrshefte für Zeitgeschichte*, No. 18, Munich 1970.

----------, *The Hitler State: The Foundation and Development of the Internal Structure of the Third Reich*, London 1981.

----------, "Hitler and the Genesis of the Final Solution: An Assessment of David Irving's Thesis," Yad Vashem Studies, vol. XIII, Jerusalem 1979.

Berenstein, Tatiana, "Eksterminacja zydowskiej w tzw, dystrykcie Galicja," in: BZIH, H. 61, Warsaw 1967.

Boshyk, Yuri (ed.), *Ukraine During World War II. History and its Aftermath*, Edmonton 1986.

Braham, Randolf, *The Politics of Genocide. The Destruction of Hungarian Jewry*, New York 1982 (2 vols).

Bullock, Alan, Hitler: *A Study in Tyranny* (rev. ed.), New York 1962.

Burleigh, Michael (ed.), *Confronting the Nazi Past*, London 1996.

----------, *Germany Turns Eastward: A Study of 'Ostforschung' in the Third Reich*, Cambridge 1988.

Cesarani, David (ed.), *The Final Solution: Origins and Implementation*, London 1994.

Dabrowska, D.; Wein, A.; Weiss, A. (eds.), *Pinkas Hakehillot. "Eastern Galicia" - Encyclopaedia of Jewish Communities in Poland*, vol. 3, New York 1980.

Dawidowicz, Lucy, S., *The War against the Jews 1933-1945*, London 1987.

Diekmann, Christopher, *The War and Killing of the Lithuanian Jews: National Socialist Extermination Policy*, Oxford 2000.

Fest, Joachim, *Hitler*, London 1974.

----------, *Das Gesicht des Dritten Reiches. Profile einer totalitärien Herrschaft*, Munich 1993.

Fleming, Gerald, *Hitler and the Final Solution*, London 1985.

Friedman, Tuviah, *Schupo-Kriegsverbrecher von Stanislau vor dem Wiener Volksgericht -Dokumentationssammlung*, Haifa 1957.

----------, *Nazi Hunter*, London 1961.

Garrard, John, "The Nazi Holocaust in the Soviet Union: Interpreting Newly-Opened Russian Archives," in: *East European Jewish Affairs*, vol. 25, 2, London 1995.

Gellately, Robert, *The Gestapo and German Society*, Oxford 1988.

Gilbert, Martin, *Auschwitz and the Allies: How the Allies responded to the news of Hitler's Final Solution*, London 1981.

----------, *The Jews of Russia: Their History in Maps*, London 1986.

Gregor, Neil, *Nazism*, London 2000.

Bogdan Musial, *Deutsche Zivilverwaltung und Judenverfolgung im Generalgouvernement*, Wiesbaden 1999

Kahane, David, *Lviv Ghetto Diary*, Massachusetts 1990.

Kaplan, Chaim; Katsh, Abraham (ed.), *Scroll of Agony: A Warsaw Diary*, Indianapolis 1999.

Kehr, Helen: Langmaid, Janet, *The Nazi Era 1919-1945: A Select Bibliography of Published Works from the Early Roots to 1980*, London 1982.

Kevles, Daniel, *In the Name of Eugenics: Genetics and the Uses of Human Heredity*, London 1986.

Klee, Ernst, *'Euthanasia' in NS-Staat: Die 'Vernichtung lebensunwerten Lwebens,'* Frankfurt-am-Main 1986.

Klemperer, Victor, *The Language of the Third Reich: LTI, lingua tertii imperii : A Philologist's Notebook*, London 1999.

Knoop, Hans, *The Menten Affair*, London 1979.

Krausnik, Helmut; Martin Broszat, *Anatomy of the SS State*, London 1968.

----------, Hans-Heinrich, Wilhelm, *Die Truppe des Weltanschauungskrieges: Die Einsatzgruppen der Sicherheitspolizei und des SD, 1938 -1942*, Stuttgart 1981.

Landau, Ronnie, *The Nazi Holocaust*, London 1992.

Lewin, Abraham; Antony Polonski (ed.), *A cup of Tears: A Diary of the Warsaw Ghetto*, London 1990.

Lifton, Robert Jay, *The Nazi Doctors: Medical Killing and the Psychology of Genocide*, New York 1986.

MacPherson, Malcolm, *The Last Victim*, London 1984.

Magosci, Paul-Robert, *Galicia: A Historical Survey and Bibliography Guide*, London 1985.

Marrus, Michael R., *The Holocaust in History*, New York 1989.

Mayer, Arnold J., *Why Did The Heavens Not Open: The Final Solution in History*, London 1990.

----------, *Der Krieg als Kreuzzug. Das Deutsche Reich, Hitler's Wehrmacht und die Endlösung*, Reinbeck 1989.

Marshall, Robert, *In the Sewers of Lviv: The Last Sanctuary from the Holocaust*, London 1990.

Mazower, Mark, *Dark Continent*, London 1999.

----------, *Inside Hitler's Greece: The Experience of Occupation, 1941- 1944*, London 2001.

Mommsen, Hans, *Realisation of the Unthinkable*, Jerusalem 1983.

Mulligan, Timothy, *The Politics of Illusion and Empire. German Occupation Policy in the Soviet Union 1942-43*, New York 1988.

Musial, Bogdan, "The Origins of Operation Reinhard: The Decision-Making Process for the Mass Murder of the Jews in the Generalgouvernment," in: *Yad Vashem Studies*, vol. XXV111, Jerusalem 2000.

Musmanno, Michael A., *The Eichmann Commandos*, London 1969.

Ogorreck, Ralf, *Die Einsatzgruppen der Sicherheitspolizei und des SD im Rähmen der Geneses der Endlösung*, Berlin 1996.

Orth, Karin; Herbert, U.; Dieckmann, C. (eds.), *Die nationalsozialistischen Konzentrationslager 1933 bis 1945. Entwicklung und Struktur*, Göttingen 1998.

----------, *Das System der nationalsozialistischen Konzntrationslager. Eine politische Organisationsgeschichte*, Hamburg 1999.

----------, *Die Konzentrationslager-SS. Sozialstrukturelle Analysen und biographische Studien*, Göttingen 2000.

Pacy, James S.; Wertheimer, Alan P. (eds.), *Perspectives on the Holocaust: Essays in Honour of Raul Hilberg*, London 1995.

Pauley, Bruce, *Hitler and the Forgotten Nazis: A History of Austrian National Socialism*, Chapel Hill 1981.

----------, *Western Galicia and Silesia*, vol. 4, London 1984.

Piper, Franciszek, *Auschwitz. How Many Perished: Jews, Poles, Gypsies*, Oswięcim 1996.

The New Order in Poland, Polish Ministry of Information, London 1942.

Proctor, Robert N., *Racial Hygiene: Medicine under the Nazis*, Oxford 1988.

Rashke, Richard, *Escape from Sobibor: The Heroic Story of the Jews Who Escaped from a Nazi Death Camp*, Boston 1982

Reitlinger, Gerald, *The Final Solution: The Attempt to Exterminate the Jews of Europe, 1939-1945*, London 1953.

Ringelblum, Emanuel, *Chronicle of the Warsaw Ghetto*, Warsaw 1983.

Russell of Liverpool, *Scourge of the Swastika*, London 1954.

Salsitz, Amalie, *Against All Odds*, New York 1990.

Schellenberg, Walter, *The Schellenberg Memoirs*, London 1956.

Shirer, William L., *The Rise and fall of the Third Reich*, London 1960.

Spektor, Shmuel, "Aktion 1005 - Effacing the Murder of Millions," in: *Holocaust and Genocide Studies*, No. 5, London 1990.

Sword, Keith, *The Soviet Take-Over of Polish Eastern Provinces 1939-1941*, London 1991.

Sydor, Charles W., *Soldiers of Destruction: The SS Death's Head Division, 1933- 1945*, Princeton 1977.

Tory, Avraham; Gilbert, Martin (eds.), *Surviving the Holocaust. The Kovno Ghetto Diary*, Cambridge (Mass.) 1990.

Trunk, Isaiah, *Judenrat: The Jewish Councils in Eastern Europe Under Nazi Occupation*, New York 1972.

Vern, Thomas Larry, "Friedrich-Wilhelm Krüger: Höherer SS-und

Polizeifuehrer Ost," in: Smelser, Ronald; Syring, Enrico (eds.), *Die SS: Elite unter dem Totenkopf: 30 Lebensläufe*, Paderborn 2000.

Wiernik, Yankiel, *A Year in Treblinka*, New York 1945.

Weindling, Paul, *Health, Race and German Politics between National Unification and Nazism 1870-1945*, London 1989.

Willenberg, Samuel, *Revolt at Treblinka*, Warsaw 1992.

Wistrich, Robert S., *Who's Who in Nazi Germany*, London 1982.

Yahil, Leni, *The Holocaust: The Fate of European Jewry 1932-1945*, Oxford 1990.

Zygmunt, Albert, *The Murder of the Lviv Professors - July 1941*, Wroclaw 1989.

Miscellaneous Papers presented at the *Action Reinhardt* Conference held in Lublin, Poland, 7-9 November 2002.

The Beginning of Action Reinhardt; Liquidations of the First Ghetto in the Lublin District.

Peter Witte, *Functioning of the Death Camps in Belzec and Sobibor.*

Tomasz Kranz, *The Role of KZ Majdanek in Action Reinhard.;*

Robert Kuwalek, *The Transit Ghettos in the Lublin District.*

Janina Kielbon, *Deportations of Jews to the Lublin District from outside the General Government.*

Andrzej Zbikowski, *Katzmann's Report and Extermination of Galician Jews.*

Felicja Karay, *Work Camps for Jews during Action Reinhardt.*

Thomas Sandkühler, *Economical Exploitations: Nazi Planning and Direct Implementations.*

Wolfgang Scheffler, *German Perpetrators and Postwar Trials.*

Helga Grabitz, *Trials of the Perpetrators in Germany.*

Witold Kulesza, *Prosecuting the Perpetratord in Poland - The Polish Administration of Justice.*

Peter Black, *Trawnikimänner, Non-German Auxiliary Staff during Action Reinhard.*

Patricia Heberer, *Continuity in Killing Operations: 'T4' Perpetrators and Action Reinhardt.*

Klaus Michael Mallmann; *Security Police in the Krakow District.*

Shmuel Krakowski, *Jewish Resistance in the General Government.*

Glossary

Aktion Reinhardt: The coded name used for the Nazi program in their Jewish Genocidal policies.[533]

T4: The center for state sponsored murder of so-called 'incurables'; T4 is a shortened title taken from the address of the central office in Berlin, Tiergartenstrasse 4.

BDC: Berlin Document Center - Personnel files of members of the SS. [534]

BdO: Befehshaber der Ordnungspolizei (Commander of Orpo – Order Police).

BdS: Befehlshaber der Sicherheitspolizei und des SD (Commander-in-Chief of the Sipo-SD).

DAW: Deutsche Ausrstüngs-Werke (German Arms Factories).

Einsatz/Einsatzgruppen: Groups/Security Police and SD.[535]

GDG: Gouverneur des Distrikts Galizien (Governor of Galicia).

GDL: Ibid. (Governor of Lublin District).

GedOb: Generaldirektion der Ostbahn (Director of Eastern Rail).

Gestapo: Secret State Police.[536]

GG: General Government. Main part of occupied Poland made up of four districts (later five including Galicia).

GPK: *Grenzpolizei - Kommissariat*: A regional frontier HQ of the Grenzpolizei-controlled Grenzposten (outposts).

Gauleiter: The supreme territorial or regional Nazi Party authority, employed in Germany and some annexed territories. The geographical units were termed *Gaue*, headed by Gauleiter (the term is singular and plural).

Gestapo: Secret State Police.

Hilfspolizei: Auxiliary Police, recruited from Nazi Party formations that assisted the regular police and security services in various functions but were not part of the Ordnungspolizei (Orpo).

HHE: Used to identify the main protagonists of genocide: Himmler-Heydrich-Executive within the RSHA (Reich Security Main Office).

HSSPF: Höhere SS- und Polizeiführer *(Senior SS and Police Commander)*: Himmler's personal representative in each district and liaison officer with the military district commander and regional authorities (Nominally the commander of all SS and police units in the occupied territories).

KdF: Hitler's Chancellery.

KdO: Kommandeur der Ordnungspolizei (See Ordnungspolizei).

KdS: Kommandeur der Sicherheitspolizei und des SD (See Sipo-SD). Hans Krüger was the KdS Regional Commander in Stanislawow. Krüger's immediate superior was Dr. Schöngarth, the KdS commander of the SD in Krakow. The KdS were the cadre responsible for mass executions and resettlement. The KdO (units) were on the periphery of events and only utilised when requested by the KdS commanders.

KdSch: Kommandeur der Shutzpolizei (Commander of the city police).

Kreishauptleute/Kreishauptman: City Governors during the occupation in Galicia. Many were with the SD and were very active in the Jewish resettlement program.

Kriminalassistent: Lowest grade of criminal police (Criminal Investigation Department).

Kriminalkommissar: The lowest rank in the upper officer class of the CID (= Obersturmführer). Promotion to Kriminalrat (=Hauptsturmführer). For the outsider, the rank alignment is very complicated: An officer can hold the rank of Kriminalkommissar but also hold a higher rank of the SS as SS-Hauptsturmführer. In many of the Security offices, the lower grade CID officer can out-rank his boss with SS rank, and although this situation should not present any problems, sometimes it led to an awkward awareness within the office.

Kripo: Kriminalpolizei (CID).

NSDAP: Nazi Party.[537]

OT: Organisation Todt was a semi-military-government agency established in 1933. Its main function was the construction of strategic highways, armament factories and military installations.

Orpo: Ordnungspolizei (Order Police): Separate from the Gestapo and Criminal police. The Orpo within Germany handled civilian matters such as traffic patrols and routine police business. However, in the occupied territories or regions—notably Poland and Russia—Orpo often had Einsatzgruppen roles, including carrying out mass killings. Since 1933, the Ordnungspolizei and Shutzpolizei had become the foot soldiers of the Nazi Security Service.

Reichsleiter: Member (s) of an executive board of the Nazi Party.

RFSS: Reichsführer-SS (Chief of all the police cadres—Himmler).

RSHA: Reichssicherheitshauptamt (Reich Security Main Office), formed in 1939 under Reinhardt Heydrich. The department included the Gestapo, the Criminal Police and the SD.[538]

SA: **Sturmabteilung** (Brown Shirts, Storm Troopers).[539]

Schupo: Shutzpolizei. Auxiliary police recruited in the eastern occupied territories from the local population.

Sipo-SD: SD Sicherheitsdienst:(+Sicherheitspolizei=Sipo-SD of the RSHA).

Selbstschutz: A militia as used by Globocnik in the early stages of Jewish oppression in the Lublin area.

Sonderdienst: A militia that replaced the Selbstschutz in name only.[540]

SS-Schutzstaffel: (Lit. "Defense echelon").

SSPF: SS- und Polizeiführer (commander of a police district i.e. Globocnik in Lublin).

Volksdeutsche: Ethnic Germans, that is, people of German origin whose families had lived outside Germany for generations. Reichsdeutsche referred to German nationals living within the pre-1939 boundaries of the Third Reich.

WVHA: Wirtschaftsverwaltungshauptamt der SS: Economic Division RSHA, which administered and supervised the vast web of concentration camps (but not including the Reinhardt camps).[541]

YVA: Yad Vashem Archives.

ZAL: Zwangsarbeitslager (Labor Camps - Janowska etc.).

zbV: Einsatzgruppen zur besonderen Verwendung (Einsatzkommando, zbV for special purposes.

Notes

[1] See: Kola, *Belzec,* Aerial Photograph, National Archives, Washington DC, USA: Film Roll No: GX 8095 33 SK, exposure 155, dated 15 May 1944, and 26th May 1940 (copies in the archives of the ROPWiM in Warsaw), reproduced in: *Air Photo Evidence,* 93-94. Although the author examined the 1940 and 1944 aerial photos on-site at Belzec, further examination of these photos has subsequently been carried out with the assistance of William Rutherford (UK) and Thomas Wise (USA) who are both experts in this field. It is with their assistance that the author has drawn his conclusions.

[2] For the deportation operations from those districts see: T. Berenstein, *'Eksterminacja ludności żydowskiej w dystrykcie Galicja 1941-43',* in: Biuletyn Żydowskiego Instytutu Historycznego, No 61, Warsaw, January - March 1967, 41 and n., and figs. 1-11 (source base of these estimates). For an outline history of the Lvov railway, edited in recent years, and information about directing Jewish transports from Lvov ghetto to Belzec in 1942-43, Cf. *Lwiwska zaliznicja-Istorija i suczasnist,* (L'viv 1996), 37.

[3] The four dedicated death camps had specific areas of operation: Sobibor (Lublin district, Netherlands, Slovakia, Reich-Protectorate, France and Minsk); Treblinka: (Warsaw, Radom, Bialystok and Lublin districts, Macedonia-Thrace, Reich, and Theresienstadt); Belzec: (Lublin, Galicia, Kraków, Germany and Austria); Chełmno: Wartheland/Reich, via Łódz. KZ/death camps -Lublin (Majdanek) Lublin District, Warsaw District and France. Auschwitz (Birkenau); Europe. (See: Hilberg, *Destruction,* vol. 3, 893, table 9-8). Another misunderstood fact that very often goes unnoticed is the present-day rail line from Kraków (west Galicia) that branches off from Jaraslow to Belzec. During the resettlement transports of 1942-43, all traffic destined from the south and west was routed through Rawa-Ruska and Lvov.

[4] Klukowski, *Diary,* 73.

[5] Adapted plan of Belzec village by kind permission of Martin Gilbert. See: Gilbert, *Holocaust Journey,* 430.

[6] TAL/OKBZ: Report dated 11 April 1946. The construction commenced on 1 November 1941. Initially, an area of 255 m x 250 m was cleared by local labour under the supervision of the SS. In 1947 the dimensions were amended to 275 m x 263 m. See also: Statement of Karl Werner Dubois who served in Belzec from April 1942 - May 1943 who gives the dimensions as 250 m x 200 m.

[7] TAL/OKBZ, Statement of Stanislaw Kozak, 14 October 1945. The file contains over 50 testimonies from local inhabitants in Belzec and Sobibor Lubelski that relate to the building of the camp and the activities of the Germans and Ukrainian guards during this period. See also: TAL/ZStL, *Belzec Case*: Sketches of Belzec camp drawn by former SS-NCOs Jührs, Unverhau, Gley and Girtzig.

[8] Gilbert, *Holocaust Journey,* 431; Kola, *Belzec,* 19; E. Sztrojt in: Kola, *Belzec,* 7; Arad, *Belzec,* 437. The location of the mass graves shown in Reder's map of Belzec is corroborated by the recent investigation.

[9] See: Kola, n 3: The Archives of the Council of Protection of Memory of Combat and Martyrdom (ROPWiM) in Warsaw. They are: (A), report from investigation results in the case of the death camp in Belzec (carried out during 10-13 October 1945); (B), protocol of excavating the cemetery in the death camp in Belzec on 12 October 1945, together with the protocol of the inspection and court (medical) forensic opinion. Among the archives of the ROPWiM are copies of aerial photographs of the Belzec

area taken during World War II. One taken on 16 May 1944 by the Luftwaffe indicates traces of levelling of the camp area to cover traces of mass graves and the camp buildings.

[10] See: Szrojt, *Belzec*.

[11] TAL/ZStL, *Belzec Case:* Statements of Heinrich Gley, 10 May 1961, Heinrich Unverhau 10 July 1961, Hans Girtzig, 18 July 1961, Kurt Franz, 14 September 1961, Robert Jührs, 11 October 1961, Karl Schluch, 11 November 1961.

[12] YVA, M 7/2-2. Diary of Wilhelm Cornides, entry for 31 August 1942. See also: Hilberg, *Documents,* 208: Sandkühler, *Endlösung*, 173.

[13] I am grateful for Billy Rutherford's expertise in arriving at these conclusions.

Tables

Arad, Yitzhak, *Belzec, Sobibor, Treblinka: The Operation Reinhard Death Camps*, New York (rev. ed.) 1999: **AR**

Berenstein, T, "Eksterminacja ludnosci zydowskiej w dystrykcie Galicja 1941-43," in: *Biuletyn Zydowskiego Instytutu Historycznego*, No 61, Warsaw, January - March 1967:**TB**

Gilbert, Martin. *Dent Atlas of the Holocaust,* London, 1993: **MG**

Yad Vashem Archives: **YVA**

[14] Activities within and outside the General Government (**GG**), focussing directly on Jewish residents.

March 1942

[15] In March 1942, 27,800 (16 transports, Lublin), and 16,700 (11 transports, Lvov) were deported to Belzec. See Dr Jozef Wassatek, unpublished document (Lublin) re deportations to Belzec. See also Reitlinger, *The Final Solution* (London 1958), 268, and Yitzhak Arad (hereafter YA), Appendix A, 383-9.

[16] County of Zamosc (Lublin). MG, Map 107. Jews in first deportation to Belzec were taken to Tomaszow Lubelski ghetto. Many Jews from the surrounding district were used as labor in the building of Belzec camp in the experimental period. Resident Jews in the village were very few, as most had fled to the Russian zone.

[17] County of Bilgoraj (Lublin). MG, Map 111.

[18] Dr Jozef Wassatek: conclusions.

[19] Ibid.

[20] County of Drohobycz (Galicia): MG Map 111. See also YA (2,000), YVA O-7/32 TB, table 4 (1,000), 24-25. March 42. See also YVA LL/2, 3/42, 3000 Jews deported to Belzec.

[21] Ibid. MG, Map 107.

[22] County of Hrubieszow (Lublin): MG, Map 107. Further deportations to Sobibor: 2.6.1942.

[23] County of Krasnystaw (Lublin): MG, Map 111. See also YA (2200), YVA O-7/32, 17.3.1942. Second transport 24. 3. 42 contained Jews from Germany, see also above, TB table 7 (2,200, 24.3.1942, 2 transports from Czechoslovakia).

[24] County of Pulawy (Lublin): MG, Map 111. See also YVA O-7/32, TB, 30.3.1942, table 9.

[25] Ibid.

[26] County of Lublin (Lublin): MG, Map 111. Lublin bore the brunt of the first resettlement transports to Belzec and nearly all the Jewish population of over 30,000 were transported to Belzec over a two-week period. MG shows two transports dated 17 (1,600) and 18-24 March (10,000). Others quote differing numbers in March and April, but overall the Jewish population of Lublin was surely murdered in Belzec. See also YA (17/3 - 14/4, 30,000); YVA (16 transports from Lublin to Belzec); TB, table 1, (17/3 - 20/4, 30,000). At a press conference on 9.7.1942, Stanislaw Mikojaczyk, the then Deputy Prime Minister in-Exile, stated: "We learned that part of the Jews from the Lublin District—26,000 of them—were directed during the night of 23-24 March, 1942, to camps at Belzec and Trawniki."

[27] County of Rawa Ruska (Galicia): TB table 8. In late February 1942 some of the first victims came from this town and were engaged in building the camp. They were all murdered during the first gassing experiments.

[28] County of Lvov (Galicia): MG, Map 111. See also YA (15/3 - 1/4), YVA (11 transports from Lvov to Belzec), YVA 0-1/32 and TB, table 1.

[29] County of Debica (Krakow): MG, Map 107. One of the very first transports to Belzec: See also YVA KK/5, 13.3.1942.

[30] County of Rawa Ruska (Galicia): See YA, YV. TR 10/517, 7-9: See also MG, Map 111, and TB, table 7.

[31] County of Pulawy (Lublin): MG, Map 111; YVA O-7/32 (Jews from Pulawy and Austria); TB, 31.3.1942.

[32] County of Lublin (Lublin): MG, Map 111. See also YA, YVA O-7/32, TB, table 8 (Jews from Austria, Germany and Czechoslovakia). Now that Piaski was the main point of Jewish embarkation to Belzec, a sequence of events was in place: For every Jew deported from Piaski to Belzec, a Jew from outside the district would replace that Jew in Piaski (e.g., 5,000 Piaski-Belzec, was replaced by 5,000 from Germany-Piaski).

[33] County of Rawa Ruska (Galicia): MG, Map 111, YA, YVA. See also Dr Wassatek, who quotes 2,000 on 19.3.1942.

[34] County of Brzezany (Galicia): MG, Map 111, and YVA.

[35] County of Rzeszow (Krakow): YVA. Further deportation to Belzec: 7.7.1942. Rzeszow was also a main transit ghetto.

[36] County of Krasnystaw (Lublin): MG, Map 111, and TB (via Lublin): Further deportation 15.9.1942 to Treblinka.

[37] County of Stanislawow (Galicia): MG, Map 111. See also YA (5,000, 31.3.1942), YVA O-1/32 (including 1,000 Hungarian Jews): TB, table 9 (5,000, 31.3.1942).

[38] In the County of Zamosc (Lublin): The nearest town to Belzec (5km).

[39] County of Lublin (Lublin): YVA.

[40] In the County of Drohobycz (Galicia): TB, table 4.

[41] County of Stanislawow (Galicia): MG, Map 111; YVA O-1/32; TB, table 9.

[42] County of Lvov (Galicia): MG, Map 111. See also YA (25-26), YVA O-7/32, TB, table 7. In May, when Jews from Zolkiew were being marched to Krasnystaw, there were shouts from local Poles: "Hey Jews, you are going to burn (Hey, Zydzi, idziecie na spalenie)." A survivor later commented: "we had heard of the death camp Belzec, but we didn't believe it." Statement of Itzhak Lichtman, see Sobibor Verdict.

April

[43] We have further complications with regard to operational dates at Belzec that are in conflict with some assessments and conclusions. The inconsistency surrounds the actual period when Belzec was closed for the re-construction of the second series of gas chambers. Unlike Treblinka, where gassings continued in the first gas chambers at the same time the second, much larger chambers were being built. The first gas chambers were inadequate due to the flimsy airtight construction. In practice, only one out of the three chambers in Belzec was operational. The facts, as we know them, arrive from and surround the statements made by Josef Oberhauser on 26.2.60 and 20.4.60, where he states Wirth left Belzec for Berlin directly after the February experimental gassings and returned with an increase in staff in time for the gassings commencing 17 March 1942. In the latter statement (12.12.62), Oberhauser refers to the suspension and new construction in late June, early July. Oberhauser, who finally left Belzec with Wirth on 1 August 1942.

[44] County of Bilgoraj (Lublin): YVA, 4.4.1942.

[45] Jewish Commission Report (Krakow): 1945 (YVA). See also Gilbert, Holocaust, 319.

[46] County of Zamosc (Lublin): Map 115; YA (1,300).

[47] County of Krasnystaw (Lublin): MG, Map 116; YVA; YA; TB, table 7, 8.4.1942.

[48] County of Kolomyja (Galicia): MG, Map 115, TB, table 5, YA (5,000). These were the first transports from Kolomyja to Belzec via Lviv and Rawa Ruska. Once the ghetto was cleared of these Jews, other Jews from the surrounding area replaced them in the ghetto: Gwozoziec, Horodenka (YA, 1,400) Jablonow, Kosow, Kuty, Obertyn, Peczenizyn (YA, 1,200), Pistyn, Sniatyn (YA, 5,000), and Zablotow (YA, 400). This was the system which operated throughout the occupied areas. Another factor was that after each resettlement transport the ghetto was reduced in size. See also YVA 0-1/32.

[49] Gilbert, Holocaust, 317.

[50] County of Krasnystaw (Lublin): MG, Map 115. YVA, YA, TB: table 7, 13.4.1942.

[51] County of Janow (Lublin): MG, Map 115; YVA; YA (2500); TB, table 2, (2,500), 12.4.1942.

[52] County of Krasnystaw (Lublin): MG, Map 115; YVA; TB, table 7, 13.4.1942.

[53] County of Rawa Ruska (Galicia): MG, Map 115. 28-30.4.1942.

[54] County of Lublin (Lublin): MG, Map 115 (also Holocaust, 317); YVA; YA; TB, 9-10.4.1942.

[55] Ibid. YVA (10 transports from Lublin to Belzec), YA, TB, table 1, 1-3 April, 1942 and 26-29 April, 1942. The overall deportations from Lublin lasted from March through April. That is reflected by the conclusions of Gilbert and YA (totals 30,000 in March).

[56] County of Lviv (Galicia): YVA, 23-29.4.1942 (11 transports from Lviv to Belzec).

[57] County of Lublin (Lublin): MG, Map 115, TB, and table 1.

[58] County of Janow (Lublin): MG, Map 115, 12.4.1942.

[59] County of Tarnopol (Galicia): YVA, 23.4.1942.

[60] County of Stanislawow (Galicia): VA, TB, table 9, PH (5000), 1.4.1942. The old, sick, the beggars were the first Jews to be deported to Belzec. The fit and healthy were being sent to the Janowska labor camp: Stanislawow, 16.4.1942, 500 Jews to Janowska, Jaworow, 5.4.1942, Jews to Janowska labor camp, Grodek Jagiellonski Jews to Janowska labor camp.

[61] County of Zamosc (Lublin): MG Map 115; YA; YVA; TB, table 11, 11.4.1942 (First day of Passover). Several hundred were also shot on the spot (Gilbert, Holocaust, 320).

[62] Dr Jozef Wassatek refers to 270 deported on 13 April 1942 from Siennica Rozana.

May

[63] County of Pulawy (Lublin): Schwarz, 137, Blatt, 29 (indicates Sobibor).

[64] County of Zamosc (Lublin): MG, Map 119.

[65] County of Bilgoraj (Lublin): Gilbert, Holocaust, 331.

[66] Ibid. YVA, TB, table 11, 24.5.1942.

[67] MG, Map 124. 1.5.1942. 2,100 Jews deported from Dortmund. There were further deportations on 27 May, 1942. It is probable that these transports went direct to Izbica or Piaski before onward journey to Sobibor or Belzec. At this time, Sobibor was taking the majority of transports as Belzec was in the process of re-building. On 10 May 1942, 1,300 Jews from the town of Chemnitz were deported to the Belzyce ghetto and in all probability finished up in Belzec or Sobibor.

[68] County of Zamosc (Lublin): YVA; TB, table 11.

[69] Ibid. MG, Map 119, YA (1000), YVA, TB table 11, 23.5.1942.

[70] Ibid. MG, Map 119, YVA, TB, table 11: 22.5.1942.

[71] See Schwarz, 143.

[72] County of Bilgoraj (Lublin): MG, Map 119; YA; YVA; TB, table 3, 8.5.1942.

[73] In the County of Zamosc (Lublin): MG, Map 119, YA (581-800), YVA, TB, table 11 (800), 22.5.1942.

[74] Ibid. YVA, TB, 27.5.1942. Many Jews from Germany and Czechoslovakia passed through Zamosc.

June

[75] Only in May 1942 did the Nazi regime begin the systematic mass deportations of Reich Jews that Hitler had decided upon the previous autumn. A similar fate befell the transports from Slovakia and Western Europe soon thereafter. Between 4 and 15 May, 12 transports containing 10,000 Reich Jews were deported to Chelmno where they were gassed. Jews from Vienna were deported to Maly Trostenets on 5 May, followed by a further 17 transports June 1942. On 22 June 1942, it was pointed out by Dr Frauendorfer, the Director of Labor in the Generalgovernement, that expulsions of Jewish labor from the ghettos was causing economic difficulties. Frauendorfer explained that Jews were part of the 100,000 skilled workers employed in the armaments industry; 800,000 workers were sent to Germany, and a further 100,000 (including Jews) were employed by the military. He further pointed out that he was solely dependent on Jewish labor, and therefore, Jewish skilled labor should be utilized and not be fodder for the SS resettlement program. While Globocnik was pulling one way to exterminate the Jews, the military were pulling the other way to retain Jewish skilled labor. A compromise was reached in September/October, 1942.

[76] County of Czortkow (Galicia): YV L L/6 3 (report dated 2 June 1945).

[77] County of Kolomyja (Galicia): Deportations probably from the ghetto that included Jews transferred from other towns in the district. YVA (1-6 shows two transports: 1st and 4th June), TB, table 6, June 1942.

[78] County of Czortkow (Galicia): YVA LL6, 6.6.1942.

[79] County of Krakow (Krakow): MG, Map 128 (7,000), YVA; YA (5,000, 1 - 6), TB, table 7, two very large transports between 1 and 6 June 1942. See also YVA KK/1, 6,000 on 1.6.1942, and 4,000 on 6.6.1942. From all other sources 10,000 is the probable number. See also Tadeusz Pankiewicz, Krakow Ghetto Pharmacy, NY, 1985, 40-53.

---

[80] County of Lviv (Galicia): YVA, this transport from Janowska camp joined up with the Kolomyja transport for Belzec in mid June. See also YVA LL/1, 24.6.42, 4,000 deported to Belzec. Lviv was spared further transports until 12 August 1942.

[81] County of Rawa Ruska (Galicia): YVA, 19.6.1942.

[82] County of Krakow (Krakow): MG, Map 128; 11-19 June 1942.

[83] County of Tarnow (Krakow): MG, Map 128, YVA, YA, 11-18 June 1942, these were very large transports. See also YVA KK/3, 11-18, June 1942, 12,000. SS-Oberführer Scherner, Police Leader, Krakow, personally directed these transports. These were the first big deportations since the Krakow transports. 40,000 Jews in the open ghetto faced 30 Schutzpolizei, 100 Polish police officers, 150 Gendarmerie, a unit of *Sonderdienst* and the Polish labor service (*Baudienst*). Two separate operations were taking place simultaneously: örtliche Aussiedlung (local resettlement) where thousands were either taken to the forests or to the local cemetery, where they were shot into pits. The residue, some eleven and a half thousand, were deported to Belzec. These actions stalled on 18 June, when the remaining (some 20,000) work Jews were sealed into the ghetto. Further actions of this kind took place in August, September and November 1942. When this transport arrived at Belzec on 13 June 1942, there was a spontaneous act of resistance. When the work Jews were removing the bodies from the gas chambers and they saw the situation, they attacked the German and Ukrainian guard. It was reported four Germans and nearly all the Jews were killed. See Archives of PZPR (Polish United Worker's Party), Documents for 1942 - Sikorski Archive London.

[84] See Schwarz, 138.

July

[85] July was a crucial month when all inhibitions were abandoned by virtue of a direct order from Himmler, who demanded rapid and complete implementation, regardless of the looming labor shortage facing the Third Reich.
See Browning, Nazi Policy, 56: "A Final Decision for the 'Final Solution'? The Riegner Telegram Reconsidered."

[86] County of Przemysl (Galicia): YVA O-7/32, YA. 27.3.1942 (via Przemysl).

[87] Ibid. YVA O-7/32, YA, 29.7.1942

[88] In the County of Debica (Krakow): MG, Map 131, (1-19), YVA O-7/32, YA. 21-25.7.1942.

[89] County of Przemysl (Galicia): YVA O-7/32, 27.7.1942, YA.

[90] County of Krosno (Krakow): YVA O-7/32, 29.7.1942.

[91] County of Czortkow (Galicia): YVA O-7/32.

[92] Arad, Belzec, 384.

[93] County of Rawa Ruska: Arad, Belzec, 384.

[94] Ibid., 384.

[95] County of Tarnow (Krakow): YVA O-7/32, 22.7.1942.

[96] County of Rzeszow (Krakow): MG, Map 131, (7-13,), YVA O-7/32 (7-19), YA, 7-18, July 1942.

[97] County of ZLoczow (Galicia): MG, Map 131, and YVA O-7/32, 15.7.1942.

[98] County of Bilgoraj (Lublin): YVA O-7/32, YA, (400, 9.7.1942).

[99] Ibid. MG, Map, 131.

[100] County of Krakow (Tarnow): YA 24-25.8.1942. See Gilbert, Holocaust Journey, 198.

[101] County of Czortkow (Galicia): YVA O-7/32, YA. 7/42.

[102] County of Rawa Ruska (Galicia): MG, 131, YVA O-7/32, TB, table 8, 27.7.1942.

[103] See Schwarz, 147 (Central ghetto).

August

[104] MG, Holocaust, 410-111). From unpublished sources: Conclusions record 40,000 (9 transports) in the Krakow district, 14 transports from Galicia (79,222), and 2 transports) Lublin (2,800): A total of 122,022, Jews deported to Belzec. Martin Gilbert records 76,000 Jews from Lviv and other towns in East Galicia to Belzec. From West Galicia, Jews from 30 communities were deported to Belzec, including 16,000 from the region of Nowy Sacz and 12,500 from Przemysl. Over 145,000 from the Galician district gassed in Belzec; Berenstein concludes a similar number.

[105] County of Jaslo (Krakow): MG, Map 141.

[106] County of Bilgoraj (Lublin): MG, Map 137, YVA, TB, table 3, 9.8.1942.

[107] See Schwarz, 137.

[108] County of Jaslo (Krakow): Unknown numbers shot or deported to transit ghettos.

[109] County of Krakow (Bochnia): MG, Map 141 (2600), YA, 3-6.8.1942, TB table 7. See also YVA L L/2 4 (report 28.5.1945).

[110] County of Krakow (Krakow): MG, Map 139, YA, YVA (25.8.1942).

[111] County of Lviv (Galicia): MG, Map 139, YA (1,200-1,500, 12.8.1942), YVA, TB, table 7, (1,260), 12.8.1942.

[112] County of Drohobycz (Galicia): MG, Map 139, YA (5000, 4-6), YVA, 6-8.8.1942.

[113] County of Krosno (Krakow): unknown numbers shot or deported via Krakow. See TB table 4 (5,000).

[114] County of Czortkow (Galicia): YA.

[115] County of Czortkow (Galicia): MG, Map 139; YA. 28.8.1942, TB table 11.

[116] County of Przemysl (Galicia): YA, YVA, TB, table 3, 27.8.42 (3,000).

[117] County of Czortkow (Galicia): MG, Map 139, YA (2,000), 27.8.1942), TB, table 3, 28.8.1942. See also YVA LL/6 26.8.1942, (2,800), including many Hungarian Jews. The remaining 312 Jews were all transferred to the Kamionka labor camp.

[118] Ibid.

[119] County of Stryj (Galicia): MG, Map 139, YVA, TB, table 10, 26.8.1942 (3,000).

[120] County of Drohobycz (Galicia): MG, Map 139, transport on 6.8.1942 (2,000), further transport on 17.8.1942 (3,000). YA (8-17, 2,500, 23-24, 2,300), YVA, TB, table 4, (5,000).

[121] County of Jaslo (Krakow): unknown numbers deported via Jaslo.

[122] County of Bilgoraj (Lublin): MG, Map 140, 18.8.1942.

[123] County of Rzeszow (Krakow): MG, Map 137, YA, YVA.

[124] County of Jaslo (Krakow): MG, Map 141.

[125] County of Lviv (Galicia): MG, Map 140, YVA, TB, table 7, 21.8.1942.

[126] County of Lviv (Galicia): YA, TB, table 7, 13.8.1943.

[127] County of Krosno (Krakow): MG, Map, 141, TB table 7, 13.8.42.

[128] County of Jaslo (Krakow): MG, Map 141, YA: 16-20.8.1942.

[129] County of Tarnopol (Galicia): MG, Map 139, YA (200), TB, table 11, 28. 8.1942.

[130] See Schwarz, 140, TB table 11.

[131] County of Krosno (Krakow): MG, Map 141, YA, YVA, TB, table 3, 10-15.8.1942. There were further deportations on 13.8.1942, from Rymanow and Krosno via railway station at Wroblik Szlachecki.

[132] County of Jaraslow (Krakow): MG, Map 140, YA (10,000) YVA, and TB. 21.8.1942. All transports via Pelkin Labor camp.

[133] County of Lviv (Galicia): MG, Map 137/9 (40,000/1-10), YA (50,000, 10-23). TB table 1, 1-10 and 10-22.8.1942. See Gilbert, Holocaust, 410.

[134] County of Tarnopol (Galicia): MG, Map 139, YA, YVA, TB, table 11, 28-31.8.1942.

[135] In the County of Nowy Sacz (Krakow): MG, Map 141, YA, YVA, TB, 24-28.8.1942.

[136] County of Nowy Targ (Krakow): MG, Map 141, YA, YVA, TB, 28-30.8.1942.

[137] County of Krakow (Krakow): Resettlement via Skawina, Krakow, and Tarnow etc. MG. Map, 141.

[138] County of ZLoczow (Galicia): MG, Map 139 (472), YA, YVA, TB, table 11, 28-30.8.1942.

[139] County of Przemysl (Galicia): MG, Map 141, YA, YVA, 3.8.1942.

[140] County of Rzeszow (Krakow): MG, Map 141, 10.8.1942.

[141] County of Rzeszow (Krakow): MG, Map 141.

[142] County of Drohobycz (Galicia): MG, Map 139, YA (4,000, 4-6), YVA, TB, table 4, (600 to Janowska), 4-6.8.1942.

[143] County of Zloczow (Galicia): MG, Map 139, YA, YVA, TB, table 11, 29.8.1942.

[144] County of Drohobycz (Galicia): MG, Map 139, YA, YVA, TB: 29.8.1942, table 4, 6.8.1942.

[145] County of Tarnopol (Galicia): MG, Map 139, YA, YVA, TB, table 11 (500), 31.8.1942.

[146] County of Krakow (Krakow): MG, Map 141, YA, YVA, 28.8.1942.

[147] County of Stanislawow (Galicia): MG, Map 139, YVA, 12.8.1942, and TB table 11.

[148] County of Drohobycz (Galicia): MG, Map 139, YA, YVA, TB, table 4, 5-6.8.1942.

[149] County of Nowy Sacz (Krakow): MG, Map 141, YA, YVA, 17.8.1942, TB table 11.

[150] Ibid. YVA, TB, table 4, 8.1942.

[151] County of Lviv (Galicia): YVA, 12.8.1942.

[152] County of Drohobycz (Galicia): YVA, TB, table 4.

[153] County of Bilgoraj (Lublin): MG, Map 137, YA, 9.8.42, YVA, TB, table 3, 9.8.1942. See also Gilbert, Holocaust, 408.

[154] County of Bilgoraj (Lublin): MG, Map 137, YA, YVA, TB, table 3, 9.8.1942.

[155] County of Tarnopol (Galicia): MG, Map 139, YA (29-31), YVA, TB, table 11, 3000, 28-31.8.1942.

[156] County of Tarnow (Krakow): YVA KK/3, 28.8.1942, 8,000-9,000 deported to Belzec. See TB table 4.

[157] County of Czortkow (Galicia): Ibid.

[158] County of Tarnopol (Galicia): YA, 31.8.42.

[159] County of Drohobycz (Galicia): MG, Map 139, YVA, TB: table 11 (3,000).

[160] County of Drohobycz (Galicia): MG, Map 139, YVA (4-8), YA, TB, table 4, (150 to Janowska). 21.8.1942.

[161] County of Krakow (Krakow): MG, Map 141, TB table 3. See also YVA L L/2 4 (report 28.5.1945).

[162] County of Zamosc (Lublin): MG, Map 137, 13.8.1942, TB, (500-600), 11.8.1942.

[163] County of Zloczow (Galicia): MG, Map 141, and YVA, 29.8.1942. See also, Yacov Gurfein statement to the Israeli police 23.6.1960, ref. 280: File 13-142/4BP.

[164] County of Tarnopol (Galicia): YA, YVA, TB, table 4, 31.8.1942.

[165] Ibid. YA, YVA, 31.8.1942.

[166] County of Zloczow (Galicia): YA, 30.8.1942.

[167] County of Bilgoraj (Lublin): MG, Map 137, 10.8.1942.

[168] Ibid. MG, Map 137 TB, table 3.

September

[169] Many thousands of Jews were sent to Belzec from Lviv (Janowska), which we shall never know about. Klaparow junction, Lviv, was the main transit location for all transports arriving from the south and west. It was also the feeding and collection point for Janowska labor camp. Transports en-route to Belzec also brought fit workers from other districts on the same transport. The fit Jews were off-loaded and replaced by unproductive Jews from the camp destined for resettlement. On the notorious transport from Kolomyja on 10 September 1942, 1,000 Jews were off loaded and sent to the Janowska labor camp and were replaced immediately with 1,000 naked Jews selected from Janowska. See Nuremberg Document, N0-PS 1611 and 3688. See also YA, 48-53, and Hilberg, Destruction Vol. 2, 52.

[170] YA.

[171] County of Bilgoraj (Lublin): YVA, 9.9.1942 (the day of Yom Kippur). (*Note: Doesn't agree with 162, 167-170)

[172] County of Czortkow (Galicia): YA, 26-27.9.1942, TB table 3.

[173] County of Zloczow (Galicia): MG, Map 151, YA (2500), YVA, TB, table 11, 19.9.1942.

[174] County of Brzezany (Galicia): YVA, 20.9.1942, TB table 2.

[175] County of Brzezany (Galicia): MG, Map 153, YA, YVA, (200-300), TB: table 2, 21-22.9.1942 (Yom Kippur). There were two main deportations in early and late September 1942.

[176] Ibid. MG, Map 153, YA, YVA, TB, table 2, 3.9.1942.

[177] Ibid. YA, YVA, TB, table 3, 22.9.1942.

[178] Ibid. MG, Map 153, YA, YVA, TB, table 2, 22.9.1942.

[179] Ibid. MG, Map 153, YA, YVA, TB, table 2, 21, 22.9.1942.

[180] Ibid. YVA, YA, TB, table 2, 21.9.1942 (Yom Kippur).

[181] Ibid. YVA, YA, TB, table 2, 21.9.1942 (Yom Kippur).

[182] Ibid. MG, Map 153, YA, YVA, TB, table 2, 21-22.9.1942 (Yom Kippur).

[183] Ibid. MG, Map 153, YA, YVA, TB, table 2, 21-22.9.1942 (Yom Kippur).

[184] Ibid. YVA, 26-30 September including the communities of Husiatyn, Suchystaw, Oryszkowice and nearby villages.

[185] County of Czortkow (Galicia): YVA, TB, table 3, 26-30.9.1942.

[186] Ibid. YA, 26.9.1942, TB, table 3.

[187] Ibid. YA, YVA, TB, table 3, 30.9.1942.

[188] Ibid. YVA, TMR, YA (700) 26.9.1942, TB, table 3.

[189] Ibid. YA, YVA, TB, table 3, (1,000), 26.9.1942.

[190] Ibid. YVA, TB, Table 3, 30.9.1942.

[191] Ibid. MG, Map, 151, YVA, 20.9.1942 (via Czortkow).

[192] Ibid. MG, Map 154, YA, YVA, 25-27.9.1942, TB, table 3.

[193] County of Tarnow (Krakow): YVA. 13.9.1942.

[194] County of Bilgoraj (Lublin): YA, YVA, 14.9.1942.

[195] County of Jaslo (Krakow): YVA, 14.9.1942.

[196] County of Stanislawow (Galicia): YVA, 15.9.42.

[197] County of Kolomyja (Galicia): First deportation September 7-10, MG, Map 145 (8700), YVA LL/7 (8000). Second deportation: a further deportation (YVA LL/7) of

3,000 Jews in the sub-district was deported on 19.9.1942 to Janowska KZ and Belzec. See also YA who quotes on 17.9.1942, 7,000 deported from Kolomyja probably included the YVA ref. (3,000). In total the September deportations are approximately 15,000. See also TB, table 6, Kolomyja was the holding transit ghetto for surrounding towns.

[198] County of Kamionka Strumilowa (Galicia): MG, Map 144, YA, 15.9.1942, TB, table 5. YVA.

[199] Ibid. YVA, YA: 15.9.1942, TB, table 5.

[200] Ibid. MG, Map 151, YA, YVA, (end of September), TB: table 5, 17.9.1942.

[201] Ibid. YVA. Jews from the surrounding communities were moved to Sniatyn prior to Belzec.

[202] County of Czortkow (Galicia): TB, table 3.

[203] In the County of Krakow (Krakow): MG, Map 144, YVA, YA, 10-18 September.

[204] County of Lublin (Lublin): MG, Map 143 (via Majdan Tatarski, 2.9.1942).

[205] County of Lviv (Galicia): YVA. 11.9.1942.

[206] County of Miechow (Krakow): MG, Map 143, 3.9.1942, 144, 6.9.1942. 1,000 shot in the streets during deportation YA, YVA, 7.9.1942.

[207] County of Lublin (Lublin): TB, table 8. Many thousands were deported via Piaski Transit ghetto to Sobibor and Belzec.

[208] County of Tarnopol (Galicia): MG, Map 154, YVA, and TB. 23-30.9.1942 (via Tarnopol).

[209] County of Rzeszow (Galicia): YVA, 9.1942. TB, table 11.

[210] County of Nowy Targ (Krakow): YVA KK/7. Final roundups were made in the district: Zakopane, Nowy Sacz, Skawina, and Gdow.

[211] County of Drohobycz (Galicia): MG, Map 143, YVA, TB, and table 4.

[212] County of Tarnopol (Galicia): TB, table, 3, 21-22.9.1942.

[213] County of Stanislawow (Galicia): MG, Map 144, YA, YVA, 12.9.1942. TB, table 9 (first day of Rosh-Hashanah).

[214] County of Stryj (Galicia): MG, Map 143, YA, YVA, 1.9.1942. See also YVA LL/3, 9/42, 5,000 to Belzec, TB, and table 10.

[215] County of Stryj (Galicia): YVA, TB, table 10, 3-5.9.1942.

[216] Ibid. MG, Map 143, YA (5,000), YVA, TB, table 10, 4-5.9.1942.

[217] Ibid. MG, Map 143, YA (500), YVA, TB, table 10, 3-5.9.1942.

[218] Ibid. MG, Map 143, YA, YVA, TB, table 10, 4.9.42.

[219] Ibid. MG, Map 143, YA, YVA, TB, table 10, 4-5.9.1942.

[220] Ibid. MG, Map 143, YA, YVA, TB, table 10, 2-4.9.1942.

[221] Ibid. MG, Map 143, YA, YVA, 5.9.1942. TB, table 10, 4-5.9.1942.

[222] Ibid. MG, Map 143, YA, YVA, TB, table 10, 4-5.9.1942.

[223] Ibid. YA (750), 30.9.1942, YVA, TB, table 11.

[224] County of Tarnow (Krakow): MG, Map 144, YA, YVA, 6-16 (5,100). September 1942. A new slave labor camp opened up at Pustkow on 16.9.1942.

[225] YVA, L L/2 4.

[226] County of Zamosc (Lublin): MG, Map 144. 6.9.1942. TB, table 11.

[227] In the County of Tarnopol (Galicia): MG, Map 143, YA, TB, table 10, 1.9.1942.

[228] Ibid. MG, Map 154, YVA, and TB: table 10, 23-30,9.1942.

[229] County of Stryj (Galicia): YVA, 5.9.1942.

October

[230] Between 16 and 19 October 1942, 12,000-16,000 from Zamosc via Izbica (foreign Jews) arrived in Belzec. See Polin, Belzec, 282, n, 21. I have not included this number, as I have been unable to verify and corroborate this source. 4,000 is listed.

[231] County of Krasnik (Lublin): MG, Map 160, YA, YVA, 1-14.10.1942 (via Krasnik).

[232] Ibid. 500 women and children shot. All the rest deported to Majdanek or the Budzyn forced labor camp.

[233] County of Bilgoraj (Lublin): MG, Map 165, 15-31.10.1942.

[234] County of Stryj (Galicia): YVA, YA. 15-31.10.1942.

[235] County of Brzezany (Galicia): YVA, YA. 26-30.10.1942.

[236] Ibid. YVA, YA, TB, table 2, 10.10.1942.

[237] County of Czortkow (Galicia): MG, Map 161, YVA, YA, TB, table 3, 17.10.1942. See also YVA LL/6, 1,000+. In addition, 2,500 deported from Monasterzyska see MG, Map 165.

[238] County of Brzezany (Galicia): YVA, YA, 26.10.42.

[239] Ibid. YVA, YA, TB, table 2, 10.10.42.

[240] County of Lublin (Lublin): YVA, TB, table 8, 11.10.1942.

[241] County of Stryj (Galicia): YVA, YA, TB, table 10, (29/11 to Lublin, 30/11 to Belzec). 18.10.1942.

[242] County of Czortkow (Galicia): YVA, YA, 19.10.1942.

[243] Ibid. MG, Map, 162, YVA, YA, 5.10.1942. See also YVA LL/6, 300 to Belzec, 500 to Janowska KZ, 3.10.1942.

[244] County of Drohobycz (Galicia): MG, Map 165, and YVA. 23-29.10.1942. See also YVA LL/2, 10/42, TB table 4.

[245] Ibid. YVA, YA, TB, table 4, 10.10.1942.

[246] Ibid. MG, Map 165, YVA, YA: 22.10.1942 (2,000), also 17-18.10.1942 (2,000). TB: table 4, (1,000 17-18 Oct).

[247] County of Krasnik (Lublin): MG, Map 160. 1-14.10.1942.

[248] County of Lublin (Lublin): MG, Map 160, 1-14.10.1942. (May have been deported to Sobibor).

[249] County of Lviv (Galicia): YVA, 14.10.1942.

[250] County of Tarnopol (Galicia): YVA (via Skalat).

[251] See Kolomyja.

[252] County of Kamionka Strumilowa, MG Map, 165, YVA, TB, table 5, YA: 28.10.1942. 10.7.1943, 5,000 Jewish laborers shot.

[253] County of Kolomyja (Galicia): MG, Map 162, YVA, YA, TB, table 6, 3-13.10.1942. (Kosow, Kuty, Jablonow, Pistyn, Zablotow).

[254] In the County of Lublin (Lublin): MG, Map 160. 1-14.10.1942. May have gone to Sobibor.

[255] County of Czortkow (Galicia): YVA, 8.10.1942, and local villages.

[256] See Kolomyja.

[257] County of Krakow (Krakow): MG, Map 165, YA, YVA 28.10.1942. See also Tadeusz Pankiewicz, Krakow Ghetto Pharmacy, NY, 1985, 53.

[258] County of Janow (Lublin): TB.

[259] County of Krasnystaw (Lublin): MG, Map 165. 15-31.10.1942.

[260] See Lubaczow.

[261] See Kolomyja.

[262] County of Lublin (Lublin): YVA. 23.10.1942.

[263] In the County of Kamionka Strumilowa (Galicia): YVA, TB. 22-23.10.1942 (Via Sokal).

[264] County of Rawa Ruska: YA, 10.10.1942 (2,000-3,000, Oct/Nov., 1942 (via Oleszycek and Rawa Ruska).

[265] County of Lublin (Lublin): MG, Map 160, and YVA, 11.10.1942 (Many Slovakian Jews) may have gone to Sobibor.

[266] County of Rawa Ruska (Galicia): YVA, YA, TB, table 8.

[267] County of Janow (Lublin): MG, Map 160, YVA, YA: 1-14.10.1942 (via Krasnik).

[268] County of Lviv (Galicia): YVA, YA 10.10.1942, TB table 7.

[269] County of Lublin (Lublin): MG, Map 160, 14.10.1942 (may have gone to Sobibor).

[270] County of Lviv (Galicia): YVA. 22-24.10.1942 (via Sokal).

[271] See Lubaczow.

[272] See Kolomyja.

[273] County of Brzezany (Galicia): MG, Map 165, YVA, YA (1,200), TB, table 2, 30.10.1942.

[274] County of Tarnopol (Galicia): YVA.

[275] County of Tarnopol (Galicia): TB, table 11.

[276] County of Kamionka Strumilowa (Galicia): YVA: 22-24.10.1942 (via Sokal).

[277] County of Lviv (Galicia): YVA, YA, TB, table 7, 10.10.1942.

[278] County of Opatow (Radom): YA. 29.10.1942.

[279] County of Tarnopol (Galicia): MG, Map 165, YVA, YA. 21-22.10.1942, TB table 11.

[280] See Kolomyja.

[281] County of Kamionka Strumilowa (Galicia): MG, Map 165, YVA, YA, TB, table 5, (2,000 to Lublin). 22-28.10.1942.

[282] County of Stryj (Galicia): MG, Map 165, YVA, YA. 17-18.10.1942. See also YVA LL/3, 7.10.1942, 3-4,000 Jews deported to Belzec.

[283] County of Bilgoraj (Lublin): MG, Map 165, TMR, YA, TB, table 7, 20-21.10.1942.

[284] County of Tarnopol (Galicia): YVA, TB, table 11, 5-7 October 1942.

[285] County of Kamionka Strumilowa (Galicia): YVA, YA. 22-24.10.1942 (via Sokal to Belzec), TB table 5.

[286] County of Czortkow (Galicia): MG, Map 162, YVA, YA. 5.10.1942, TB table 3.

[287] See Schwarz, 147.

[288] County of Janow (Lublin): MG, Map 165 (500), YVA, YA (1100). 15-31.10.1942.

[289] County of Krasnik (Lublin): MG, Map 160. 1-14.10.1942.

[290] County of Kamionka Strumilowa (Galicia): YVA, YA, TB, table 5, 22-24.10.1942 (via Sokal to Belzec).

[291] See Kolomyja.

[292] County of Krasnik (Lublin): MG, Map 160, YVA, YA: 1-14.10.1942 (via Krasnik).

[293] County of Zamosc (Lublin): MG, Map 165, YVA, TB, table 11, 15-30.10.1942 (via Izbica).

[294] County of Opatow (Radom): MG, Map 165, YA. 15-31.10.1942.

[295] County of Tarnopol (Galicia): MG, Map 165, YVA, YA. 21-22.10.1942.

[296] County of Tarnopol (Galicia): YVA.

[297] County of Bilgoraj (Lublin): MG, Map 166, YVA, YA (5,000), TB, table 3, 2.11.1942 and 9.11.1942 (YA).

[298] County of Krakow (Krakow): Map 173, 10.11.1942. See also YVA KK/2, YVA.

[299] County of Stryj (Galicia): YVA, YA, 20-23.11.1942.

[300] County of Czortkow) Galicia): YVA, 26-27.11.1942.

[301] County of Drohobycz (Galicia): MG, Map 166, YA, YVA (5.11.42), TB, table 4, 30.11.1942, 600 Jews were transported naked to avoid a disturbance, which was nothing unusual. On 22.6 and 21.7.1944, hundreds of Jews to Auschwitz.

[302] County of Zloczow (Galicia): MG, Map 173, YA, 2.11.1942, YVA, TB, table 12.

[303] County of Brzezany (Galicia): MG, Map 166, 4.11.1942, TB table 2.

[304] County of Tarnow (Krakow): YVA, 15.11.1942.

[305] County of Czortkow (Galicia): YVA, YA (2,500), 27.11.1942, TB, table 3 (3,000). After the deportation to Belzec, the 2000 Jews left in the ghetto were all shot in February 1943.

[306] County of Tarnopol (Galicia): YVA, 5.11.1942. See Trembowla.

[307] County of Drohobycz (Galicia): YA. 9.11.1942, YVA, TB, table 4 (30.11.1942).

[308] County of Bilgoraj (Lublin): MG, Map 166, YVA, YA (2000), TB, table 3, 1-6.11.1942.

[309] County of Janow (Lublin): YA.

[310] County of Tarnopol: YVA, YA, Oct-Nov. See Trembowla.

[311] County of Lviv (Galicia): MG, Map 173, YA (1,300), TB, table 7, 7.11.1942.

[312] County of Bilgoraj (Lublin): MG, Map 166, YVA, YA (1,800), TB, table 3, (1,300), 2.11.1942.

[313] County of Lviv (Galicia): MG, Map 166. 1-6.11.1942.

[314] County of Zamosc (Lublin): MG, Map 173. 10.11.1942.

[315] County of Rzeszow (Krakow): MG, Map 173. 15.11.1942.

[316] County of Kolomyja (Galicia): YVA, TB, table 6, 1.11.1942.

[317] In the County of Tarnopol (Galicia): YVA, 8.11.1942 see Tarnopol.

[318] County of Janow (Lublin): YVA, YA, TB, table 6, 1.11.1942.

[319] County of Bilgoraj (Lublin): YA (20.11.1942), YVA, TB: table 3, 2.11.1942.

[320] County of Lviv (Galicia): YVA, YA, TB, table 7, 25.11.1942.

[321] County of Lviv (Galicia): MG, Map 173, YVA, YA, (8,000-10,000). 18.11.1942. See also YVA LL/1. It is estimated that between 15,000 and 25,000 Jews were deported from Lviv/Janowska to Sobibor December 42 - June 1943. See also TB, table 1.

[322] County of Tarnopol (Galicia): YVA. See Trembowla.

[323] County of Janow (Lublin): YA: Oct/Nov 1942 (via Krasnik).

[324] County of Lviv (Galicia): MG, Map 173, and YVA. 28.11.1942.

[325] County of Rawa Ruska (Galicia): YA (via Lubaczow).

[326] County of Przemysl (Galicia): MG, Map 173. 18.11.1942.

[327] County of Lviv (Galicia): MG, Map 173, YA, YVA, TB, table 7, 7.11.1942.

[328] County of Rzeszow (Krakow): MG, Map 173. 10.11.1942.

[329] County of Tarnopol (Galicia): MG, Map 173. 25.11.1942.

[330] Ibid. MG, Map 173, YA, YVA, TB, table 11, 9.11.1942.

[331] County of Stryj (Galicia): MG, Map 173, YA, YVA, TB, table 10, (700). 11.11.1942.

[332] County of Bilgoraj (Lublin): YA. 20.11.1942.

[333] County of Lviv (Galicia): YA, 29-30, November 1942, YVA, TB table 7.

[334] County of Bilgoraj (Lublin): MG, Map 167, YVA, YA, TB, table 6, 2-3.11.1942.

[335] County of Tarnopol (Galicia): YA, YVA, TB, table 11, 8.11.1942.

[336] In the County of Tarnow (Krakow): YVA, 15.11.1942.

[337] County of Stryj (Galicia): MG, Map 173, and YVA. 27.11.1942.

[338] County of Tarnopol (Galicia): YA, YVA, TB, table 11, 5.11.1942.

[339] County of Stryj (Galicia): YA. 15.11.1942.

[340] County of Janow (Lublin): YA (2000), YVA. 1-3.11.1942.

[341] County of Tarnow (Krakow): MG, Map 173, 10-11.11.1942, YA, 15.11.1942, 2,500.

[342] County of Janow (Lublin): YA.

[343] County of Zamosc (Lublin): MG, Map 173. 15.11.1942.

[344] County of Tarnopol (Galicia): MG, Map 173, YA, /TB, 8.11.1942.

[345] County of Tarnow (Krakow): YA, 15.11.1942.

[346] County of Zloczow (Galicia): YVA, 2-3 November 1942.

[347] County of Lviv (Galicia): YA, YVA, TB, table 7, 22-23.11.1942.

[348] Gilbert, Holocaust, 500. Last Jews held over from the ghetto liquidation.

December

[349] From the second half of December 1942, no further transports arrived in Belzec and the murder ceased. 200,000 Jews slated for deportation from Romania to Belzec never materialized. This meant that there were no more victims for this camp. However, Sobibor, Treblinka, Majdanek and Auschwitz were still open for business. The priority in the camp now centered on completing the burning of the corpses, decommissioning and removal of all traces of Jewish destruction, which was completed at the end of April 1943. The last 300 Jewish work brigades, who had been kept behind to dismantle the camp, were lured by Christian Wirth into a transport and taken to Sobibor where they were all shot. The remaining Ukrainian guard suffered no lesser fate: a special unit of the Gestapo attended the camp and eliminated them. See Hilberg, Destruction Vol. 2, 492.

[350] County of Brzezany (Galicia): MG, Map 180.

[351] Ibid. YVA. 4-5.12.1942, YA, TB table 11.

[352] Ibid. MG, Map 180.

[353] Ibid.

[354] County of Czortkow (Galicia): YVA LL/6. MG, Map 180.

[355] Ibid.

[356] Ibid.

[357] Ibid.

[358] County of Krosno (Krakow): MG, Map 180, 4.12.1942.

[359] County of Brzezany (Galicia): YVA, YA, 4-5.12.1942.

[360] In the County Zloczow (Galicia): YA, YVA, 5.12.1942.

[361] County of Rawa Ruska (Galicia): MG, Map 180, YVA, YA, 7-11.12.1942. It was about this time that 1000-1500 Polish Christians were sent to Belzec for political reasons. See TAL/OKBZ: statement of Stefan Kirsz and Tadeusz Stoboda, 19 February 1946.

[362] Ibid. YVA, by road to Belzec.

[363] Ibid. YVA.

[364] Ibid. YVA, 7.12.1942.

[365] Ibid. YVA, 7.12.1942.

[366] Ibid. YVA, 7-11.12.1942.

[367] County of Brzezany (Galicia): MG, Map 180, YVA, YA (1,500). 8.12.1942.

[368] County of Zamosc (Lublin): This small town is the nearest to Belzec and yet, it was the last town to be cleared of Jews.

[369] County of Lublin (Lublin): Blatt, 33, transport to Sobibor, numbers u/k.

[370] County of Lviv (Galicia): Map 183. 27.1.1943, 1,300 Jews shot.

[371] County of Lublin (Lublin): Blatt, 33, transported to Sobibor date u/k.

[372] Ibid. MG, Map 183, 15.1.1943, 2,500 Jews shot in nearby forests.

[373] County of Kamionka Srumilowa (Galicia): TB: table 5, liquidation of ghetto 20.1.1943.

[374] County of Krakow: See Piper, 57, transport to Auschwitz 19 January 1943.

[375] County of Rawa Ruska (Galicia): Map 183, 6.1.1943, hundreds shot.

[376] County of Lviv (Galicia): Map 183 5-7.1.1943, 15,000 shot.

[377] YVA. Zaslaw was the main transit ghetto for Sanok. 15.1.1943 camp liquidated, many shot. Unknown number deported, probably to Auschwitz/Sobibor. The record shows Belzec (closed). One known survivor who "jumped" the train: Yacov Gurfein (See n. Zaslaw 29.8.1942).

[378] County of Stanislawow (Galicia): Map 183. 26.1.1943, 1,000 Jews shot.

February 1943

[379] County of Drohobycz (Galicia): MG, Map 193. 15.2.1943, 600 men shot. 16.2.1943, 600 women and children shot.

[380] County of Czortkow (Galicia): MG, Map 193. 1.2.1943, 2,000 Jews shot.

[381] County of Lublin (Lublin): Blatt, 33, transport to Sobibor date u/k.

[382] County of Stryj (Galicia): MG, Map 193. 5.2.1943, 200 Jews shot.

[383] County of Kolomyja (Galicia): MG, Map 193 February 1943, 1500 Jews shot. TB, table 6, liquidation of ghetto 2.2.1943.

[384] County of Lviv (Galicia): TB, table 7, liquidation of ghetto and slave labor camp, table 10.2.1943.

[385] County of Stanislawow (Galicia): MG, Map 193, 22.2.1943, 10,000 Jews shot in forest. TB, table 9, liquidation of ghetto.

[386] County of Stryj (Galicia): MG, Map 193. February 1943, 2,000 Jews shot, assisted by Police Guard Battalion 1 (Posen).

[387] County of Czortkow (Galicia): MG, Map 193, 12.2.1943, 40 Jews shot.

[388] County of Lublin: See Piper, 55, transport to Auschwitz 5 February 1943.

March 1943

[389] YVA L L/2 4 (report 7.6.1945).

[390] County of Krakow (Krakow): Map 199, 13.3.1943, ghetto liquidated, 2,000 shot, 2,000 to Auschwitz. See also Piper, 55.

[391] County of Lviv (Galicia): Map 199, 17.3.1943. 1,500 Jews to Sobibor.

[392] County of Drohobycz (Galicia): MG, Map 199, 14.3.1943. 900 Jews deported or shot.

[393] County of Rzeszow (Krakow): MG, Map 199. Slave labor camp opened.

[394] County of Lviv (Galicia): MG, Map 199, 25.3.1943. thousands murdered in Borek forest.

April 1943

[395] County of Brzezany (Galicia): MG, Map 201, 12.4.1943, 2,000 Jews shot by SS.

[396] County of Czortkow (Galicia): MG, Map 202, 19.4.43.

[397] Budzyn forced labor camp is 3 km north of Krasnik. All forced labor camps were cruel but this was one of the worst. Between November 1942 and February 1944, over 800 Jews were butchered. Many of the Jews had arrived from Warsaw, Belzec, Janow-Lubelski, Janiszow, Konski-Wola, Minsk, Bobriusk, Smolensk, Vienna and Slovakia. Over 3,000 Jews here served the Heinkel aircraft works nearby, and as such were

spared the liquidations of 3 November 1943 (Harvest Festival). The Commandant was Josef Leipold who, to avoid war duty, shot himself in the foot. Leipold was transferred to Brunnlits camp, Czechoslovakia where Oskar Schindler operated. Replacing him was SS-Scharführer Feix who had recently been transferred from Belzec death camp. On 8 April 1943, the 71 Jews had come from Belzec. Among them: Rachel Klocendler (Krasnik) Chaja Wurmann and Kac (Belzyce).

[398] County of Lublin (Lublin): Blatt, 33, transport to Sobibor 28 April 1943.

[399] County of Lviv (Galicia): MG, Map 201, 18.4.1943, 3,489 Jews shot by SS, six communities listed destroyed.

[400] MG, Map 201

[401] County of Lviv (Galicia): MG, Map 203, 18.4.1943.

[402] County of Lublin (Lublin): Blatt, 33, transport to Sobibor, 29 April 1943.

[403] Ibid.

[404] See Sabrin, 279 (Soviet Commission of Enquiry).

[405] See Blatt, 33.

[406] Ibid.

[407] Ibid.

[408] Ibid. MG, Map 201, 9.4.1943, 500 Jews shot by SS.

[409] Ibid. Map 201, TB, and table 3.

[410] County of Brzezany (Galicia): MG, Map 201-7, 9-17.4.1943, 1000 Jews shot by SS. On 4.6.1943, a further 400 Jews were shot.

[411] County of Zloczkow (Galicia): MG, Map 201, April 1943, 100 Jews shot by SS.

[412] County of Lviv (Galicia): TB, table 1, Liquidation of ghetto. 1-20 April 1943.

[413] County of Przemysl (Galicia): MG, Map 201, April 1943, mass revolt by Jews in labor camps. Many shot by SS.

[414] County of Lviv (Galicia): MG, Map 201, 9.4.1943, 1,700 Jews shot by SS. TB, table 7, 300 Jews to Janowska KZ.

[415] County of Drohobycz (Galicia): MG, Map 201, 14.2.1943, TB, table 4. 1,000 Jews shot.

[416] County of Tarnopol (Galicia): MG, Map 201/8, 7.4.1943, 750 Jews shot by SS. On 28.7.43, a further 400 shot.

[417] County of Lublin (Lublin): Blatt, 33, transport to Sobibor 30 April 1943.

[418] County of Zloczkow (Galicia): MG, Map 201, 5.4.1943, 5,000 Jews shot by SS in nearby forest. TB: table 12, liquidation of ghetto 2-4, April 1943.

[419] County of Tarnopol (Galicia): TB, table 7, 6.4.1943, liquidation of ghetto.

May 1943

[420] See Blatt, 33. 8.5.43.

[421] TAL: statement of Jenta Silbernadel (report Israeli police 27 July 1962). The 500 (women and children) were shot into pits at the rear of the synagogue by SS-Scharführer Feix (Belzec) and Ukrainians. 100 women were taken to Budzyn labor camp where the witness, Silbernadel remained until June 1944.

[422] County of Zloczkow (Galicia): MG, Map 205, 1.5.1943, clashes between Wehrmacht and partisans. TB, table 12, slave labor camp and ghetto liquidated 22.5.1943.

[423] County of Kamionka Strumilowa (Galicia): MG, Map 205, 21.5.1943. TB, table 5, liquidation of ghetto, many Jews sent to Janowska KZ.

[424] YVA: L L/2 4 (report 7.6.1945).

[425] County of Drohobycz (Galicia): YVA, 10.5.1943.

[426] County of Lublin (Lublin): Blatt, 33, transport to Sobibor. It is estimated that over 25,000 Jews from Lviv and Stryj districts were deported or shot about this time.

[427] County of Zloczkow (Galicia): TB, table 12, and liquidation of ghetto 22.5.1943.

[428] County of Tarnopol (Galicia): MG, Map 205, 9.5.1943.

[429] County of Kamionka Strumilower (Galicia): MG, Map 205, 27.5.1943. TB, table 5, liquidation of ghetto 28.5.1943.

[430] County of Stryj (Galicia): MG, Map 205, 22.5.1943.

[431] County of Czortkow (Galicia): MG, Map 205, 27.5.1943. See also YVA L L/6 3 (report 2.6.1945).

[432] County of Lublin (Lublin): Blatt, 33, transport to Sobibor 1-7 May 1943.

June 1943

[433] MG, Map 206: According to reports, 434, 329 Jews had been deported to Belzec or shot between June 1942 and June 1943.

[434] County of Zamosc (Lublin): MG, Map 207. The last Jews (300) from Belzec death camp sent to Sobibor where they were shot. There were two survivors including Chaim Hirszman, who escaped by breaking out of the wagon en route.

[435] County of Czortkow (Galicia): MG, Map 207, 5.6.1943. TB: table 3: between 9-12.6.1943, the final liquidation of the ghetto.

[436] County of Drohobycz (Galicia): MG, Map 251, 22.6.1943. All sent to Auschwitz. TB: table 4, liquidation of ghetto, 600 to Plaszow KZ and Mauthausen KZ.

[437] County of Brzezany (Galicia): MG, Map 207, 12.6.1943.

[438] County of Czortkow (Galicia): MG, Map 207 (700), TB, table 3, YVA L L/6 3 (report 2.6.1945) liquidation of ghetto and camps.

[439] Ibid. TB, table 3, 16-18.6.1943, final liquidation of the ghetto. On the 23 June 1943, final liquidation of slave labor camps and other locations. See also YVA L L/6 3 (report 2.6.1945).

[440] YVA: L L/2 4 (report 7.6.1945).

[441] County of Drohobycz (Galicia): MG, Map 207, 21.6.1943. Mass shootings in arms factories, ghetto liquidated assisted by Police Guard Battalion 1 (Posen). See also YVA L L/2 4 (report 7.6.1945).

[442] County of Tarnopol (Galicia): MG, Map 207, 4.6.1943. TB: table 4, 12.6.1943, ghetto liquidated. 13.6.1944 Jews sent to Plaszow KZ (table 2).

[443] County of Lviv (Galicia): MG, Map 207, 21-27.6.1943. Many Jews deported to Sobibor.

[444] County of Zloczow (Galicia): TB, table 12; the liquidation of slave labor camp.

[445] County of Tarnopol (Galicia): MG, Map 207, 6.6.1943, the liquidation of ghetto.

[446] Ibid. TB, table 11 the liquidation of slave labor camp.

[447] County of Tarnopol (Galicia): Ghetto liquidated 28.6.1943.

[448] County of Rawa Ruska (Galicia): MG, Map 207, 8.6.1943.

[449] County of Tarnopol (Galicia): TB, table 11: the liquidation of ghetto.

[450] County of Brzezany (Galicia): MG, Map 207, 6.6.1943.

[451] County of Czortkow (Galicia): MG, Map 207, 9.6.1943, the liquidation of ghetto.

[452] County of Stryj (Galicia): TB, table 10: the liquidation of ghetto 5-6 June 1943.

[453] County of Drohobycz (Galicia): TB: table 4, liquidation of ghetto.

[454] County of Tarnopol (Galicia): MG, Map 207, 20.6.1943. TB: table 11, liquidation of ghetto 20.6.1943 the liquidation of slave labor camp 23.6.1943 assisted by Police Guard Battalion 1 (Posen).

[455] County of Tarnopol (Galicia): MG, Map 207, 3.6.1943.

[456] County of Czortkow (Galicia): MG, Map 207, 6.6.1943. See also YVA L L/6 3 (report 2.6.1945).

[457] County of Chelm (Lublin): MG, Map 207: the final transport of Jews to Sobibor.

[458] County of Tarnopol (Galicia): TB, table 11, the liquidation of ghetto.

July 1943

[459] County of Drohobycz (Galicia): 21.7.1943, many deported to Auschwitz.

[460] County of Stryj (Galicia): MG, Map 208, 13.7.1943.

[461] County of Lviv (Galicia): TB, table 7: the liquidation of slave labor camp.

[462] County of Czortkow (Galicia): TB, table 11: the liquidation of slave labor camp.

[463] County of Kamionka Strumilowa (Galicia): MG, Map 208, 10.7.1943.

[464] County of Lviv (Galicia): Blatt, 33, transport to Sobibor 4 July 1943.

[465] County of Tarnopol (Galicia): MG, Map 208, 28.7.1943.

[466] Ibid. 21.7.1943: the liquidation of slave labor camp.

[467] County of Zloczow (Galicia): TB, table 12: the liquidation of slave labor camp.

August 1943

[468] County of Krakow (Krakow): See Piper, 56, transport to Auschwitz 31 August 1943

[469] County of Czortkow (Galicia): MG, Map 210, 14.8.1943.

[470] County Lublin (Lublin): Blatt, 33, transport to Sobibor, number and date not known.

[471] County of Krakow (Krakow): Blatt, 33, transport to Sobibor 8 August 1943. See also YVA L L/2 4 (report 7.6.1945).

[472] County of Drohobycz (Galicia): Gilbert, Holocaust, 476. See also YVA L L/2 4 (report 7.6.1945).

[473] County of Kolomyja (Galicia): MG, Map 210, slave labor camp liquidated.

[474] Ibid. MG, Map 210, the slave labor camp liquidated.

[475] County of Lviv (Galicia): MG, Map 210, the slave labor camp liquidated.

September 1943

[476] YVA: L L/2 4 (report 28.5.1945).

[477] County of Lublin (Lublin): Blatt, 33, transport to Sobibor 29 September 1943, No. U/k.

[478] County of Lublin (Lublin): Blatt, 33, transport to Sobibor 10 September 1943, No. U/k. Forced labor camp near Trawniki. When Belzec closed down, several of the SS-garrison were transferred there: Juhrs; Zierke; Schluch; Tauscher and Schwarz.

[479] County of Krakow (Krakow): See Piper, 56, transport to Auschwitz, 2 September 1943. With six trains, three local shootings, carried out by no more than 600 armed Germans, the 40,000 Jews of Tarnow ceased to exist.

[480] County of Przemysl (Galicia): See Piper, 56, transport to Auschwitz 2 September 1943.

[481] County of Krakow (Krakow): See Piper, 56, transport to Auschwitz 19 September 1943.

[482] Ibid. MG, Map 222, 25.10.1943.

[483] County of Warsaw (Warsaw): Blatt, 33/90: transport to Sobibor 20 October 1943. 100 Jews sent from Treblinka to dismantle Sobibor Camp. Five wagons numbered 22757, 130789, 19796, 22536, and 70136, carrying the demolition crew entered Sobibor. On 1

November 1943, another three wagons arrived as a support crew. On 23 November, when the work was completed, the camp commandant (Wagner) together with SS-Scharführers Jührs and Zierke (Belzec) shot the Jewish workers into a pit. They were then cremated by the Ukrainian guards. On the same day, total destruction of all Jews commenced in the Lublin district (statement of Francziszek Zabecki, stationmaster of Treblinka to the AKW.

November 1943
[484] County of Chelm (Lublin): MG, Map 223 Jews of the body-burning brigade shot. Three survived.

After the Sobibor revolt, a high level conference was held in Krakow on 19 October 1943. Among those present: Dr Hans Frank, SS-Oberführer Bierkamp (succeeded Schöngarth), Major-General Hans Grunwald, Chief of the Schützpolizei and HSSPF Frederick Krüger. It was decided to liquidate the entire Jewish population in the Lublin district. On 3 November 1943, under the code "Erntefest," (Harvest Festival), a total of 43,000 Jews were murdered in six days. In a letter dated 4 November 1943, Globocnik informed the HHE that Reinhardt had been officially concluded on 19 October 1943. County of Chelm (Lublin).

[485] YVA: L L/6 3, report 2.6.1945.

[486] County of Drohobycz (Galicia): MG, Map 223, 14.12.1943.

[487] County of Lublin (Lublin): MG, Map 223, 5.11.1943, slave labor camp destroyed.

[488] County of Lviv (Galicia): MG, Map 223, 19.11.1943, Janowska camp revolts.

[489] County of Lublin (Lublin): MG, Map 223, 3.11.1943, Lipowa St. camp destroyed.

[490] Ibid. MG, Map 223, 3.11.1943, mass liquidation assisted by Reserve Police Battalions 101, and 41, Mounted Police Third Squadron, Police Guard Battalion 1 (Posen), Motorised Gendarme Battalion.

[491] Ibid. MG, Map 223, 5.11.1943, mass liquidation.

[492] County of Rzeszow (Krakow): MG, Map 223 November 1943, 1,000 Jews to Auschwitz. See Piper, 56.

[493] Ibid. MG, Map 223, 4.11.1943, 2,800 to Auschwitz. 6.11.1943, 500 shot by SS.

[494] County of Lublin (Lublin): MG, Map 223, November 1943, mass liquidation.

[495] County of Drohobycz (Galicia): MG, Map 251, 22.6.1944 - to Auschwitz.

[496] County of Czortkow (Galicia): MG, Map 225, 18.1.1944, 300 Jewish partisans shot in forests.

1944
[497] County of Drohobycz (Galicia): MG, Map 223, 14.12.1943.

[498] County of Galicia: See Piper, 57, transport to Auschwitz 28 March 1944.

[499] County of Drohobycz (Galicia): 13.4.1943, TB, table 4.

[500] County of Galicia: See Piper, 57, transport to Auschwitz 22 June 1944.

[501] County of Drohobycz (Galicia): 21.7.1944, TB, table 4.

[502] County of Krakow: See Piper, 57, transport to Auschwitz 31 July 1944.

[503] County of Galicia: See Piper, 57, transports to Auschwitz 6 (two Jews) and 15 (seven Jews) August 1944.

[504] This transport was probably re-directed from Belzec, which was re-building its gas chambers and was unable to deal.

505 Jews transported from outside Poland usually arrived at the "holding ghettos" at Izbica, Piaski, Chelm, Wlodawa and Krasnystaw. As the backlog of Jews were cleared in Belzec or Sobibor, Jews from these transit ghettos were transported to whichever death camp was free to receive them. Either the camp or ghetto administrators of incoming transports kept no records, or where Jews from these "holding ghettos" were destined.

506 These were the remaining work Jews from Belzec, which was now shut down. Only one Jew survived, Chaim Hirszman, who broke out of the transport before it reached Sobibor. All the others were shot on arrival.

507 The last Jewish prisoners were taken to Sobibor and shot.

508 After Belzec closed in December 1942, it is estimated that over 25,000 Jew from Lviv (Janowska Camp) and Stryj ghetto were sent to Sobibor and murdered. The German armaments factories had employed these Jews.

509 After the Sobibor revolt, these 100 Jews were brought from Treblinka to dismantle the camp. After they had completed this all were shot. See Blatt, 33.

510 Exact numbers are shown here, which reflects the efficiency of the Nazi resettlement machine in Western Europe. No such care was taken in Galicia.

511 Ibid.

512 Bialystok-Sammellager.

513 Rest-ghetto.

514 Kobylka -Sosnowka.

515 Rest-ghetto.

516 Legionowo-Ludwisin.

517 The Miedzyrzec Podlaski Rest ghetto.

518 Nowe Miasto nad Pilca.

519 Radom Glinice: Ghetto 2.

520 Radom - Ghetto 1.

521 Rest Ghetto.

522 Rawa Mazowiecka.

523 Skarzysko-Kamienna.

524 Warsaw-Falenica.

525 Warsaw-Rembertow.

526 Brzesc Kujawski.

527 Taken from a number of sources. I have also included references to police regiments where applicable. There are many gaps in this table where the research has not been completed but is ongoing. Numbers have been withheld due to lack of positive verifiable information. To be sure, there were many thousands.

528 The Rembertow Rest ghetto.

529 The Swidry Stare ghetto.

530 Acknowledgement to Peter Witte and Lucas Pribyl: pribyl@ti.cz

531 Ibid. Letzte Aktualisierung: 18.1.2000. There were no direct transports from the cities of the Protectorate to transit ghettos or killing centers, with the notable exceptions of transports from Prague to Lodz on: 16.10.1942, Transport "A" – 1,000 persons; 21.10.1942, Transport "B" – 1,000 persons; 26.10.1942, Transport "C" – 1,000 persons; 31.10.1942, Transport "D" – 1,000 persons; 03.11.1942,Transport "E" – 1,000 persons and one transport sent directly to Minsk from Brno on 16.11.1942, Transport "F" – 1,000 persons. All other transports were dispatched to Theresienstadt and no doubt onward to the holding ghettos and killing centers.

---

[532] * Identified Jewish slave labor camps where Jews were deported to Belzec.   **
Locations of mass shootings. See Alexander Benin Bernfes Archive, Zbrodnie
Hitlerowskie Na Ziemiach Polska Wlatach, 1939-45 (Nazi Crimes in Poland 1939-45).

[533] For overview to the name of Aktion Reinhardt: Ian Kershaw in "Hitler - Nemesis
1936-1945," London 2000, 484, n 124 suggests that the name for Aktion Reinhardt
appears to have been taken from the State Secretary in the Reich Finance Ministry,
Fritz Reinhardt, and hinted at the regime's interest in the material outcome of the mass
murder of around 1.75 million Jews (mainly from Poland). When account was
rendered, money and valuables worth around 180 million Reich Marks were placed in
the Deutsche Reichsbank for the future use of the SS. Mistakenly, SS men involved in
the Action attributed the name to Reinhardt Heydrich (Benz, Graml and Weiss,
Enzyklopadie des Nationalsozialosmus). For interpretation of "Einsatz," "Action," and
"Reinhardt," see also the fascinating appraisal by Peter Witte in A New Document on
the Deportation and Murder of Jews during "Einsatz Reinhardt" 1942: Holocaust and
Genocide Studies, V15, Winter 2001, 474-5 (hereafter New Document). Note: Since it
is apparent that Belzec was not operational until March 1942, and Heydrich's
assassination was in May, 1942, naming the "Action" in memory of Heydrich prior to
his death (June) seem improbable. It is interesting to note that on 15 September 1942,
the phrase "Aktion Reinhardt" is openly used in German radio traffic: see PRO HW
16/21. Steven Tyas made this information available and hereafter is shown
(PRO/Tyas).

[534] Berlin Document Center (jetzt: Bundesarchiv, Aussenstelle Zehlendorf) is the central
archival for research concerning former members of the SS. In this thesis, the author
has referred to copies held in Yad Vashem, Israel. Further references have also relied
on the comprehensive bibliography as shown in the publications of Dieter Pohl
(Ostgalizien) and Thomas Sandkühlrer (Endlösung).

[535] The Einsatz groups—and it is important that the full title be held in mind at all times—
were the Offices of Sipo-SD operating in the field behind the armies (Einsatzgruppen).
When police control had been established in the newly occupied territory, the mobile
Einsatz Groups were disbanded and became regional offices under the commanders of
Sipo-SD in the occupied territories.

[536] Gestapo (State) and SD (Party) are inextricably linked due to the fact of their
indistinguishable criminal enterprises.

[537] No one was compelled to join the Nazi Party, much less to become one of the leaders.
Many joined for business, social, or selfish reasons. There was no legal compulsion to
join.

[538] R.S.H.A. A department of the SS. Substantially all of its personnel belonged to the SS.
It was under the command of Heydrich (later Kaltenbrünner). In addition to the SD,
which was always an SS formation, it included the Gestapo and the Reich Criminal
Police, both of which were State agencies.   For this reason the R.S.H.A. Also
recognized as a department of the Reich Minister of the Interior.

[539] The SA should not be underestimated as to their contribution to the Nazi war effort,
particularly as a combat unit for defense of the Party. They were used extensively as
guards in Danzig, Posen, Silesia and Baltic Provinces. Particular attention is drawn to
their actions in the Kovno and Vilna ghettos in guarding of Jews when digging up and
burning corpses: See IMT Speeches, 45. Affidavit of Szloma Gol: International
Military Tribunal: "Speeches of the Prosecutors": The Trials of German Major War
Criminals (London, 1946), 45. Hereafter IMT Speeches.

---

[540] See for formation and daily duties of the Sonderdienst: Zygmunt Klukowski, Diary from the Years of Occupation 1939-1944 (translated from the Polish by George Klukowski) ed. Andrew Klukowski and Helen Klukowski May, Chicago, 1993.

[541] The W.V.H.A. was under the leadership of SS-Obergruppenführer Pohl who was charged with the administration of concentration camps (KZs), and the exploitation of labor.

Photographic credits:

Page 1: SS group on parade at Belzec: United States Holocaust Memorial Museum (USHMM) and Tomaszow Lubelski Regional Museum

Page 20: Himmler and Heydrich: www.Holocaust Research Project.org

Page 30: Camp Commandants: www.Holocaust Research Project.org

Page 39: Euthanasia map: Michael Peters, Germany

Page 52: Michael Tregenza collection, Lublin, Poland

Page 81: Jews in camp: USHMM; Tomaszow Lubelski Regional Museum

Page 82: Rudi Kamm: Tomaszow Lubelski Regional Museum

Page 86: Kurt Franz and group in Hartheim: www.Holocaust Research Project.org

Page 113: Jewish Kapos in Belzec: USHMM; Tomaszow Lubelski Regional Museum

Page 117: Narrow gauge rail: Tomaszow Lubelski Regional Museum; www.Holocaust Research Project.org

Page 118: Gas chambers first phase: Author

Page 127: Three SS men: www.Holocaust Research Project.org

Page 130: Chart management line: Author

Page 148: Second phase gas chambers: Author

Page 158: Painting Kolomyja: Author; Joseph Bau Gallery, Israel

Page 161: Rail map southern Poland: Author

Page 165: Camp second phase: Author

Page 167: Four paintings by Wacław Kołodziejczyk: Tomaszow Lubelski Regional Museum: www.Holocaust Research Project.org; Michael Tregenza collection, Lublin; Author

Page 171: Göckel: Michael Tregenza collection, Lublin; Tomaszow Lubelski Regional Museum

Page 198: Rice factory in Trieste: www.Holocaust Research Project.org

Page 218: Two men drilling in Belzec: Author

Page 219: Archaeologist group in Belzec: Author

Page 220: Excavator: Michael Tregenza collection, Lublin

Page 234: Time Line: Michael Peters, Germany

CPSIA information can be obtained at www.ICGtesting.com
Printed in the USA
LVOW10*1322040215

425694LV00004B/10/P

9 780976 475934